SYSTEMIC CHANGE

Touchstones for the Future School

EDITED BY

Patrick M. Jenlink

IRI/Skylight Training and Publishing, Inc.
Palatine, Illinois

Systemic Change: Touchstones for the Future School
First Printing

Published by IRI/Skylight Training and Publishing, Inc.
200 E. Wood Street, Suite 274
Palatine, Illinois 60067
Phone 800-348-4474, 708-991-6300
FAX 708-991-6420

Creative Director: Robin Fogarty
Managing Editor: Julia Noblitt
Editors: Monica Phillips, Marge Pilot
Proofreader: Troy Slocum
Graphic Designer: Heidi Ray
Illustration and Cover Design: David Stockman
Type Compositor: Donna Ramirez
Production Coordinator: Michelle Herron

Printed in the United States of America.
ISBN 0-932935-63-X

Library of Congress Catalog Card Number: 95-79278
850-8-95
Item number 1344

ACKNOWLEDGMENTS

Understanding the complexity and the interdependence of systems has been brought to life through the experience of preparing this book. The large number of authors who have worked in concert with various editors and production people exemplifies the dynamic and often self-correcting nature of a human activity system with a common purpose. An important lesson learned throughout this process was that taking an idea from the design phase to the implementation phase is evolutionary in nature, not only in process but also in the level of consciousness created along the way.

Another important lesson learned is that we are all responsible actors in the process, but there is ultimately one person who must facilitate at every step of the way—a major responsibility. In creating *Systemic Change: Touchstones for the Future School,* the system facilitator has been Julia Noblitt, managing editor. Her patience and understanding, along with her expertise, have provided order where there was chaos and given a sense of wholeness to the book. On a personal note, Julia often provided a needed connectedness to reality when I found myself drifting in time and space. She has proved to be an invaluable systems facilitator. I'm eternally indebted to Julia.

Secondly, I'd like to acknowledge the invaluable roles that Jim Bellanca and Robin Fogarty have played in facilitating the evolution of the book. They have provided positive feedback and guiding direction from the beginning. Their critical examination of the conceptual framework and the content of the book helped to provide focus for the purpose we all shared for the book.

Thirdly, but certainly with equal importance, I would like to acknowledge all the authors for their trust and commitment to the idea of the book. In a time when systemic change in education is at the forefront, these individuals have made a major contribution through their creativity and originality, as well as through their strong sense of the importance of approaching educational change from a systems and systems design mindset. Few words can express my gratitude for their patience and participation in preparing this book. They truly are human touchstones in transcending mindsets about educational change.

I would also like to acknowledge the other actors who are too numerous to mention, and are often unknown. They are behind-the-scene enablers for an activity of much complexity. To all the production folks, I extend my thanks. To the many colleagues who shared ideas and gave their counsel, thank you and hopefully I can play a similar role in the future. To all my friends and family, I can only say that without your strong support and understanding, this book wouldn't have been possible. Thank you all.

Finally, a note of appreciation to Michael Fullan, who, in the final phase of the book, was contacted to write a foreword because of his prominence in educational systems change. He graciously accepted, and to him I am grateful.

The enterprise of any human activity system is best judged by the creativity and contribution given to both its purpose and future; the actions speak for themselves. The future will arrive with or without human guidance, and I believe we have made a difference. Thank you all for contributing to the promise and potential of a better educational system for our children and their future.

Patrick M. Jenlink

CONTENTS

—

SECTION ONE

DESIGNING EDUCATION FOR THE FUTURE

SECTION TWO

EMPOWERING SCHOOLS FOR SYSTEMIC CHANGE

CONTENTS

FOREWORD

—

Michael Fullan

Patrick Jenlink and his colleagues have put together the most comprehensive treatment available on the topic of systemic change in education. Systemic reform is perhaps the most overused and misunderstood concept in education today. It is used loosely to refer to almost any attempt that a given author considers to be major. In fact, systems thinking has a strong tradition in theory, albeit with a much less well-developed knowledge base in practice. This book focuses reform for the future by bringing together systems theory with detailed examples of strategies and cases that illustrate the power of the concept.

The chapters in Section 1 provide the theoretical basis for systems thinking by linking it explicitly to redesigning education and schools for the future. Section 2 identifies and portrays the most powerful and fundamental "strategic" concepts needed for designing and mapping out approaches to systemic reform: Stakeholder participation, empowerment, evaluation, professional development, and information management systems.

While Section 2 outlines the broad strategies, the chapters in Section 3 take us to a more detailed level of strategizing by examining collaboration, evaluation and assessment, and the management of change in learning organizations.

The final section of the book proceeds to a more integrated level of analysis by presenting six well-developed case studies of actual examples of systemic reform in action at the school, district, and state level.

At a time when everyone is struggling to grasp the meaning and potential of large-scale reform, *Systemic Change* marshals a set of interrelated chapters that provides us with a multilevel lens on the meaning of educational reform. This book has something for everyone—from the individual school community attempting to transform its school to the macroanalyst or planner interested in designing and assessing systemic change.

The value of the chapters is not only that they give us solid accounts of particular cases and strategies, but also that they inspire us to go further in the pursuit of shaping schools of the future that have built-in capacities for continuous improvement.

PREPARING FOR OUR FUTURE
Transcending Existing Mindsets of Schools and Change

—

Patrick M. Jenlink

Not all changes, even desirable ones, contain the power of transcendence. It is possible for you to have a change of orientation and still continue to exist in a linear, cause-and-effect system. Transcendence operates outside such a system. Transcendence evokes the power to start from scratch, outside the realm where previous causal actions are in play. Because transcendence is an ever-new state of being, once you enter into it, each new moment is alive with fresh possibilities—possibilities that may never have seemed possible before.

—*Robert Fritz*

We are in the dawning of a new global age, and on the horizon stretching before us is the future. The future will be dramatically different from the present, and it is already calling us into preparation for major changes being brought to life by forces of change that will require us to transcend current mindsets of the world we know.

How are the forces shaping the world going to change the nature of modern organizations? How must the current educational system change in order to meet the demands of the twenty-first century? What are the touchstones essential to transcending current mindsets about schools and educational change? These are questions that confront us now, as we enter the dawning of a new century and the light of a different future shines bright, bringing stark contrast to the old and new paradigms of a changing world. Perhaps our greatest challenge lies in unfettering the American mind from the industrial age mindsets that have continued to constrain us to a model of schooling that is archaic and obsolete.

THE CHANGING MODERN ORGANIZATION

History shows that organizations vary, along with the nature of environmental change (Bell 1973; Toffler 1990; Reich 1991). The agrarian revolution led us into the industrial age, which gave way to the post-industrial age and brought us rapidly into the information age. We are now experiencing a rapid transition into what has been characterized as the global age. New forms of organizations are emerging that are far different than the organization of two, three, and four decades ago. Learning organizations (Senge 1990), knowledge organizations (Drucker 1993), and network organizations (Hastings 1993) exemplify how the forces of change are altering the basic business organization. As organizations are influenced more and more by the global forces of change, global learning organizations and business ecosystems are being projected as the fourth wave of businesses in the twenty-first century (Marquardt and Reynolds 1994; Maynard and Mehrtens 1993). In the midst of this change in mindsets of organizations, we find that we have become a society of organizations wherein knowledge is the recognized coinage of exchange and leverage for a new generation of knowledge workers (Drucker 1993).

We have ridden the waves of change (Morgan 1988) across the last century, experiencing major shifts in the mindsets that govern and guide organizational, cultural, economic, technological, geopolitical, and social affairs. And now we face the new realities (Drucker 1989) of a changing world and the promises of a new future.

A CHANGING SOCIETY

Equally, the waves of change that have influenced organizations have also touched the larger society. Reflections of changes in society of the last century are recognizable in many of the major social systems through which youth connect to their adult lives.

There are two primary systems in which we spend most of our lifetime. One is the family and the other is the workplace. A third system prepares us for the transition between these two systems; it is the educational system. In the agrarian age, the family system was characterized by the extended family, and the family farm or family-owned business helped complete a portrait of agrarian life. Expanding a view of society at this time was the one-room schoolhouse as well as transportation by horse and wagon.

The industrial age changed these systems in fundamental ways. The factory became the dominant model of existence from the workplace to the schoolhouse. Transportation evolved into the automobile, and advancements in technology, most notably the telephone, began a revolution that would connect the world in ways unexperienced. The fundamental change initiated by the industrial revolution has continued into the information age with significant impact on the family and workplace. Unfortunately, the educational system has fallen behind in meeting the demands created by the global changes we are experiencing today.

With the changes of the family system—evolving from the extended family to a nuclear model, and more currently, the single-parent and two-working-parent family—new demands have been placed on the educational system to help mediate the tension placed on the children by a changing family structure. Likewise, with dramatic shifts in the workplace brought on by advances in technology and a changing global environment, new and additional demands have been placed on the educational system to prepare youth to enter the workforce better equipped. Unfortunately, these increasing demands, brought on by changing family and workplace systems, have left education in a position of assuming responsibilities that can no longer be addressed within the existing educational system. Preparing children for their place in a global workforce as functioning knowledge workers will require new and expanding competencies that will enable students to negotiate their roles as contributing citizens in the twenty-first century.

WHAT MUST CHANGE IN AMERICAN EDUCATION TODAY?

American education is at a critical juncture. The new changes in the workplace will drastically shift expectations for student competencies and school-to-work transition requirements. As the infrastructure of the workplace evolves into a learning community and knowledge becomes the social center of activity, the expectation for schools will be to prepare the next generation of students to function in the new work environment. Students will increasingly need skills for critical thinking, problem posing and problem solving, and integrative reasoning. As the advances in information technology enable organizations to create networking infrastructures, students will need to develop new levels of computer skills.

Knowledge- and learning-transfer competencies, along with knowledge creation, will be increasingly in demand as organizations take on the character of learning organizations. Systems thinking and visioning, team learning, and personal mastery competencies are further examples of how schools must redesign the students' learning life environment for the future.

Additional demands will be placed on the educational system to prepare students to work in diverse multicultural settings that are becoming more and more a part of the real-world workplace. Connecting students to the future will require a changed educational system. It will require an entirely new system that leaves behind the industrial age model for schools. But educational change is neither easy nor often successful.

Piecemeal change efforts, often characterized as fragmented or tinkering at the edges, have proven less than satisfactory. While enjoying some initial success, past and more recent attempts at change do not produce fundamental, long-lasting change. Consequently, there is an increasing call for systemic change (Banathy 1991, 1992; Glickman 1993; Goodlad 1984; Perelman 1987; Reigeluth 1994).

Fundamental changes in the educational system begin at the deepest level of purpose, values, and beliefs about learning and all corollary components that support learning, such as curriculum, instruction, assessment, policy, etc. Where we have experienced considerable failure in our efforts to work within the system to bring about change, we must now move outside the existing system and work to create a new twenty-first century educational system. This will require that mindsets about schools and educational change be confronted and changed if we are to prepare for the future.

TOUCHSTONES FOR TRANSCENDING MINDSETS OF SCHOOLS AND CHANGE

Leaping out of the existing twentieth-century school system requires transcending existing paradigms of educational change and transgenerational mindsets of schools, schooling, and the education found within the existing system. Transcendence is achieved by engaging stakeholders in a disciplined inquiry approach to educational systems change (Banathy 1991) that negotiates outside the constraints of the existing system. Educational systems design connects stakeholders with the fundamental elements of purpose and identity, core values and beliefs, characteristics of an educational system oriented toward the twenty-first century, functions essential to creating the new learning system, and the enabling or support systems for the new educational system. This type of fundamental change (Reigeluth 1994) is not without major shifts in the way we think about and understand schools or educational change. It will require substantive shifts in personal and collectively held mindsets for those who choose to participate in the process. Changing mindsets will, in turn, require becoming sensitive to the touchstones for personal change.

Touchstones for Changing Mindsets

Breaking free from existing mindsets will require participants engaging in change to get in touch with themselves, individually and collectively. Critical self-examination along with reflection are important. Personal mastery (Senge 1990) is another step that must be taken to change mindsets. Table 1 suggests examples of touchstones for changing mindsets.

To change, a place must be created for the new mindset, and that requires the discarding or death of the old mindset. William Bridges (1991) suggests that there are three overlapping and interactive phases that we process: endings, neutral zones, and beginnings. Most people fail because they try to begin something before they have ended what they are trying to replace. When we think about shifting mindsets, we are really talking about changing frames of reference that serve as an interpretative lens for our interactions with the world around us. In addition to the frames of reference, we are also changing basic patterns or routines that are used in association with the frames of reference, which enables us to operationalize our world. Shifting mindsets is a complex process, and before we can assimilate a new mindset, the old one must necessarily be left behind. During the transition period between ending and beginning, we are in a neutral zone. The neutral zone provides an opportunity for grieving the loss and for creat-

---

TOUCHSTONES FOR CHANGING MINDSETS

- Systems thinking and practice in personal/professional life

- Personal mastery and self-development

- Critical self-inquiry and personal reflection

- Identify and understand existing mindsets

- Dialogue and communicative action

- Developing alternative futures through visioning

- Discarding old language and creating new

- Focusing inward on managing interpersonal transitions

- Connecting with sense of purpose and identity

- Understanding the death and grieving cycle of change

Table 1   Touchstones for Changing Mindsets

ing bridges to the new mindset. The touchstones provided in table 1 are ways to connect stakeholders with past and future mindsets. While most change is introduced in social context, the real work in changing mindsets is an individual affair and occurs in a personal psychological context.

Existing Mindsets of Schools

As Reigeluth (1994) notes, the industrial age ushered in what may be the only time in American history that we have experienced systemic change of such societal proportions with respect to the educational system (a change from the one-room schoolhouse to the factory model of education). The information age has yet to offer equal fundamental change for schools and the educational system. This type of deep substantive change required of the existing educational system must be one that is systemic and considers changing the *whole* system. Breaking out of the factory model mindset of schools has proven to be very difficult. In large part this can be attributed to the models for educational change, which haven't changed substantively since the industrial revolution's impact on schools. Equally, the difficulty for change lies in the shared mindsets of what schools, schooling, and education are that often exist in as many as three generations of citizens living today. Table 2 compares the characteristics of the twentieth-century factory model of schools to those of a school for the twenty-first century.

The unchangeability of education and the intractable nature emphasized by failed reform ef-

forts accents the power of the rigid paradigms that have come to characterize schools. Shifting the paradigm of schools will require that stakeholders who have a vested interest in our children and their future transcend their existing mindsets about educational change.

Existing Mindsets of Change

Perhaps one of the greatest problems that American education faces today is understanding change. As William Bridges (1991) suggests, it is not the tangible, observable change that fails, but rather our inability to manage the personal psychological transitions that each of us must engage in to be a participant in change. It is not the experience of change (which is external), but what we do with the experience (which is internal) that determines our successes and failures with change.

As we enter the information age, schools and the schooling process will need to shift dramatically to come into alignment with twenty-first-century thinking, which is systems oriented. Systems thinking will require a reexamination of change itself. Unfortunately, we are still caught in the mid-twentieth-century mindset that viewed the problem with schools as lack of change. As we prepare to enter the twenty-first century, we now understand *"the current problem is change itself. It's the problem of 'survivors' of yesterday's change projects, and everyone is a survivor"* (Bridges 1991, 123). Table 3 provides some contrast between traditional twentieth-century change and a more systemic twenty-first-century change.

20TH-CENTURY SCHOOL	21ST-CENTURY SCHOOL
• Factory model	• Learning community model
• Learn what to learn	• Learn how to learn
• Teaching as telling, information dissemination by teacher	• Teaching as facilitating, socially constructed knowledge by students and teacher
• Closed boundaries for learning	• Open boundaries for learning
• Individualism	• Collectivism and community
• Teacher poses problems, defines learning context	• Students cojoin with peers and teachers to pose problems, coresponsibility for learning context
• Convergent problem solving, one best way	• Divergent and convergent problem solving, many ways
• Competitive learning environment, win-lose	• Cooperative and collaborative learning environment, win-win
• Parent external to formal learning relationship and process	• Parent or guardian integral learning team member

Table 2   Comparing Two Paradigms of School

The key to transcending existing mindsets of educational change and preparing education to enter the twenty-first century will require that individuals find and activate the touchstones for shifting from continued applications of old paradigms of change to embracing a twenty-first-century paradigm of systemic change. As stakeholders begin to transcend old paradigms and embrace a new mindset of educational change, they will be faced with a new set of touchstones essential to changing education systemically.

OLD MINDSET OF CHANGE	NEW MINDSET OF CHANGE
• Working within existing system to fix parts and improve old system	• Working outside existing sytem to create new system
• Change is short term	• Change is continuous and lifelong
• Planning process that perpetuates	• Designing process that creates
• Views problem as within system	• Views problem as entire system
• External change agent	• Stakeholders as change agent(s)
• Limited stakeholder involvement	• High stakeholder involvement
• Individual and team oriented	• Team and community oriented
• Autocratic leadership	• Shared leadership
• Focus on improving programs	• Focus on creating learning system

Table 3   Contrasting Mindsets of Educational Change

TOUCHSTONES FOR CHANGING SCHOOLS THROUGH SYSTEMIC CHANGE

Systemic change in education connotes a new holistic view of education and its relationship to the larger environment. Various authors and researchers (Banathy 1991, 1992; Reigeluth and Garfinkel 1994) have noted that systemic change is about changing the entire system rather than fixing any single part. Systemic change requires seeing the interrelatedness and interconnectedness of parts to the whole, of understanding that a change in part of the system necessarily influences the whole system. Additionally, there has been some distinction between *systematic,* which suggests consistency; *systemwide,* which suggests change within an entire system; and *systemic,* which suggests transcending the existing system to design a new system. Transcending the existing system (the mindsets of schools, schooling, and education within) will require that those embarking on the systemic change journey (Banathy 1991) first change their mindsets about change and secondly engage in a design process for liberation from the existing system.

Examples of touchstones for creating a new twenty-first century educational system are listed in table 4. Those who will be the architects and designers of a new learning system for tomorrow's children must be sensitive to the concept of transcendence. They must also understand the importance of the roles touchstones play in creating a self-renewing school system and in designing a new educational system.

CONCLUSION

What the future holds for us is only speculative at best. We won't know for sure until we arrive. What we do know is that our current educational system is not adequate for the task of preparing today's students for tomorrow's world. Given the changes we are presently witnessing and what is envisioned for the future, our present educational system will not meet the demands. Changing the educational system from within is not the answer. We need to liberate ourselves from the industrial age system we currently have in place. We must engage in fundamental systemic change that designs a new twenty-first-century educational system. Transcending the existing system will require major shifts in commonly held mindsets about school, schooling, and education, as well as how we approach educational change. One thing is for certain: we will find ourselves in the future whether we take responsibility or not. The choice is ours. If we do not assume our responsible role in guiding our destiny, it will be our children who bear the consequences.

TOUCHSTONES FOR SYSTEMIC CHANGE IN SCHOOLS AND EDUCATION

- Transcending existing mindsets of schools, schooling, education, and change

- Reconnecting American people with the purpose of schools, schooling, and education in a democratic society and reconnecting people with their responsibility to education

- Applying systems theory, thinking, and practice to schools, schooling, and education

- A disciplined inquiry approach to educational systems design

- Inclusion of a broad base of diverse stakeholders as user-designers in the process

- Scaffolding change through new vistas of evaluation as critical inquiry, professional development as learning, communication as dialogue and communicative action, leadership as shared responsibility, and management of change as continuous facilitation of transitions and transformation

- Collectively creating a common language for systemic change with all stakeholders

- Understanding educational systems design as learning change for the future

Table 4   Touchstones for Systemic Change in Schools and Education

REFERENCES

Banathy, B. H. 1991. *Educational systems design: A journey to create the future.* Englewood Cliffs, N.J.: Educational Technology Publications.

————. 1992. *A systems view of education: Concepts and principles for effective practice.* Englewood Cliffs, N.J.: Educational Technology Publications.

Bell, D. 1973. *The coming of post-industrial society: A venture in social forecasting.* New York: Basic Books.

Bridges, W. 1991. *Managing transitions: Making the most of change.* Reading, Mass.: Addison-Wesley Publishing Company, Inc.

Drucker, P. 1989. *The new realities: In government and politics, in economics and business, in society and world view.* New York: Harper and Row Publishers.

————. 1993. *Post-capitalist society.* New York: Harper Business.

Glickman, C. D. 1993. *Renewing America's schools.* San Francisco: Jossey-Bass, Inc.

Goodlad, J. I. 1984. *A place called school.* New York: McGraw-Hill.

Hastings, C. 1993. *The new organization: Growing the culture of organizational networking.* Great Britain: McGraw-Hill International (UK) Limited.

Marquardt, M., and A. Reynolds. 1994. *Global learning organization: Gaining competitive advantage through continuous learning.* Burr Ridge, Ill.: Irwin Professional Publishers.

Maynard, H. B., Jr., and S. E. Mehrtens. 1993. *The fourth wave: Business in the 21st century.* San Francisco: Berrett-Koehler Publishers.

Morgan, G. 1988. *Riding the waves of change: Developing managerial competencies for a turbulent world.* San Francisco: Jossey-Bass, Inc.

Perelman, L. J. 1987. *Technology and transformation of schools.* Alexandria, Va.: National School Boards Association.

Reich, R. B. 1991. *The work of nations.* New York: Alfred A. Knopf.

Reigeluth, C. M. 1994. The imperative for systemic change. In *Systemic change in education,* edited by C. M. Reigeluth and R. J. Garfinkel. Englewood Cliffs, N.J.: Educational Technology Publications.

Reigeluth, C. M., and R. J. Garfinkel. 1994. *Systemic change in education.* Englewood Cliffs, N.J.: Educational Technology Publications.

Senge, P. M. 1990. *The fifth discipline: The art and practice of the learning organization.* New York: Doubleday.

Toffler, A. 1990. *Powershift: Knowledge, wealth, and violence at the edge of the 21st century.* New York: Bantam Books.

DESIGNING EDUCATION FOR THE FUTURE

The future is not a result of choices among
alternative paths offered by the present,
but a place that is created —
created first in the mind and will,
created next in activity.

The future is not some place we are going to,
but one we are creating.

The paths are not to be found, but made,
and the activity of making them changes
both the maker and the destination.
                                        —*John Schoor*

Intentions are fairly easy to perceive, but frequently do not come about.
Design is hard to perceive. It is design and not intention that creates the
future.

                                        —*Kenneth Boulding*

The history of educational reform in America is replete with good intentions and missed opportunities to bring about fundamental change. As society emerges into the information age, and we enter what is rapidly becoming known as the era of knowledge organizations, we find the disparity widening between a changing society and an unchanging educational system. On the horizon is a new awareness that transformation of schools, and our education system, will first require major shifts in the paradigms that govern our daily lives. The transformation must begin at the individual level and increasingly work its way into the mainstay of organizational life that we call schooling in America. To this end, educational systems design is viewed as the next generation of intellectual technology to bring about the fundamental changes required for schools in the twenty-first century.

The first touchstones for designing future schools are provided in this section. The contributions that follow provide the foundation for the essential orientation in bringing about fundamental change in America's educational system and creating new schools for the future. The perspectives shared connect the reader with systems theory and thinking as a way of understanding and overcoming the intractable and characteristic failure in educational reform efforts. Educational systems design is introduced as a philosophy and nascent discipline that will provide the guidance system for directing educators and stakeholders in their efforts to create new schools equipped for the twenty-first century.

The first chapter in this section introduces systems design as the new currency for educational change. The author discusses the meaning and applications of a systems view in the design of educational systems. Important to systemic change is the development of community competence in comprehensive design. In the second chapter, systems theory concepts and terminology and their applications to educational systems design is further explored. The third contribution in this section explores systemic change in educational systems as a dynamic process, wherein stakeholders are engaged in designing the destiny of their school and community.

A Systems View and Systems Design in Education

—

Bela H. Banathy

While an unchanging dominant majority is perpetually rehearsing its own defeat, fresh challenges are evoking fresh creative responses from newly recruited minorities, which proclaim their own creative power by rising, each time, to the occasion.

—Arnold Toynbee

Systemic is a buzzword in high currency in the public and private domains. We say that we are seeking "systemic solutions" to "systemic problems" by following a "systemic approach." If we are ambitious, we combine "systemic" with "long term" and "comprehensive" as we contrast these with short-term, piecemeal, disjointed efforts. Recently, the notion of systemic has become a key slogan in a search for educational reform. There is hardly an article, a request for proposal (RFP), a position paper, a proposal, or a status report in the educational reform arena that would not claim to be systemic.

An article by Lynn Olson in the September 9, 1992, issue of *Education Week* gives us some clues to answering this question. In "Fed Up with Tinkering, Reformers Now Touting 'Systemic Approach,'" the author observes that "vexed by the lack of success of school reform efforts of the past decade, a growing group of scholars and lawmakers is arguing that the incoherent and fragmented nature of the initiatives may be part of the prob-

lem. What is needed, they say, is 'systemic reform.'" But, Lynn Olson says that "pinning down just what advocates mean when they speak of 'systemic reform' is difficult." As I read the comments quoted in the article about being systemic, what systemic means, and why we need it, and, as I recall the large number of similar statements about systemic approaches in educational reform initiatives, I am reminded of the parable of a group of blind men who try to describe an elephant by touching its various parts. Not knowing what they are touching, they gave a wide variety of fragmented and erroneous descriptions of the thing.

Reform scholars decry the confusion, saying such things as "current claims of being systemic underestimate the complexity of educational systems"; "85 percent of the people who use the term have no more meaning for it than for radical change"; "there is so much we don't know, it is incredible"; and "the understanding and use of the term is a far cry from what the sociologist means by systemic." So we can ask, "*Why* does this confusion exist?" This question must be answered if we have any hope of bringing about systemic solutions to education's systemic problems. In this chapter, I offer a discussion that might be helpful. The ideas are elaborated in two of my recent books, *Systems Design of Education* and *A Systems View of Education.*

The incoherent and fragmented nature of educational reform initiatives reflects the prevailing fragmented approach to the study of education. This approach depends on scholarship in a variety of disciplines, each claiming a part of the "educational pie." This division can provide only a partial interpretation of the system studied and develops descriptions that are based on disparate theoretical frameworks. For example, in education we study the sociology of the classroom, the psychology of learning, the technology of instruction, the economics of education, the anthropology of school culture, and the politics of governance. Compartmentalized inquiry, combined with the use of widely differing orientations, methods, and languages of the separate disciplines, results in nonintegrated, disjointed, and incomplete knowledge and characterization. Thus, the disparate, disciplines-based theoretical frameworks currently used in educational inquiry cannot offer a conceptualization and depiction of education as a total system. It cannot portray the complex interactions and systemic connectedness among the various components of the system, or the mutually interacting and recursive dynamics of systems processes. To sum it up, the present orientation of educational inquiry cannot provide an adequate theoretical basis for reconceptualizing education as a complex social system, and, consequently, it cannot offer useful approaches to systemic educational reform.

A SYSTEMS VIEW OF EDUCATION

For any system of interest, a systems view enables us to explore and characterize not only the system, but also its environment and its components and parts. We can acquire a systems view by integrating systems concepts and principles in our thinking and learning. A systems view empowers us to think of ourselves, the environments that surround us, and the groups and organizations in which we live

in a new way—the systems way. This new way of thinking and experiencing enables us to understand and describe (1) the characteristics of the "embeddedness" of education systems operating at several interconnected levels (e.g., institutional, administrative, instructional, and learning experience levels); (2) the relationships and mutual interdependencies of systems operating at those levels; (3) the purposes and the boundaries of educational systems; (4) the relationships, interactions, and information, matter, and energy that are exchanged between our systems and their environments; (5) the dynamics of interactions, relationships, and patterns of connectedness among the components of systems; (6) the properties of wholeness and the characteristics that emerge at various systems levels as a result of systemic interaction and synthesis; and (7) the behavior and change of systems and their environments over time. The systems view generates insights into ways of knowing, thinking, and reasoning that enable us to pursue the kind of inquiry described above. Systemic educational renewal will become possible only if the educational community will develop a systems view of education and embrace it as its approach to reform.

Systems science incorporates three interrelated streams: systems philosophy, systems theory, and systems methodology. In contrast to the analytical, reductionist, and linear orientation of the classical scientific worldview, *systems philosophy* brings forth a reorientation of thought: an expansionist, dynamic, theological, and holistic mode of thinking. The scientific exploration of isomorphism of systems has brought forth a general *systems theory*, a set of interrelated concepts and principles organized in systems models. *Systems methodology* provides a set of strategies, methods, and tools that instrumentalize and apply systems thinking and theory in the design, development, and management of complex systems. The integration of these three streams of discipline inquiry is called *systems inquiry.*

Systems inquiry and systems applications have been applied in the world of business and industry, information technology, health services, architecture and engineering, and environmental issues. However, in education—except for instructional technology—systems inquiry is highly underconceptualized and underutilized, and it is often manifest in misdirected applications. With very, very few exceptions, systems philosophy, systems theory, and systems methodology as subjects of study and applications are not yet on the agenda of our educational professional development programs. And, as a rule, capability in systems inquiry is not yet in the inventory of our educational research community. It is my firm belief that unless our educational communities embrace systems inquiry and our research agencies learn to *pursue* systems inquiry, the notions of systemic reform and systemic approaches to educational renewal will remain hollow and meaningless buzzwords.

The notion of systemic enfolds large sets of concepts that constitute principles common to all kinds of systems. Acquiring a systems view of education means that we learn to think about education as a system, understand and describe it as a system, and design it so that it will manifest systemic behavior. We need to put the systems view into practice and apply it in educational inquiry. Once we individually and collectively develop a systems view, then (and only then) can we become systemic in our approach to educational reform; only then can we apply the systems view to the reconceptualization and redefinition of education as a system; and

only then can we engage in the design of systems that will nurture learning and enable the full development of human potential.

During the past decade we have applied systems thinking and systems inquiry in education and other social systems. As a result, we now have systems models and methods that enable us to work creatively and successfully with education as a complex social system. I have organized these models and methods in four complementary domains of organizational inquiry (Banathy 1988): (1) the systems analysis and description of educational systems by the application of three systems models: the systems environment, functions/structure, and process/behavioral models (Banathy 1972, 1992); (2) systems design, the conducting of comprehensive design inquiry with the use of design models, methods, and tools appropriate to education (Ackoff 1981; Nadler 1981; Banathy 1991); (3) implementation of the design by systems development and institutionalization (Ackoff 1991; Checkland 1981; and Nadler 1981); and (4) systems management and the management of change (Checkland 1981; Morgan 1986; Senge 1990). Figure 1 depicts the relational arrangement of the four domains of organizational inquiry. In the center of the figure is the integrating cluster.

Of interest to us in this chapter is systems design as a disciplined inquiry that offers potential for

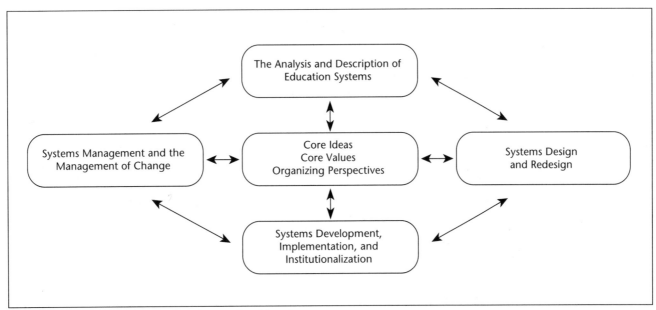

Figure 1   A Comprehensive System of Educational Inquiry

the development of truly systemic educational reform.

THE SYSTEMS DESIGN OF EDUCATION

In education we are already in the next century. Whatever we offer in our schools today will define the creative capacity, competence, and character of the generation that will shape the society of the twenty-first century. Nonetheless, many of us share the realization that today's schools are far from being able to do justice to the education of future generations. There is a growing awareness that our current design of education is out of sync with the new realities of the information/knowledge era (Bell 1976; Drucker 1989; Harmann 1988; Reich 1991). Those who are willing to face these new realities understand that (1) rather than improving education we should transcend it; (2) rather than revising it, we should re-vision it; and (3) rather than re-form it, we should transform it by design. We now call for a metamorphosis of education. From the cocoon a butterfly should emerge. Improvement does not give us a butterfly, only a faster caterpillar.

In times of accelerating and dynamic changes, when a new stage has unfolded in social evolution and the information/knowledge era has transcended the industrial age, inquiry should not focus on the improvement of existing systems. Staying within the existing boundaries of education constrains and delimits perception and locks us into prevailing practices. At best, improvement or restructuring of the existing system can attain some marginal adjustment of an educational design that is still rooted in the perceptions and practices of the nineteenth-century machine age. But, adjusting a design rooted in an outdated image creates far more problems than it solves (Markeley and Harmann 1982). We have already found this out. The escalating rhetoric of educational reform has created high expectations, but the realities of improvement efforts have not delivered on those expectations.

We are now faced with the challenge of acquiring a new way of thinking and with learning the new practice of systems design. But first, we have to understand the what's and the how's of system design.

Systems Design: A New Intellectual Technology

Systems design, in the context of social systems such as education, is an inquiry that is future creating, decision oriented, and disciplined. In education we engage in design in order to devise and implement a system that will create the society we wish to have. We seek to design a system that meets the educational requirements of a "just system" for future generations.

The design of open social systems is a relatively new intellectual technology. In sharp contrast with the earlier mechanistic "social engineering" approaches, social systems design emerged recently as a manifestation of open systems thinking and a corresponding participative systems design approach. It was elaborated by such systems scholars as Ackoff (1981); Checkland (1981); Churchman (1972), Cross (1982), Jantsch (1976); Jones (1980), Nadler (1981), Ulrich (1983); and Warfield (1990). Open social systems inquiry surfaced just in time to enable us to redesign our societal systems and realign them with the "new realities" of the information/knowledge age. My own contribution has been to introduce systems design to the educational community (Banathy 1991).

It is most unfortunate that, as a rule, systems design is not on the agenda of our schools of education and it is not practiced by the educational profession. Most of us still use outdated social planning approaches that reduce the problem to "manageable" pieces and seek solutions to each. We believe that solving the problem incrementally, piece by piece, will correct the larger issue we aim to remedy. But, systems thinkers know that optimal performance of the parts does not prevent the bankruptcy of the whole. And systems designers tell us that getting rid of what is not wanted does not give us what is desired. In sharp contrast with traditional social planning, systems designers seek to bring about a comprehensive, interconnected, interdependent, interacting, and internally consistent system of solution ideas that are manifested in the design of the new system.

A FRAMEWORK FOR TRANSCENDING AND ENVISIONING

I created a framework that enables us to leap out from and transcend our existing system (Banathy 1991). Using the framework, we can create an option field of design inquiry and explore a wide range of design alternatives. Exploration leads to choices. And the synthesis of choices provides the image of a new system. The framework has three dimensions: (1) the *focus* of the inquiry, (2) its *scope,* and (3) its *relationship* with other systems. Each dimension offers four options. Figure 2 provides an example of creating an option field and drawing alternative boundaries for design inquiry.

Focus Options

The four focus options mark the four levels of the systems complex of education: governance, administration, instruction, and learning experience. In societies where the state or the church operates education, governance dictates. In our country, the system is built around administration. Recently, in some restructuring programs, authority is shifted to the instructional level. The fourth choice calls for designating the learning experience as the primary level and building the whole systems complex around it. When learning comes to focus, the learner becomes the key entity of the system, and the primary task is to provide resources,

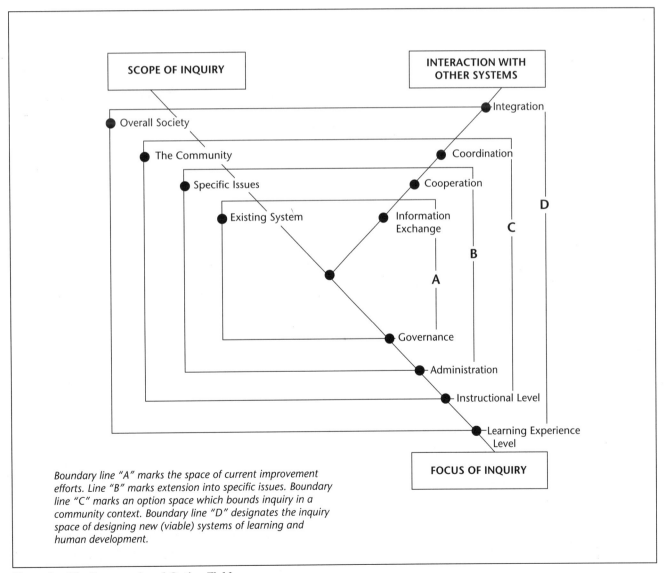

Boundary line "A" marks the space of current improvement efforts. Line "B" marks extension into specific issues. Boundary line "C" marks an option space which bounds inquiry in a community context. Boundary line "D" designates the inquiry space of designing new (viable) systems of learning and human development.

Figure 2   The Framework and Option Field

arrangements, and opportunities for learning. A learning focus will require a major boundary change and, consequently, will call for the design of a new system.

Scope Options

The scope of the inquiry also has four boundary options: (1) staying within the existing system, (2) considering certain issues in the environment, (3) making the community the context of design, and (4) selecting the whole society as the context of the inquiry. Improvement stays within existing boundaries. So does restructuring, as it is concerned with the reassignment of authority or the rearrangement of system components. The implications of choosing the first and second options mean that we do not change boundaries; therefore, we cannot talk about design.

The third option extends the boundaries as the community becomes the context of the inquiry. This scoping option means transcending the boundaries of "schooling" and contemplating a new design that includes all systems in the community that can provide resources, opportunities, and arrangements for learning and human development. Contemplating a community-based system, we also recognize the uniqueness of our communities and design systems that reflect this uniqueness.

The fourth option reaches into the overall society as the context of design. By exploring this option, we are raising crucial questions: What are the educational implications of the new realities of the information/knowledge era? What are the implications of the massive changes and transformations that have emerged in the sociocultural, socioeconomic, sociotechnical, scientific, and organizational spheres? Answers to these questions will guide us in the redefinition of the societal functions of education, the development of a new learning agenda, and the organization of new ways of learning and human development. Choosing this fourth option calls for a major boundary change and, consequently, for the design of a new system.

Relationship with Other Systems

This dimension of the framework offers the following options: (1) exchange of information with other systems in the environment, which is typical practice today; (2) occasional cooperation with other systems; (3) coordination with other systems that might share educational and human development resources and opportunities; and (4) integration with all other social service systems. This last option will create a "new education species"—a community-based system of learning and human development that leads to the realization of a learning society.

IMPLICATIONS OF USING THE FRAMEWORK

Possible implications of using the framework are marked in figure 2. If we stay within the boundaries marked "A" and "B," we might attend to problems in the existing system and respond to them by improvement or restructuring, but we are not engaged in design. Options "C" and "D," on the other hand, create two expanding design inquiry spaces. The further we go out on any of the dimensions of the framework, the more novelty we create, the more complex the system will be, and the more involved, intensive, and time/resource consuming the design task will be.

If we use the options framework and make choices among the various options, a conversation unfolds around several questions:

- Why did we select a particular option? As we probe into the why's, we begin to articulate, share, and harmonize our values, assumptions, preferences, and ideas that support our choices.

- Is there internal consistency among the choices we made? Exploring this question we begin to probe into examining the selected alternatives within the whole context of our inquiry.

- Are our choices compatible with our stated values and ideas and are they supportive of each other? Now we explore how particular choices affect each other and test their compatibility with our collectively stated core values and core ideas.

For example, selecting the learning experience level as our focus, we shall recognize that we need a much larger base for learning resources and opportunities than is available in the classroom. We need to create learning territories beyond the walls of our current buildings. This will require at least coordination, and possibly integration, with other systems in the community.

If the system we aspire to create is expected to coevolve with the societal environment in which it is embedded, and if we wish to work continuously with ongoing changes, we must select the overall society as the functional context for design.

If our aspiration is to integrate learning with human development, establish lifelong learning, and bring to life a learning society, then we shall seek the integration of all those systems in the community that offer opportunities, resources, and arrangements for learning and human development.

ENVISIONING THE IMAGE OF THE NEW SYSTEM

> *A young nation is confronted with a challenge for which it finds a successful response. It then grows and prospers. But as time passes the nature of the challenge changes. And if a nation continues to make the same once successful response to the new challenge, it inevitably suffers a decline and eventually failure.*
>
> —*Arnold Toynbee*

At the end of the twentieth century, our nation is faced with the new challenge of a new era. This challenge requires a new educational response. It requires the envisioning of a new image of education and—based on the image—it requires the transformation of education by design.

Systems design creates a normative description, a representation of a future system. This creation is grounded in our vision, our values and ideas, and in our aspirations of what that future system should be. The framework discussed above enables designers to transcend the boundaries of the existing system and explore alternative design options. In the course of this front-end work, designers collaboratively clarify their vision of the new system and articulate their shared core values and ideas. Then, based on all these, they formulate the image of the new system. The image is the first "broad-stroked picture" of the future system. The more intensive and inclusive the exploration of the option field, the clearer the vision. The more core values and core ideas formulated and integrated, the more compelling and powerful the image. Table 1 introduces an image that is grounded in option "D," as shown in figure 2 (Banathy 1991). Seven markers of the future and existing system are presented in this table: (1) relationship with society; (2) relationship with other systems; (3) the overall function of education; (4) the scope of the educational experience; (5) the key imperative; (6) types of arrangements for learning; and (7) resources to use. The image of the desired future system is juxtaposed with a speculative representation of the image of existing school systems.

The image presented here is revolutionary, but the move toward it can be evolutionary. This image is speculative and serves the purpose of triggering conversations and further explorations. The image is only an intent. It expresses an *idea* of creating a new system. However, intention does not give us a system, only design does.

As Kenneth Boulding (1985) once said, "Intentions are fairly easy to perceive, but very often do not come about and are not fulfilled. Design is hard to perceive. But it is design and not intention that creates the future" (p. 221). That is why understanding how to organize and engage in it is so critical. It is also why developing competence in design is an attainment of the highest value.

TRANSFORMATION

Systems design in the context of human activity systems is a future-creating, decision-oriented, disciplined inquiry. It aims at the creation of a system that will bring to life our aspirations and transform that image into reality. First, I will introduce a design architecture that creates the inquiry space of transformation. Then, I will map the journey that creates the future system.

THE IMAGE OF A FUTURE SYSTEM	THE IMAGE OF THE EXISTING SYSTEM
1. Education should reflect and interpret society as well as shape the society through coevolutionary interaction as a future-creating, innovative open system.	1. Education is an instrument of the transmission of culture and knowledge, which focuses on maintaining the existing state and operates in a rather closed-system mode.
2. Education should integrate with other social and human service systems in creating systems of learning and human development.	2. Education acts as an autonomous social agency separated from other societal systems.
3. Education should provide lifelong learning experiences for the full development of all individuals.	3. Education now provides instruction to individuals during their schooling years.
4. Education should provide for learning experiences that are sociocultural, ethical, moral, economic, political, scientific, technological, aesthetic, and that promote physical, mental, and spiritual wellness.	4. Education focuses on the basics and preparation for employment.
5. Education should be organized around the learning experience level (i.e., arrangements should be made in the learner's environment that allow him or her to master learning tasks).	5. Education is now organized around the instructional level, enabling teachers to present subject matters to students.
6. Use a variety of learning types: self-directed, other directed, cooperative team learning, and social and organizational learning.	6. Today, teacher-class and teacher-student interactions are the primary means of schooling.
7. Use the large reservoir of learning resources and arrangements available in the community to support learning.	7. The use of resources and arrangements is very much confined within the classroom.

Table 1   Seven Images of the Future and Existing System

The Design Architecture

Systems design operates in five interrelated "inquiry spaces." These spaces are integrated by their interaction into a system of inquiry. Figure 3 depicts this architecture. The five spaces are connected by arrows that show their interactions and create the dynamics of systems design.

- In the *exploration/image creation space* (EICS) we do the following: (1) formulate our reason for engaging in design; (2) establish the boundaries of the design inquiry; (3) interpret the educational implications of new societal realities; (4) generate core ideas and core values; and (5) envision the image of the future system. (The image was created with the use of the framework. See fig. 2.)

- In the *design information space* (DIS) we introduce findings generated in the EIC space and display knowledge about the following: learning and the learner; approaches, methods, and technologies that mediate learning resources; methods of systems design; and knowledge required in the ongoing design inquiry.

- In the *design solution space* (DSS) we create and explore design alternatives as we search for the desired solution.

- In the *design evaluation/experimentation space* (DEES) we test the alternatives against these criteria: (1) our stated vision; (2) our core values/ideas; (3) the image; and (4) the design specifications.

- In the *design modeling space* (DMS) we display the following: (1) the models of the new system; (2) the model of its systemic environment; and (3) the implementation plan.

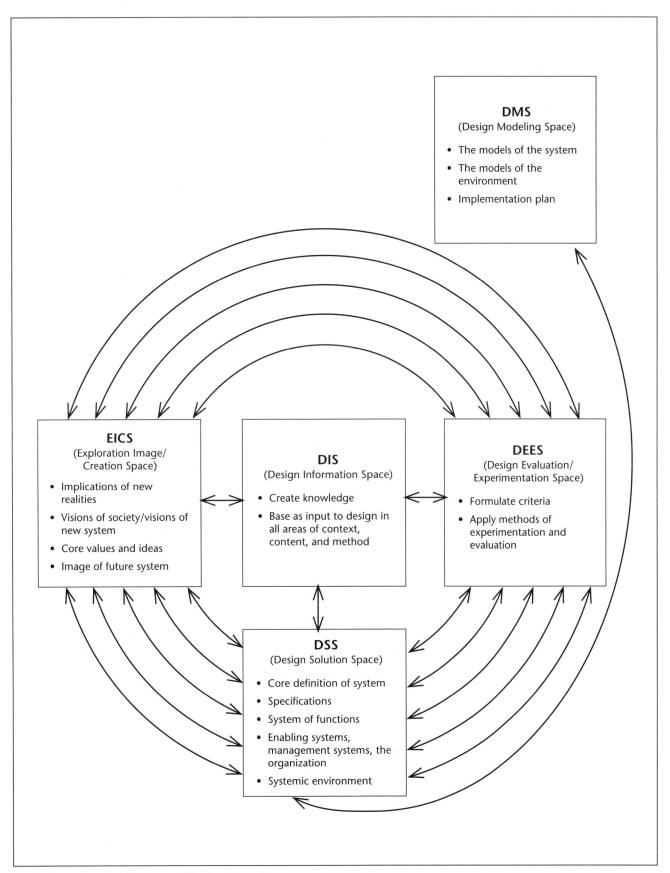

Figure 3   Design Architecture and Design Dynamics

The Design Journey

Figure 3 shows the five spaces of the design architecture that we spiral through to create and evaluate various potential design solutions. The arrows show nonlinear, dynamic interaction among the design spaces. The interaction is recursive and mutually affecting.

Spiral One: Formulating a Core Definition

During spiral one—the core definition of the future system—we formulate the mission of an educational system. We ask what the new system is about. More specifically, we ask, "What is our aspiration in serving humanity, the larger society, our community, the learners, people who serve the system, and all those who are affected?" We ask about future generations and what the shared aim is that can give everyone a clear direction and commitment. A synthesis of answers provides us with a comprehensive definition of the future system. Thus, the mission is elaborated in terms of specific purposes. The core definition spiral is connected with the knowledge base that informs the decisions we make. First, it spirals through testing, where we evaluate the core definition based on the criteria we formulated to evaluate the generated design solutions. Then, we spiral back to the frontal (EIC) space, where we might reformulate our core ideas in view of the core definition.

Spiral Two: Developing Specifications

During the second spiral we formulate specifications, based on the image and the core definition. To interpret these specifications, we might ask questions such as these: Who are the clients of the system? What services should we offer them? What characteristics should those services have? When, where, and how should we provide those services? Who should own the system? (I.e., Who should own the educational system? How should ownership be distributed? What rights and responsibilities should owners have? What rights and responsibilities should clients and stakeholders have?) How should the system relate to other systems in the environment? Do the specifications respond to the

core definition? In the forward-moving spiral, the selected specifications are then evaluated in the DEES. The spiral now moves on to the EICS, where we review how the specifications, core values and ideas, and the image affect each other. The specification spiral connects with design information, where we draw on the knowledge base in formulating specifications.

Spiral Three: Selecting Functions

The crucial design work during spiral three involves the selection of functions. These are the questions we ask: What are the key functions that have to be carried out that enable the system to attain its mission and purposes and meet its specifications? How do these functions interact and constitute a system of functions? What are the component functions or subfunctions? How can we organize the subfunctions in subsystems of functions? By answering these questions we unfold the systems complex of functions that constitute the first systems model of the new system. The functions spiral connects to the knowledge base and is tested against the core definition and specifications. Next, the functions spiral moves into the DEES and then back to the EICS.

Spiral Four: Design the Enabling Systems

This spiral is comprised of three component spirals. First, we design the management system by asking what design will enable it to guide the functions, energize and inspire people in the system, ensure the availability of needed information and resources, and provide for continuous organizational learning. Next, we design the organization that will have the systemic capacity and human capability to carry out the functions. We ask what systems components (and what kind of people in those components) have the required capabilities. We also ask how we should integrate the selected components in relational arrangements and what resources should be allocated to whom. The third component spiral produces the design of the systemic environment in which the new system is embedded and which is capable of providing the resources and information required by the system.

Each spiral goes through several iterations as we explore, test, and select solution alternatives. Moving with a spiral, initially we are in a "divergent mode," where we create a number of alternatives. But gradually we "converge" and try out and evaluate the various alternatives in order to select the most desirable solution.

Modeling the Design Solution

The term *model* is used here as a mental or conceptual representation, a description of the future system. In human activity systems, we model the design solution by constructing three systems models: systems/environment, functions/structure, and process/behavioral (Banathy 1992). These models jointly provide a comprehensive characterization of the new system. We also formulate a plan for the design-based development and implementation of the new system.

ORGANIZING PERSPECTIVES

Organizing perspectives guides our thinking and actions about design. Explicitly stated and shared perspectives ensure the attainment of consensus about design and generate support for carrying out the design tasks.

Participation

Participation is based on the cardinal principle that design is authentic and sustainable only if it involves all those who will inhabit the system and will be served and affected by it. Genuine participation in design enables informed contribution and the incorporation of individual and collective values and aspirations. Participation enhances commitment to implementation and empowers design.

Commitment to Idealized Design

Commitment to idealized design means creating the most inspirational design, one that acts as a magnet and pulls us toward its realization. Only the pursuit of the ideal is worth the effort required to carry out design. Only when the ideal model of the future system is created shall we consider the

constraints and enabling resources for an implementable design. The ideal will be always on the horizon and will guide our purposeful move toward it. The ideal might be truly revolutionary, but its realization can be evolutionary.

Learning Design

Design is learning, and by learning to design—and engaging in it—we learn as an organization and as individuals. As individuals we learn about the contributions we can make to the system. As an organization we learn to continuously reexamine our values, perspectives, purposes, and models of operation, and we gain insights and ideas for shaping the future of our system.

Design Never Ends

As we move toward the horizon, the horizon moves ahead of us. New realities emerge, the environment and our perspectives might change, and we might reimagine the ideal in light of those changes.

Nurturing Human Values and Human Quality

We design systems that value and serve people. We design systems that build and nurture human quality. We believe that it is our destiny—and it is within our power—to guide our evolution and the evolution of our systems and to shape our individual and collective future by design.

REFLECTIONS

We now realize that systems design is a missing inquiry in education. Therefore, we should embrace systems design as an essential part of our professional repertoire. We can attain this by developing organizational capacity and individual and collective capability in systems design. Confronted with "new societal realities" and new educational requirements of a rapidly changing world, people look to the professional education community for guidance in the design of their educational systems. This expectation confronts us with the challenge to individually and collectively acquire systems thinking and develop competence in systems design.

The viability and relevance of the educational profession will be judged based on the extent to which we spearhead the evolution of education, place ourselves in the service of transforming education, and help create just systems of learning and development for future generations. Education creates the future and there is no more important task and no more noble calling than participating in the creation.

———

REFERENCES

Ackoff, R. 1981. *Creating the corporate future.* New York: John Whiley & Sons.

Banathy, B. 1991. *Systems design of education: A journey to create the future.* Englewood Cliffs, N.J.: Educational Technology Publications.

———. 1992. *A systems view of education: Concepts and principles for effective practice.* Englewood Cliffs, N.J.: Educational Technology Publications.

Bell, D. 1976. *The coming of post-industrial society.* New York: Basic Books.

Boulding, K. 1985. *Human betterment.* Beverly Hills: Sage.

Checkland, P. 1981. *Systems thinking, systems practice.* New York: John Whiley & Sons.

Churchman, W. 1972. *The design of inquiring systems.* New York: Basic Books.

Cross, N. 1982. *Developments in design methodology.* New York: John Whiley & Sons.

Drucker, P. 1989. *The new realities.* New York: Harper & Row.

Harmann, W. 1988. *Global mind change.* Indianapolis: Knowledge Systems.

Jantsch, E. 1976. *Design for evolution.* New York: George Braziller.

Jones, C. 1980. *Design methods.* New York: John Whiley & Sons.

Markeley, O., and W. Harmann. 1982. *Changing images of man.* London: Pergamon Press.

Morgan, G. 1986. *Images of organizations.* Beverly Hills: Sage Publications.

Nadler, G. 1981. *The planning and design approach.* New York: John Whiley & Sons.

Reich, R. 1991. *The work of nations.* New York: Alfred A. Knopf.

Senge, P. 1990. *The fifth discipline.* New York: Doubleday.

Ulrich, W. 1983. *Critical heuristics of social planning.* Bern: Verlag Paul Haupt.

Vickers, J. 1983. *Human systems are different.* London: Harper & Row.

Warfield, J. 1990. *A science of generic design.* Salinas, Calif.: Intersystems Publications.

2

SYSTEMS THEORY
An Approach to Redesigning Education

Joe B. Hansen

When placed in the same system, people, however different, tend to produce similar results.

—*Peter Senge*

The words "system," "systemic change," "systems approach," and other similar terms are heard with increasing frequency in educational circles, especially among advocates of "systemic reform." However, only a small portion of those who use these terms have more than a rudimentary understanding of the concept of a system and the valuable theory of systems that has evolved to explain what systems are and how they function. This view is shared by Betts (1992), who says,

> Unfortunately the word system has been popularized without a fundamental understanding of its implications, to the point where everything is a system but nothing really is treated like one. Many people say they are using a systems approach, but almost no one really is. (p. 38)

Many education professionals remember the 1960s and 1970s and may therefore recall with some distaste the adaptation of some *systems theory* concepts to education. Specifically, I am referring to management by objectives (MBO), program planning and budgeting systems (PPBS), programmed instruction, and other such applications that made procedural demands on users and yielded little in terms of measurable improvements, either managerially or instructionally. Unfortunately, in many instances, those were maladaptions of processes and techniques from the world of scientific management and systems engineering rather than adaptations of a *systems theory* approach. The result of those efforts created in the minds of many educators an association of the word "system" with complex, detail-laden procedures and forms for use in program budgeting, management by objectives, and other processes that always seemed to be creating paperwork burdens and somehow missing the big picture of education. Now, nearly thirty years later, education is rediscovering the concept of system. The first time around we got lost in the details and the trappings without capturing the philosophy and richness of thought that systems theory had to offer. Had we not done so, we might have found education at a new, higher plane than it is today. This time around we hope to get it right.

This book is about the application of systems thinking to education as an approach to educational reform. It is not about the details and trappings of systems engineering, although it may embody some engineering concepts. This chapter provides an introduction to systems theory concepts and terminology and their applications to educational redesign.

BASIC SYSTEMS CONCEPTS AND PRINCIPLES AS THEY APPLY TO EDUCATION

The term *system* has many legitimate and useful applications for describing and analyzing the way education is organized and conducted. We may, in fact, think of many education systems and subsystems that interact in myriad ways to define what we think of as the American education system. There are also state systems, county systems, citywide systems, and local systems. Each is a legitimate application of the construct system. In this section, I will explore the concept of a system and apply systems theory to education by drawing from the works of systems and educational theorists.

Among the more influential advocates of the need for a systems view of education is Seymour Sarason (1991), who, in his book *The Predictable Failure of Educational Reform*, advocated that a total systems view of education was essential if meaningful reform was ever to occur. In Sarason's words,

> System is a concept we create to enable us to indicate that in order to understand a part, we have to study it in relation to other parts. It would be more correct to say that when we use the concept *system* it refers to the existence of parts, that those parts stand in diverse relationships to each other, and that between and among those parts are boundaries (another abstraction) of various strength and permeability. Between system and surround are also boundaries, and trying to change any part of the system requires knowledge and understanding of how parts are interrelated. At the very least, taking the concept of system seriously is a control against overly simple cause-and-effect explanations and interventions based on tunnel vision. (p. 15)

This failure to recognize and understand the relationships among the interrelated parts of a system is, in Sarason's view, the major reason that repeated attempts at educational reform in the United States have failed, and will continue to fail if not properly addressed.

Sarason has appropriated the systems view from the social sciences—sociology and social psychology, in particular—where the study of complex human social systems has been taking place for more than a hundred years.

Two Basic Types of Systems

Systems theorists define two basic types of systems: open and closed. Prior to the advent of open systems thinking, most systems models were of a closed nature. They relied on laws of Newtonian physics and assumed such conditions as might exist in a laboratory environment, where a chemical reaction can be controlled in a beaker, isolated from extraneous input that might interfere with the desired outcome. These models shared a common feature: the system did not interact with its environment. Instead it was thought of as being enclosed within permanent boundaries, isolated from interaction with other systems. Some writers have attributed the disintegration of the Soviet Union to its closed nature, which prevented it from importing intellectual energy to sustain itself (Banathy 1991).

Open Systems

An educational system is a social organization, and all social organizations are open systems (Katz and Kahn 1966). Therefore, I will focus my attention on open systems exclusively throughout this chapter.

School systems are moderately open (Betts 1992; Banathy 1991). According to Katz and Kahn (1966), open systems share the following nine common characteristics:

- importation of energy
- throughput
- output
- systems as cycles of events

- negative entropy

- information input, negative feedback, and the coding process

- steady state and dynamic homeostasis

- differentiation

- equifinality

In addition to these nine characteristics, Betts (1992) has added synergy, hierarchy, and purposiveness, or teleology. I will discuss each of these terms briefly, and illustrate how it applies to education.

Importation of Energy

A primary distinction between open and closed systems is the exchange of energy across boundaries. Living organisms are open systems, taking in fuel, oxygen, and other requisites from their environment and returning waste products and useful elements such as nitrogen and carbon dioxide. Most large-scale organizations are dependent on the social effects of their output for energy renewal (Katz and Kahn 1966). In other words, the system's output affects the system's environment in some way that stimulates a return of energy from the environment to the system. When this exchange is mutually beneficial, symbiosis occurs, an interdependent relationship between system and surroundings.

As a social system, an education system is open to energetic input from the environment through a variety of mechanisms. Policy direction is provided by its elected board of education. The board represents the will of constituents, who have a stake in the system although they are outside of it. Local PTA/PTO, school site councils, advisory accountability committees, and various other representative groups influence the way in which schools and school systems conduct the education process. In many instances, funding is also subject to an electoral process. Educational reform ideas influence the operation of the system. They find their way into the system through varied sources (e.g., literature, preservice and inservice training, state and federal legislative mandates, and even public input). All of these sources of energy serve to both sustain and transform an education system.

Throughput

The throughput is the transformation of imported energy into output by means of the processes and functions of the organism and organization (Katz and Kahn 1966). For example, the human body converts starch and sugar into heat and action; the factory transforms raw materials into products; and the school transforms a multitude of inputs such as educational theory, monetary resources, characteristics of incoming pupils, community attitudes, values, and instructional resources into applied knowledge and skills manifested in the students who pass through the system.

Output

Open systems export some products into the environment (Katz and Kahn 1966). In the case of a biological organism, it may be nitrogen and carbon dioxide. In the factory example, it is a consumer or capital good such as an automobile or industrial robot. In the case of a school, it is a citizen who can solve problems, find and use information effectively, and function successfully in society. The mission statement of the school or the school district will express the value ideal associated with the output.

Systems as Cycles of Events

The exchange of energy between a system and its environment is cyclical in nature. The product returned to the environment becomes the source of energy for repetition of the cycle of activity. In biology, the nitrogen and carbon dioxide help sustain and stimulate the production of plants, which provide sources of energy, directly and indirectly, for the sustenance of the organism that may consume them or other organisms that consume them. The computer manufacturer's product generates the needed revenue to purchase more components and provide a return to investors. The output of a school, however, contributes to a complex set of interactions with society that influences the flow of energy back into the system.

For example, a student may become a politician who influences tax legislation that directly affects school funding, or she may become a scientist, contributing a new scientific theory or discovery that becomes incorporated into the curriculum. The student will most likely become a taxpaying citizen who eventually has children of her own in the system. She may even join the PTA and become an advocate for school reform, expressing herself through letters to board members and meetings with the teachers and principals who influence her children.

Over time this repetitive cycle may result in changes within the school system. Such changes can be organizational, philosophical, or curricular in the instructional process. These changes occur naturally in response to the influence of environmental, social, and economic factors, which themselves are transformations of inputs in the larger system of society. By the same token, subsystems will contain their own cycles of activity, or loops, within the larger system, based on the exchange of energy within the system's internal environment.

Entropy and Negative Entropy

Entropy is a concept within systems theory whereby all forms of organization—biological, social, or physical—move toward cessation of activity and ultimate death. A classic example within physics is found in the second principle of the law of thermodynamics, which states that a system tends toward a state of equilibrium in which its elements become arranged in a random, disordered fashion. Heating a bar of iron on one side with a blowtorch will result in a speeding up of the heat-exposed molecules on that side. Eventually, some of the energy from the heated molecules will dissipate into the surrounding environment to increase the activity of neighboring molecules until all molecules within the bar are at an equal temperature and rate of movement. Further dissipation of heat energy will heat the surrounding environment until the bar and its environment are the same temperature. Entropy continues until the physical system reaches the state of the most probable distribution of its elements (Katz and Kahn 1966). Another way of thinking about entropy is that if a nonliving system is isolated or placed in a uniform environment, all motion usually comes to a standstill as a result of various sources of friction or resistance.

Differences of electric or chemical potential, as well as differences of temperature, are equalized. This results in a permanent state of cessation of activity known as thermodynamical equilibrium, or maximum entropy (Schrodinger 1968).

Negative entropy is the reversal of the entropic process of perpetuating the differentiation of a system rather than decreasing it to a moribund state of torpor. Because they are open systems, which import negative entropy, social systems differ from physical systems in that their structures tend to become more elaborated rather than static. This is evident in school systems in the elaboration of the curriculum; the differentiation of roles of administrators, counselors, psychologists, social workers, nurses, and teachers, and their diverse endorsements and certifications; and the increasing complexity of regulations and legal requirements that school systems now face.

Examples of increasing the negative entropy of a school system include increasing school funding through legislative action or a mill levy, the introduction of a new instructional methodology or assessment system, and the creation of new partnerships with business and industry. Each of these actions would result in new structures within the system, creating new functions and activities and thereby counteracting the effects of entropy on the system.

Information Input, Negative Feedback, and the Coding Process

The inputs into a system may be of an informational nature as well as energy bearing, or energic. Informational inputs provide important signals about changes in the environment that have implications for the way the system operates. Feedback is one type of informational input. Feedback may be either positive or negative. Positive feedback from the environment signals the system to continue on its current course. It may be selective, focusing on a particular program, department, or aspect of the curriculum, or it may be more diffuse and general. Information feedback to the system will vary in terms of specificity and quantity. More-specific information is generally useful for formulating plans or making specific choices among alternatives. General information, on the other hand, is more useful for policy guidance (Hansen 1992). Systems can react only to those inputs to which they are attuned. The process of transforming the input signal into useful information is known as coding (Katz and Kahn 1966).

Negative feedback signals the system that something is wrong. It suggests an alteration to the system's current course, which is central to systems theory. A thermostat, for example, controls the temperature in a room by (1) sensing when the temperature has deviated from the acceptable range, and (2) sending a signal to the heating or cooling unit to increase the output of either heated or cooled air.

School systems need thermostat mechanisms to monitor the social, political, and economic climate in which they operate. Examples of such mechanisms might include community needs/satisfaction surveys, focus-group or town-hall meetings, client hotlines, citizen advisory groups, and program evaluations. These mechanisms become sensors for detecting conditions that will produce negative feedback. They can collect, codify, and process that negative feedback, thereby causing corrective actions to occur within the system. Without such feedback mechanisms, school systems can become nonresponsive, isolated entities that are more closed than open and thereby more subject to the effects of entropy.

System theorists (Katz and Kahn 1966; Miller 1955) postulate that if there is no such corrective device, a system will consume too much energic input or energy and will eventually cease to exist as a system. Obviously, the implication for a public school system is complicated by legal requirements. Nonetheless, it is conceivable that a school system that fails to respond to signals for change from its environment will ultimately suffer the dire consequences of reduced funding, legal sanctions, or a loss of enrollment that could, if not stemmed, lead to failure and eventual death of the system. Therefore, a healthy school system should actively develop and maintain its feedback mechanisms and seek to maximize the effective use of the feedback obtained. It must also have mechanisms in place for utilizing such feedback in a process of continuous improvement. It is not enough to merely capture and contain the feedback, it must be used to make corrective changes in both the substance and processes of curriculum, instruction, support subsystems, and system administration.

Steady State and Dynamic Homeostasis

A healthy system is constantly searching for a dynamic balance through self-regulating mechanisms. Relationships among elements, subsystems, and suprasystems are constantly changing while searching for equilibrium and avoiding entropy (Betts 1992). Dynamic homeostasis is the process by which, once established, a system will act to preserve its essential character. This is accomplished through constant exchange of inputs and outputs with the external environment, where the inputs are either energic or informational and the outputs are the products of the system. In an animal or a human, homeostasis is maintained through the ingestion of essential nutrients, the regulation of body temperature, and the release of bodily waste. The animal or person may grow, and through the process of cell regeneration may even become a different physical being, but its essential character does not change. A similar process occurs in a social system. The system may change in response to energic or informational inputs, but its essential nature will remain the same. That is to say that a school system's purpose and basic operational characteristics will likely remain unchanged, even though there may be a staff turnover, funding fluctuations, reform movements, and other political, social, and economic events that will affect it. To ensure survival, systems will act to acquire some margin of safety beyond that required for existence (Katz and Kahn 1966). Social systems will tend to incorporate within their own boundaries those external resources essential for survival. The equilibrium established by the system will be a long-term condition, based on its purpose. Homeostasis will be based on preserving the essential character of the system, not on maintaining a specific form with all specific functions continuing intact.

The widely held perception that public education is a conservative institution that resists change at all costs may stem from fears based on professional educators' misperceptions that changes in the system will disrupt its equilibrium. This view confuses long-term equilibrium with stability, where stability is viewed as nonchange. Understanding equilibrium as a long-term dynamic process may help educators alter their view of change as a threat to systemic equilibrium.

School systems are subject to specific restraining forces that affect the ways in which they can change and still maintain dynamic homeostasis. For example, the willingness of voters to support property-tax levies is one such constraint. Social constraints in terms of the acceptability of certain curricular variations, such as sex education or AIDS education, are a variable in the school community. The former chancellor of the New York City Public Schools, Joseph Fernandez, found severe community resistance to his program to distribute condoms to students to prevent the spread of AIDS. This public resistance ultimately led to his dismissal. Conservative religious groups' recent upsurge of interest in and activism toward public education is another example of such a constraint.

The vital role of public education in a free society creates conditions that spawn many self-interest groups who monitor the education system and keep it operating within certain acceptable boundaries defined by mainstream values. These boundaries are reflective of the social, economic, and political environment. Dynamic homeostasis for a school system is established within those boundaries over a long period of time.

Differentiation

Open systems progress from simple to more-complex structures as they evolve and grow. This is true of biological and social systems. In social systems, and, in particular, school systems, increased differentiation is constrained by environmental variables such as those discussed above. Limits are determined by societal values, public opinion, economic factors, and other intrinsic factors. Currently, we are experiencing a societal trend toward simplified

organizational structures with less middle management. The Total Quality Management (TQM) approach of W. Edwards Deming has had a profound, if belated, effect on American management theory. We are beginning to experience a crossover of this influence from industry to the public schools. This is not the first time such a crossover has occurred. Much of the scientific approach to education of the sixties and seventies crossed over from the teachings of Frederick Taylor, some thirty-five years earlier.[1] The effects of this more recent crossover include site-based management accompanied by reductions in central administrative staff. Thus, we see a "dedifferentiation" such as that described by Gouldner (1959) in which a system reorganizes at a lower level of complexity in response to a disturbing stimulus. A system's ability to dedifferentiate is dependent on the degree of functional autonomy of its parts and the tension between the parts and the system. Dedifferentiation may lead to new growth and further differentiation as the original sources of tension are relieved. Therefore, we may expect to see new and different structures in the education system. We may also see a thriving and growing system of education based on these new structures. Some may describe this phenomenon as educational renewal.

Equifinality

The principle of equifinality states that "in any closed system the final state is unequivocally determined by the initial conditions: for example, the motion in a planetary system where the positions of the planets at a time t are unequivocally determined by their position at time t_0. Or, in a chemical equilibrium, the final concentrations of the reactants naturally depend on the initial concentrations" (Bertalanffy 1967, 121). The principle of equifinality as applied to open systems suggests that a system can reach the same final state from differing initial conditions and a variety of paths.

The application of the principle of equifinality to educational systems would suggest that a system

1. For a discussion of the influence of scientific management theory on education accountability and reform, see J. B. Hansen's article, "Is Mandated Accountability as a Tool for Educational Reform an Oxymoron?," in the April 1993 issue of *Measurement and Evaluation in Counseling and Development.*

could move toward a desired end state regardless of the condition or status it manifests at a given point in time. This principle implies that a degree of plasticity exists in school systems that should be taken into account by those who fear that structural changes to the organization will necessarily have detrimental results.

Synergy

Another characteristic of systems is that they exhibit synergy. That is to say that a system is more than just the sum of its parts because the relationships among the elements of the system add value to the whole (Betts 1992). According to Katz and Kahn (1966), system theory is basically concerned with problems of relationships, structure, and interdependence among elements, rather than with constant attributes of objects. While synergy may be difficult to observe directly, in an education system it nevertheless occurs with some frequency.

Hierarchy

The hierarchy of a system is determined by the number of levels that exist within it. Each successively higher level encompasses all processes at each lower level and is increasingly complex as the number of elements and their relationships or subsystems increase. The energy required to maintain the system increases at an even greater rate than does the complexity. Arbitrary or manmade hierarchies require more energy to maintain than natural ones (e.g., birth order within a family) (Betts 1992).

Purposiveness

A system must have some purpose for which it exists and seeks to sustain itself. For an ecosystem, the purpose may be the survival and continuation of the varied species of living organisms it supports. For an organization or system such as education, the purpose may be less clear. It is currently in vogue for organizations to go to great lengths to establish vision, mission, and goals to clarify their purpose and communicate it to their employees. When the goals of an organization are not the same as its members', dissonance results. However,

the input, output, and functions of an organization may define its purposes more accurately than the stated intent of its leaders (Katz and Kahn 1966). Therefore, it is crucial for the long-term health of the system that each member (employee and student) of the system understand not only the purpose, but also the relationship between that purpose and his or her own role in the system.

Banathy (1991) distinguishes between unitary and pluralistic systems. *Unitary* systems have a single clear goal, whereas *pluralistic* systems have multiple goals, some of which may conflict with others. School systems operate under numerous legal mandates that create a variety of purposes or goals, some of which may be in conflict with others, thereby requiring greater energy to maintain the system and the relationships within it (Betts 1992).

THE MODERN SCHOOL SYSTEM

Alternative Systems Views of a School System

Various educational theorists and scholars have developed systems theoretic views of education. In this section, a brief overview of three different systems perspectives on education is provided. First is the hierarchical model of Dolan (1991), followed by the systems design approach of Banathy (1991), then the Total Quality Management systems view of Herman (1992).

Hierarchical Model

Patrick Dolan (1991) attributes much of the alleged dysfunctionalism of the modern school system to the fact that it is based on a hierarchical model that originated in ancient times and has since become obsolete. This model worked well through the era of the Roman empire, providing the framework for military governance. According to Dolan, this model is also the basic organizational model of the (Catholic) church, which provided the mold from which all subsequent military, government, and industrial organizations were formed. Dolan suggests that this model is no longer functional because it is designed for one-way communication only, from the leader to all those below. To Dolan, the restructuring of education must begin with the communication system. Changes in communications must be made at the boundaries of the subsystems to promote a more open, two-way exchange within the system, and between the system and its environment. In other words, the education system model must move further toward becoming an open system.

Figure 1 shows how a typical school district is organized. This pyramidal structure is characteristic of military forces, churches, monarchies, and, until recently, most postindustrial social and business enterprises. Such systems are relatively closed and are designed for information to flow from the top down rather than from the bottom up. They contain many barriers to communication that occur at the boundaries of the subsystems (Dolan 1991). These barriers tend to isolate the subsystems from one another, thereby inhibiting, rather than promoting, interaction. This restricts

the flow of vital energy within the system and between the system and its environment. In a pluralistic system, such as a school district, this can result in a self-perpetuating cycle of isolation and alienation from the system's goals because the subsystems and their components are focused on their own goals. This happens because the one-way communication grid does not encourage the flow of information from lower to upper levels of the hierarchy, telling the upper levels that the system needs to make internal adjustments so that it can stay on its plotted course.

At least two strategies are necessary in order to overcome the problems of the hierarchical system model. One is to reduce the number of layers in the hierarchy, thereby promoting more direct interaction between the top, policy-level decision makers and those at the operational level (i.e., the teachers). A second necessary strategy is to establish and sustain a continuous flow of information

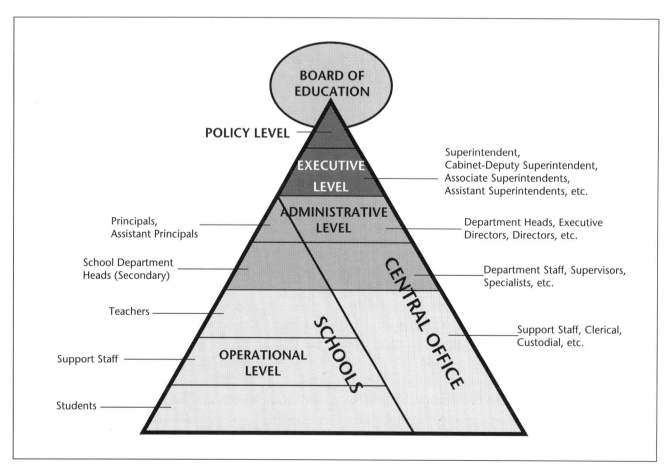

Figure 1   The Hierarchical Organization of a School District

across subsystem boundaries to create a means of removing or weakening the barriers between subsystems. A specific example of this in a larger district would be a cross-divisional or cross-departmental coordinating council. In the Colorado Springs Public Schools we have established such a council. It is the Curriculum, Instruction, and Assessment Coordinating Council (CIACC), which is made up of representatives from the Division of Instruction and the Division of Data and Technology Systems. The Division of Instruction has responsibility for curriculum development, instructional supervision, and school management. The Division of Data and Technology Systems has responsibility for student data systems, management information services, planning, evaluation, and measurement. The CIACC meets monthly during the school year to discuss and make decisions about issues of common interest to the two divisions, such as developing new assessment techniques, meeting state accountability requirements, reviewing instruction and assessment policies, setting up and monitoring pilot programs in assessment, and so on. The existence of the CIACC helps to ensure that there is a continuous flow of information back and forth across the boundaries between these two organizational units, each of which has a separate mission, but which share the need to support the mission and goals of the system as a whole. Without such a structure as the CIACC, the potential for misunderstanding and conflict of interests between these two entities would increase considerably.

A Design-Based Approach to Systemic Reform

Banathy (1991) asserts that there is an ever-widening gap between education, which is relatively slow to respond to the need for change, and the rest of our rapidly changing society. He also says that the current model based on the industrial society is outmoded and has lost its viability and usefulness. Banathy advocates that we must go beyond reform to *transform* our outdated school system model. He says that making adjustments to the current model won't work because the model is based on an outmoded mindset of *determinism*, which fails to deal with interactions among all the constituent parts of the system. According to Banathy, our ef-

forts at educational reform in the past have failed because (1) they were piecemeal and incremental; (2) they failed to integrate solution ideas into a complex, interactive whole or system; and (3) they remained within the boundaries of our current system. Focusing on the system as it exists instead of designing a new system will not work. Banathy calls for the design of a new educational system based on a *vision* of how things should be. This vision would then result in an *image* of a new system that would address societal needs and would be focused around the current and anticipated future issues.

Banathy's approach to systemic change may be the most extreme and comprehensive to have emerged thus far. It fails, however, to acknowledge the natural and historical fact that most change does occur incrementally and that evolution accounts for more change than revolution does. It would also appear that Banathy does not accept the principal of equifinality as being applicable to education systems or he would recognize its implication for making incremental changes in order to reach the desired end state.

Total Quality Management as a System in Education

> *Educational stakeholders must realize that school districts are systems which are comprised of a series of subsystems, and the sooner these subsystems work collaboratively together to develop an effective and efficient total school district system, the quicker the school district will develop high quality services and products which will please all categories of its customers.*
>
> —*Jerry Herman*

Herman's words characterize the philosophy of a true systems thinking approach to education that is needed today to bring about the long-sought-after transformation of education that will put American schools back at the forefront of education, globally. Herman has adapted the principles of TQM to education through an approach that "begins with a commitment to quality and customer satisfaction, using TQM as the means to accomplish these goals" (Herman 1992, 21).

Herman's TQM model for school systems is depicted in figure 2. This overall systems view contains the following five subsystems: TQM employee, TQM student, TQM external environmental, TQM strategic planning process, and TQM tactical process. An important feature common to all of these subsystems is the assessment component that provides a "recycle" or feedback loop to the system. This allows continuous improvement of the subsystem's processes and outputs. Herman's model employs both *formative* and *summative* assessments in each of its five subsystems.

Herman's TQM Student Subsystem contains the essential features found in more recent approaches

to education that are based on certification of student performance, such as "outcome-based education" and "standards-based education." As shown in figure 3, outcome-based quality specifications for student achievement are first determined, then quality achievement specifications for individual students are developed. Instruction is provided based on the desired outcomes and quality standards, and the quality of learning is then assessed.

Figures 2 and 3 illustrate how an assessment subsystem functions to provide appropriate information to other subsystems, using a TQM framework. Chapter 11 will provide the interested reader with further discussion of assessment subsystems.

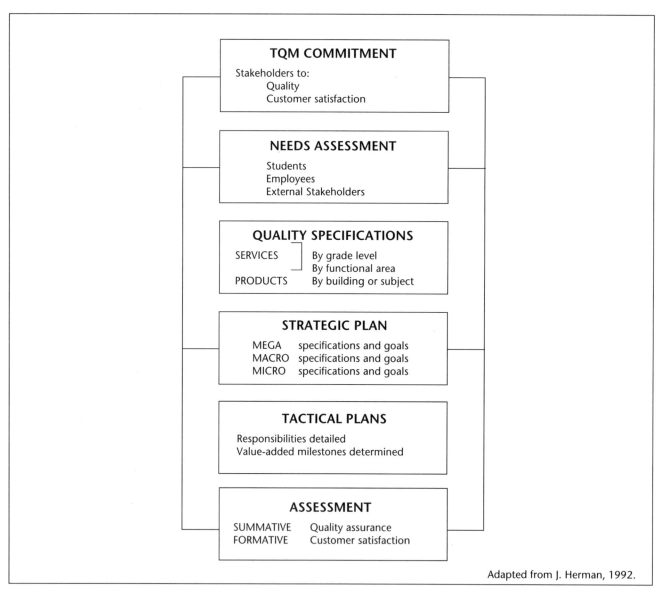

Adapted from J. Herman, 1992.

Figure 2 TQM Model for School Districts

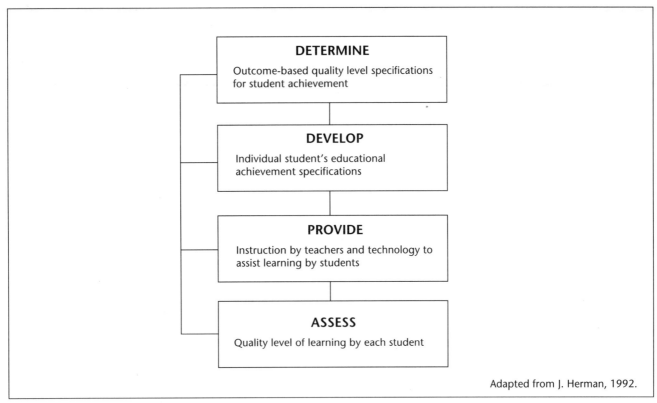

DETERMINE
Outcome-based quality level specifications for student achievement

DEVELOP
Individual student's educational achievement specifications

PROVIDE
Instruction by teachers and technology to assist learning by students

ASSESS
Quality level of learning by each student

Adapted from J. Herman, 1992.

Figure 3   TQM Student Subsystem

An Open-System View of Education

Dolan, Banathy, Herman, Betts, and Sarason correctly identified an education system as comprising subsystems that interact, require communication, and process information. A critical feature of each of these views is that the system defined by them is, at least ideally, an open system. Figure 4 graphically depicts a school system as an open system, the most significant unit of which is the individual school. Alternatively, one could focus on the classroom or the administrative structure of the system and by so doing derive a different, though equally valid, perspective.

As illustrated in figure 4, in an open-system view of a school district, a number of sources of input and energy exert their influence and create the system dynamics. In this view, the school system appears as an independent, teleological system. That is to say, it is a system with a definite purpose: the education of the child, pupil, or student. All resources are directed toward this end. External sources of energy include state and federal government, the public, business and industry, changes in societal values, legally mandated site councils, and advisory committees. Internal sources include professional associations/unions, employee groups, and structural levels (e.g., elementary, middle, and high school).

Major Subsystems—Their Interfaces and Information Needs

As described by Sarason, Dolan, Banathy, and Herman, an education system is comprised of various subsystems, each of which performs a vital function for the suprasystem and each of which interfaces with other subsystems through the flow of information and energic input. The major organizational subsystems and interfaces in this open-system view of education are illustrated in table 1.

Policy Level

Each of these subsystems has information needs that derive from its purpose or central mission. These information needs vary across subsystems in terms of both content and level of detail (Hansen

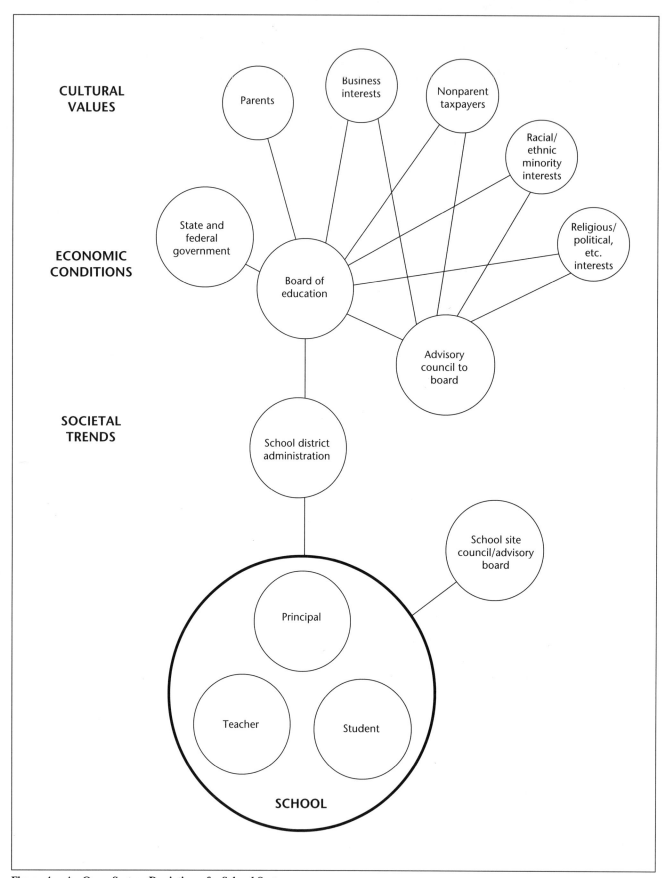

CULTURAL
VALUES

ECONOMIC
CONDITIONS

SOCIETAL
TRENDS

Parents

Business
interests

Nonparent
taxpayers

Racial/
ethnic
minority
interests

State and
federal
government

Religious/
political,
etc.
interests

Board of
education

Advisory
council to
board

School district
administration

School site
council/advisory
board

Principal

Teacher

Student

SCHOOL

Figure 4   An Open-System Depiction of a School System

LEVEL	MEMBERS	RESPONSIBILITIES
Policy	Board of education (public and administrative interface)	Provide policy guidance and maintain a connection with the values and interests of the community at large.
Executive	Superintendent and top-level central administration, including deputy and assistant superintendents	Interface with board of education, school administration, and the public through open meetings and advisory groups; responsible for maintaining system integrity through sound fiscal management, providing and developing leadership, developing curriculum, providing vital support functions, monitoring system effects, reporting results, and assuring compliance with legal mandates.
Administrative	Program directors, department heads, central support service coordinators/supervisors, and specialists	Interface with principals and teachers, primarily for the delivery of needed curricular, instructional, assessment-related, business, and physical plant support services.
Operational	Individual school, including principal, teaching staff, support staff, and students	Interfaces with parents, advisory groups, PTO/PTA, etc.; responsible for maintaining safe and orderly learning environment and teaching students.

Table 1   Major Organizational Subsystems and Interfaces of an Open System

1992), as illustrated in table 2. For example, the board of education as the main policy body exists for the purpose of representing the general public in the formulation of policy decisions to guide the district administration and staff. This purpose requires a broad perspective in which the needs of the taxpayers and the needs of the students are viewed simultaneously and are balanced against each other. The board must stay focused on the big picture of the needs of the entire system. Therefore, the board's information need is for summary information about the larger issues that affect the district as a whole, such as enrollment growth trends that might have implications for building new schools or closing old ones. They need information on how well the students in the district are

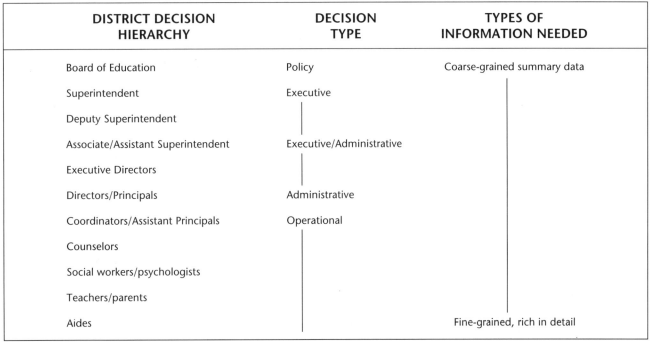

Table 2   Relationship of Informational Detail to Educational Decision-Making Hierarchy

achieving with respect to the broad outcomes in critical areas of learning, such as basic skills, thinking skills, social studies, science, etc. And they need information on the extent to which the students are being prepared adequately for their major life roles as workers, lifelong learners, and responsible citizens. By contrast, the board of education does not need information on the achievement or performance of individual students or staff unless that performance has implications for district policy. Nor do they need line-item details about the budget. They need information that tells them the extent to which the district's planned and actual spending supports the broad policy goals, educational priorities, and strategic-plan directions they have established for the district.

This relationship between type of information needed and hierarchical level of the system that needs it is illustrated in a flow diagram in figure 5.

As shown in figure 5, the board of education is responsible to the community at large, from which it receives energic input in the form of votes, protests, statements of support, and other information. The community, in turn, receives information from the board about how well the school district as a whole is performing its mission of educating students.

Executive Level

The executive level is the highest administrative level of the decision hierarchy. This level comprises the superintendent, deputy superintendents, and other superintendent level personnel. Typically, the people at this level make up the superintendent's cabinet. This group of top-level administrators is responsible for providing the leadership that will enable the district to fulfill its mission and achieve the goals adopted by the Board of Education. While this group does not formally make policy, since only the board can do that, it makes policy-level recommendations to the board and ensures that the resources are in place for the system to function in order to achieve the board's goals. Therefore, the decisions made at this level tend to be districtwide decisions with a long-term as opposed to a short-term focus. Exceptions to this occur in the case of legal issues involving personnel or labor laws that may deal with individuals.

The information required for these executive-level decisions tends to be somewhat more detailed than that required by the Board of Education but is still concerned with the district as a whole. Top-level executives needs indicator data on how well the system is doing as a whole and how well each component within their area of responsibility is performing. They make detailed observations about the employees who report directly to them, but rely on the process of delegation of authority and responsibility to provide them with summary data from the lower levels for which they are responsible. With respect to student achievement data they are interested in trends, indicators of strength and weakness in the curriculum, comparisons with other districts, and equity and opportunity to learn. They want to know whether the math curriculum, for example, is preparing students for the world of work and the challenges of higher education. They need to know if there is a particular school or group of schools that are exceptional, either positively or negatively, and, if so, what is causing the exceptionality. They also need data to inform them of the district's status with respect to various state and federal accountability mandates. They would rarely need data on individual classes within a school or on individual students. Most of the achievement data needs would be districtwide.

Administrative Level

At the administrative level, subsystem information needs are more intensive than at the executive level in both the scope and degree of detail required. Program managers need information on the success of their programs in teaching students their content and processes. Department heads need detailed information on their expenditures relative to their allocated budget. Curriculum supervisors need information on the extent to which the curriculum is being implemented effectively and how well it is working in terms of student learning and teacher acceptance. Assistant superintendents or cluster leaders need information on how effective the schools under their supervision are at successfully teaching students specified out-

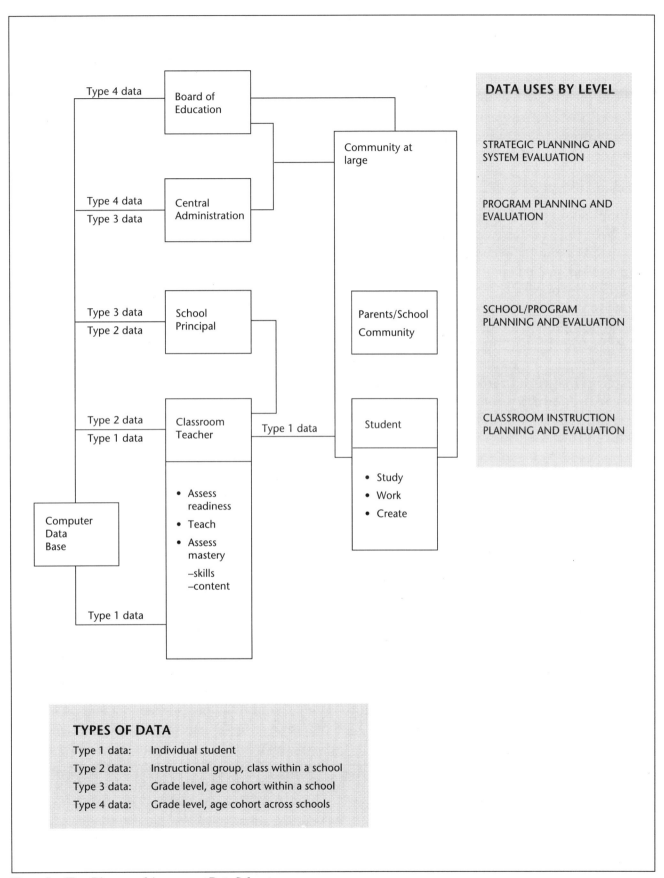

Figure 5   Flow Diagram of Assessment Data Subsystem

comes. They also need information on the perfor-mance of the principals they supervise. The feed-back this subsystem requires from the system is used to make short-term or tactical adjustments as well as to plan for longer-term or strategic goals. Therefore, the information used at this level must contain more detail than that required at the ex-ecutive or policy level.

Operational Level

The information needs at the school level are nar-rower, focusing more on what is happening within this subsystem and between it and the other sub-systems. More-detailed information on student performance is needed by teachers, who must con-stantly assess the extent to which individual stu-dents are learning what they need to know and be able to do. The teachers use the information they collect through the assessment process to make adjustments in their instructional plans. The prin-cipal needs information on how well this year's fifth grade is doing in math relative to previous cohorts and external referents. He or she also needs to know how well the school is doing in meeting the goals it has set for the year and how well each teacher or instructional team is doing.

In summary, the information needs of these major subsystems for policy, executive administra-tion, and operations vary in both content and level of detail, with the greater need for detail occurring at the school level and even more so at the class-room level within the school. The information con-tent and detail required by a subsystem are a function of the purpose of the subsystem and the types of decisions that must be made by the people within that subsystem. I have discussed this rela-tionship elsewhere (Hansen 1992) and have shown that the need for information forms a gradient that varies from fine-grained detailed information at the classroom level to coarse-grained summary in-formation at the policy level, as shown in figure 6.

Student Performance Information Needs

An important common element in the information needs of these subsystems is information on stu-dent performance and achievement with respect to the generally-agreed-upon learning outcomes, goals, or standards of achievement. Assessment of student achievement and performance plays a vital role in the education system. It provides useful in-formation to decision makers at all levels on the system's success in producing the intended results established by the system. In Chapter 11, I will de-scribe the role of assessment in greater detail and provide a model for a comprehensive assessment and reporting system that fulfills the information requirements of the education system. This model focuses on the purpose for which assessment infor-mation is needed and identifies the most appropri-ate type of assessment for the selected purpose.

SUMMARY AND CONCLUSIONS

This chapter has introduced the reader to some fundamental systems theory concepts and applied those concepts to an educational system. By doing this it is my hope that readers, especially those with some responsibility for designing or redesigning educational systems, will begin to view those sys-tems somewhat differently. It is also my hope that such readers, whether professional educators, policy makers, students, or interested members of the public, will recognize the complexities of the educational systems they interact with and will be-gin to apply those concepts and principles as they think about educational reform. The frequent and sometimes naive use of systems terms when refer-ring to educational reform efforts indicates that educational reform advocates need to have a better understanding of the principles of systems theory.

Whether one takes a position similar to that of Banathy (1991), which calls for the redesign of public education, or a more moderate position of improving education through incremental change, it is crucial to the success of any reform effort that a systems view prevails in order for the planned re-forms to be maximally effective. This is true be-cause of the complex interrelationships that exist between and among subsystems and between a sys-tem and its environment. Systems have the capabil-ity of sealing off structural and process changes that affect a single subsystem and of developing new subsystems that help them maintain their long-term dynamic homeostasis consistent with their established teleology. This sealing off is not necessarily done consciously by people within the system, but is instead an inherent quality of systems. As illustrated in this chapter, a well-established system can maintain this dynamic homeostasis and resist efforts to change it if those efforts address only one or a few subsystems. Therefore, to maintain the system, educational reformists must understand how the subsystems work and must consciously anticipate the effects of their efforts on specific subsystems. They must also consider the consequent effects of the changed subsystem on other subsystems with which it interacts. If their reform efforts are to succeed, reformists need not only to carefully analyze and understand the information needs of the system and its major subsystems, they must also understand the way the system exchanges information with its environment.

REFERENCES

Banathy, B. H. 1991. *Systems design of education.* Englewood Cliffs, N.J.: Educational Technology Publications.

Betts, F. 1992. How systems thinking applies to education. *Educational Leadership,* November, 38–41.

Dolan, W. P. 1991. *World class schools: A blueprint for change.* Overland Park, Kans.: W. P. Dolan and Associates.

Gouldner, A. W. 1967. Reciprocity and autonomy in functional theory. In *System, change and conflict,* edited by N. J. Demerath and R. A. Peterson. New York: The Free Press.

Hansen, J. B. 1992. Matching levels of accountability with information needs. Paper presented at the American Evaluation Association's annual conference in Chicago.

Herman, J. J. 1992. Total quality management basics: TQM comes to school. *School Business Affairs,* April, 20–28.

Katz, D., and R. L. Kahn. 1966. The social psychology of organizations. Chap. 2 in *Common characteristics of open systems.* New York: Wiley.

Miller, J. G. 1955. Toward a general theory for the behavioral sciences. *American Psychologist* 10:513–31.

Sarason, S. 1991. *The predictable failure of educational reform.* San Francisco: Jossey Bass.

Schrodinger, E. 1968. Order, disorder and entropy. In *Modern systems research for the behavioral scientist,* edited by W. Buckley. Chicago: Aldine.

Senge, P. M. 1990. *The fifth discipline: The art and practice of the learning organization.* New York: Doubleday.

von Bertalanffy, L. 1967. The quest for a general system theory. In *System, change and conflict,* edited by N. J. Demerath and R. A. Peterson. New York: The Free Press.

EDUCATIONAL CHANGE SYSTEMS
A Systems Design Process for Systemic Change

Patrick M. Jenlink

—

The human mind is able to create an inner world that mirrors the outer reality but has an existence of its own and can move an individual or a society to act upon the world. In human beings this inner world— the psychological realm—unfolds as an entirely new level and involves a number of phenomena that are characteristic of human nature. They include self-awareness, conscious experience, conceptual thought, symbolic language, dreams, art, the creation of culture, a sense of values, interest in the remote past, and concern for the distant future.

—Fritjof Capra

An examination of the literary mindscape of educational change over the past three decades yields a picture of confusion and general state of fragmentation in efforts of change related to schools, schooling, and American education. A closer examination of the real-world landscape of change and reform efforts in schools over the past ten years indicates that approaches to change have focused on parts of the system, but seldom consider the context for change systemically. We work to effect change within the existing system in a piecemeal fashion, localizing efforts to a specific part of the system, failing to understand the interrelatedness of the system's parts. This fragmentation arises out of an "incoherence in thinking" and resultant "incoherence in thought," which guides our decision processes and influences our worldviews of education as a complex and integrated social system (Bohm and Edwards 1991).

Moreover, this incoherence influences how we perceive and interpret complex problems in the educational system. Subsequently, it often results in confusion and conflict for the stakeholders who engage in attempts to provide informed solutions of change for the complex problems under consideration. In part, this incoherence is a cultural artifact of the existing system, and, therefore, those passing through the system are subject to, and participants in, the very incoherence that plagues their attempts to remedy the system. In other words, it is difficult to effect change in a system using a nonsystemic way of thinking that created the need for change in the first place. This paradox is recognized as a systemic fault (Bohm 1994) that must be considered in any efforts toward fundamental or systemic change.

This chapter offers the reader a systemic change process grounded in six years of field research and work with schools involved in systemic change and educational systems design.[1] This process represents a future-oriented systems inquiry approach to transcending existing mindsets about schools, education, and educational change efforts currently dominating the American educational system. Furthermore, systemic change is viewed as a democratic decision-oriented approach to changing fundamental values and beliefs about schools and education in the larger context of a dramatically changing global society.

Given that recent research and writing on the topic of educational change has attended to the predictable and intractable nature of educational reform, as well as the implicit problems plaguing practitioners and researchers in their efforts to change schools and schooling, this chapter will focus on a process for systemic change rather than establish a need for systemic change (Banathy 1991, 1992; Cuban 1990; Fullan 1991, 1993; Reigeluth and Garfinkel 1994; Reigeluth 1993; Sarason 1990). To this end, three sections are presented in this chapter that establish the following: (1) a foundational idea of systemic change and some clarifying characteristics and idiosyncracies; (2) a theory-, research-, and experience-based conception of a change systems dynamic essential to effecting successful systemic change through systems design; and (3) an educational systems design process that provides for a creative and requisite alternative to change in schools, schooling, and the educational system.

SYSTEMIC CHANGE

The relevant and critical literature of systemic educational change directs the reader to an emerging meaning for systemic change as a fundamental shift in value systems, embedded belief structures, and individual as well as shared mindsets of schools, schooling, and education. It is a process wherein changing one part of the system necessarily requires changing all parts of the system as well (Banathy 1991; Reigeluth 1994). Axiomatic to systemic change is understanding that the context for change is the entire system rather than a part. Also axiomatic to systemic change is a systems inquiry

approach to educational systems design. Underlying the systemic change process is the need for inner (personal-psychological) and outer (social-psychological) learning, which recognizes that *learning to change* is requisite to change in complex systems and must be connected with systems thinking, generative learning, higher levels of conscious awareness, and the development of an evolutionary consciousness (Banathy 1991; Fullan 1993; Senge 1990).

The integration of systems philosophy, theory, and practice into a disciplined form of systems inquiry and design (Ackoff 1981; Banathy 1988, 1991, 1992; Reigeluth 1993) provides for systems design/systemic change as a nascent discipline. Implicit in systems design is the creation of an *image ideal* that serves as the center of creativity and change for educational systems. Evolving from this image ideal, as schools and stakeholders implement the new design, is a dynamic living architecture that interacts heuristically with system stakeholders and their environment, creating a purpose-seeking and future-oriented self-renewing learning system for children and society.

Implicit in systems design/systemic change is the adoption of systems thinking and new conventions of language and communication that reconnect stakeholders and their educational system. Interrelated to these new conventions of systems thinking, language, and communication is systems design as a creative and generative learning process.

Change *in* System vs. Change *of* System

Most educational change and reform efforts to date are best characterized as change in the system. Systemic change suggests change *of* the system rather than change *within* the system. While there is some validity in attempting change within the existing system, this mindset brings with it much of the artifacts and baggage of past initiatives. In large part, when individuals go within the system they are confronted with entrenched practices, rigid mindsets, and deep underlying assumptions about schools and change. Often, these entrenched practices seriously challenge new efforts and lead to failure and abandonment. The presence of *systemic faults* (Bohm 1994) contributes to the overarching problems encountered in change efforts and provides for additional concern when attempting change within existing systems of learning. Systemic fault refers to the application of nonsystems thinking and thought to a systems problem. For example, when we attempt to solve a problem within an existing system, we are often focusing on the problem as context for change rather than the system. Nonsystemic thinking, incoherence created by diverse mindsets of randomly acting stakeholders, and lack of a common language for change all contribute to the presence of systemic faults that compromise change efforts. When we approach current educational problems with the same level of thinking and thought processes and consciousness that created the problem, solutions and proposed change efforts tend to be more superficial than fundamental, limited by the capacity and competencies of stakeholders to see the real problem that resides in nonsystemic thinking.

When we leap out of the existing system and engage in systems design, the change that occurs overcomes the systemic faults because a change in our thinking and thought processes is a primary part of building the competencies and capacities essential to engaging in the process. The entire system, including the inherent systemic faults, becomes the focus of design, rather than a fragmented part of the system.

Old and New Mindsets of the Educational Change Process

Mindsets are the mental maps or models that each individual carries and which serve to help a person conceptualize, interpret, and select various strategies for interacting with his or her personal and professional world.[2] How does a mindset of systemic change differ from one of more traditional change? Differences are created from each person's conception, based on acquired theories and experience of what educational change is. A wide range of experiences in past change initiatives and current educational needs gives challenge to old mindsets and provides the necessity for new mindsets to emerge.

While it is not the primary focus of this chapter to argue mindsets, it is deemed critical to the reader that some provision be made to bring clarity to our thinking about systemic change. Mindsets play a critical part in the thinking and thought process and often contribute to the systemic faults we encounter during educational change. Table 1 offers clarifying insight into the meaning of systemic change. Nineteen dimensions of the change process common to educational change are shown, which provide two different mindsets of educational change. The two mindsets should not be viewed as necessarily mutually exclusive. Each is provided as a context for better understanding the existing or potentially conflicting mindsets that often bring an incoherence to our thinking and working within change processes.

Systems Design/Systemic Change as Process Ideal

Ideals serve important functions in human existence. They are the "holy grail" that guides individuals' quests throughout their lives. The power of the quest lies in the journey rather than the destination. Seeking self-actualization and new levels of consciousness are examples of ideals we set before ourselves.

Using the educational systems design to transcend existing systems and design new learning systems is an example of an ideal (Banathy 1991, 1992). Systems design is an inseparable part of systemic change; the ideal is in the process of creating, not in the content of the process. It is in the process ideal of transcendence that systems design "evokes the power to start from scratch, outside the realm where previous causal actions are in play. Because transcendence is an ever-new state of being, once you enter it, each new moment is alive with fresh possibilities—possibilities that may never have seemed possible before" (Fritz 1989, 277–78). Once schools and stakeholders and system design facilitators engage in the systems design process, it becomes a lifelong journey of creative growth and learning.

DIMENSION	OLD MINDSET— TRADITIONAL CHANGE	NEW MINDSET— SYSTEMIC CHANGE
Metaphor	Innovation-diffusion, medicine, hard-systems, Newtonian	Hologram, learning community, soft-systems, quantum
Characteristics	Mechanistic, particularistic, piecemeal, fragmented, technical and incremental, consultant-designer based	Holistic, organic, interrelated and interconnected, integrative and evolutionary, user-designer based
Purpose	To work within existing educational system to bring about change (Banathy's Type A Change); aimed at impacting existing system	To leap out of old system and create a new educational system (Banathy's Type B Change); aimed at building capacity of stakeholders to create/design
Focus	Problem within existing educational system; fix existing system, concerned with structure of problem, identify solution	Problem is existing system; design new system, implementation of new design, continuous self-renewal
Scope	Project, program, innovation, particulate initiative, select dimensions, specific boundaries	Systemwide, understands change in relationship to whole, all dimensions, boundaryless
Mindset	Views schools as purposive in nature; change as planning, improvement of existing educational system, linear	Views system as purpose seeking; change as designing, creating a new educational system, dynamic
Motivation for Change	State or federal legislation or mandate (governed by political climate), economic pressures, negative dissatisfaction, need for error correction in existing system	Internal self-examination, positive dissatisfaction, self-renewal, natural decay in existing system with need for self-organizing to new levels
Primary Change Agent	External consultant as expert in educational change	Internal stakeholders as user-designers and learners in change
Role of Change Agent	Infusion of innovative ideas; consultant as expert, planner, director, developer, trainer	Creation of ideas; stakeholders as user-designers, developers, implementors, evaluators, learners
Locus of Control	Generally in the hands of funding sources and external agents (legislature, state); administration oriented	Community/school stakeholders as users of the educational system; user-designer oriented
Temporal	Short-term intervals, episodic in nature, beginning and ending	Long-term intervals, continuous in nature, beginnings with no endings
Stakeholder Involvement	Minimal and select, generally selected by administration, limited perspectives constrained by focus and locus of control	Broad base of stakeholders, diverse representation, multiple perspectives emerging constantly
Assumptions	People are unable to handle responsibility of change themselves, require experts; change will happen when educators are in compliance with regulations or normative standards set by controlling agencies	People are capable of handling the responsibility of change, may require varying levels of facilitation; change will occur when time/space continuum is provided with resources and liberation
Evaluation	External consultant, compliance-driven, studies innovation's impact on existing system and reports to funding agents, policy and management; methodologies include quantitative-experimental, qualitative-naturalistic; accountability (program, project, innovation)	Enables stakeholders in rigorous self-examination and critical inquiry as a function of designing a new system; methods include qualitative-naturalistic, reflection, dialogic research, action learning research; accountability (system) and design integrity

Table 1   Old and New Mindsets of the Educational Change Process

TABLE 1—CONTINUED		
Communication	Limited to consultant and contracting agent, top-down, filtered; consultant-expert language of change imported into context of change, innovation diffusion through training, information sharing, discussion and debate	Inclusion of all stakeholders as user-designers, bottom-up, open; socially constructed language within context of change, disciplined inquiry, knowledge construction, reflection and dialogue
Professional Development	Build capacity of individuals, focused on developing specific actors associated with a particulate innovation in the system; focused on training and development paradigm, staff-oriented skill development, develop curriculum, etc.	Capacity building of user-designer community—all stakeholders of the system; sees stakeholders as the system versus participants within the system; moves from a training to learning paradigm
Leadership	Superintendent viewed as primary leader, often with external consultant providing visionary direction or guiding the leaders' vision; principal as leader at a building level with school improvement team or building-level team often the action group	Views superintendent or building administrator as critical member of design team, with design team providing the leadership for the system change; leadership is at all levels of system and community
Resources	Limited internal resources (dollars, time, people) allocated as available or based on priority placed on innovation, more often external funding (state) viewed as critical to sustaining change (limited federal funds), budget-driven (money viewed as controlling variable)	Dedicated internal resources (dollars, time, people), change is the priority with design of new system guiding allocation of resources, external funding augments initial phases of change but not viewed as critical to sustaining change
Policy	Rigid, fixed decision rules, governing components of the school, systematic	Flexible, constantly revisioned decision rules, systemwide and holistic in focus

A CHANGE SYSTEMS DYNAMIC FOR EDUCATION

What is primarily needed is a growing realization of the extremely great danger of going on with a fragmentary process of thought. Such a realization would give the inquiry into how thought actually operates that sense of urgency and energy required to meet the true magnitude of the difficulties with which fragmentation is now confronting us.

—David Bohm

Changing complex social systems like schools involves negotiating multiple intercolliding systems that interrelate and contribute to the total identity of the system as well as provide a source of identity for individuals within the system. Myriad factors contribute to the increasing difficulty of attempting to change schools. Six of these factors are of immediate concern when considering systemic change.

Considerations for Systemic Change

First, the dynamic nature of complex systems is generally not understood at a high level of sophistication by most stakeholders. Only recently has the literature begun to provide support for comprehending the complexity of change in social systems (see Banathy 1991, 1992; Fullan 1993; Reigeluth and Garfinkel 1994; Reigeluth 1993; Senge 1990).

Second, since people derive their identity as a participant in the system (either as an internal or external stakeholder), changing systems threatens stakeholder identity and thus elicits resistance. Threats arise when the integrity of organizational or individual worldviews is challenged and/or undermined by forced or mandated change. Personal and organizational mindsets are formed from our experiences within and from complex social systems. In unconscious and significant ways, we derive our personal identity from the cultural fabric of the system (Bohm and Edwards 1991). In a similar fashion, the organization takes its own identity from the systems culture in which it interacts.

Third, there exist few real-world examples of fundamental change or systemic change processes that could serve to guide such a process. Banathy (1991) and Reigeluth (1993) provide two design-oriented approaches to systemic change, but there is limited practical experience in the field. Additionally, the absence of a field-based and research-grounded systemic change process presents a major dilemma to educators or change agents interested in this type of fundamental change. In the absence of strong processes or experiences to connect to, individuals and systems tend to fall back on familiar cognitive structures and routines to guide the change process, thus rendering systemic change victim to old mindsets and familiar patterns of lesser resistance.

Fourth, most change efforts to date have championed a consultant-based approach to change rather than a stakeholder-based approach.[3] Furthermore, most change efforts are passively democratic in the decision-making process and are often only representative in nature. When processes or models of change fail to recognize the need for an active participation of a diverse and broad base of stakeholders in decision matters within change process, loss of ownership ensues and growing resentment and resistance to change occurs. Change efforts that are top-down and mandated rather than grassroots and generated by a shared assumption of necessity, common purpose and sense of concern for children, tend to be forced and fragmented.

Fifth, a cognitive dimension that creates some difficulty in effecting systemic change includes the dynamic nature of language and thought, thinking and learning, and the building of the mindsets or mental models and deep structures or assumptions of schools, schooling, and educational change (Bohm 1980, 1994; Capra 1988; Senge 1990). The building of these mindsets is guided by the interaction of our perceptions, thought, and assumptions (opinions) as we interact and negotiate our professional and personal lives. Language forms thought and thought shapes language. As we engage in systemic change, language and thought and thinking and learning play critical roles in our learning and unlearning the cognitive maps and associated routines that govern our lives and give rise to the deep structures of schools and the schooling processes.

Sixth, a critical factor in negotiating change in complex systems is the management of the transitions, which are very different, though interrelated, to change. As Bridges (1991) notes, *"change is situational: the new site, the new boss, the new team roles, the new policy. Transition is the psychological process people go through to come to terms with the new situation. Change is external, transition is internal"* (p. 3). Educational change efforts are generally first introduced in the external social settings or social-psychological space of groups, teams, entire faculties of schools, etc. The potential for failure or success of change resides in managing the intra- and interpersonal psychological space where assumptions, mindsets, and emotions for familiar and interpretative structures reside. Managing the external change effort or process is only one dimension of the systemic change process. While managing change is important, providing facilitation and support for stakeholders as they experience internal psychological transitions is essential to the success of systemic change.

Changing the System Requires Changing Ourselves First

In systemic change, the individual is the nexus of the change process. Changing the deep fundamental structures of a system begins with changing the internal mental structures of people, their mindsets, which govern and give rise to the external system structures. This type of change alters the identity relationship stakeholders have with the system. Schools and communities as social systems are complex webs of relationships constructed by people through their interactions. Schools and communities also consist of dynamic relationships between people, their culture, and the environment. Internal and external relationships form connections that create the contexts for learning in which children, parents, and educators live their educational lives. As people interrelate in the system, they communicate through language, sharing culturally transmitted symbols and artifacts of their existence.

"Growth, change, and ultimately evolution occur as individuals, organizations, and society increase the depth of their relationships by continually broadening and strengthening their interdependent connections" (Land and Jarman 1992, 189). Change, either *in* or *of* complex systems, requires that the individuals the system comprises must change or make a transition on an intrapsychological level before change on an interpsychological level is possible (Bridges 1991). A change in identity is inevitable for all involved, and the option in guiding the change within ourselves is available through authentic participation.

Transitions on an intrapsychological level include shifts in assumptions, mindsets, conceptual language structures, and thinking/thought processes. In short, "old ways have to be relinquished before new systems will work . . . people have to let go of a piece of their identity to protect the integrity of the whole" (Bridges 1991, 31). And each shift does not occur independently of the other. Language, thought, and thinking processes are all interwoven

into a dynamic that directs individual associations within the complex web of relationships. Figure 1 suggests that language and thought interact through and in conversation. This interaction is influenced by individual perceptions governed by personal assumptions and mindsets. As language shapes thought and thought shapes language, they are mutually influenced by perceptions. This dynamic also influences individual and organizational learning, and contributes to the evolutionary nature of change in the whole system. Learning change is first about learning about ourselves—learning our personal assumptions, mindsets, competencies, capacity for fundamental change. It is about becoming self-aware. It is about learning a new inner voice (Vygotsky [1934] 1988) and language as well as new external conventions of language and communication.

We are all responsible for the changes sought in society because we are the change we seek to bring about. Perhaps Land and Jarman (1992) state it most succinctly when they say, "transcending where we are can occur when we recognize that we are infinitely able to empower ourselves to change when it is appropriate. Changing our conscious belief to one of self-empowerment will be the doorway to changing everything else. As individuals shift, so too will organizations and the larger society" (p. 219).

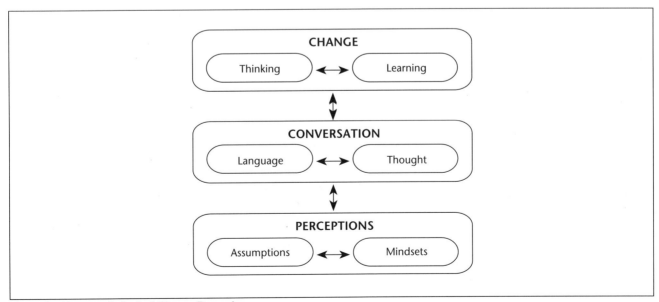

Figure 1   Intrapsychological Change Dynamic

Change Systems Dynamic

When one considers that change in a system begins within the individual stakeholders of the system, the previously discussed factors become important considerations in preparing for systemic change. It is in the dynamic interrelationships of these factors that we find the beginnings for a change systems dynamic fundamental to systemic change.[4] Of critical importance are the elements of thinking and thought that are inseparable from language and learning, and which are critical to changing ourselves. Also central to this change systems dynamic is a decision-oriented disciplined inquiry approach to systems design that guides the systemic process for change. Finally, there is an empowering potential of a dynamic that is designed for change within individuals, their human activity systems (Checkland 1981), and the whole social system. Figure 2 gives the reader a general framework for the change systems dynamic as six of the dimensions are explored in detail.

In the following paragraphs I will elaborate a clearer picture of the change systems dynamic by selecting six primary elements from the previous discussion—five of which will be addressed in the remainder of this section. The sixth element, educational systems design, will be discussed in the third section of the chapter, and a set of design axioms that interrelate with the change axioms presented in this section will be provided. At the end of the discussion for each of the five dimensions, there are a set of systemic change axioms, which are guides for the reader. Together, the elaborations and axioms create the foundation for a change systems dynamic essential to successful systemic change.

It should be made clear that each of the six dimensions of the change systems dynamic discussed must be viewed and understood as dynamically interrelated and interdependent with all the others. Confusion and conflict will plague the change process and result in an incoherence in thinking if those who choose to use the change system dy-

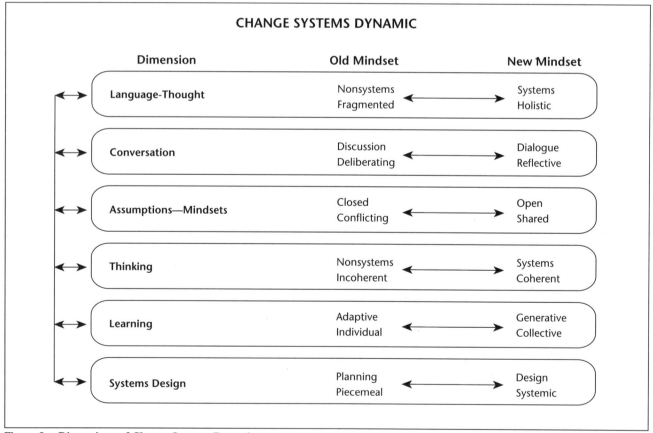

Figure 2   Dimensions of Change Systems Dynamic

namic attempt to apply one element of the system at a time.

Change Axiom: Changing complex social systems like educational systems and schools will require a disciplined decision-oriented inquiry approach to systems design.

Change Axiom: Complex social systems are difficult to change and require a dynamic system of change that recognizes the interrelated and interdependent nature of language and thought, conversation, thinking and learning, and the inter- and intrapsychological contexts of change.

Language and Thought in Systemic Change

Language plays a strong role in the shaping of our overall worldviews as well as in expressing them. Language "is clearly of key importance in thought, in communication, and in the organization of human society in general" (Bohm 1980, 27). The words that make up our language, whether in educational change processes or classroom learning of students, hold a special relationship to thought. "The realm between thought and word is a living process; thought is born through words. . . . But thought that fails to realize itself in words also remains a 'Stygian shadow'" (Vygostky 1988, 255). There is a certain transition that occurs from perception to thinking, and a generalized reflection of reality takes form in the basic characteristic of words. From perception to thinking, and thinking to thought, meaning of words, and ultimately our language (see fig. 1) depends "not only on the context that is being observed and our immediate perception, it also depends on how our perceptions are shaped by our thoughts, as well as on what we do, to test our conclusions, and to apply them in practical activities" (Bohm 1980, 43).

In examining the educational reform and change literature, characteristics or patterns of language emerge that reflect the general discourse of the moment. Such terms as school improvement, restructuring, and systemic change carry a particular cognitive valence as well as presence of deep underlying beliefs and assumptions about change in educational settings (see Banathy 1992; Elmore 1990; Lieberman 1986; Murphy 1991; Reigeluth and Garfinkel 1994). These variant forms of educa-

tional change language contribute to levels of confusion and conflict when participants in change processes attempt to communicate only when informed by the literature they have read. (See table 1 for examples of common terminology associated with more traditional change literature and that associated with systemic change.)

When individuals and collectives attempt to engage in meaningful discourse, there is a level of incoherence in thinking (see fig. 2) that emerges and contributes largely to confusion in the overall change process. As Bohm (1980) notes, "every language form carries a kind of dominant or prevailing worldview, which tends to function in our thinking and in our perception whenever it is used, so that to give a clear primary structure to language is usually very difficult" (p. 46). Comparable to a mindset, or worldview, according to Land and Jarman (1992),

> is that set of shared assumptions that make up our fundamental idea of how the world works—how things fit together. It is largely unquestioned, it is "the way things are." We accept the traditional wisdom of a worldview . . . we are not conscious of the thoughts forming our worldviews. It is simply the way things have always been and always will be. (p. 9)

It is necessary, therefore, in the study of educational change language to give serious and sustained attention to its worldview, both in content and function. In systemic change, knowing the language is of particular importance when one considers that language is a "representation of the images and concepts that occur in the brain . . . knowing the systems principle language helps the mind push for a broader and more inclusive set of images" (Nadler and Hibino 1990, 169).

Change Axiom: Language is a dynamic cultural artifact that takes an important role in effecting change in complex social systems like education.

Change Axiom: Language conveys and helps to create meaning and understanding among all stakeholder participants in educational change efforts.

Change Axiom: Old languages of school or educational change must be subject to close scrutiny in deter-

mining viability or appropriateness of use in any systemic change or systems design process.

Change Axiom: *A common change language is essential in matters of creating fundamental change in complex social systems. A common language must be socially constructed, guided by knowledgeable facilitators competent in conventions of change language, and shared on basis of meaning and understanding.*

Change Axiom: *Social language is subject to systemic faults and habits of thought in both structure and utilization; therefore, stakeholders and facilitators who participate in change must engage in systems thinking as a part of constructing a systemic change language.*

Change Axiom: *Systemic change will require communicative competencies in systems language appropriate to educational systems design.*

Conversation and Dialogue

Transmitting symbolic meaning is a primary function of language. Language represents associations and abstractions commonly held by an individual or collectives, and which are necessary for conveyance of meaning within the communication process. An equally important function of language is the shaping of individual and social thought while simultaneously serving as the reciprocal medium in which thought fashions language. When we focus on the importance of language in renegotiating the assumptions and mindsets that govern our worldviews, it is important to provide appropriate containers within which our change conversations are conducted (in this sense, container is a metaphor for conventions of conversation that support discussion and dialogue). Dialogue is a primary form of conversation for educational systems design and systemic change (see fig. 2).

Dialogue's purpose is to create a setting where "conscious collective mindfulness" can be maintained (Isaacs 1993, 31). As conversation, dialogue focuses on bringing to the surface and altering the tacit infrastructure of thought. Making the tacit infrastructure of thought explicit enables participants in dialogue to experience and potentially alter the deep underlying assumptions or opinions

that serve as self-defeating or self-deceptive conventions of reality.

Dialogue as design conversation is a process ideal. It is not what we create that is so important; it is the process of creation, which frees us from our existing systems of captivation. Dialogue creates the space necessary for design to take place, a space that extends beyond the incoherent patterns created by diverse worldviews and concealed assumptions. It provides a space wherein participants may disclose their assumptions and share their worldviews in suspension of judgment, giving way to creating a collective consciousness that can communicate and think together.

Dialogue differs from discussion or debate because it requires creating an increasingly conscious environment in which a special kind of "cool inquiry" can take place (Isaacs 1993). Discussion or debate does not require these types of environments. Quite the contrary, participants tend to act out their discourse roles rather unconsciously under the control of their differing assumptions. And often the interactions become heated arguments focusing more on defending one viewpoint over another. Participants characteristically engage in deliberation of the discussion's content. The result is resistance to change and further fragmentation of the system. People adopt defensive routines and negotiate barriers that exist primarily in their minds. Wilber explains the defensive and often fragmentary nature of discussion: "The simple fact is that we live in a world of conflict and opposites because we live in a world of boundaries. Since every boundary line is also a battle line, here is the human predicament: the firmer one's boundaries, the more entrenched are one's battles" (Wilber 1979, 19–21).

Dialogue offers an opportunity for stakeholders engaged in change to negotiate boundaries and make transitions within a safe space. It also allows them to engage in creating a collective, mindful consciousness and a community for creative change through collective inquiry and reflection. (Review fig. 1 while integrating the various conventions of language, conversation, thinking, etc., presented in the text.) Defense routines are set aside, assumptions and opinions are suspended for friendly discourse, and judgments are suspended, thus providing the opportunity to examine self- and self-in-the-system relationships.

Change Axiom: Conversation as a medium of change in complex social systems like schools and education may lead to fundamental change or further crystallization of existing mindsets.

Change Axiom: The form of conversation (i.e., discussion or dialogue) used in systemic educational change directly influences language and thought systems and may lead to fragmentation and breakdown in relationships. Careful attention must be given to purpose and design of the conversation within systemic change processes.

Change Axiom: Dialogue is a primary form of conversation best suited to educational systems design as a creative process.

Change Axiom: Suspension of assumptions and judgment within gatherings of stakeholders is a critical element of systemic change conversations. It is important to stakeholders in negotiating a context of trust and safety wherein participants may begin to disclose and deconstruct deep structures of schools, schooling, education, and change processes.

Change Axiom: Stakeholder competencies and capacity for creating and sustaining a change conversation through a common change language must be fostered and developed very early in the systemic change process.

Thinking Systemically to Overcome Habits of Thought

Bohm (1994) offers an important insight to understanding how systems of thinking and thought sometimes break down. His insight may help schools overcome the fragmented and intractable nature of educational reform. He suggests that thought has been constantly evolving, forming its own system and constantly interacting with the culture of our educational system. This interaction is facilitated by old mindsets and nonsystemic thinking (see fig. 2). Over time, this interaction contributes to the evolution of fragmentary forms in our language and thought processes. It becomes easy

to understand how this fragmentary form in our language and thought systems contributes to the growing concern and demand for a systemic approach to educational change. This is especially true when, as Bohm relates, "the system has a fault in it—*a systemic fault*. It's not a fault here, there or there, but it is a fault that is all throughout the system. . . . It's everywhere and nowhere. You may say 'I see a problem here, so I will bring my thought to bear on this problem.' But 'my' thought is part of the system. It has the same fault as the fault I'm trying to look at, or a similar fault" (Bohm 1994, 19).

In application of this notion, the systemic fault in educational reform lies in applying old thought structures to problems they helped create. We can no longer attempt to address present or future problems at the same level of consciousness or use habits of thought with which they were created. Otherwise, it becomes an educational paradox not resolvable within the existing system of educational practice. Our habits of thought contribute much to how we negotiate our roles in educational change processes. Overcoming systemic faults and compromising habits of thought will require a new conscious awareness. As Bohm (1980) offers,

> When we really grasp the truth of the oneness of the thinking process that we are actually carrying out, and the content of thought that is the product of this process, then such insight will enable us to observe, to look, to learn about the whole movement of thoughts and thus to discover an action relevant to this whole, that will end the "turbulence" of movement which is the essence of fragmentation in every phase of life. . . . What is primarily needed is a growing realization of the extremely great danger of going on with a fragmentary process of thought. Such a realization would give the inquiry into how thought actually operates that sense of urgency and energy required to meet the true magnitude of the difficulties with which fragmentation is now confronting us. (p. 19)

Dialogue as medium of exchange in the systems design container offers stakeholders access to negotiation of existing thinking and thought processes, leaping out of old systems of thinking and creating an emptiness or creative space in which to design a future-oriented educational system for schools.

Change Axiom: Educational systems design and systemic change requires systems thinking and disciplined approaches to systems inquiry.

Change Axiom: Facilitators and stakeholders as user-designers in systems design and systemic change must develop the appropriate competencies and capacity for systems thinking to engage in fundamental change. A self-aware state (proprioception) is important to changing existing thinking and thought systems.

Change Axiom: Assumptions and mindsets as well as perception govern heavily the thinking and thought systems used in educational change.

Change Axiom: Facilitators and stakeholders as user-designers are subject to systemic faults created by old thought processes. Habits of thought tend to act as systems of reflexes, often exacerbating existing educational problems.

Change Axiom: Collective thinking and reflection are essential to changing assumptions and mindsets and are supported best through dialogue.

Learning for Systemic Change

Systemic change is about learning change in ourselves. Systems design is about learning change for a new system. As Fullan (1993) notes, "focusing on the individual is not a substitute for system change, *it is the most effective strategy for accomplishing it*" (p. 135). Learning change in ourselves and for a new system will require new vistas of learning that are creative, generative, and transcendent in nature. Language, thought, and conversation are important and evolutionary components of learning as a part of the change systems dynamic. The type of learning suggested must begin with the individual stakeholders, but must also consider the power of team and organizational learning. "Organizations learn through individuals who learn. Individual learning does not guarantee organizational learning. But without it no organizational learning occurs" (Senge 1990, 139).

Learning is the process of constructing, deconstructing, and reconstructing complex cognitive systems and is influenced by the power of perceptions of our environments. Furthermore, learning (individual, collective, and organizational) is shaped by, and simultaneously shapes, our language and thought systems. When we engage in thinking processes, such as critical thinking or systemic thinking, we are guided in our cognitive processes by our mindsets, assumptions, and thoughts. Collective thinking is influenced by shared mental models and empowered through dialogic conversation. The juxtaposition of language and thought, thinking and learning, and conversation gives clear meaning and understanding of how change in one element creates a necessity for changing all processes. When we seek to bring about systemic change, the change begins within individuals and moves outward to the larger system under consideration.

Finally, where systems design is learning for change of the system, it is imperative that stakeholders and change facilitators make a transition from learning processes that are adaptive or single-loop learning and reinforce existing normative structures (Argyris and Schon 1978; Senge 1990). Schein (1985) shares insight into these normative structures as he explains how culture is a learned product of collective experience. He sees it as

> basic assumptions and beliefs that are shared by members of an organization, that operate unconsciously, and that define in a basic "taken for granted" fashion an organization's view of itself and its environment. These assumptions and beliefs are learned responses to a group's problems of survival in its external environment and its problems of internal integration. (p. 6)

Overcoming these cultural learnings will require us to attend to the individual and the learning society (Fullan 1993). Fullan directs our attention to the importance of inner and outer learning, where "inner learning (intrapersonal sense-making) and outer learning (relating and collaborating with others) run together but they are also separable" (Fullan 1993, 137).

Individuals and school systems must embrace creative, generative, design-oriented learning processes that empower participants in the systems design/systemic change process in order to transcend the existing educational system (Banathy 1995; Land and Jarman 1992; Nelson 1993; Senge 1990). Of importance to the systems design process is the use of teams and conversation for design learning.

Senge (1990), setting out five disciplines of the learning organization, identified team learning, in combination with systems thinking, shared visions, mental models, and personal mastery, as an essential element to understanding learning within collective settings. He elaborates team learning as the following:

> The discipline of team learning starts with "dialogue," the capacity of members of a team to suspend assumptions and enter into a genuine "thinking together.". . . The discipline also involves learning how to recognize the patterns of interaction in teams that undermine learning. The patterns of defensiveness are often deeply ingrained in how a team operates. If unrecognized, they undermine learning. If recognized and surfaced creatively, they can actually accelerate learning. (p. 10)

Where design and team learning are creative and generative experiences, change and growth are the outcome for both the individuals involved in change and the system. "Learning results in changes in knowledge, beliefs, and behaviors. Learning also enhances organizational capacity for innovation and growth" (Watkins and Marsick 1993, 8–9).

Land and Jarman (1992) identify creative learning as "consciously developing an atmosphere where creativity, mutual support, interdependence, and non-judgment are fostered thereby supporting individuals and groups to discover their potential" (p. 230).

Nelson (1993) offers important insight into systems design and creative learning: "In recursive fashion, systems design as a creative process can be used as a form of intellectual technology to design and implement new complex forms of serving systems such as educational systems (including primary, secondary, undergraduate, graduate, vocational, and continuing education). Systems design also provides the necessary means to create coherency be-

tween form and content in a systemically designed educational system" (p. 146). Frantz (1994) creates additional insight into the nature of design learning "as a value-driven human activity process which fosters the emergence of images of a system's future that are:

- clear enough to permit its components to organize themselves into that future;

- powerful (attractive, meaningful, value-actualizing) enough to pull them through the inevitable difficulties in doing so; and

- complete enough to specify the activities required to accomplish the system's mission(s)" (p. 55).

Banathy (1994) further explains educational systems design, in the context of systemic change, as learning

> by learning to design and engaging in it, we learn as an organization and as individuals. As individuals we learn what contribution we shall make to the whole, and as an organization we learn to reexamine continuously our collective values, perspectives, purposes, and modes of operations; and thus gain insight and develop knowledge, based on which we can make continuous contributions to the life and betterment of the system. (p. 33)

Learning is a key dimension of a change systems dynamic, which serves as the nexus for learning change in individuals and learning for change of the educational system—systemic change. Interacting through dialogue, language, and thought helps guide the learning and unlearning processes essential to inner transition and outer growth. Learning also enables participants in systemic change to make important internal and external connections to the fluid structures constantly evolving within the culture of the system.

Change Axiom: *Systemic change requires learning change in ourselves and learning change of the educational system. Learning change is a systems design process wherein we design ourselves and the educational system simultaneously with a constant focus on creating a future-oriented learning system for children.*

Change Axiom: Learning, language, thinking, thought, and assumptions and mindsets are dynamic and interrelated processes and systems that contribute to change in individuals, collectives, and complex social systems.

Change Axiom: With individuals, learning begins on an inner psychological plane and moves to an outer social-psychological plane.

Change Axiom: Learning is influenced by context and culture, and participants in the systemic change process must understand the strong influences that culture contributes to protecting deep social structures.

Change Axiom: A scaffolding system for cognitive development and ongoing support is required in authentic systems design and systemic change processes. Managing transitions on the inner psychological level is a part of the scaffolding system. We must attend to the cognitive and affective transitions, maintaining a collective mindful consciousness of all stakeholder needs as they move through endings of the old system to beginnings of the new system.

Change Axiom: Facilitators and stakeholder participants must develop the competencies and capacities to engage in changing both current learning processes and practices.

The change systems dynamic presented so far has elaborated five of the six dimensions displayed in figure 2. The background text has provided important grounding in the role and dynamic nature of language, thinking and thought, dialogue, and learning as related to systemic change. Based on experience and field research in three districts (two in Michigan and one in Oklahoma) and research theory, it is believed that understanding these elements is essential to systemic change in education. The reader is cautioned to embrace one final thought: the fullest understanding of the conventions of language, thought, conversation, and learning necessary to bring about systemic change in schools can only be acquired through a direct, lived experience of systemic change that is guided by the disciplined inquiry of systems design.

Thus far, the text has depicted that it is the dynamic interactions of these various processes through experience that empowers us to change

ourselves and the system. Closely related is the need to unlearn much of who we are in terms of our old assumptions, mindsets, language and thought systems, and ways of thinking, learning, and communicating. The acquisition of the specific competencies related to each area examined is critical, as is the undertaking of ongoing capacity building as individuals, teams, and organizational systems.

One remaining element of the change systems dynamic, the educational systems design dimension, has yet to be explored. Up to this point, the chapter has focused more on philosophical, theoretical, and experience-based evolutionary underpinnings that played a critical role in the three districts that served as the crucible of creation and design that produced this change systems dynamic. The next section of the chapter provides an outline of the systems design process and gives some linkages for the reader by offering a set of design axioms[5] that serve to guide the design process. Additionally, the reader will be given access to some lessons learned from the field that have emerged throughout the past six years. In either case, the axiom or the lessons learned, the reader is cautioned to remember that there are no absolutes in systemic change, only possibilities for guiding our destiny and creating our future through a disciplined inquiry of discovery and creativity.

EDUCATIONAL SYSTEMS DESIGN

The design road is the road less traveled by the educational community, but once taken and followed, it will become a journey to create the future and not just retrace the past. The educational reform movement is not out of the woods yet. It stands at a juncture where it can either continue on the well-traveled road of improvement or select the less-traveled road of systems design.
—Bela Banathy

Educational systems design is an ideal creating process that enables stakeholders to transcend their existing system as they translate the ideal into reality. Grounded in systems philosophy, theory, and practice, it is a decision-oriented, disciplined inquiry approach that focuses on the entire system as the dynamic context for design. Implicit in the design process is a need to abandon old mindsets of change. This includes examining and changing existing conventions of language, thinking, conventions of discourse, and learning as they relate to fundamental change. Systems design seeks to create a future-oriented system by embracing and living a democratic ideal of participation. It is important to understand systems design as an intellectual technology (Banathy 1994; Nelson 1993), recursive in fashion that brings with it the capacity for creating coherence in thinking and thought through design learning.

This section of the chapter will complete the change systems dynamic introduced previously and integrate the various elements of the dynamic. The systems design process outlined in the following text relates six years of field experience in working with schools in systemic change initiatives. The reader should understand that the presentation of the process in different sections of text does not connote linearity or temporality. The process is dynamic and thus many of the various processes elaborated will occur simultaneously, specifically the changes required within and by the other dimensions of the larger change systems dynamic.

In the following sections, several design axioms are presented for consideration in systems design for systemic change. In addition, a brief discussion of lessons learned is presented in each section, which reflects professional experiences as a facilitator in systems design/change.

Design Conversation

Design conversation uses various conventions of conversational discourse as the creative medium of exchange between all stakeholders engaged in the design process. (The reader might find it useful to now apply systems design language/concepts to fig. 1 to form a clearer picture of the design process.) The design conversation also creates a space—a neutral zone or emptiness—where stakeholders make the transition from old to new. Creating this space is "about letting go of whatever is getting in the way of one's relationship to oneself or others. It may

involve suspending assumptions, attributions, judgments, or expectations. In order for this to occur, however, we must first realize we have these assumptions (or mental models)" (Spear 1993, 13). Carefully selecting the conversational medium is important to creating a secure climate for disclosure, suspension, and abandonment of old ways. Building a culture of trust through design conversation requires some sensitivity to people and their identity with the old ways. As Bridges (1991) notes, carefully crafted endings to old patterns are important. You must be careful, however. "You are trying to disengage people from it, not stomp it out like an infection. And in particular, you don't want to make people feel blamed for having been part of it . . . the past, which people are likely to idealize during an ending, was itself a time of change" (Bridges 1991, 31).

While these conventions include discussion and dialogue, the primary power of the design conversation is derived from a dialogic relationship (Bohm 1990; Bohm and Edwards 1991) as the creative medium. The important issue here is that user-designers take responsibility for designing their own form of conversations, informed by the potential (positive and negative) of different forms of conversation. It is important in the design of the conversational setting that the user-designers create a container in which the conversation will be held. Attention should be given to the number of participants and group dynamics as well as the physical setting to assure a creative experience.

Design Axiom: *Design of conversation is a process for creating the preferred convention of design conversation. The purposes of conversation in systems design are guided by the purpose of the systems design process.*

Design Axiom: *User-designers must understand that different forms of conversation (i.e., discussion and dialogue) are not necessarily mutually exclusive of each other. A systems design process often requires that an informing convention of conversation be used versus a collective sharing convention of conversation.*

Design Axiom: *Designing the conversation requires the design of a container to hold the conversation. The form of the container, dynamic relationships, size, etc., may necessarily change over time, and consequently influence the nature of the conversation.*

Design Axiom: Design conversations are heuristic in nature and undergo evolutionary change as user-designers engage in creative conversations of design. Language and thought interacting with the design medium and container give rise to shifting patterns in the design.

Design Axiom: Design conversations are forums for learning change within ourselves and learning change of the system.

Lessons Learned: Experience has demonstrated that falling into and out of dialogue and discussion forms of conversation is frequent. Old patterns of discourse are difficult to leave behind and require patience on the part of the facilitator and user-designers. Old habits and defense routines surface quickly, and changing of mindsets is a long and arduous process. Facilitators must take particular care in mediating the tensions within conversational forums of design or the creative dimension will lose out to fragmentation and the design process will break down. The success of design conversation is influenced heavily by changes in the old language of habit to a new language of design. It is particularly difficult for stakeholders to understand how language and thought are interrelated and how they contribute to either coherence or incoherence of thinking directly related to the design/change. Facilitators should be aware that introducing the idea of designing a design conversation is often confusing and must be given appropriate attention. It is important for facilitators to videotape conversations and other design processes. The recorded conversation can then be used as a context for the design team to distance themselves from their work and engage in collective reflection. This is a powerful tool for enabling user-designers to become self-aware of the process and their role in empowering or constraining the process.

Stakeholders as User-Designers

At the heart of any change process is the people who implement and live the change on a day-to-day basis. Unfortunately, many of the past change efforts have focused more on changing peoples' behaviors collectively within their roles in organizations and have afforded far less attention to change in the deep underlying assumptions and mindsets individually and collectively held by stakeholders. A misaligned focus of this nature gives rise to one of the more common systemic faults plaguing educational change. Another systemic fault in most conventional change processes lies in the scope and nature of stakeholder inclusion, from the first stages of design through implementation and continuous growth and renewal.

Banathy (1991), Carr (1994), and Reigeluth (1993) give critical insight and support to the need for a diverse and broad base of participation by stakeholders in the change process. Banathy's work has particularly influenced the adoption of a user-designer approach (or stakeholder approach). The imperative to stakeholder involvement originates in understanding the power and potential for success lies in the multiple perspectives and in the need for participant buy-in or ownership in the newly designed system.

Design Axiom: Stakeholders must develop a shared assumption of necessity for fundamental systemic change as well as a necessity for selecting educational systems design as the process for accomplishing systemic change. The success of stakeholder involvement in the process lies in their authentic ownership.

Design Axiom: Selection and inclusion of stakeholders in the design process must be authentic and reflect a strong democratic ideal honoring diversity (including race, gender, age, etc.). Identification of the stakeholder audiences should be accomplished by a nonbiased and nonthreatening team of individuals and not a single administrator or a few select individuals.

Design Axiom: Stakeholders must be recognized as critical participants in the design process and not representatives without voice in decision matters. Ownership of the new design will come when stakeholders are recognized as vested users and designers (user-designers) of the educational system.

Design Axiom: Stakeholder participation requires basic competencies and knowledge requisite to systems design and fundamental change. An invitation to participate as a user-designer brings with it the responsibility of the school district and those in responsible roles to provide the foundations needed to build capacity in each design team member.

Design Axiom: Begin with a core design team of twelve to seventeen members and expand the team's membership by establishing site or advocacy design teams that will be facilitated by the core design team. The expanded design team will engage in specific design functions.

Lessons Learned: Identification, invitation, and inclusion of stakeholders as user-designers is not easy. Baggage from past encounters with educational change leaves potential participants skeptical and often bitter. Experience has demonstrated that capacity building is often resource intensive and time intensive. It has also been the experience that new conventions of capacity building are prerequisite. Old models of staff development must give way to systems thinking and practice as well as understanding development as an experience-based learning process. The design process generally begins by designing learning opportunities and is guided by a design facilitator. A stakeholder approach to educational systems design/systemic change brings some requirements for expanding the core design team over time. Beginning with a core team of twelve to seventeen members and then expanding it by creating site design teams or advocacy teams for specific design tasks engages a larger number of stakeholders in the process, which results in a stronger network for communication and sharing. Over time, the core team members may take on new roles as design facilitators for the emerging site or advocacy design teams at the building level. Experience indicates that stakeholders can move toward a self-renewing system, empowered by user-designers and assisted by a design facilitator who guides the scaffolding process of development. A process for renewal of the design team must be designed by the team early on, thereby bringing new members in and allowing old members to transfer to a less active role. It is important to remember that as user-designer team members they remain critical players in the overall systemic change process.

Providing a Scaffolding System for Change

"The single biggest reason organizational changes fail is that no one thought about endings or planned to manage their impact on people" (Bridges 1991, 32). Managing change and people's transitions during change form two interrelated dimensions of the scaffolding system for systems design and systemic change. Managing change as the external experiences and managing transitions as the internal psychological transitions includes six major areas of support: (1) systems design; (2) individual, team, and organizational/system development; (3) evaluation (critical inquiry and organizational learning); (4) information management; (5) language and communications systems; and (6) management and leadership.

Changing mindsets, developing the requisite competencies, and fostering capacity building are the major foci of the scaffolding system.[6] Design team members as well as the larger body of stakeholders in the school system and community require support as a critical part of the design process. Over time, the scaffolding system will change and evolve with the changes in the system, taking on new functions. Creating communities of conscious collective mindfulness requires a reinforcing structure, a support system that scaffolds participants in such ways that leads to reflection, shared insight, and renewal for design of future experimentation.

Systems design and systemic change "demands a new mindset. That new mindset requires a very significant transition, as the old expectations are painfully abandoned and a long, difficult journey is made . . . You have to manage the big transition from the old assumptions and expectations of isolated and piecemeal change to the new ones" (Bridges 1991, 75). As discussed in the previous section introducing the change systems dynamic, stakeholders derive their identities from the cultural fabric of the existing system. Interacting through various conventions of language and thought and sharing in deep structures of the school and schooling process, individuals require structured and caring means of cognitive scaffolding (Tharp and Gallimore 1988) and affective support. Scaffolding creates a system for making the transition from old mindsets to new, providing a trustful and safe space for individuals to negotiate endings and beginnings as they travel through the neutral zone (Bridges 1991). Scaffolding also provides the support for nurturing and developing a collective consciousness through creating a community of learners.

Design Axiom: All stakeholders should have access to scaffolding and support, whether they are a part of the core user-designer team, members of the expanded design team infrastructure, or informal participants in the systemic change process. Managing transitions as part of design is requisite for all.

Design Axiom: Constructing the scaffolding system is a prerequisite to beginning the design process. And, beginning something new starts with ending the old. The scaffold is necessary to support all elements of systems design and change, but the scaffold must remain subject to the recursive conventions of design and the need for self-renewing change.

Design Axiom: Identification and design of initial capacity and competency building processes should be guided by a core team of stakeholders as user-designers who understand the critical importance of being equipped to use the intellectual technology of systems design.

Design Axiom: Scaffolding requires the adoption of new mindsets of professional and organizational development. Development must become learner-centered and incorporate systems thinking and practice.

Lessons Learned: Scaffolding is often confused by old mindsets of staff development, evaluation, information management, communication, leadership and management of change, and a planning-oriented approach toward change. Changing mindsets is about changing people's identity as it relates to the existing system. People need a lot of help in making these transitions and negotiating new identities as they construct new mindsets. Defensive routines often appear in the form of denial, which quickly escalates from the personal to the collective (from *illusion* to *delusion* to *collusion*). Resistance leading to failure occurs most often when participants fall back into old familiar patterns and routines that create paths of least resistance. The critical issue here is that everyone must change, including the facilitator. And this change demands caring and respectful support. Participants should be informed as early as possible of the scope and intent of the change. It often helps to sensitize people to how their relationship to the system will change and what role they are expected to take. Using dialogue conversations as a way of examining assumptions and expectations has been useful in creating climates of trust and building collective consciousness essential to design. Experience indicates that the architecture for a scaffolding system for systemic change must be a part of the design and not parallel to the design process. Stakeholders are often given to adopting a support system for change that they are unwilling to abandon as the needs of the changing system evolve. Care should be given to providing an architecture that is capable of self-awareness and self-renewal.

The Importance of Understanding Context

Changing complex social systems must consider the context from which stakeholders derive their identity and their relationships to a changing world. Context reflects the relationships of stakeholder interactions with one another through language and thought, collective thinking, and shared learning experiences. Context also reflects the inner and outer connections that stakeholders have with the school system and that the school system has with the larger societal environment. Examining the context gives understanding to the structures of schools and schooling subject to design and change in creating a new system. Examining context also gives awareness to societal needs and creates understanding of the functions that a new educational system must play in the changing world. The issue here is not one of focusing on problems within the existing system, but rather of creating a sensitivity to the systemic context for change. Change facilitators should guide user-designers along paths of critical inquiry necessary to informing the stakeholders of the underlying need for change. In essence, the user-designers must create their own assumption of necessity for fundamental change. The key here is in the stakeholders' taking responsibility for the decision-making processes leading to transcendence of the existing system.

Changing a system requires that stakeholders and change facilitators first create contextual competencies, both internal and external, that inform the design process (Morgan 1988). It is also important to create this sensitivity in order to begin to disclose and make transparent (Jourard 1971) the systemic faults and deep structures of thought that cause resistance and set up defensive routines against fundamental change.

The evaluative system integral to empowering the systems design process must be one that advances a self-evaluative ideal and which includes a critical inquiry and organizational learning concept. The design team should focus on asking what kinds of contextual knowledge they need to inform and learn from the design process. Internal and external considerations must be made. Where self-critical inquiry focuses internally on the existing school system, a collective inquiry into the larger external context of education should seek to identify societal changes and advances in learning theory, educational practice, and relevant design considerations for a future-oriented educational system.

The exploration of the external world should not only inform the design process of important considerations in design, but it should also inform the participants in the design process of viable alternatives to existing mindsets and assumptions about schools and learning for children. In-depth exploration of the internal context should include critical examination and unfolding of the prevailing mindsets and assumptions about schools and schooling incorporating a broad-based approach to stakeholder involvement.

Internal contextual competencies should include such issues as language, communication and information management processes, existing resources available to the design process, past and current experiences in change efforts, and perceived needs for change. Creating a shared assumption of necessity for fundamental change must include contextual knowledge of both an internal and external nature. External competencies should include such issues as needs for sustaining a democratic society and workforce requirements for youth in transition. Stakeholder and facilitator alike should develop external competencies such as

those associated with shifting global trends and the functions of schools and education in a knowledge-based economy.

Design Axiom: *Creating contextual knowledge, understanding, and competency is an initial and continuous process of systems design. Internal contextual knowledge informs change within the individual as well as the design of the new system and implementation process for the new system. External contextual knowledge informs the design of the new system and creates awareness of the need to design a self-renewing system that interrelates to the needs of a rapidly changing global society.*

Design Axiom: *Context is deeply embedded with the cultural structures of language, knowledge, thought, and values and beliefs, all of which contribute to the prevailing shared worldviews or mindsets. Contextual competencies must be developed that enable user-designers to deconstruct and construct new structures.*

Design Axiom: *Contextual sensitivity is key to informing the systems design process. Changes in the context alter the relationship of design, implementation, and redesign of the system over time, thus creating a need for a constant contextual understanding. There is a mutual interdependency of the design process, context, and user-designer participation.*

Design Axiom: *New mindsets of evaluation that reflect self-evaluation, critical inquiry, reflection, and organizational learning must be developed as part of a inquiry system for creating ongoing contextual competencies and understanding.*

Design Axiom: *Creating contextual competencies is not limited to formal participation as user-designers. Informal participant stakeholders should also be party to developing related competencies, in particular those that empower all participants to shift from old to new mindsets.*

Lessons Learned: The purpose for creating contextual understanding must be clearly articulated for all stakeholders. Nonsystemic mindsets are particularly rigid toward the need for examining context. Experience has demonstrated that baseline data should be created early because it is key to informing the overall process for designing the design process. Internal contextual knowledge is sensitive to governing assumptions, mindsets, and processes for change that typically lie concealed within the minds of stakeholders. Making explicit the tacit or hidden structures is difficult. Creating external contextual knowledge and competencies creates an awareness of future possibilities for educational systems. Overcoming the parochial worldview in which stakeholders and communities become entrenched is difficult and requires moving outside the existing context and creating access to new perspectives. It is essential to involve as wide a representation of diverse stakeholder groups as possible. This should include special interest groups as well as the general stakeholder audiences. A variety of methods can be used. Internally, focus group and individual interview methods provide good examples of techniques for inquiry. Externally, carefully selected conferences, national workshops, and school-site visitations offer examples for knowledge acquisition that provide opportunity for collective inquiry. Experience has demonstrated that developing contextual competencies must be a direct responsibility of the participants. While it is critical for the facilitator to develop his or her own contextual competencies, they cannot become the sole source of knowledge informing the design process. Avoid expertism.

Designing the Design Process

Designing the design process is crucial to creating the endings we seek to create within ourselves and for the existing system. Design also plays an equally important role in creating the ideal, which guides the new beginnings for a future-oriented educational system. Designing the design process includes creating the scaffolding system, evaluation system, and information management and communication systems. Initially, user-designers engage in designing other key elements of the change systems dynamic, including a new change language, design conversations, and learning systems for design.

Facilitators should guide stakeholders to examine existing process models and design architectures grounded in theory and practice. Banathy (1991, 1992, 1994) and Reigeluth (1993) provide particularly relevant examples that give alternative system

design processes for consideration. Reigeluth's principles for systems design provide a well-articulated set of guiding principles that are well-grounded theoretically. Banathy (1991) offers a design journey process that guides educational systems design along four spirals of inquiry. He also offers a set of three systems models (systems-environment, functions-structure, motion-picture model), which serve as a lens for understanding systems design of education (Banathy 1992). A final note is made concerning a framework and option field model that Banathy (1995) presents for assisting the user-designer in determining the scope and focus of the system design.

Additionally, Checkland (1981) and Checkland and Scholes (1990) offer a soft-systems methodology that, while oriented toward designing solutions to complex problem sets, provides valuable insight for user-designers to incorporate in their design. Ackoff (1981) offers a useful concept for idealized design and support for a user-designer approach. Each of these different sources have contributed to the overall evolution of the systems design/systemic change process outlined in this chapter. Additional influences include the works from critical theory, organizational learning, language, and conversation—specifically, dialogue and quantum physics.

Designing the design process begins with determining the purpose of the systems design process and then developing the key elements of it. Facilitators are responsible to the user-designer participants in helping with the articulation of purpose. But they should not assume responsibility for determining the purpose. Responsibility rests where the ownership of the system will reside. Likewise, facilitators carefully guide stakeholders in identification and articulation of the key elements of the process, providing caution only when the process model being constructed reflects some incoherent thinking or implicit systemic fault. Again, the primary decision making should reside in the democratic body where ownership will ultimately rest: the users of the system.

The important issue for facilitators and user-designers alike is the building of necessary knowledge and competencies of systems philosophy, theory, practice, and design as well as a strong background in dialogue, conversation, conventions of language and communications, and individual-or-ganizational learning and development. Building the required capacity to undertake changing a complex system is requisite to embarking on the journey. However, as discussed earlier in this chapter, becoming involved in the systems design process is essential to changing individually, which directly contributes to changing the system.

Key and imperative considerations in an idealized educational systems design include the following: a clearly articulated purpose(s) statement that reflects a democratic voice; a set of core values and ideals that represent guiding assumptions essential to a self-renewing social system; characteristics or specifications that detail the system and give clarity and substantive meaning to the system; a set of functions that connect the educational system to the larger societal or suprasystem it serves; and the required enabling systems essential to providing support for fulfilling and sustaining the functions of the educational system as a living, dynamic system in harmony with its environment.

At each level there would be additional sublevels that further explicate the design of the system and provide the necessary architectural detail to transcend the existing system and give life to the ideal of the new design. As an example, user-designers would identify specific goals that detail the overarching purpose(s), identify subfunctions and subenabling systems, and so on. Each level gives clearer articulation to the ideal and specificity in ways to translate the design to reality.

Design Axiom: Designing the design process should be a democratic, decision-oriented process guided by a disciplined approach to systems inquiry. Formal stakeholders as user-designers and the process facilitator are responsible to informal stakeholder participants being informed about the design process.

Design Axiom: Facilitators are responsible to all stakeholders, but not for the stakeholders. Decisions must be made from a position of ownership, for the system resides in the user of the system.

Design Axiom: Designing the design is a recursive process that embraces the ideal of democratic self-renewal. A recursive inquiry into the design process and the design

itself should be an integral aspect of the designing process. Constantly redesigning the process ensures that a static point does not enter the system—i.e., systemic fault—which contributes to failure in the system.

Design Axiom: User-designers and facilitators should identify a sufficient level of detail for each dimension of the design to translate the ideal of the design into reality. Included is a clearly articulated purpose(s), core set of values and ideals, characteristics, functions, and enabling systems that reflect an ideal for the new system.

Lessons Learned: Design is messy and extremely difficult work that is time intensive for facilitators and stakeholders alike. There are no shortcuts to systems design or systemic change. Preparing for the design is a fundamentally challenging effort for those who must shift their mindsets from old ways of planning and change within the system to a design orientation focused on creating an entirely new system. Designing the design process is often misunderstood as simply selecting a good facilitator who advocates a particular design process. While selecting a good facilitator is important, stakeholders must understand that it is important for them to make the overall decisions in matters of designing the design process. It cannot be left to an outside expert if ownership of the system is to be maintained by stakeholders. Experience indicates facilitators often fall into traps of co-optation by administration or management and must be constantly monitored. Facilitation also brings with it the temptation to take the expert role and assume responsibility for decisions in matters of systems design selection. However, when the expert role is assumed, both the facilitator and stakeholders suffer the consequences. Stakeholders may be prone to selectively abandoning parts of the design, particularly when building new competencies and increased capacity for change threatens their identity or places additional demands on their time and resources. Facilitators must provide the necessary assistance in the design process to guard against this abandonment.

Implementing the New System

Designing a new system brings with it a corollary need for a process for implementation of the new design. In some frames of reference, the term "planning the implementation is used" (Reigeluth 1993, 128). For our purposes, the concept of design is maintained. There are some important considerations primary to the implementation process. First, facilitators and user-designer participants should observe that managing transitions does not end with the design of a new system, but rather it is an ongoing part of the process through implementation and beyond. Oftentimes, stakeholders are still captive to their old mindsets even when implementation is well underway. The larger context of the school and community may be in a different phase of transition than the formal design team members, and this could create the need for managing transitions on a macrolevel.

Second, user-designers must have a clear and present sensitivity to the internal dynamics of the design, stakeholders, and implementation context. During the design process many transitions have occurred in mindsets and the deep structures of the old system. There is a potential of instability that makes negotiating implementation often chaotic and challenging. A well-established set of contextual competencies will assist the facilitator and stakeholders as they set out to implement the design.

Third, the implementation process, as it serves to translate the design into reality, contributes to the change in context, design, and the stakeholders who were not anticipated or prepared for. Facilitators and user-designers alike should be prepared for uncertainty as a condition of the complex and dynamic nature of systemic change.

Fourth, a key to the success of implementation lies in how we learn from the process. Critical inquiry and organizational learning are important elements of the implementation process, connecting stakeholders with what is going on during the process and providing them with valuable positive feedback to assist in managing the transitions accompanying implementation. Other issues and concerns will emerge for participants in systems design as they move to the point of implementation. User-designers and facilitators should rely heavily on both the scaffolding system and the critical inquiry system during the implementation process.

Design Axiom: Design of the implementation process is integral to and mutually dependent on the design of the new system. It is an ongoing and continuous learning process that extends the design learning process and provides a context for constant inquiry into the appropriateness of the design and/or needed redesign of the system.

Design Axiom: Implementation of a new design requires a carefully aligned process that will translate the ideal design into reality. The values and beliefs of the implementation process should be in harmony with those of the new design and constantly in consideration of the values and beliefs of the implementation context.

Design Axiom: Implementation must consider the state of transition in the broad social context in which design is destined.

Design Axiom: Scaffolding implementation holds an equally important role in the support provided for designing the new system. In a way, the implementation process is a scaffolding of the design at a different level of the system.

Lessons Learned: Implementation is often a difficult time for many stakeholders because they begin to realize that the possibility of the system changing is increasingly certain. Facilitators may experience some heightened levels of discomfort and possibly some new levels of resistance, generally with the informal stakeholder participants. Experience indicates that informal stakeholders may hold the design team(s) and facilitator responsible for their discomfort and may accuse them of attempting to implement a design that is not shared by all stakeholders. Facilitators will need to pay particular attention to these increasing tensions and monitor group and community dynamics for indicators of resistance and rebellion to the new design. Expanding the design team and creating a communitywide network of information sharing concerning the design process is critical. Also, facilitators feel an increasing demand on their energies while everyone prepares for the major shift in their world. Change is predictably unpredictable, and no one should assume that because the design is ready and the implementation process is in motion, everything will go off as designed. Even the best of designs often encounter unexpected turbulence at times, and the participants should prepare for possibilities. This a time when managing transitions is the most critical for all involved, even the facilitator. Each design experience is a new creative experiment that brings new opportunities and challenges to facilitator and user-designer alike.

Evaluation—Critical Inquiry and Organizational Learning

New systems of inquiry that consider the integrity of the systems design process as well as the design are important. Old mindsets of evaluation must be replaced with a new systemic evaluation mindset that reflects the integration of systems thinking and practice as well as systems design. Jenks (1994) offers some insight into this new mindset when he suggests that "the evaluation focus must be expanded to the entire educational system—as a system—rather than being limited to what is more traditionally done—evaluating programs or components of the system for their worth" (p. 36). Fetterman (1994) offers additional insight into the importance of empowering stakeholders through a self-determining process that embraces creative and self-evaluating processes. The evaluator of the empowerment evaluation process is seen more as a coach or facilitator who enables participants to shape the direction of the evaluation and actively make social change happen.

Wherein systems design is a disciplined decision-oriented systems inquiry process, the practice of critical systems inquiry becomes an important ingredient in the systemic evaluation. Complementing the inquiry nature of systems design, evaluation practice serves to inform the different interactive phases of design: preparing for design, creating contextual understanding and competencies, scaffolding, designing the design process as well as the design, implementing the new design, and continuous self-renewal. Also, when we consider that systems design involves design learning (Banathy 1991; Nelson 1993) and that there is a dynamic relationship between systems design and language, and between thought and dialogue and design conversation, a view of the inquiry nature of systemic evaluation lends to the generative or heuristic learning essential in design. Implicit in this new

mindset of systemic evaluation is self-reflection and collective thinking, both contributing to the evolution a self-renewing process of critical inquiry. Evaluation in systems design becomes a nexus of learning change within the stakeholder as user-designer and learning change of the system as a creative generative force for change.

Design Axiom: A new evaluation mindset(s) and system must be adopted by stakeholders that replaces old mindsets and evaluation practices.

Design Axiom: User-designer participants design the evaluative process and engage in self-evaluative practice assisted by an evaluator-facilitator who guides user-designers in the design and practical inquiry processes.

Design Axiom: The scope of the evaluation process is the entire system rather than component parts or individual programs and is guided by a disciplined approach to systems inquiry.

Design Axiom: Evaluation as a subsystem of systems design is subject to self-critical examination as required for redesign and renewal of the new systems design and implementation process.

Design Axiom: Evaluation, as critical and collective inquiry by user-designers, is generally viewed as part of the generative design learning process that guides the development and implementation of a new design.

Lessons Learned: Changing from old mindsets of program evaluation to new mindsets of systemic evaluation is a very difficult affair, especially when funding sources and requirements for governmental accountability still expect the old evaluation models. Also, evaluation mindsets often convey a negative valence that encourages stakeholders to resist, especially the informal stakeholders more distanced from the formal design process. Engaging stakeholders as user-designers in self-evaluative practice requires facilitation and scaffolding through differing stages of development, ranging from expert-assistance to self-assistance. A particularly difficult issue that must be confronted is the time-intensive nature of engaging in collective inquiry and action learning methodologies. Understanding the evaluative process as a key to learning systems change as well as empowering systems design must be a constant focus of scaffolding and development. Facilitators are often confronted with user-designers and informal participants who abandon the evaluation process because of its time intensiveness and their direct responsibility for the evaluation. The facilitator may also express varying levels of concern and resistance to the focus on user-designer involvement in evaluation—self-evaluation. User-designer abandonment and/or resistance to self-evaluation must be attended to early in the design and change process. Similarly, facilitator tension and resistance to self-evaluation must be monitored because it may influence the user-designer participants. A systemic evaluation process provides very useful insight and helps create a level of self-awareness essential to changing the systems design process by user-designers. Systemic evaluation, because it plays such a critical role throughout the systems design process, serves as a nexus for learning within the design and change process.

Seeing the "Whole" Change Systems Dynamic

It is important for those electing to use this dynamic to step back from the conceptualization and begin to visualize the interdependent and interrelated nature of the dimensions presented in section two of the chapter with the systems design process in this section. Earlier in the chapter, the reader was cautioned that a potential user of the system must understand how important language, thought, conversation, and learning are in the overall systemic change process. The set of axioms provided for change and design create a system for guiding and facilitating systemic change through systems design without dictating a course of action. Understanding the axioms as an interdependent and interrelated system enables potential user-designers to begin to construct their own knowledge for thoughtful action through the experience of systemic educational change.

REFLECTIONS

The lessons learned indicate that educational systems design for systemic change is an odyssey of

transcending existing mindsets and transforming ourselves and the system. There is no easy road to change in complex social systems like American education. The challenges come from within ourselves and the outside world that is constantly rearranging itself in a turbulent state of change. Perhaps the greatest challenge comes from changing an educational system that is familiar to many generations of citizens and stakeholders and provides some sense of common identity through our educational experiences. Embarking on an odyssey of fundamental change requires that we give up much of our current identity and seek to create for ourselves anew. When we understand that systemic change begins by first changing ourselves, then we will have met the first great challenge in our journey to transcend our existing systems and create a new educational system for our children and their future.

NOTES

1. I have worked over the past six years with two districts in Michigan that committed to systemic change and one district in Oklahoma that underwent a systemic consolidation and change process. During this time, I served as a research and systems design/systemic change facilitator in the districts as they undertook designing and implementing fundamental change. The systemic change process outlined in this text reflects successes and failures, as well as a set of systemic change axioms, that evolved from the change efforts of these districts and other change efforts in which I have taken part.

2. *Mindset* is a concept that shares common meaning with the terms *mental model, worldview, paradigm,* and *frames of reference.* These terms will be treated synonymously in the text, and the reader should note that a mindset may be held by an individual or shared collectively within collaboratives, teams, organizations, and communities. Mindsets comprise what is considered *active memory,* that is, an individual interprets his or her environment by applying certain conceptual frames that provide theoretical understanding for the world. Associated with these conceptual frames are learned routines or strategies that enable the individual to interrelate to a situation or to effect action. Mindsets are influenced by our thinking and thought processes as well as our language and learning processes.

3. The term *stakeholder* reflects an individual or individuals that, as part of the school, community, and larger society, have a vested interest in schools and education. Included here are students, parents, teachers, administrators, support person-

nel, business and industry, elderly citizens, and all members of society, regardless of gender, race, or other discriminating factors. For purposes of this text, all stakeholders are considered to be users of the educational system, whether formal or informal in their role and relationships. Stakeholders and user-designers may be treated interchangeably for purposes of this discussion.

4. Banathy (1988) introduced four basic requirements of a change system that influenced the formulation of the change systems dynamic: (1) the potential to define, develop/adapt, deliver, implement, and institutionalize elements of a change process to meet changing societal expectations; (2) the ability to address itself to the complex and embedded nature of educational systems; (3) the capacity to establish compatibility between the real world and the ideal world; and (4) the ability to carry out a set of specific functions. The change systems dynamic builds on the concept set forth in these requirements.

5. The design axioms and change axioms are interdependent and interconnected as part of a system of axioms that provide a guidance system for systemic change. It will be noted that there is intentional similarity in language and structure of various change and design axioms, such as those dealing with conversation and design conversation. All the axioms concerning change and design should be considered in context of the change systems dynamic. As a dynamic system, the axioms help create meaning and understanding for the process of systemic change while guiding stakeholders and facilitators through educational systems design.

6. Scaffolding is a metaphor taken from the Vygotskian constructivist theory for cognitive development, which reflects the need to provide facilitation or expert assistance for participants in various social contexts of learning and problem solving. In systems design, as stakeholders engage in addressing the complex problems embodied in systemic change, there are varying degrees of capacities and competencies with which stakeholders approach the change process. From a constructivist perspective, participants have a zone of proximal development wherein they are able to achieve certain levels of problem solving or create design solutions unassisted by the facilitator. When the sophistication or difficulty of the design context exceeds the participants' level of unassisted participation, a design facilitator provides the assistance necessary for stakeholders as user-designers to learn the competencies and grow in the capacity of becoming self-assisting designers. In essence, the design facilitator enables the empowerment of the user-designer and the system design process through his or her knowledge and experience-based facilitated assistance.

REFERENCES

Ackoff, R. L. 1981. *Creating the corporate future.* New York: John Wiley and Sons.

Argyris, C., and D. A. Schon. 1978. *Organizational learning: A theory of action perspective.* Reading, Mass.: Addison-Wesley Publishing Company.

Banathy, B. H. 1988. Systems inquiry in education. *Systems Practice,* 1(2):193–212.

———. 1991. *Systems design of education: A journey to create the future.* Englewood Cliffs, N.J.: Educational Technology Publications.

———. 1992. *A systems view of education: Concepts and principles for effective practice.* Englewood Cliffs, N.J.: Educational Technology Publications.

———. 1994. Designing educational systems: Creating our future in a changing world. In *Systemic change in education,* edited by C. M. Reigeluth and R. J. Garfinkel. Englewood Cliffs, N.J.: Educational Technology Publications.

Bohm, D. 1980. *Wholeness and the implicate order.* New York: ARK Paperbacks.

———. 1990. *On dialogue.* Ojai, Calif.: David Bohm Seminars.

———. 1994. *Thought as a system.* New York: Routledge.

Bohm, D., and M. Edwards. 1991. *Changing consciousness: Exploring the hidden source of the social, political and environmental crises facing our world.* San Francisco: Harper Collins Publishing.

Bridges, W. 1991. *Managing transitions: Making the most of change.* Reading, Mass.: Addison-Wesley Publishing Company, Inc.

Capra, F. 1988. *The turning point: Science, society, and the rising culture.* New York: Bantam Books.

Carr, A. 1994. Community participation in systemic educational change. *Educational Technology* 34 (1): 43–50.

Checkland, P. 1981. *Systems thinking, systems practice.* Chichester, U.K.: John Wiley & Sons.

Checkland, P., and J. Scholes. 1991. *Soft systems methodology in action.* New York: John Wiley & Sons.

Cuban, L. 1990. Reforming, again, again, and again. *Educational Researcher* 19 (1): 3–13.

Elmore, R. 1990. *Restructuring schools: The next generation of educational reform.* San Francisco: Jossey-Bass.

Fetterman, D. M. 1994. Steps to empowerment evaluation: From California to Cape Town. *Evaluation and Program Planning* 17 (3): 305–13.

Frantz, T. G. 1994. Systems for design learning: Evolving perspectives. *Educational Technology* 34 (1): 54–61.

Fritz, R. 1989. *The path of least resistance: Learning to become the creative force in your own life.* New York: Fawcett Columbine.

Fullan, M. G. 1991. *The new meaning of educational change.* 2d ed. New York: Teachers College Press.

———. 1993. *Change forces: Probing the depths of educational reform.* New York: The Falmer Press.

Isaacs, W. N. 1993. Taking flight: Dialogue, collective thinking, and organizational learning. *Organizational Dynamics* 22 (2): 24–39.

Jenks, C. L. 1994. Evaluating an educational system systemically. In *Systemic change in education,* edited by C. M. Reigeluth and R. J. Garfinkel. Englewood Cliffs, N.J.: Educational Technology Publications.

Jourard, S. M. 1971. *The transparent self.* New York: Van Nostrand Company.

Land, G., and B. Jarman. 1992. *Breakpoint and beyond: Mastering the future today.* San Francisco: Harper Collins Publishing.

Lieberman, A., ed. 1986. *Rethinking school improvement: Research, craft, and concept.* New York: Teachers College Press.

Morgan, G. 1988. *Riding the waves of change: Developing managerial competencies for a turbulent world.* San Francisco: Jossey-Bass.

Murphy, J. 1991. *Restructuring schools: Capturing and assessing the phenomena.* New York: Teachers College Press.

Nadler, G., and S. Hibino. 1990. *Breakthrough thinking.* Rocklin, Calif.: Prima Publishing and Communications.

Nelson, H. G. 1993. Design inquiry as an intellectual technology for the design of educational systems. In *Comprehensive systems design: A new educational technology,* edited by C. M. Reigeluth, B. H. Banathy, and J. R. Olson. New York: Springer-Verlag.

Reigeluth, C. M. 1993. Principles of educational systems design. *International Journal of Educational Research* 19 (2): 1171–31.

———. 1994. The imperative for systemic change. In *Systemic change in education,* edited by C. M. Reigeluth and R. J. Garfinkel. Englewood Cliffs, N.J.: Educational Technology Publications.

Reigeluth, C. M., and R. J. Garfinkel, eds. 1994. *Systemic change in education.* Englewood Cliffs, N.J.: Educational Technology Publications.

Sarason, S. B. 1990. *The predictable failure of educational reform.* San Francisco: Jossey-Bass.

Schein, E. 1985. *Organizational culture and leadership.* San Francisco: Jossey-Bass.

Senge, P. M. 1990. *The fifth discipline: The art and practice of the learning organization.* New York: Doubleday/Currency.

Spear, S. 1993. The emergence of learning communities. *The Systems Thinkers* 4 (5): 11–14.

Tharp, R. G., and R. Gallimore. 1988. *Rousing minds to life: Teaching, learning and schooling in social context.* Cambridge, U.K.: Cambridge University Press.

Watkins, K. E., and V. J. Marsick. 1993. *Sculpting the learning organization: Lessons in the art and science of systemic change.* San Francisco: Jossey-Bass.

Wilber, K. 1979. *No boundary: Eastern and western approaches to personal growth.* Boston: Shambhala.

Vygotsky, L. [1934] 1988. *Thought and language.* Translated and edited by A. Kozulin. Cambridge: The Massachusetts Institute of Technology.

EMPOWERING SCHOOLS FOR SYSTEMIC CHANGE

The educational system is not an abstract machine. It is people. To change a system is to change what those people value, where they think they are headed, what they talk about, how they talk to one another and what they do day to day. It is to change the policies that give the system direction, and the rules and regulations that specify how individuals work and what they work on. It is to change how the system is managed and how it inspires or crushes initiative and creativity. It is to create new incentives and disincentives, new norms, new cultures, new forms of leadership. In short it is to change every aspect of the system.

—Education Commission of the States, 1992

There are no experts when it comes to answering the question: what ought a system be like? Here, every stakeholder's opinion is as good as any other's.

—Russell Ackoff

Changing the system, the whole system, begins first with changing ourselves in new and fundamental ways. We must begin with the deep underlying assumptions we hold to be true about what change is, who should be involved, how we prepare for change, and how we presently evaluate change. In the past, change has been viewed as piecemeal, fragmented, "tinkering around" within the existing system, and generally extrinsic in nature, with more attention to the technical or practical day-to-day aspects of the school. As we reexamine our mindsets about change, we now understand that change must be holistic, constantly examining the influence of change in any part of the system on all interrelated and interconnected parts. We also now understand that if we are to bring about substantive fundamental change, there must be critical self-examination of the purpose(s) of schools and schooling as well as of our own personal values and beliefs, followed by close examination of the theory, practice, and technical dimensions of schools and schooling.

What we also know is that critical self-examination must encourage and engage all stakeholders to participate in the change process, rather than the limited and selective approaches that have historically served schools engaged in change. We must move from the constraining force of limited perspectives to the creative force of multiple perspectives. Invitation for inclusion of all stakeholders must replace the more autocratic and representative models of inclusion. We must set about releasing the power and potential within the schools' stakeholders through engaged participation in designing and changing their schools.

Also, empowering schools requires developing the capacity and competencies of individual stakeholders to participate in changing the system. The shifts in mindset required for empowering schools and stakeholders to engage in systemic change will necessitate new avenues of access to information about the schooling process as well as evaluative insight concerning the process of change. Information must be created, shared, and utilized in new generative ways supportive of changing whole systems.

The touchstones for future schools included in this section connect the reader to a second, yet equally important, level of important considerations for systemic change. Designing future schools will require new resources as well as new mindsets. Systemic change demands a new level of participation by stakeholders with higher stakes: the future of their school, community, and society. Fundamental change begins deep within ourselves and evolves outward through our new perspectives of what the future will be. Empowering stakeholders through design, evaluation, professional development, and information systems technology is a step toward future schools.

The first contribution in this section focuses on the stakeholder approach to design for public schools. Critical in this design approach is the identification, recruitment, and sustainment of stakeholder involvement in systemic change. The next chapter offers a new mindset for empowerment evaluation, wherein stakeholders are empowered to create and carry out the evaluative process essential to systemic change. A core value of this process is in the focus on helping people help themselves. The third chapter connects the reader with new directions for professional development. Facilitating and participating in systemic change will require new skills and knowledge not currently a part of the landscape of educational change. The final contribution to this section emphasizes the critical role of instructional information management systems in the overall scope of systemic change. Deepening practitioners' vision and understanding of the instruction and instructional processes is requisite to examining the deep underlying assumptions about schooling and to bringing about fundamental change.

STAKEHOLDER PARTICIPATION IN SYSTEMIC CHANGE
Cornerstones to Continuous
School Improvement

—

Alison A. Carr

I'm concerned about the lack of parental involvement in inner-city school systems. I'm concerned about the increasing amounts of violence and academic failure in our schools. I'm concerned about the increasing polarization of various socioeconomic groups in this society. I'm concerned about the relationship between the business world and the educational system. I'm referring to how they choose to support certain educational institutions, ignore others, and control others. I think we as a society should send a clear message to the business world and to the political leaders that they have a responsibility to support the schools that are in trouble and to be supportive of children in those socioeconomic groups that are in trouble.

—*A father, on why he wants to be involved in the stakeholder change group at his child's school*

Why should parents become involved in their children's educational institutions? Why should these institutions want parental involvement? What overt and covert messages are sent to parents and community members when they enter into teamwork with schools? What are the benefits of involving whole communities of people embracing differing ideologies in the process of re-creating systems of human learning? Isn't that painful? Why do it at all?

Stakeholder participation can take varied forms and comes from a tradition of inclusivity, but many efforts which pay lip service to lofty goals of commu-

nity empowerment fail to deliver with sometimes dire consequences. In this work I examine definitions and traditions of stakeholder approaches and why this approach is particularly necessary to systemic change efforts. It is important to recognize that stakeholders must be involved in all portions of the change process. They must be involved during the analysis, development, and evaluation of changes. However, in this chapter, I will focus on the importance of and processes necessary to broad-based community participation in design efforts. I will offer several practical methods for involving communities in their schools and examine some thorny problems associated with stakeholder empowerment.

DEFINITIONS AND TRADITIONS OF STAKEHOLDER PARTICIPATION

The idea that various individuals or groups who have compelling interests in schooling should be involved in some significant way is a fairly popular approach to school change. For many years, stakeholders' views, input, opinions, and voices have been sought for inclusion in the process of making schools better places. The term stakeholder approach has several meanings and interpretations but is rooted in the stakeholder approach to evaluation (Stake 1986). Stake offers reflections on the meaning of the word stakeholder:

> The lay meaning of the term (stakeholder) pertains more to having a share in the success and failure of the enterprise. (p. 29)

> Risk is an essential implication of the word "stakeholder." A stake may be lost. It might be improved. Whether or not the stake is protected, even treated fairly, is part of the concept of stakeholder evaluation—as some see it. The ultimate value of stakeholder approaches to program evaluation will probably involve the fairness and justice of educational and social provisions. (p. 147)

Other definitions of stakeholders may be more pragmatic. Mauriel (1989) points to stakeholders as "those attempting to influence the allocation of resources or intended direction of the school system" (p. 147). Similarly, Bowles (1989) defines stakeholders as "any individuals, groups, or institutions that may have an interest or stake in the resolution of actual or potential conflict over the allocation of resources, values, or power." Power is central to the definition of stakeholder, though oftentimes stakeholders, other than professional educators, are not given substantive power (Dawson 1982).

Beyond definitions based on the history of stakeholder approaches to educational program evaluation, the term stakeholder has taken on great importance in current change initiatives. Whether a school is engaged in TQM, systemic change, school design, or restructuring efforts, the importance of stakeholder participation has been seen as central to substantial change in schools. Thus we

see extensive use of terms such as "customer" or "client" in the traditions of TQM now being applied to schools where these concepts are similar if not equivalent to stakeholders.

Naturally, we in the educational community have endeavored throughout our history to involve stakeholders in the schools though we have often called it by other names. The history of community participation and control has waxed and waned through the decades (Davies 1981). From locally controlled one-room schools to state-controlled systems of mass education to local boards of education, we have invented various checks and balances to see that many needs are served by our schools. We have sought a balance among three primary factions: parents, the state, and commercial interests. This is the tradition from which the current wave of stakeholder participation springs. It is important to understand this historical context of the community participation and stakeholder involvement movement in order to effectively practice broad-based community inclusion.

WHY IS STAKEHOLDER INVOLVEMENT IMPORTANT?

One notable agreement in educational systems design literature is the importance of community participation. Reigeluth (1992) and Banathy (1991) express concern over the state of community "buy-in" at the outset of design efforts. Reigeluth emphasizes the importance of assessing community readiness and gaining commitment from stakeholder groups *before* beginning educational systems design efforts. Further, Reigeluth points to the importance of fundamental support for change efforts: "The change process is far more likely to be successful if there is grass-roots community support for fundamental change" (p. 120). Banathy echoes the importance of community support. He feels that it "has to be generated by inviting and encouraging a genuine involvement of representatives of the community in the design activity" (p. 168). Once again, it is important to emphasize the necessity of community involvement *throughout* the change process including, but not limited to, the design activity.

IDENTIFYING COMMUNITY STAKEHOLDERS

Within a school community, there are major groups which have interests in the school or are affected by the educational system. Such groups can be considered the major stakeholders in the community of interest (Reigeluth 1993). Among these groups are the political, religious, and commercial leaders in the community, the social service and educational personnel, as well as the student and parental populations. Thiemann and Ruscoe (1985) view the entire community as stakeholders in the public schools. They divide stakeholders into three broad groups who have interests in public schools: taxpayers, employers/employees, and voters. They identify several community groups that can help one to identify stakeholder groups.

> The Chamber of Commerce, the Better Business Bureau, and the League of Women Voters can provide lists of formal and informal groups. Contact fraternal, social, and religious agencies for lists of their members. (p. 42)

Early identification of stakeholder groups is crucial to successful selection efforts that hope for *effective* involvement of community members. "Without such involvement," write Stevenson and Pellicer (1992), "change is perceived as a 'top-down' process, misunderstood and often resented by those charged with its implementation" (p. 137). Haphazard identification of stakeholder groups can lead to resentment and sabotage of educational design efforts.

In order to select a balanced educational change team, it is necessary to identify the stakeholder groups who need to be considered for representation. It is also imperative that educational professionals recognize that each stakeholder group has its own set of members, social norms, and status. Group representatives will enter the educational change process with a set of concerns and interests in education before any community meetings are held. The operational ideologies with which these team members and stakeholder group representatives enter change efforts are the source of both innovation and conflict (Carr 1992).[1] Further discussion of ways to identify, recruit, and select members of

design teams from the community of interest are presented here.

HOW STAKEHOLDER PARTICIPATION WORKS

Stakeholder participation in public school design efforts differs somewhat from stakeholder participation in evaluation efforts explored earlier in this chapter. However, there are some commonalities as well. It is important to consider both the theoretical assertions of how stakeholder participation works and the realities of such attempts to involve broad-based support and input in new designs of human learning systems.

Systems Theory

Theoretically, stakeholder participation is important because it gains the support of those who are interested in the schools. Theories of change and diffusion (Havelock 1973) encourage the inclusion of those who have a compelling interest in the innovation. Systems theory emphasizes stakeholder participation because bringing those with competing ideologies together over a problem is more likely to expose some of the important interconnections among systemic components. Design based on committee work, while more difficult to accomplish, is also more likely to highlight effects that changes in one part of the system have on others because representatives of various systemic components work together through the design. In combination with increased community "buy-in" and political support for changes in the current system, this systemic tendency of group-supported design is a major reason why systems theory resoundingly endorses stakeholder participation.

Realities

In reality, stakeholder participation in design efforts is a very difficult task. Entertaining competing ideologies in the process of creating something new is time consuming, and many teams get bogged down in the process and begin feeling they are not really "doing" anything productive. Negotiating all the interests fairly without autocratic leadership is very difficult, but there are even more basic difficulties associated with stakeholder participation. For example, it is very difficult to *find* those who are interested. There are two main reasons why this is hard to do: first, there is little to guide practitioners in terms of who should be included and how to include them; and second, there is an apathy in society for educational outcomes.

Who are the stakeholders? Interested groups will vary by community and that is why it is so difficult for anyone to suggest an exhaustive list of who should be involved. I have offered an open-ended list of possibilities (Carr and Reigeluth 1993) that includes representatives from the political, religious, commercial, social service, educational, parental, and student populations. This is by no means exhaustive and suggests only a beginning in terms of who might be considered a stakeholder in any given community.

There is value implied by who is included in a list of stakeholders. Mauriel (1989) suggests the following list of stakeholders: federal, state, and local government officials, State Department of Education, support staff, building administration, teaching staff, parents, nonparent residents, business community, society at large, and the board and central office administration. This list is taken from Mauriel (1989), who places the board and central office administration at the center. Certainly no one is left out of any list that includes "society at large"; however, the value implied by lumping large portions of the local community together in this way while giving more space to government officials and educational administrators expresses a certain value about who should be making decisions in our schools.

In contrast, I suggest that exclusive decision-making power should be shared equally with parents, social service agents, government leaders, business constituents, religious leaders, minority rights groups, and even students where possible (see fig. 1). This slant on who should be involved certainly does express a value about what our democratic schools might be like. Practitioners who are working in certain communities might find Mauriel's list more appropriate to their political climate. One list is not necessarily better than another, it is simply more well-suited to certain environmental conditions and values about the process.

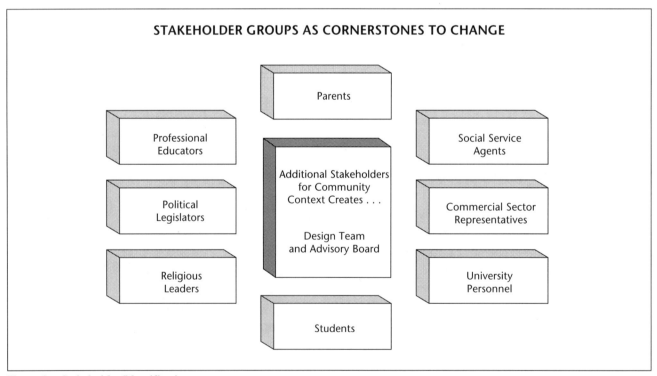

STAKEHOLDER GROUPS AS CORNERSTONES TO CHANGE

Parents

Professional Educators

Social Service Agents

Additional Stakeholders for Community Context Creates . . .

Design Team and Advisory Board

Political Legislators

Commercial Sector Representatives

Religious Leaders

University Personnel

Students

Figure 1   Stakeholder Identification

The two-team approach (Reigeluth 1993) generally invests more power in the design team than the advisory board. Another trend in many schools is to involve school personnel in the design team (teachers, administrators, staff) while relegating parents and community members to advisory boards where professional educators are also represented. This does not create the sort of balance necessary to adequately represent the interests of various stakeholder groups. It is important for practitioners to avoid this tendency, despite the attractiveness of logistics, such as common meeting times, that are shared among professional educators.

The second major reason why it is difficult to recruit stakeholders is because of a basic lack of interest or apathy in our communities and even in our society as a whole. Most people in a community are less than interested in what happens inside their school walls—especially if they do not have school children currently attending their local public school.

The only stakeholder group who has had sustained and compelling interest in educational outcomes has been the commercial sector. My concerns about the active role that business has played in shaping our schools are better saved for another opportunity. However, it is important that practitioners recognize the vested interests commercial sector representatives bring to design efforts. Many well-intentioned business people are actively involved in the shaping of curriculum, but there is often a tendency to focus on the needs of their particular organization in terms of future employees. This can be a dangerous bias if it is overemphasized. Most often such overemphasis comes in the form of more money and power in communities where children may not want to grow up to work at the Chrysler plant.[2]

However, the exemplary model that business has provided in terms of committed participation has not been followed by other stakeholder groups. The apathy a community feels for its schools reveals itself in a variety of ways, but, primarily, parents and community members simply do not attach themselves in significant ways to educational systems. This attitude translates into actions: parents and community members don't show interest in signing up for teams, don't attend meetings, and don't say much when they do attend. Experiences in stakeholder evaluation illustrate this problem poignantly:

> We went knocking on doors. We found the vast majority of parents have very, very, very low interests. It's absurd! The good reaction is that they express a sort of general interest in seeing their kids do well in school. That's the upper half of the reaction. The others felt absolutely powerless to do anything. The school people said, "You want to know what happened the last time we asked the parents to come in? We sat there all night with our tea and donuts—alone. If you want parents then you're going to have to go out and lasso them." (Stake 1986, 82–83)

The issue of how we, as a society, heighten interest in the educational enterprise is not one which I can solve here, though it is an area that I hope to pursue in future research and writing. Instead, I hope to deal with some of the realities of "lasso-ing" those parents and community members and gaining community commitment to innovative schools.

PROCESSES OF STAKEHOLDER INVOLVEMENT

Assessing the Community Readiness

Reigeluth (1992) and other educational systems designers have advocated the importance of assessing the readiness of a given community that has expressed an interest in systemic change. This is an important step not to be overlooked. In Reigeluth's work a somewhat counterintuitive suggestion is made: a community must be *dissatisfied* with its current system substantially enough to create a groundswell for change. Most school personnel prefer to think of ways in which they can *boost* the image of the school. However, according to Reigeluth, systemic change is more likely to be borne out of discontent than apathy, which is bred in contentedness. Finding evidence of this dissatisfaction in a community is a good indicator that the ground is fertile for the seeds of systemic change. Although it would certainly be preferable to see a community drawn to systemic change in an effort to transform already functioning schools into innovative systems of human learning, my experience and the writings of systems theorists does not support this as a realistic approach much of the time.[3]

Recruitment

During my work with a major midwestern urban school district in selecting members of parent/community advisory teams (PCATs), I found that despite the best recruiting efforts, there was little variation among school sites with regard to membership and retention. An example here should help illustrate my point. One school I worked with made a strong commitment to recruiting minority (in this case African-American) parents for their PCAT. In response to this goal, they went to over two hundred homes and visited with parents in a discontiguous locale from which minority students were bussed. The school personnel involved in this effort included a guidance counselor, teachers, the vice principal, and the principal. They also held four "town meetings" (discussed in depth later) in elementary schools in this same discontiguous area. However, despite these efforts, they were able to attract only four minority participants. Given the demographics of the school and comparing it to other similar schools in the study, it is true that this was a higher number, but only by one or two members. In addition, they were no more successful than other schools in retaining the minority members they were able to attract.

All this is not to suggest that extra efforts shouldn't be expended to try to attract and retain populations who may otherwise be difficult to include or who have traditionally been disenfranchised from the process. Much to the opposite, it is to suggest that something larger is going on in many cases that are systemically keeping certain people out of the schools. In response to this, such efforts as those taken on by this particular school may not be enough. They were able to attract several additional members, and that's a good start. However, the teams needed to have clear purpose and some level of power in order to show participants the value of their involvement. The conclu-

sion to be drawn is that some efforts pay off in bigger ways than others. Recruitment, while an important step, is not the end of the membership concern; we must also pay continual attention to retention.

Selection

Selection is an area I've focused much of my research energies on (Carr 1992; Carr 1993; Carr and Reigeluth 1993). Here I present a basic model of selection for community and parent populations. The guidelines are not necessarily applicable to professional educator selection, which may require different sorts of selection strategies.

This model[4] is the result of formative research (Roma 1990) in which guidelines, distilled from literature, are tested out and refined based on field tests. In this case, selection guidelines were reviewed and refined by several administrators and then tried out to the extent possible in real settings where selection was currently taking place. The study from which these guidelines come examined the selection practices of six middle schools in a large, urban, midwestern school district. Throughout the study, the guidelines were refined to represent what was learned in the field, and the current form of the model is presented here.

Criteria

To assist those interested in selection criteria for educational design efforts, table 1 provides a checklist of criteria for these two primary roles: design and advisory (Reigeluth 1993). These criteria can be used in a checklist fashion to assist team directors in selecting community members or as a collaborative tool to help teams select new or additional members. Each group of educators will have different needs for their community members' involvement and may wish to alter this list.

These guidelines are presented as rules of thumb. It is expected that different team selector(s) will require different skills and values in prospective team members. Local values, current team makeup, and even the current status of school/community relations may impact selection of community members for service on design teams.

ADVISORY BOARD	DESIGN TEAM
1. Contributes to team balance: • Race • Educational level • Economic status • Profession • Neighborhood • Grade level of child (if applicable)	1. Contributes to team balance: • Race • Educational level • Economic status • Profession • Neighborhood • Grade level of child (if applicable)
2. Represents stakeholder group(s): • Education community • Parent community • Student population • Business/commercial • Political • Religious • Social Service	2. Represents stakeholder group(s): • Education community • Parent community • Student population • Business/commercial • Political • Religious • Social Service
3. Sees need for systemic change in education	3. Sees need for systemic change in education
4. Represents diverse viewpoint	4. Represents diverse viewpoint
5. Is process oriented	5. Is task/outcomes oriented
6. Is consensus oriented	6. Is collaboration oriented
7. Secondary Criteria • Is a community opinion leader • Is credible, respected in larger community • Is persuasive • Has public relations abilities • Is open minded • Is influential	7. Secondary Criteria • Is a school opinion leader • Is credible, respected in school community • Is cooperative • Has interpersonal relations abilities • Is open minded • Is insightful

Table 1   Revised Selection Criteria for Advisory and Design Teams

These factors are variable and must be considered on a case-by-case basis by each person or group selecting future team members. In addition, some of the secondary criteria are vitally important in truly systemic change teams, but may not be readily observable in many or most of the candidates. To the extent that these are viewed as important by selectors and are observable, they can be prioritized more highly.

Selection Procedures

Decide to Form a Selection Delegation

It is not recommended that only one person select team members. If an individual working alone, say the school principal, identifies all team members, the community may view the team(s) as being "stacked" rather than representative of the whole community. Therefore, it is recommended that a delegation be formed in order to identify and select team members. In this method, a delegation of interested stakeholders who are *not* going to serve on the design team or the advisory board are asked to select members for both teams based on predetermined criteria.

The most common criticism of selection delegations is that, if the criteria are not followed, partisan choices may result. Sumption and Engstrom (1966) suggest that the "group" membership ties which result from the delegation approach may be emphasized to the point that team members are not able to collaborate. As long as the criteria are kept in the forefront of the selectors' minds, it is unlikely that such conflicts will emerge.

Another potential difficulty with delegations is that delegates might make great team members themselves; however, if they are voting on themselves and a team they will serve on, competing and personal interests may interfere with optimum team member selection. The final difficulty with selection delegations is that they take time. Time must be spent selecting the delegation and their meeting to choose participants for advisory and design teams. Nevertheless, the success of community participation efforts depends on the caliber of volunteers selected.

The decision to employ delegations is a decision to utilize exclusive selection procedures. While it may seem more humane, or expedient, to include all volunteers who come to your school, it is important to maintain a manageable team. Exclusive selection gives your team continuity, commitment, and balance, which are not possible if the makeup of your team is not under close scrutiny.

We recognize the desire to include all volunteers and suggest strongly that a single, committed, well-balanced team be put in place with subcommittees or pyramid teams set up also in order to make best use of all stakeholders and gain broad-based support without compromising the effectiveness of the design team or advisory board.

Recognizing the desire to include all volunteers, we strongly suggest that a single, committed, well-balanced team be put in place with subcommittees or pyramid teams. This way, best use can be made of all stakeholders and broad-based support can be achieved without compromising the effectiveness of the design team or advisory board. In this process it is important to make it clear to all applicants why they were not chosen for service on the primary team(s) to avoid hurt feelings and maintain honesty in stakeholder relationships.

Hold Town Meetings

One way of identifying people to serve on a selection delegation—and a way of identifying possible candidates for the teams—is to set up several town meetings, where interested individuals, teachers, students, community members, school board members, and administrators can be brought together. During town meetings the focus should be exclusively on the new initiative—not mixed in with other agenda items and announcements. This may

contribute to confusion about the role of the new teams being formed or the fuzzy boundaries between the new teams and old or existing teams such as the PTA. Thus, a brief description of the new initiative and the teams being formed should be presented at these meetings.

During these meetings representatives of various constituencies should be identified to serve on the selection delegation. It is imperative that these individuals be visible opinion leaders of their groups, but not members of the advisory or design teams. Opinion-leader delegates earn early community buy-in, which will pay off during the design and implementation processes. Identifying opinion leaders, however, requires careful observation throughout town meetings in order to pinpoint those opinion leaders who cannot or will not serve on an advisory or design team but who might be involved in the selection delegation.

Town meetings are also an opportunity to gather a set of names as a core of prospective team candidates. Simple forms that can be completed showing interest in service should be made available to attendees. The forms should avoid long questions or expectations of essay answers, which may discourage representation of stakeholder groups whose members have weak literacy skills. The form should simply ask for name, address, phone number, occupation, relationship to school (optional), and possibly a *short* statement about why the individual is interested in volunteering for service on the design or advisory team (optional). One additional item of interest is "Significant Volunteer Activities." This may lead to an understanding of the candidate as a representative of a stakeholder group in a voluntary capacity. An oral announcement encouraging community members who would like more information to phone or stop by the school is highly recommended, as it may encourage members of the community who cannot complete the form to offer service to change their educational system. See figure 2 for a sample Community Team Candidate Volunteer Form.

During the town meeting all attendees should be encouraged to nominate themselves or others whom they feel would positively influence the design of their school. The function of the team and the time commitment required should be made clear during the meeting. Volunteers who are not sincerely committed to offering their time to systemic restructuring efforts or who are more interested in "honorary" positions should be discouraged. Candidates must be willing to give their time and themselves for the betterment of their schools.

Alternative methods of recruiting might include sending fliers home with students or mailing newsletters directly to parents' homes. This may be an effective method for gaining parental participation, but may not reach many other stakeholder groups in the school community. These types of open invitations attract parents who have traditionally been involved in schools; however, reaching nontraditional parents and moving them to action usually requires more active recruiting strategies. During recruitment efforts, whether they are in the form of fliers, meeting announcements, or town meetings, it should be made clear that several teams are forming and that the selection delegation is tasked with finding the "best match" for a

volunteer's profile and the teams' needs. In this way, exclusive selection will be explained early in the process, in the hope that no one will feel rejected, only placed on different teams.

Town meetings are only one of a number of viable recruiting techniques. I have observed several additional recruiting techniques that offer some advantages for some schools. For example, I have seen selectors invite candidates to school for lunch to explain the purpose of the team, meet them, and spend time getting to know their personalities. This approach has the advantage of enabling selectors to observe some of the more difficult criteria. However, it may take several small lunches to meet all interested candidates, and it can be slightly disruptive. Another approach I've observed is to issue invitations to candidates during open houses or musical performances. These events offer excellent opportunities to reach parents who may not typically attend PTA meetings, but they may not afford enough time to really discuss the initiative and will not allow you much of a chance to see what the

---

COMMUNITY TEAM CANDIDATE VOLUNTEER FORM

Name: _____

Address: _____

Phone (home): _____ (work): _____

Occupation: _____

Significant volunteer activities: _____

_____

_____

Relationship to our school: _____

_____

Why are you interested in volunteering to work for change in our school? _____

_____

_____

_____

Figure 2   Sample Community Team Candidate Volunteer Form

applicants are like. However, you are able to reach large numbers of people in this way. Many approaches are acceptable; it is a matter of finding the approach that feels the most comfortable and effective to you.

Select Delegates

Once the decision has been made to create selection delegations, and names of candidates for all teams have been collected at town meetings, a short period of time should be spent choosing members of stakeholder groups who can serve on the selection delegation. Selection delegations should be kept to under ten people, since groups of this size will have a tendency to come to consensus more quickly. The difficulty with keeping the selection delegation small, in most cases, is attaining representation of all stakeholder groups. This difficulty is likely to resurface during team selection, but keep in mind that each delegate or team member may represent more than one stakeholder group.

Some administrators prefer to form several small, three- or four-person delegations, each representing a different stakeholder group, which meet and select representatives for the design team and advisory board. This strategy is not recommended for two reasons. First, the competing ideologies that delegates bring to the selection task are not socially negotiated if all of the delegates represent the same stakeholder group. Second, the loyalties of the selected candidate are likely to be tied strongly to the stakeholder group that elected him or her. This can concretize opposing ideologies, resulting in a team that disputes, but never decides.

There are also several advantages to a single-selection delegation. First, delegates' competing ideologies are aired during the selection process. Thus the facilitator for the restructuring process has an opportunity to gain experience dealing with these competing ideologies in the selection delegation and is better prepared to face similar challenges in work with the design team and advisory board. Second, the single-delegation approach may cause the delegates to be more sensitive to competing ideological issues, therefore causing

them to choose team members who are at least minimally compatible. Finally, several small delegations never get a sense of what the whole team looks like, while the single-delegation approach lends a sense of balance and wholeness to the selection process.

Although the delegates may be chosen by the principal alone, it might be better to bounce ideas off of at least one other person—perhaps the PTA president or another "outsider." Extensive time should not be spent setting up the delegation, but care should be taken to avoid the perception (or the reality) that the delegation (and any resulting team) is "stacked." This perception can be harmful to community empowerment. Finally, a "stacked" team will represent biased views and will impact the resulting design.

Hold Delegation Meeting(s)

Once the delegates and possible candidates have been identified, meetings of the delegation should be scheduled to adopt the criteria and procedures they will use and to discuss and select the candidates according to their criteria and procedures. Selection should be a thoughtful process, not a rushed one. Despite this, you want to set up your team and get going on the business at hand—designing innovative educational solutions. It may take one meeting to select team members, or it may take several. This is a decision each school must make for itself.

It is important to impress upon the delegates the necessity of confidentiality in the selection process. Some comments may be made that should not be reflected back to the community because they could hurt feelings or cause community schisms to form, which may pose serious opposition later in the process.

Selection criteria and procedures should be reviewed, adapted, and adopted, and the delegates should be clear about their task and the role the members they select will take in the advisory board and design team.

Candidate application forms should be shared with the delegation. Delegates should be asked to openly discuss the potential of any given candidate for service on design or advisory boards. In an effort to facilitate discussion, a set of items that may be considered for each candidate is presented in figure 3. This figure represents a suggested sequence and a set of selection criteria which may be used in delegation meetings.[5] Such forms can be copied or made into transparencies for group discussion purposes. Showing the group the direction of their discussion can be helpful in keeping them on task.

Since the number of successful candidates is not *absolute,* it is easiest to divide candidates into simple "yes" or "no" decisions at first. An alternative to this approach is to set aside several "slots" that need to be filled based on identified stakeholder groups.

This can be effective as long as several individuals are considered for each slot. In this way a "short list" can be created and issues of balance in ethnicity, gender, and socioeconomic status can be considered in addition to the stakeholder group representation. This process can be more complicated to manage, and simple "yes" or "no" selections may precede the slating of a short list to combine these two strategies.

After initial decisions have been made, it is important to present the entire list to the delegation to ensure their acceptance and recognition of the whole field of candidates as the list is being formed. Despite an initial acceptance of the slate,

---

CANDIDATE DISCUSSION FORM

1. Review of candidate application

2. Discussion based on (change as needed):

   Balance of:
   • Race
   • Educational level
   • Economic status
   • Profession
   • Neighborhood
   • Grade level of child (if applicable)

   Stakeholder:
   • Education community
   • Parent community
   • Student population
   • Business/commercial
   • Political
   • Religious
   • Social Service
   • Other (list)

3. Sees need for systemic change? ☐ Yes ☐ No

4. Represents diverse viewpoint? ☐ Yes ☐ No

5. Process or Outcomes oriented? (circle one)

6. Consensus or Collaboration oriented? (circle one)

7. Any applicable secondary criteria?

VOTE: ☐ YES ☐ NO

Figure 3   Sample Candidate Discussion Form

it is important to remember that changes can be made and candidates who are not on the initial slate may be reconsidered later if commitment cannot be confirmed for slated candidates. Therefore, it is important that these decisions again remain confidential.

Drawn from the pool of "yeses," the final team slate should be discussed. It is recommended that the design team receive first consideration because it will require the strongest cohesion and commitment. Therefore, it may be easier to put the most delicate puzzle together first, and follow it by selecting the advisory board members. Each of the candidates should be discussed at length, extolling their strengths and weaknesses at this point in the process.

Throughout the selection process, the slate should be continually referred to, as opposed to selecting two or three members and then setting that list aside to consider the next candidate as an individual. Each candidate will be part of a team and should be considered in light of the balance within the whole group. At the conclusion of these discussions, there should be a single slate for the design team and a separate slate for the advisory board that the delegation can accept as a whole. Since some candidates may decline to serve, it is important to have alternates for those candidates ranked.

One final word of caution: It is important that the selection process does not relegate to the advisory board those who couldn't quite "measure up" to design team standards. These two teams have distinct criteria, and the advisory board should not become a "second chance lottery."

Confirm Commitment

Once the team members have been chosen, it is important to confirm their commitment. This is a very important step—without it your team may have high levels of turnover. If sufficient commitment is lacking among several of the candidates, an additional meeting of the delegation may be necessary to approve a revised slate—that is a lot of work that you'd like to avoid if at all possible. Therefore, once the slate has been selected, it is advisable to contact each candidate by phone and

confirm their commitment. Impress upon the candidates the importance of their service and explain how the selection was carried out so they know this is an important service opportunity. Also indicate at the time of the call that other members have expressed willingness to participate and that if the candidate cannot commit to consistent attendance and participation, you will invite another person on the list to participate instead. Make clear the consequences of accepting and/or declining the invitation to serve.

It is also important to pay close attention to how you explain to those candidates who are not invited to serve on the primary teams how you went about selecting and why they were not selected. If it is clear that there were simply enough white women already serving on the team, this will answer many unspoken questions that the declined candidate may have. It's important to deal carefully with the feelings of those who are turned away. If you have elected to use a pyramid team or subcommittee structure, you may honestly tell candidates that the delegation felt their contribution would be better served on the team to which they've been assigned. This is a delicate process which should be carefully conducted.

Hold a "Coming Out" Event

It is very important to have a planned "coming out" event for the new team members. Interested parties should know who has been selected to serve on the teams and, therefore, who they can go to both to get information about the change effort and to give their input for the school design. This event can also be cause for celebration, which can generate much-needed enthusiasm. Do not ignore the potential of such an event or skip it in order to get down to work as quickly as possible. A "coming out" event should be a part of every school's team building to enhance team bonding, community buy-in, and constituent identification.

Ensure Self-Renewal of Teams

Self-renewal is important for any working system, particularly educational change systems (Havelock 1973). Generally, after the team is formed, it has self-renewing capabilities. It can select its own replacement members. However, balanced representation must be ensured, and selection criteria must continue to be considered in selecting replacement members. It is a good idea to set up specific contingency plans for member replacement at one of the early team meetings. Such a plan should include the use of the criteria used to select the current team members and any additional criteria that need to be added based on the recent experience of selecting or on the input of current team members. This plan should be written down and put on file, where it can be easily accessed. In addition, this plan should be flexible so that as new needs or criteria are identified for inclusion in the next round of selection, they can be easily added.

Retain Members

The issue of retention is one that I am currently very interested in. During my experiences with PCATs, I found that retention rates differed somewhat predictably. Minority parents were not only harder to recruit, they were harder to retain, and their participation at meetings they did attend was substantially lower than majority parents. I found that one of the biggest reasons that parents did not remain on the teams they had originally committed to was because of a lack of sense of purpose. When interviewed, many parents suggested that the reasons they did not attend were focused on logistics. For example, transportation, work schedules, and baby-sitter arrangements all made it difficult for many parents (particularly minority parents in this case) to attend the meetings. If the parents had felt that their input was vital to the functioning of the group and that the group was involved in substantive problem solving in their child's school, they admitted that they would have found ways to be there in many cases.

I have not completed my work on the issue of retention, but would suggest to practitioners who are currently forming teams and are interested in recruitment and selection that retention strategies are equally important and deserve substantial effort and thinking. Following are a few ideas for maintaining higher retention rates that go beyond using the proper commitment confirmation and selection procedure.

Be very clear from the outset what the goal and purpose of the team is. If the team will have decision-making power, be clear where the limitations of that are and how it might be exercised. Training in this regard is essential. Also, it is important to have a variety of team "bonding" experiences. The coming out event mentioned earlier is an example of that. Other ideas include environmental challenge experiences (e.g., going on a difficult hike where members have to help one another to succeed) or team social functions. If the school community has participants in different locales, move the meetings around to meet all needs in terms of transportation and easy access; don't limit yourselves to the school site only. These and other ideas are possibilities for increasing the commitment to the entire team. Follow-up phone calls coming from members of a team you feel close to can be more impactful than from "just another school representative." It is important that issues of retention be considered carefully and that specific strategies be adopted that meet the needs of individual groups and communities.

CONCLUSION

There is little doubt that the stakeholder approach to design is costly both in terms of time and money necessary to make it a success. It can also be costly in terms of emotional taxation. For educational systems design practitioners, facing the realities of openly negotiating values leading to a vision of what our schools should be is a daunting task. Asking these same practitioners to then *invite* all the most disparate ideological representatives to sit around a table and hash that out is even more frightening. It is the creation, in my view, of the school as the ground for social negotiation. It involves politics, power, values, attitudes, and diplomacy, and demands of practitioners the most delicate skills of facilitation.

In order to succeed in this effort, we must have a deeper understanding of membership issues such as balance, retention, and selection. It would be wise to continue to learn why certain populations drop out at higher rates than others. In addition, it is imperative that the issue of community apathy be addressed in formal research studies. Qualitatively understanding this apathy, comparing our society with others to identify salient characteristics that contribute to this apathy, and isolating aspects of schooling that contribute to this attitude are important steps to take in future research. Despite the obstacles, it is my view that stakeholder participation is necessary to encourage a truly democratic system of schooling in our society.

NOTES

1. A complete discussion of the opportunities and obstacles of broad-based community involvement in systemic educational design or restructuring was presented to the 34th Annual Conference of the International Society of Systems Sciences and has been accepted for publication in an upcoming special issue of *Educational Technology* focusing on educational systems design.

2. For a more complete discussion of this debate, see Carr (1992).

3. It should be noted, however, that a group of systemic theorists known as the International Systems Institute is looking seriously at this issue at the Annual Conference of Comprehensive Systems Design held in Asilomar, California, each winter. This group considers issues of cultivating a design culture in the society.

4. This original version of this model was published in *Educational Technology* (Carr and Reigeluth 1993), and the study that produced the revised version of the model as presented in this paper was first published in my dissertation (Carr 1993).

5. These selection criteria were first presented at the International Conference for Technology and Education, Paris, France. For a more complete discussion of the importance and derivation of these selection criteria, see Carr and Garfinkel (1992).

REFERENCES

Banathy, B. H. 1991. *Systems design of education.* Englewood Cliffs, N.J: Educational Technology Publications.

———. 1992. Comprehensive systems design in education: Building a design culture in education. *Educational Technology* 22 (3): 33–35.

Bowles, B. D. 1989. In *Strategic leadership for schools: Creating and sustaining productive change*, edited by J. J. Mauriel. San Francisco: Jossey-Bass.

Carr, A. A. 1989. Please Mr. Iacocca, no assembly line schools. *The Criterion*, May, 2. NSPI Front Range Chapter publication.

———. 1992. Community participation in systemic restructuring: Opportunity or obstacle to change? Paper presented at the 36th Annual Conference of the International Society for the Systems Sciences, Denver, Colo.

———. 1993. Selecting community participants for systemic educational restructuring: Who should serve? *Dissertation Abstracts International.*

Carr, A. A., and C. M. Reigeluth. 1993. Community participation in educational systems design: Member selection criteria and procedures. *Educational Technology* 33 (7): 36–46.

Carr, A. A., and R. Garfinkel. 1992. Community participation in school restructuring. In *Proceedings of the Ninth International Conference on Technology and Education*, vol. 3, 1625–27, edited by N. Estes and M. Thomas. Austin: University of Texas at Austin.

Davies, D. 1981. Citizen participation in decision making in the schools. In *Communities and their schools*, edited by Don Davies. New York: McGraw-Hill.

Dawson, D. 1982. Educational hegemony and the phenomenology of community participation. *The Journal of Educational Thought* 16 (3): 150–59.

Havelock, R. G. 1973. *The change agent's guide to innovation in education.* Englewood Cliffs, N.J.: Educational Technology Publications.

Mauriel, J. J. 1989. *Strategic leadership for schools: Creating and sustaining productive change.* San Francisco: Jossey-Bass.

Reigeluth, C. M. 1992. Principles of educational systems design. *International Journal of Educational Research* 19 (2): 117–31.

Roma, C. M. 1990. Formative evaluation research on an instructional theory for understanding. Unpublished doctoral dissertation, Indiana University, Bloomington.

Stake, B. 1986. *Quieting reform.* Urbana: University of Illinois Press.

Stevenson, K. R., and L. O. Pellicer. 1992. School-based management in South Carolina: Balancing state-directed reform with local decision making. In *Restructuring the Schools: Problems and Prospects*, edited by J. J. Lane and E. G. Epps. Berkeley, Calif.: McCutchan Publishing Corporation.

Sumption, M., and Y. Engstrom. 1966. *School-community relations: A new approach.* New York: McGraw-Hill.

Theimann, F. C., and G. C. Ruscoe. 1985. Garnering stakeholders' support for educational excellence. *NASSP Bulletin*, 41–44.

EMPOWERMENT EVALUATION
A Learning Tool for Systemic Change in Education

—

David M. Fetterman

Empowerment evaluation is an innovative approach to evaluation. It has been adopted in higher education, government, inner-city public education, nonprofit corporations, and foundations throughout the United States and abroad. A wide range of program and policy sectors use empowerment evaluation, including accelerated schools, doctoral programs, substance abuse prevention, HIV prevention, crime prevention, welfare reform, battered women's shelters, agriculture and rural development, adult probation, adolescent pregnancy prevention, tribal partnership for substance abuse, and programs focusing on self-determination and individuals with disabilities. Descriptions of these programs that use empowerment evaluation appear in *Empowerment Evaluation: Knowledge and Tools for Self-Assessment and Accountability* (Fetterman, Kaftarian, and Wandersman 1995). A second book titled *Empowerment Evaluation* (Fetterman n.d.) provides additional insight into this new evaluation approach, including information about how to conduct workshops to train program staff members and participants to evaluate and improve practice on a whole-school basis with an orientation toward systemic change. (See Banathy 1991, 1992, and Reigeluth 1994 concerning the interpretation of systemic change adopted in this discussion.) In addition, this approach has been institutionalized within the American Evaluation Association and is consistent with the spirit of the standards developed by the Joint Committee on Standards for Educational Evaluation (Fetterman 1995; Joint Committee 1994).

Despite its increasingly wide use, empowerment evaluation is not a panacea, nor is it designed to replace other forms of evaluation. It meets a specific evaluation need: to help program participants evaluate themselves and their program—as well as their entire school system—to improve practice and foster self-determination. Empowerment evaluation is as much an orientation toward change (systemic in nature and design) as it is an evaluative method or approach to transform a system. Empowerment evaluation has been used to promote change within healthy, transformative educational systems and help educators and others change the system by examining the purpose of what they are doing, their core values and ideas, and basic assumptions. In this capacity it may also influence other forms of evaluation and audit to adopt a more collaborative and participatory tone.

Empowerment evaluation is still evolving; there is much to learn, explore, refine, and improve. As with other forms of evaluation, we constantly learn more about the craft as we practice it.

Definition and Focus

Empowerment evaluation is the use of evaluation concepts, techniques, and findings to foster improvement and self-determination. Improvement can focus on a particular program or project or an entire system. However, even when the focus is on a particular program, it is viewed through a lens of the larger system. "Think globally, act locally" applies to empowerment evaluation. A global or holistic perspective is often focused on values and beliefs and enables participants to address fundamental and substantive issues of change. Adopting a systems orientation (Checkland 1981) enables stakeholders to view their own schools as interconnected, dynamic entities in which changes in one segment have implications for all of the other elements of the educational system.

Empowerment evaluation employs both qualitative and quantitative methodologies, although it can be applied to individuals, organizations (at both intra- and extraorganizational levels), communities, and societies or cultures. It is attentive to empowering processes and outcomes. Zimmerman's work on empowerment theory provides the theoretical framework for empowerment evaluation. According to Zimmerman (n.d.):

> A distinction between empowering processes and outcomes is critical in order to clearly define empowerment theory. Empowerment processes are ones in which attempts to gain control, obtain needed resources, and critically understand one's social environment are fundamental. The process is empowering if it helps people develop skills so they can become independent problem solvers and decision makers. Empowering processes will vary across levels of analysis. For example, empowering processes for individuals might include organizational or community involvement, empowering processes at the organizational level might include shared leadership and decision making, and empowering processes at the community level

might include accessible government, media, and other community resources.

> Empowered outcomes refer to the operationalization of empowerment that allows us to study the consequences of citizens' attempts to gain greater control in their community or the effects of interventions designed to empower participants. Empowered outcomes also differ across levels of analysis. When we are concerned with individuals, outcomes might include situation-specific perceived control, skills, and proactive behaviors. When we are studying organizations, outcomes might include organizational networks, effective resource acquisition, and policy leverage. When we are concerned with community-level empowerment, outcomes might include evidence of pluralism, the existence of organizational coalitions, and accessible community resources.

Empowerment evaluation has an unambiguous value orientation: it is designed to help people help themselves and improve their programs and systems using a form of self-evaluation and reflection. Program participants conduct their own evaluations and typically act as facilitators. An outside evaluator often serves as a coach or additional facilitator depending on internal program capabilities. In essence, empowered stakeholders function as self-evaluative and self-reflective practitioners who focus on improving schools and schooling. Zimmerman's (n.d.) characterization of the community psychologist's role in empowering activities is easily adapted to the empowerment evaluator:

> An empowerment approach to intervention design, implementation, and evaluation redefines the professional's role relationship with the target population. The professional's role becomes one of collaborator and facilitator rather than expert and counselor. As collaborators, professionals learn about the participants through their culture, their world view, and their life struggles. The professional works *with* participants instead of advocating *for* them. The professional's skills, interest, or plans are not imposed on the community; rather, professionals become a resource for a community. This role relationship suggests that what professionals do will depend on the particular place and people with whom they are working, rather

than on the technologies that are predetermined to be applied in all situations. While interpersonal assessment and evaluation skills will be necessary, how, where, and with whom they are applied cannot be automatically assumed as in the role of a psychotherapist with clients in a clinic.

Empowerment evaluation is necessarily a collaborative group activity, not an individual pursuit. An evaluator does not and cannot empower anyone; people empower themselves, often with assistance and coaching. This process is fundamentally democratic. It invites (if not demands) participation, examining issues of concern to the entire community in an open forum. This process helps to establish and sustain schools as learning organizations in which information is continually generated and fed back into the system to improve practice. Following Banathy's (1991), Reigeluth's (1994), and Carr's (1994) conceptions of educational systems design, empowerment evaluation becomes a tool to help participants become empowered learners who use continuous and ongoing learning as a vehicle to democratically redesign oneself and the educational system as a whole.

As a result, the context changes: the assessment of a program's value and worth is not the endpoint of the evaluation—as it often is in traditional evaluation—but part of an ongoing process of program improvement. This new context acknowledges a simple but often overlooked truth: merit and worth are not static values. Populations shift, goals shift, knowledge about program practices and their value change, and external forces are highly unstable. By internalizing and institutionalizing self-evaluation processes and practices, a dynamic and responsive approach to evaluation can be developed to accommodate these shifts. Both value assessments and corresponding plans for program improvement (developed by the group with the assistance of a trained evaluator) are subject to a cyclical process of reflection and self-evaluation. Program participants learn to continually assess their progress toward self-determined goals, and to reshape their plans and strategies according to this assessment. In the process, self-determination is fostered, illumination generated, and liberation actualized.

Value assessments are also highly sensitive to the life cycle of the program or organization. Goals and outcomes are geared toward the appropriate developmental level of implementation. Extraordinary improvements are not expected of a project that will not be fully implemented until the following year. Similarly, seemingly small gains or improvements in programs at an embryonic stage are recognized and appreciated in relation to their stage of development. In a fully operational and mature program, moderate improvements or declining outcomes are viewed more critically. In addition, value assessments are sensitive to the dynamic life cycles of various human activity sytems that are part of the complex learning settings of schools and education.

Despite its focus on self-determination and collaboration, empowerment evaluation and traditional external evaluation are not mutually exclusive. In fact, the empowerment evaluation process produces a rich data source that enables a more complete external examination.

Origins of the Idea

Empowerment evaluation has many sources. The idea first germinated during preparation of another book, *Speaking the Language of Power: Communication, Collaboration, and Advocacy* (Fetterman 1993c). In developing that collection, we wanted to explore the many ways that evaluators and social scientists could give voice to the people they work with and bring their concerns to policy brokers. We found that, increasingly, socially concerned scholars in myriad fields are making their insights and findings available to decision makers. These scholars and practitioners address a host of significant issues, including conflict resolution, the dropout problem, environmental health and safety, homelessness, educational reform, AIDS, Native American concerns, and the education of gifted children. The aim of these scholars and practitioners was to explore successful strategies, share lessons learned, and enhance their ability to communicate with an educated citizenry and powerful policymaking bodies. Collaboration, participation, and empowerment emerged as common threads throughout the work and helped to crystal-lize the concept of empowerment evaluation.

Empowerment evaluation has roots in community psychology and action anthropology. Community psychology focuses on people, organizations, and communities working to establish control over their affairs. The literature about citizen participation and community development is extensive. Rappaport's (1987) "Terms of Empowerment/Exemplars of Prevention: Toward a Theory for Community Psychology" is a classic in this area. Sol Tax's (1958) work in action anthropology focuses on how anthropologists can facilitate the goals and objectives of self-determining groups, such as Native American tribes. Empowerment evaluation also derives from collaborative and participatory evaluation (Choudhary and Tandon 1988; Papineau and Kiely 1994; Shapiro 1988; Stull and Schensul 1987; Whitmore 1990; Whyte 1990).

A major influence was the national educational school reform movement with colleagues such as Henry Levin. Levin's Accelerated School Project (ASP) emphasizes the empowerment of parents, teachers, and administrators to improve educational settings. We worked to help design an appropriate evaluation plan for the Accelerated School Project, which contributes to the empowerment of teachers, parents, students, and administrators (Fetterman and Haertel 1990). The ASP team and I also mapped out detailed strategies for districtwide adoption of the project in an effort to help institutionalize the project in the school system (Stanford University and American Institutes for Research 1992).

Dennis Mithaug (1991; 1993) worked extensively with individuals with disabilities to explore concepts of self-regulation and self-determination. His work provided additional inspiration. Recently, we completed a two-year grant funded by the Department of Education about self-determination and individuals with disabilities. We conducted research designed to help both providers of students with disabilities and the students themselves become more empowered. We learned about self-determined behavior and attitudes and environmentally related features of self-determination by listening to self-determined children with

disabilities and their providers. Using specific concepts and behaviors extracted from these case studies, we developed a behavioral checklist to assist providers as they work to recognize and foster self-determination.

Self-determination, defined as the ability to chart one's own course in life, forms the theoretical foundation of empowerment evaluation. It consists of numerous interconnected capabilities, such as the ability to identify and express needs, establish goals or expectations and a plan of action to achieve them, identify resources, make rational choices from various alternative courses of action, take appropriate steps to pursue objectives, evaluate short- and long-term results (including reassessing plans and expectations and taking necessary detours), and persist in pursuing those goals. A breakdown at any juncture of this network of capabilities—as well as various environmental factors—can reduce a person's likelihood of being self-determined. (See also Bandura 1982, concerning the self-efficacy mechanism in human agency.)

A pragmatic influence on empowerment evaluation is the W. K. Kellogg Foundation's emphasis on empowerment in community settings. The foundation has taken a clear position concerning empowerment as a funding strategy:

> We've long been convinced that problems can best be solved at the local level by the people who live with them on a daily basis. In other words, individuals and groups of people must be empowered to become changemakers and solve their own problems through the organizations and institutions they devise. . . . Through our community-based programming, we are helping to empower various individuals, agencies, institutions, and organizations to work together to identify problems and to find quality, cost-effective solutions. In doing so, we find ourselves working more than ever with grantees with whom we have been less involved—smaller, newer organizations and their programs. (W. K. Kellogg Foundation 1992, 6)

Their work in the areas of youth, leadership, community-based health services, higher education, food systems, rural development, and families and neighborhoods exemplifies this spirit of putting "power in the hands of creative and committed individuals—power that will enable them to make important changes in the world" (W. K. Kellogg Foundation 1992, 13). For example, one project—Kellogg's Empowering Farm Women to Reduce Hazards to Family Health and Safety on the Farm—involves a participatory evaluation component. The work of Sanders, Barley, and Jenness (1990) on cluster evaluations for the Kellogg Foundation also highlights the value of giving ownership of the evaluation to project directors and staff members of science education projects.

These influences, activities, and experiences form the background for this new evaluation approach. Empowerment theory by Zimmerman (n.d.), Zimmerman et al. (1992), Zimmerman and Rappaport (1988), and Dunst et al. (1992) also inform this approach. A brief review of empowerment evaluation's many facets will illustrate its wide-ranging application.

FACETS OF EMPOWERMENT EVALUATION

In this new context, training, facilitation, advocacy, illumination, and liberation are all facets—if not developmental stages—of empowerment evaluation. Rather than additional roles for an evaluator, whose primary function is to assess worth (as defined by Stufflebeam [1995] and Scriven [1967]), these facets are an integral part of the evaluation process. Cronbach's developmental focus is relevant and on target: the emphasis is on program development, improvement, and lifelong learning. Empowerment builds on this conception by both including and transcending the program level. People need to begin within the context of their immediate environment for their work to be meaningful and relevant. However, they also need to have a conception of how their work fits into the larger spectrum if they are going to be transforming agents of change on a global or systems level.

Training—Learning by Doing

In one facet of empowerment evaluation, evaluators teach people to conduct their own evaluations and thus become more self-sufficient. This approach desensitizes and demystifies evaluation and ideally helps organizations internalize evaluation principles and practices, making evaluation an integral part of planning. Too often an external evaluation is an exercise in dependency rather than an empowering experience. In these instances, the process ends when the evaluator departs, leaving participants without the knowledge or experience to continue on themselves. In contrast, an evaluation conducted by program participants is designed to be ongoing and internalized in the system, creating the opportunity for capacity building.

Empowerment evaluation training has been used extensively and successfully in educational settings, ranging from inner-city school districts to institutes of higher education. In each case, training that typically connotes developing skills and knowledge is designed to immerse participants in the self-reflective and evaluative process. This process forces them to reevaluate values and beliefs about evaluation, school change, and their own roles. It is designed to enhance self-determining relationships within the school system.

In empowerment evaluation, training is used to map out the terrain, highlighting categories and concerns. It is also used in making preliminary assessments of program components, while illustrating the need to establish goals, strategies to achieve goals, and documentation to indicate or substantiate progress. Training a group to conduct a self-evaluation can be considered equivalent to developing an evaluation or research design (since that is the core of the training). It is a standard part of any evaluation. This training is ongoing, as new skills are needed to respond to new levels of understanding. Training also becomes part of the self-reflective process of self-assessment (on a program or schoolwide level) because participants must learn to recognize when more tools are required to continue and enhance the evaluation process. This self-assessment process is pervasive in an empowerment evaluation. It is built into every part of a program, even to the point of reflecting on how its own meetings are conducted and feeding that input into future practice.

In essence, empowerment evaluation is the concept of "give them a fish, and you feed them for a day. Teach them to fish, and you feed them for a lifetime." The primary difference is that in empowerment evaluation the evaluator and the individuals benefitting from the evaluation are typically on an even plane, learning from each other.

Facilitation

Empowerment evaluators serve as coaches or facilitators to help others conduct a self-evaluation. For example, the Oakland Unified School District was in the process of self-evaluation to assess their progress in carrying out their five-year plan. They had a district mission, a strategic approach, and a list of desired student outcomes. They adopted an empowerment evaluation approach. Superintendent Mesa, an enthusiastic supporter of the empowerment approach, and coordinators of the overall effort—Gary Yee, a former principal in the district, and Ed Ferran, a district staff member with extensive facilitation experience—recognized the value of the participatory process. Once staff members began setting their own goals and identifying their own program performance indicators, program improvement became a powerful all-inclusive force. Staff members were asked to rate their performance, document that rating, and in some cases adjust their self-rating to accommodate group feedback. This process created a baseline against which to monitor future progress, established goals and milestones for the future, and highlighted the significance of documenting progress toward self-selected goals. It demystified the evaluation process and helped staff members internalize evaluation as a way of thinking about what they were doing on a regular basis. It also put them in charge of their own destinies. They selected the intermediate goals and objectives required to have an impact on the larger, long-term goals of improving student performance and reducing dropout and crime rates.

In my role as coach, I provided general guidance and direction to the effort, attending sessions to monitor and facilitate as needed. It was critical to emphasize that the staff were in charge of this effort; otherwise, program participants would initially tend to look to the "empowerment evaluator" as the expert, which would make them dependent on an outside agent. In some instances, my task was to clear away obstacles and identify and clarify miscommunication patterns. I also participated in the first few cabinet-level meetings in the district, providing explanations, suggestions, and advice at various junctures to help ensure that the process had a fair chance.

An empowerment evaluation coach can also provide useful information about how to create facilitation teams (balancing analytical and social skills), work with resistant (but interested) units, develop refresher sessions to energize tired units, and resolve various protocol issues. Simple suggestions along these lines can keep an effort from backfiring or being seriously derailed.

A coach may also be asked to help create the evaluation design with minimal additional support. For example, The Hebrew Union College asked for assistance in designing an action or empowerment-oriented evaluation. After some consultation and a study of relevant literature, the college reshaped its entire plan, choosing to have congregations throughout the country conduct their own self-evaluations. An empowerment evaluator was hired at a later date to help keep the process on track.

Whatever her contribution, the empowerment evaluation coach must ensure that the evaluation remains in the hands of program personnel. The coach's task is to to keep the effort on track by providing useful information based on her training and past experience.

Advocacy

In some instances, empowerment evaluators conduct an evaluation for a group after the goals and evaluation design have been collaboratively established. They may even serve as direct advocates, helping groups become empowered through evaluation. Evaluators often feel compelled to serve as advocates for groups that have no control over their own fates, such as the homeless or dropout populations. In an empowerment setting, advocate evaluators allow participants to shape the direction of the evaluation, suggest ideal solutions to their problems, and then take an active role in making social change happen.

A common workplace practice provides a familiar illustration of self-evaluation and its link to advocacy on an individual level. Employees often collaborate with both supervisor and clients to establish goals, strategies for achieving those goals and documenting progress, and realistic time lines. Employees collect data on their own performance and present their case for their performance appraisal. Self-evaluation thus becomes a tool of advocacy. This individual self-evaluation process is easily transferable to the group, program level, or system level.

Evaluators have a moral responsibility to serve as advocates after the evaluation has been conducted if the findings merit it. In a national study of dropouts, postevaluation activities included disseminating generally positive findings to appropriate policymakers and preparing a Joint Dissemination Review Panel Submission.

Advocate evaluators write in public arenas to change public opinion, influence power brokers, and provide relevant information at opportune moments in the policy decision-making forum. An excellent editorial piece about school dropouts in Chicago highlighted evaluation findings concerning minority education and school failure. Hess's work (1993) was a catalyst for citywide educational and social change. Hopper (1993) writes newspaper editorials to respond critically to cultural "givens" or stereotypes about the homeless and to participate in social change on their behalf. In an op-ed piece in *The Chronicle of Higher Education,* I wrote about lessons learned in a controversial environmental health and safety evaluation at Stanford University. This editorial piece focused on classic organizational conflicts of interest existing within college campuses and the benefits of empowering health-and-safety workers to ensure safer working environments in higher education (Fetterman 1990a). Other op-ed pieces dispel myths about gifted and talented children (Fetterman 1990b). Evaluators thus used the media to build a case for the people we work with, at-

tempting to inform a concerned and educated citizenry. These actions are in accordance with Mill's (1959) position:

> There is no necessity for working social scientists to allow the potential meaning of their work to be shaped by the "accidents of its setting," or its use to be determined by the purposes of other men [or women]. It is quite within their powers to discuss its meaning and decide upon its uses as matters of their own policy. (p. 177)

Illumination

Illumination is an eye-opening, revealing, and enlightening experience. Typically, a new insight or understanding about roles, structures, and program dyamics is developed in the process of determining worth and striving for program improvement (see Parlett and Hamilton 1976). Empowerment evaluation is illuminating on a number of levels. Two cases from the Oakland School District self-evaluation highlight the illuminating qualities of this process or approach. During one meeting, members of the district's early childhood group decided after a lengthy and somewhat circuitous discussion that they wanted to link their work with student academic outcomes or test data, something they'd never done before in assessing their performance. Working with various district administrators, they extracted the CTBS test data for children in the early childhood program from the district management information system and compared them with data for similar students in the district but not in the program. The data documented significantly higher educational achievement by students in the early childhood program. Program staff members found this to be an eye-opening experience. The next tasks were to determine whether these findings held up with additional comparisons and to dig deeper to identify the specific reasons for any differences. This led to a detailed critical review of the entire program. It also opened doors that they did not know existed, such as access to an existing student database within the district bureaucracy to help them understand the differences, measure the impact, and improve their program.

A meeting with one of the largest and most powerful units in the district resulted in a research epiphany. Unit members thought of themselves as a very successful group, in spite of the district's overall poor performance. When one facilitator asked them to provide some evidence of their effectiveness, they pointed to their work in the area of school climate. After some discussion, they suggested that leadership training was the most significant variable affecting school climate (of the variables they had control over). They claimed to have five leadership teams operating at a high level of effectiveness. After requesting and receiving documentation to support this rating, the facilitator asked if they would have more impact if they had more teams. One member of the unit said, "We could have a dramatic effect if we had more teams and we worked at more schools." She then proceeded, with the assistance of the facilitator, to chart out a growth curve with an x and y axis and a dotted line running through it at a 45 degree angle, predicting the type of positive impact anticipated from this increased effort. They agreed to set this new goal for the unit, rearrange their schedules and workloads to accommodate the expanded number of schools, and work toward this goal over the academic year, collecting documentation about their progress throughout the year. This administrator, with little or no research background, developed a testable, researchable hypothesis in the middle of a discussion about indicators and self-evaluation. It was not only illuminating to the group (and to her), it revealed what they could do as a group when given the opportunity to think about problems and come up with workable options, hypotheses, and tests.

This experience of illumination holds the same intellectual intoxication each of us experienced the first time we came up with a researchable question. The process creates a dynamic community of learners as people engage in the art and science of evaluating themselves.

Liberation

Illumination often sets the stage for liberation. It can unleash powerful, emancipatory forces for self-determination. Liberation is the act of being freed or freeing oneself from preexisting roles and constraints. It often involves new conceptualizations of oneself and others. Empowerment evaluation can also be liberating. Many of the examples in this discussion demonstrate how helping individuals take charge of their lives—and find useful ways to evaluate themselves—liberates them from traditional expectations and roles. They also demonstrate how empowerment evaluation enables participants to find new opportunities, see existing resources in a new light, and redefine their identities and future roles.

For example, school nurses in the Oakland public school system are using this approach to help them understand their own evolving role in the school district. Nurses are becoming more involved in assessing the life circumstances of the entire student population, rather than simply meeting individual student needs. They view the empowerment evaluation meeting activity as an opportunity to help define what their role will be in the future. In the process of redefining their role, they have designed specific tasks that will help them emerge as life-circumstance-oriented health care providers, including conducting a schoolwide assessment of the health conditions at the various sites, such as the percentage of students with asthma at each school site.

Empowerment evaluation can also be liberating on a larger sociopolitical level. Johann Mouton, executive director of the Centre for Science Development at the Human Sciences Research Council, and Johann Louw from the Department of Psychology at the University of Cape Town invited me to speak about empowerment evaluation and conduct workshops throughout South Africa after apartheid had ended but before the elections. These two individuals and the institutions they represent "reject racism and racial segregation and strive to maintain a strong tradition of non-discrimination with regard to race, religion, and gender." The Centre for Science Development was the national funding agency for the human sciences in South Africa, and my empowerment evaluation workshops were conducted under the auspices of the then-new Directorate: Research Capacity Building, which focused primarily on building research capacity among black scholars in the country. Over a third of the participants in the workshops were black. This was a historic achievement by South African standards.

When Johann Louw and I first met, he said he was "intrigued and interested [in the approach, since] as you can imagine, empowerment is very much on the social agenda in this country" (1993, personal communication). He invited me to work with him, assisting in the evaluation of various programs administered in and by an impoverished black community near Cape Town (see Fetterman 1994). These community members were implementing and evaluating a broad range of community participation health care programs. They used self-evaluation to monitor and build on their successes and failures. This commendable work took place despite a context of disenfranchisement, high rates of unemployment, and disease. Acts of violence were a part of daily life. (See Fetterman 1993b for a discussion of the culture of violence and the balance between hope and fear in South Africa.) This progressive self-reflective impoverished black community reflects the real spirit of hope persisting despite South Africa's culture of violence. In another example, the Independent Development Trust, under the guidance of its director, Professor Merlyn Mehl from the University of the Western Cape, is building empowerment evaluation into the process of reformulating national educational goals, including one of the country's most ambitious educational undertakings—the whole-school improvement of one thousand primary and secondary schools across the country (Mehl, Gillespie, Foale, and Ashley 1995). This new nation is rethinking and reevaluating everything, from social attitudes to land distribution. The issue of empowerment speaks to the heart of the reconstruction of South Africa.

STEPS OF EMPOWERMENT EVALUATION

There are several pragmatic steps involved in helping others learn to evaluate their own programs and the school system: (1) taking stock and determining where the program and systemic change

process stands, including strengths and weaknesses; (2) focusing on establishing goals—determining where you want to go in the future with an explicit emphasis on program or schoolwide change; (3) developing strategies and helping participants determine their own strategies to accomplish goals and objectives; and (4) helping participants determine the type of evidence required to document progress credibly toward their goals.

Step One: Taking Stock

One of the first steps in empowerment evaluation is taking stock. Program participants are asked to rate their program on a scale of one to ten, with ten being the highest level. They are asked to make the rating as accurate as possible. Many participants find it less threatening or overwhelming to begin by listing, describing, and then rating individual activities in their program before attempting a gestalt or overall unit rating. Specific program activities might include recruitment, admissions, pedagogy, curriculum, graduation, and alumni tracking in a school setting. The potential list of components to rate is endless and each participant must prioritize the list of items, typically limiting the rating to the top ten activities. Program participants are also asked to document their ratings (both the ratings of specific program components and the overall program rating). Typically, some participants give their programs an unrealistically high rating. However, the absence of appropriate documentation, peer ratings, and a reminder about the realities of their environment—such as a high dropout rate, students' bringing guns to school, and racial violence in a high school—helps participants recalibrate their ratings. In some cases, ratings stay higher than peers consider appropriate. However, the significance of this process is not the actual rating so much as it is the creation of a baseline from which future progress can be measured. In addition, it sensitizes program participants to the necessity of collecting data to support assessments or appraisals.

Shifting gears and applying the same process to systemic change, stakeholders create a baseline of data to inform progress of systems design, implementation, and evaluation. Stakeholders refocus their lens on systems design and systemic change processes, rather than the detail of the program per se. (See Banathy [1988] and Jenks [1994] for additional insight into the evaluative role in design and change processes.) These levels of analysis are not mutually exclusive. In fact, they are mutually reinforcing and needed to think globally and act locally.

Step Two: Setting Goals

After rating their program's performance and providing documentation to support that rating, program participants are asked how highly they would like to rate their program in the future. Then they are asked what goals they want to set to warrant that future rating. These goals should be established in conjunction with supervisors and clients to ensure relevance from both perspectives. In addition, goals should be realistic, taking into consideration such factors as initial conditions, motivation, resources, and program and systems dynamics.

It is important that goals be related to the program's activities, talents, resources, and scope of capability. One problem with traditional external evaluation is that programs have been given grandiose goals or long-term goals that participants could only contribute to in some indirect manner. There was no link between their daily activities and ultimate long-term program outcomes in terms of these goals. In empowerment evaluation, program participants are encouraged to select intermediate goals that are directly linked to their daily activities. These activities can then be linked to larger, more diffuse goals, creating a clear chain of outcomes.

Program participants are encouraged to be creative in establishing their goals. A brainstorming approach is often used to generate a new set of goals. Individuals are asked to state what they think the program should do. The list generated from this activity is refined, reduced, and made realistic through a critical review and consensual agreement process after the brainstorming phase.

There are also a bewildering number of goals to strive for at any given time. As a group begins to establish goals based on this initial review of their program, they realize quickly that a consensus is required to determine the most significant issues to focus on. These are chosen according to significance to the operation of the program, such as teaching; timing or urgency, such as recruitment or budget issues; and vision, including community building and learning processes.

Goal setting can be a slow process when program participants have a heavy work schedule. Sensitivity to the pacing of this effort is essential. Additional tasks of any kind and for any purpose may be perceived as simply another burden when everyone is fighting to keep their heads above water. Although this step was initially conceptualized for use on the program level because of empowerment evaluation's hands-on nature, it is equally relevant and necessary on the level of educational systems design. After establishing baseline data concerning the educational system, broad-based goals and processes must be established to tranform a community of learners from one stage of development or understanding to the next. They provide a sense of direction and specific landmarks to idenfity along the way.

Step Three: Developing Strategies

Program participants are also responsible for selecting and developing strategies to accomplish program objectives. The same process of brainstorming, critical review, and consensual agreement is used to establish a set of strategies. These strategies are reviewed routinely to determine their effectiveness and appropriateness. Determining appropriate strategies in consultation with sponsors and clients is an essential part of the empowering process. Program participants are typically the most knowledgeable about their own jobs, and this approach acknowledges and utilizes that expertise in the process of putting them back in the "driver's seat." Once again, shifting gears from a program level to a systems level, the act of developing specific strategies allows participants to engage in pragmatic activities and tasks in a credible manner, since they can see the linkages between their actions and the larger goals and processes associated with systemic change. One of the reasons for emphasizing program and systems levels simultaneously is that they are integrally interwoven in practice. Focusing on the program level as a starting point (with a global or systemwide lens) makes the day-to-day activity of systemic change real and manageable. In addition, program-level change and self-evaluation is a concrete metaphor for systems change and self-evaluation. The same steps apply to the systems level of analysis; the only difference is that the specifics of the conceptual map are more abstract and pervasive.

Step Four: Documenting Progress

In step four, program participants are asked what type of documentation is required to monitor progress toward their goals. This is a critical step. Each form of documentation is scrutinized for relevance to avoid devoting time to collecting information that will not be useful or relevant. Program participants are asked to explain how a given form of documentation is related to specific program goals. This review process is difficult and time consuming, but prevents wasted time and disillusionment at the end of the process. In addition, documentation must be credible and rigorous if it is to withstand the criticisms that this evaluation is self-serving. (See Fetterman 1994 for a detailed discussion of these steps and case examples.)

Similarly, documentation is required to monitor progress and processes associated with systemic change. Process and outcomes associated with systemic change are not difficult to discern and record. They are similar to the processes and outcomes associated with empowerment theory. Democratic and participatory decision-making patterns are significant indicators of systemic educational change. Actual decisions that emerge from this process are documentable outcomes.

CAVEATS AND CONCERNS

Is Research Rigor Maintained?

Empowerment evaluation is one approach among many being used to address social, educational, industrial, and health care problems. As with the exploration and development of any new frontier, this approach requires adaptations, alterations, and innovations. This does not mean that significant

compromises must be made in the rigor required to conduct evaluations. Although I am a major proponent of individuals' taking evaluation into their own hands and conducting self-evaluations, I recognize the need for adequate research, preparation, and planning. These first discussions need to be supplemented with reports, texts, workshops, classroom instruction, and apprenticeship experiences if possible. Program personnel new to evaluation should seek the assistance of an evaluator to act as coach, assisting in the design and execution of an evaluation. Further, an evaluator must be judicious in determining when it is appropriate to function as an empowerment evaluator or in any other evaluative role.

Does This Abolish Traditional Evaluation?

New approaches require a balanced assessment. A strict constructionist perspective may strangle a young enterprise; too liberal a stance is certain to transform a novel tool into another fad. Colleagues who fear that we are giving evaluation away are right in one respect: we are sharing it with a much broader population. But those who fear that we are educating ourselves out of a job are only partially correct. Like any tool, empowerment evaluation is designed to address a specific evaluative need. It is not a substitute for other forms of evaluative inquiry or appraisal. We are educating others to manage their own affairs in areas they know (or should know) better than we do. At the same time, we are creating new roles for evaluators to help others help themselves.

How Objective Can a Self-Evaluation Be?

Objectivity is a relevant concern. We needn't belabor the obvious point that science and, specifically, evaluation have never been neutral. Anyone who has had to roll up their sleeves and get their hands dirty in program evaluation or policy arenas is aware that evaluation, like any other dimension of life, is political, social, cultural, and economic. It rarely produces a single truth or conclusion. In the context of a discussion about self-referent evaluation, Stufflebeam (1995) states that "as a practical example of this, in the coming years U.S. teachers will have the opportunity to have their competence and effectiveness examined against the standards of the National Board for Professional Teaching Standards and if they pass to become nationally certified" (p. 331). Regardless of one's position on this issue, evaluation in this context is a political act. What Stufflebeam considers an opportunity, some teachers consider a threat to their livelihood, status, and role in the community. This can be a screening device in which social class, race, and ethnicity are significant variables. The goal is improvement, but for whom and at what price are questions that remain valid.

To assume that evaluation is all in the name of science or that it is separate, above politics or "mere human feelings" (indeed, that evaluation is *objective)*, is to deceive oneself and to do an injustice to others. Objectivity functions along a continuum. It is not an absolute or dichotomous condition of all or none. Fortunately, such objectivity is not essential to being critical. For example, I support programs designed to help dropouts pursue their education and prepare for a career; however, I am highly critical of program implementation efforts. If the program is operating poorly, it is doing a disservice both to former dropouts and to taxpayers.

One needs only to scratch the surface of the "objective" world to see that it is shaped by values, interpretations, and culture. Whose ethical principles are evaluators grounded in? Do we all come from the same cultural, religious, or even academic tradition? Such an ethnocentric assumption or assertion flies in the face of our accumulated knowledge about social systems and evaluation. Similarly, assuming that we can "strictly control bias or prejudice" is naive, given the wealth of literature available on the subject, ranging from discussions about cultural interpretation to reactivity in experimental design. (See Fetterman 1982; Conrad 1994.)

What about Participant or Program Bias?

The process of conducting an empowerment evaluation requires the appropriate involvement of stakeholders. The entire group—not a single individual, external evaluator, or internal manager—is responsible for conducting the evaluation. The group thus can serve as a check on individual members, moderating their various biases and agendas.

No individual operates in a vacuum. Everyone is accountable in one fashion or another and thus has an interest or agenda to protect. A school district may have a five-year plan designed by the superintendent; a graduate school may have to satisfy requirements of an accreditation association; an outside evaluator may have an important but demanding sponsor pushing either time lines or results, or may be influenced by training to use one theoretical approach rather than another.

In a sense, empowerment evaluation minimizes the effect of these biases by making them an explicit part of the process. The example of a self-evaluation in a performance appraisal is useful again here. An employee negotiates with his or her supervisor about job goals, strategies for accomplishing them, documentation of progress, and even the time line. In turn, the employee works with clients to come to an agreement about acceptable goals, strategies, documentation, and time lines. All of this activity takes place within corporate, institutional, and/or community goals, objectives, and aspirations. The larger context, like theory, provides a lens in which to design a self-evaluation. Supervisors and clients are not easily persuaded by self-serving forms of documentation. Once an employee loses credibility with a supervisor it is difficult to regain it. The employee thus has a vested interest in providing authentic and credible documentation. Credible data (as agreed on by the supervisor and the client in negotiation with the employee) serves both the employee and the supervisor during the performance appraisal process.

When applying this approach to the program, whole school, or community level, superintendents, accreditation agencies, and other "clients" require credible data. Participants in an empowerment evaluation thus negotiate goals, strategies, documentation, and time lines. Credible data can be used to advocate program expansion, whole school educational and administrative redesign, and/or improvement. This process is an open one, placing a check on self-serving reports. It provides an infrastructure and network to combat institutional injustices. It is a highly (often brutally) self-critical process. Empowerment evaluation is successful because it adapts and responds to existing decision-making and authority structures on their own terms (see Fetterman 1993c). It also provides an opportunity and a forum to challenge authority and managerial facades by providing data about actual program operations—from the ground up. The approach is particularly valuable for disenfranchised people and programs to ensure that their voice is heard and that real problems are addressed.

POSITIONS OF PRIVILEGE

Empowerment evaluation is grounded in my work with the most marginalized and disenfranchised populations, ranging from urban school systems to community health education programs in South African townships. They have educated me about what is possible in communities overwhelmed by violence, poverty, disease, and neglect. They have also repeatedly sensitized me to the power of positions of privilege. One dominant group has the vision, makes and changes the rules, enforces the standards, and need never question its own position or seriously consider any other. In such a view, differences become deficits rather than additive elements of culture. People in positions of privilege dismiss the contributions of a multicultural and multidimensionally represented world. They create rational policies and procedures that systematically deny full participation in their community to people who think and behave differently.

Evaluators cannot afford to be unreflective about the culturally embedded nature of our profession. There are many tacit prejudgments and omissions embedded in our primarily Western thought and behavior. These values, often assumed to be superior, are considered natural. However, Western philosophies have privileged their own traditions and used them to judge others who may not share them, disparaging such factors as ethnicity and gender. In addition, they system-

atically exclude other ways of knowing. Some evaluators are convinced that there is only one position and one sacred text in evaluation, justifying exclusion or excommunication for any "violations" or wrong thinking (see Stufflebeam 1994). Scriven's (1991) discussion about perspectival evaluation is instructive in this context, highlighting the significance of adopting multiple perspectives, including new perspectives. Carr's work (1994) is instructive on systemic change as the level of analysis, calling for a multivocal representation of stakeholders.

We need to keep open minds, but not empty heads. Skepticism is healthy; cynicism, blindness, and condemnation are not, particularly for emerging evaluative forms and adaptations. New approaches in evaluation and even new ways of knowing are needed if we are to expand our knowledge base and respond to pressing needs. As Campbell (1994) states, we should not "reject the new epistemologies out of hand. . . . Any specific challenge to an unexamined presumption of ours should be taken seriously" (p. 293). Patton (1994) might be right "that the world will not end in a subjective bang, but in a boring whimper as voices of objectivity drifting off into the chaos" (p. 312).

Evaluation must change and adapt as the environment changes, or it will either be overshadowed by new developments or, as a result of its unresponsiveness and irrelevance, follow the path of the dinosaurs to extinction. People are demanding much more of evaluation and are not tolerant of the limited role of the outside expert who has no knowledge of or vested interest in their program, school, or community. Participation, collaboration, and empowerment are becoming requirements in many community-based evaluations, not recommendations. Teachers, administrators, staff members, and students are conducting empowerment and other forms of self- or participatory evaluations with or without us (the evaluation community). I think it is healthier for all parties concerned to work together to improve practice, rather than ignore, dismiss, and condemn evaluation practice; otherwise, we foster the development of separate worlds operating and unfolding in isolation from each other.

DYNAMIC COMMUNITY OF LEARNERS

Many elements must be in place for empowerment evaluation to be effective and credible. Participants must have the latitude to experiment, taking both risks and responsibility for their actions. An environment conducive to sharing successes and failures is also essential. In addition, an honest, self-critical, trusting, and supportive atmosphere is required. Conditions need not be perfect to initiate this process. However, the accuracy and usefulness of self-ratings improve dramatically in this context. An outside evaluator who is charged with monitoring the process can help keep the effort credible, useful, and on track, providing additional rigor, reality checks, and quality controls throughout the evaluation. Without any of these elements in place, the exercise may be of limited utility and potentially self-serving. With many of these elements in place, the exercise can create a dynamic community of transformative learning.

SPREADING THE WORD

Empowerment evaluation is drawing a great deal of attention. It was the theme of the annual meeting of the 1993 American Evaluation Association, as well as the subject of my presidential address for that organization. Evaluators throughout the world—ranging from OXFAM in England to scholars in Israel and auditors in Canada and Texas—have expressed their interest in this new approach. It crystallizes what many of these evaluators are already doing—serving as a change agent to help others help themselves.

Empowerment evaluation is creating a new niche in the intellectual landscape of evaluation. This approach is political in that it has an agenda: empowerment. However, it is not liberal or conservative, ideologically, or positivist or phenomenological, per se. It knows no political or geographic boundaries. It has a bias for the disenfranchised, including minorities, disabled individuals, and women. However, empowerment evaluation can be used to help anyone with a desire for self-determination. It can be used simultaneously on the program and whole-school or system level. Empowerment evaluation is a tool to facilitate systemic educational change, building a dynamic community of learners today.

REFERENCES

Alkin, M. C., R. Daillak, and P. White. 1979. *Using evaluations: Does evaluation make a difference?* Beverly Hills: Sage.

Baggett, D. 1994. Using a project portfolio: Empowerment evaluation for model demonstration projects. *Interchange* 13 (1): 5–7. Champaign: University of Illinois at Urbana-Champaign.

Banathy, B. H. 1988. Systems inquiry in education. *Systems Practice,* 1 (2): 193–212.

———. 1991. *Systems design of education: A journey to create the future.* Englewood Cliffs, N.J.: Educational Technology Publications.

———. 1992. *A systems view of education: Concepts and principles for effective practice.* Englewood Cliffs, N.J.: Educational Technology Publications.

Bandura, A. 1982. Self-efficacy mechanism in human agency. *American Psychologist* 37:122–47.

Campbell, D. T. 1994. Retrospective and prospective on program impact assessment. *Evaluation Practice* 15 (3): 291–98.

Carr, A. 1994. Community participation in systemic educational change. *Educational Technology* 34 (1): 43–50.

Checkland, P. 1981. *Systems thinking, systems practice.* Chichester, U. K.: John Wiley & Sons.

Choudhary, A., and R. Tandon. 1988. *Participatory evaluation.* New Delhi: Society for Participatory Research in Asia.

Conrad, K. J. 1994. Critically evaluating the role of experiments. *New directions for program evaluation.* No. 63. San Francisco: Jossey Bass.

Dunst, C. J., C. M. Trivette, and N. LaPointe. 1992. Toward clarification of the meaning and key elements of empowerment. *Family Science Review* 5 (1&2): 111–30.

Fetterman, D. M. (n.d.). *Empowerment Evaluation.* Thousand Oaks, Calif.: Sage.

———. 1982. Ibsen's baths: Reactivity and insensitivity (A misapplication of the treatment-control design in a national evaluation). *Educational Evaluation and Policy Analysis* 4 (3): 261–79.

———. 1988. *Excellence and equality: A qualitatively different perspective on gifted and talented education.* Albany: State University of New York Press.

———. 1990a. Health and safety issues: Colleges must take steps to avert serious problems. *The Chronicle of Higher Education,* March 21, A 48.

———. 1990b. Wasted genius. *Stanford Magazine* 18 (2): 30–33.

———. 1993a. *Evaluate yourself.* The National Research Center on the Gifted and Talented. Storrs: University of Connecticut.

———. 1993b. Confronting a culture of violence: South Africa nears a critical juncture. *San Jose Mercury,* October 3, 1C and 4C.

———. 1993c. *Speaking the language of power: Communication, collaboration, and advocacy (Translating ethnography into action).* London: Falmer Press.

———. 1995. In response to Dr. Daniel Stufflebeam's "Empowerment evaluation, objectivist evaluation, and evaluation standards: Where the future of evaluation should not go

and where it needs to go," *Evaluation Practice* 16 (2): 177–197.

Fetterman, D. M., and E. H. Haertel. 1990. A school-based evaluation model for accelerating the education of students at risk. ERIC ED 313 495. Clearinghouse on Urban Education.

Fetterman, D.M., S. Kaftavian, and A. Wandersman. 1995. *Empowerment evaluation: Knowledge and tools for self-assessment and accountability.* Thousand Oaks, Calif.: Sage.

Gray, S. T, ed. 1993. *Leadership is: A vision of evaluation.* Washington, D.C.: Independent Sector.

Hess, G. A., Jr. 1993. Testifying on the Hill: Using ethnographic data to shape public policy. In *Speaking the language of power: Communication, collaboration, and advocacy (Translating ethnography into action)* edited by D. M. Fetterman. London: Falmer Press.

Jenks, C. L. 1994. Evaluating an educational system systemically. In *Systemic change in education,* edited by C. M. Reigeluth and R. J. Garfinkel. Englewood Cliffs, N.J.: Educational Technology Publications.

Joint Committee on Standards for Educational Evaluation. 1994. *The program evaluation standards.* Thousand Oaks, Calif.: Sage.

Linney, J. A., and A. Wandersman. 1991. *Prevention plus III (Assessing alcohol and other drug prevention programs at the school and community level: A four-step guide to useful program assessment).* Rockville, Md.: Office of Substance Abuse Prevention, U.S. Department of Health and Human Services.

Mehl, M., G. Gillespie, S. Foale, and M. Ashley. 1995. *Project in progress: The first year and a half of the thousand schools project (May 1993–December 1994).* Cape Town, South Africa: The Independent Development Trust.

Mills, C. W. 1959. *The sociological imagination.* New York: Oxford University Press.

Mithaug, D. E. 1991. *Self-determined kids: Raising satisfied and successful children.* New York: Macmillan.

———. 1993. *Self-regulation theory: How optimal adjustment maximizes gain.* New York: Praeger Publishers.

Oja, S. N., and L. Smulyan. 1989. *Collaborative action research.* Philadelphia: The Falmer Press.

Papineau, D., and M. C. Kiely. 1994. Participatory evaluation: Empowering stakeholders in a community economic development organization. *The Community Psychologist* 27 (2): 56–57.

Parlett, M., and D. Hamilton. 1976. Evaluation as illumination: A new approach to the study of innovatory programmes. In *Beyond the numbers game,* edited by D. Hamilton. London: Macmillan.

Patton, M. Q. 1986. *Utilization-focused evaluation.* Beverly Hills: Sage.

———. 1994. Developmental evaluation. *Evaluation Practice* 15 (3): 311–19.

Rappaport, J. 1987. Terms of empowerment/exemplars of prevention: Toward a theory for community psychology. *American Journal of Community Psychology* 15:121–48.

Reason, P., ed. 1988. *Human inquiry in action: Developments in new paradigm research.* Newbury Park, Calif.: Sage.

Reigeluth, C. M. 1994. The imperative for systemic change. In *Systemic change in education,* edited by C. M. Reigeluth and R. J. Garfinkel. Englewood Cliffs, N.J.: Educational Technology Publications.

Sanders, J. R., Z. A. Barley, and M. R. Jenness. 1990. Annual report: Cluster evaluation in science education. (Unpublished report.)

Scriven, M. S. 1967. The methodology of evaluation. In *Curriculum evaluation,* vol. 1, edited by R. E. Stake. AERA Monograph Series on Curriculum Evaluation. Chicago: Rand McNally.

Shapiro, J. P. 1988. Participatory evaluation: Toward a transformation of assessment for women's studies programs and projects. *Educational Evaluation and Policy Analysis* 10 (3): 191–99.

Stanford University and American Institutes for Research. 1992. A Design for Systematic Support for Accelerated Schools. In *Response to the New American Schools Development Corporation RFP for Designs for a New Generation of American Schools.* Palo Alto, Calif.: American Institutes for Research.

Stevenson, J., R. E. Mitchell, and P. Florin. 1995. Evaluation and Power in Community Prevention Coalitions. In *Empowerment evaluation: Knowledge and tools for self-assessment and accountability,* edited by D. M. Fetterman, A. Wandersman, and S. Kaftarian. Newbury Park, Calif.: Sage.

Stufflebeam, D. L. 1995. Empowerment evaluation, objectivist evaluation, and evaluation standards: Where the future of evaluation should not go and where it needs to go. *Evaluation Practice* 15 (3): 321–38.

Stull, D., and J. Schensul. 1987. *Collaborative research and social change: Applied anthropology in action.* Boulder, Colo.: Westview.

Tax, S. 1958. The Fox Project. *Human organization* 17:17–19.

van der Walt, H. 1993. *Training for self-evaluation at Ithusheng Health Centre.* Tygerberg, South Africa: Centre for Epidemiological Research in Southern Africa, Medical Research Council.

Watkins, J. M. 1992. Critical friends in the fray: An experiment in applying critical ethnography to school restructuring. In *Empowering teachers and parents: School restructuring through the eyes of anthropologists,* edited by F. Hess. Westport, Conn.: Bergin & Garvey.

Whitmore, E. 1990. Empowerment in program evaluation: A case example. *Canadian Social Work Review* 7 (2): 215–29.

Whyte, W. F., ed. 1990. *Participatory action research.* Newbury Park, Calif.: Sage.

W. K. Kellogg Foundation. 1992. *Transitions.* Battle Creek, Mich.: W. K. Kellog Foundation.

Zimmerman, M. A. (n.d.). Empowerment theory: Psychological, organizational, and community levels of analysis. In *Handbook of community psychology,* edited by J. Rappaport and E. Seldman. New York: Plenum Press.

Zimmerman, M. A., B. A. Israel, A. Schulz, and B. Checkoway. 1992. Further explorations in empowerment theory: An empirical analysis of psychological empowerment. *American Journal of Community Psychology* 20 (6): 707-27.

Zimmerman, M. A., and J. Rappaport. 1988. Citizen participation, perceived control, and psychological empowerment. *American Journal of Community Psychology* 16 (5): 725–50.

PROFESSIONAL DEVELOPMENT IN SYSTEMIC EDUCATIONAL CHANGE

—

Laurie Miller Nelson and Charles M. Reigeluth

As systemic educational change becomes a major force in school restructuring efforts, there is a growing need for educators to become proficient in facilitating and participating in systemic change. To answer this need, professional development programs in systemic educational change must be created to help educators develop an understanding of the process. This understanding should be supported through the acquisition of specific attitudes, knowledge, and skills necessary for proficient participation in the systemic change process. Professional development programs should be designed to address each of the particular needs of preservice, inservice, and postservice educators. They should also encourage collaborative efforts among all levels of education, from the elementary to the university level.

The purpose of this chapter is to examine how each of these issues can be addressed through effective professional development in systemic educational change. This discussion begins with a review of what systemic educational change is and why it is vital to the endurance of school reform, the process educators engage in during systemic change, and the issues affecting this process. The

chapter continues with a look at the rationale and purpose of professional development in systemic educational change and the ways in which it can best be accomplished.

SYSTEMIC EDUCATIONAL CHANGE

Educators and the public are concerned with improving the ways in which schools meet the needs of learners. Currently, school restructuring refers to many of the educational reform efforts aimed at helping schools become better learning environments. Yet, many of these efforts are accused of having no clear objective and no clear knowledge of the real clients (Kaufman 1993), while effecting only change at the margins and piecemeal reform (Banathy 1991; Reigeluth 1994). Systemic educational change attempts to overcome many of these shortcomings by taking a contextual approach to change that examines the interrelated components and functions of a school system (Banathy 1992). The systemic approach to restructuring advocates the development of a new paradigm of education built upon evolutionary change, systems thinking, and design theory (Banathy 1991, 1992). These three constructs are the basis from which systemic change operates and are vital to the formation of a new mindset ready to take on the task of educational restructuring. These constructs will be described in the discussion of how this mindset is developed.

Thus, systemic educational change attempts to address, through systemic redesign, many of the problems plaguing our school systems. The process by which this occurs is centered around a design team made up of those most vested in the success of the school, the stakeholders (Eason 1988). Stakeholders include teachers, parents, students, administrators, and community members. Systemic change involves stakeholders in creating a design of an educational environment that will best meet the future needs of their learners. To assist stakeholders in this process, a facilitator should support and structure their efforts as needed. There should be a significant amount of interaction and group processing among participants, as well as professional development to assist educators. Before addressing this need, we will first discuss systemic change.

THE PROCESS OF SYSTEMIC CHANGE

To be effective instigators, participants, facilitators, and maintainers of systemic change, educators must understand the overall systemic change process. They need to learn how to participate in each of its nonlinear, cyclical phases: (1) instigating change; (2) developing a new mindset toward educational change; (3) creating a vision of the ideal future society and its educational systems; (4) designing the needed learning environments and instructional, administrative, and governance systems to support this vision; and (5) operationalizing the design through effective development, implementation, and maintenance.

It is important to emphasize that these phases are not linear. Rather, individuals and teams move into these stages at different times. Also, many of the phases can occur recursively as well as interact concurrently. For the sake of clarity, and to assist in conveying their specific characteristics, the phases are described in a sequential manner.

Instigating Change

The instigation for systemic change begins with an awareness of the historical background from which our current public education system has developed. Throughout history, educational systems have emerged that reflect the needs of society during a given time period (Reigeluth 1994; Toffler 1980). The one-room schoolhouse answered the needs of the agrarian age. Then, as the agrarian age gave way to the industrial age, this was superseded by the current system of mass education. Now, we find ourselves rushing ever faster into the information age and the new demands created by the infoglut of the burgeoning information highway. Just as the one-room school could not meet the requirements of the industrial age, our current industrial age school system cannot effectively prepare learners for their roles in the twenty-first century (Branson 1987). In essence, our antiquated school systems no longer have the agility to respond to the real, contextual demands of learners preparing for the information age—a realization that provides a strong incentive for change. (This should be one element of a professional development program for systemic change.)

Through systemic change, educators attempt to insure that schools will be able to keep pace with society. This underscores the importance of designing educational environments that prepare learners for the roles necessary for success in the twenty-first century. Reich (1991) discusses these roles in *The Work of Nations*. He describes the functions of problem solvers and problem identifiers as well as "strategic brokers." Strategic brokers are those who have the skills to link the first two roles. Other information age competencies are also highlighted in the SCANS report (Secretary's Commission 1991). This report identifies three foundational requirements for all individuals—basic skills, thinking skills, and personal qualities—and four areas that a successful employee must be able to identify and manipulate—resources, interpersonal skills, information systems, and technology. The new learning environments required to educate learners for these roles and skills will be, by necessity, quite different from those that mass produced the obedient workers needed for the industrial age. This need provides a powerful justification for the redesign of our school systems. Once educators understand these global reasons for systemic change, they can begin to focus on more-localized imperatives for change identifiable within their own communities. (This is a second important element of a professional development program.)

Evaluating how well schools or districts are currently meeting their learners' needs is another activity that educators can do to instigate change. Such an evaluation requires educators to first describe the competencies and attributes their graduates will need for them to be most successful and happy in the twenty-first century, then measure their own schools against this standard (Peck 1994). As educators compare what *should* be with what is actually occurring in their schools, they can come to conclusions about what changes need to be made. This self-evaluation identifies problems and shortcomings in a nonthreatening way. Self-evaluation is much more powerful than mandates and suggestions from outside sources. It is also the most meaningful incentive for change (and should be a third element of a professional development program).

During the instigation-for-change phase, it is important to recognize that educators from within the system are also better equipped to be sensitive to the culture of the school and community. This allows them to evaluate readiness for change and identify potential problems. Decisions determining the appropriate timing of change as well as negotiations of situations requiring diplomacy are also handled more effectively by those within the school. This can enhance the opportunities for effective systemic change to take place. (All these elements are important for instigating positive, systemic change and should be addressed in a professional development program, which is discussed later.)

Developing a New Mindset

Once stakeholders determine that fundamental change is needed, they must begin developing a new mindset that allows them to understand and participate in a systemic change process within their schools. This change begins with a paradigm shift and requires a basic understanding of the underlying constructs of systemic change—evolutionary change, systems thinking, and design theory. Without these three perspectives, educators are more likely to attempt unrelated, piecemeal changes rather than using a holistic, systems approach.

The first phase of mindset development begins when stakeholders acquire an appreciation for the **evolutionary nature** of educational systems. These systems need to be adaptive and reflexive to societal changes. When society undergoes such massive changes as it did during the industrial revolution and as it is doing now with the advent of the global information age, important new educational needs and contextual conditions emerge. Schools must keep pace with these changes and coevolve with society if they are to meet society's needs. In order for this to occur, an educational system must be redesigned in such a manner that it can respond to and accommodate evolutionary changes originating from both inside and outside of the system. This process of redesign is also supported by an understanding of the principles underlying systems thinking and design theory. Combined with evolutionary change, these perspectives are integral to the change process as practitioners use them to create new educational systems.

Systems thinking (Checkland 1984) acknowledges the interconnectedness among components (subsystems) within an organized system, such as an educational system. Through systemic thinking, stakeholders are encouraged to think outside of their present definitions of schooling. This new mindset allows them to begin thinking of a school as a human activity system embedded within an environmental context of suprasystems (e.g., social, economic, governmental), peer systems (e.g., social services), and subsystems (e.g., administrative, faculty, maintenance) (Banathy 1992). Each system is interdependent with, and impacted by, the condition and functions of all other systems. This interdependency requires educators to take a global look at a school and address all the systems it influences or is influenced by. This is achieved through an examination of the interrelationships between the needs, values, functions, and purposes of all elements that impinge upon the school, its learners, and the community. This develops an understanding of the ways in which change in one system or its parts influences change in other systems. Therefore, school restructuring must be approached from the perspective of systems thinking because systemically designed schools more closely answer the current needs of learners, the community, and society at large.

In addition to evolutionary change and systems thinking, **design theory** is the other important theoretical foundation of systemic educational change. Design theory gives powerful tools and insights for using a design approach. As it relates to systemic change, a design approach is used as a way to resolve problems through customized, pragmatic design grounded in purpose and volition (Nelson 1994). This contrasts significantly with most school reform efforts and their related professional development programs that use an "adoption" approach (Rogers 1983). The adoption approach uses generic, off-the-shelf solutions that are usually devoid of any input from the actual users. In comparison, a design approach seeks to empower users to address the contextual and situational issues affecting a school system and to design the needed innovations. Therefore, it is important for stakeholders to develop design abilities that allow them to think and behave in the same ways that other types of designers do when resolving ill-defined problems (Cross 1990). Applying a design approach also encourages flexibility and adaptability during the creative phases of the change process. In these ways, design theory is a critical complement to the evolutionary and systemic nature of the change process.

As participants begin to meld an understanding of the constructs of evolutionary change, systems thinking, and design theory, a powerful new mindset for educational restructuring emerges. From this mindset, innovative designs for schools develop in anticipation of the educational needs of future learners. (Therefore, these three elements should be included in a professional development program for systemic change.)

Creating a Vision of Society

With this new mindset in place, practitioners can begin to move into the visioning stage, where they create a vision of what they want their society of the future to be like. This is not a process of guessing the future but of envisioning the future as they want it to be. The practitioners are taking an interactive versus a reactive posture to the future by being accountable for *creating* the future instead of just letting it develop unplanned (Banathy 1991). This process acknowledges the power we have to impact our own futures, rather than to act only as inert recipients.

During this phase, it should be pointed out to participants that this interactive visioning can be contrasted with the more reactive, precursor activity done during the instigation phase. During the initial phase, participants describe what they think learners need in the twenty-first century. In comparison, during the visioning stage, stakeholders take a counterposition as they describe an ideal future society. They actively plan the future rather than passively predict it. After this vision of the ideal future society is articulated, systemic change participants are ready to begin envisioning the learning environments that can prepare learners to function as members and sustainers of that society.

Designing the System

In the visioning phase, the participants conceive and outline the vision of the ideal society, then they design complementary educational systems. Again, participants in systemic change do not seek to predict, but rather to design the learning environments that will most effectively assist in realizing their ideal society. Later, they can compromise as necessary to accommodate existing constraints, then continue to strive to come ever closer to their ideal. This "idealized design" approach has proved advantageous because most constraints can often be overcome later, either in the short run or the long run.

Therefore, participants can begin by using an educational systems design, which integrates systems theory and design theory, to create an ideal design of the specific educational system for their community. During the creation of their design, stakeholders identify the needs, values, and goals that will provide the underpinnings of their educational system. This vague vision or image of an ideal educational system of the future is then solidified through a series of design spirals that successively identify and clarify the purposes, functions, and components of the new educational system. Each spiral produces a progressively clearer image of the new system. Detailed design plans of each component are created with descriptions of its function and relationships to other components within the system.

To keep the design focused on the learning needs for fostering an ideal community, it is best to start by designing the learning-experience level of the new system and the instructional system that can best foster those learning experiences. But to maintain the systemic nature of the design, it is important to keep in mind the interrelationships or impact each level of the new system has on other levels (learning experience, instruction, administration, and governance).

Once the design is clearly formed, the design team can begin to operationalize it.

Operationalizing the Design

Each level of the system is operationalized as the design team develops, implements, and maintains the components of the new design. Development of the design occurs as the team identifies and activates the specific resources needed for the school system to function. These may include such resources as personnel, instructional materials, appropriate technologies, physical facilities, and sources of funding. Once resources have been identified and acquired, the participants initiate the implementation plan.

Ideally, some elements of the implementation plan are developed and carried out concurrently with the design phase. For example, involving all major stakeholder groups from the beginning of the design work creates an understanding and a sense of ownership that avoids potentially disastrous obstacles to implementation. For this to happen, design plans must be continuously disseminated to all

stakeholders, and their input must be sought and acted upon.

Once implemented, the school system is then continuously "debugged" and improved. However, it is important not to expect any dramatic superiority of the new system for at least three to five years. In fact, the first few years may show an actual decrease on the traditional measures of educational effectiveness. This points out the importance of the participants deciding what outcomes they think are important, and making sure that there are appropriate measures for them. Also, to the extent that the ideal design was compromised in its initial implementation, the design team should pursue a plan that will gradually move it back on track. Furthermore, it should not be expected that the new system will remain forever ideal to the community. The community will continue to change; therefore, there must be a redesigning process that ensures the new system can make the adjustments needed to coevolve with it.

Gaining an understanding of the purpose and process of systemic change and developing an ability to participate in it are the major goals for professional development in systemic change. In addition, educators should be aware of the issues that influence and often act as obstacles to systemic change.

ISSUES AFFECTING SYSTEMIC EDUCATIONAL CHANGE

A variety of issues can impact the success of systemic educational change. These influences can originate inside or outside of the primary school system and include opposition to school change efforts, persistence of old paradigms of professional development, availability of needed resources, and political factors. In order to effectively mitigate the potential impact of these issues, they must be well understood.

Opposition to Change

First, there is often open opposition to school reform efforts. This may come from within the school as well as from without. Teachers, administrators, and community members who are not participating as part of the design team may misunderstand or be intimidated by the changes being discussed. This underscores the importance of strong, open lines of communication, which (1) disseminate information about the team's activities; (2) educate those who are not participating directly but are affected by changes made; and (3) solicit stakeholders' input and incorporate it into the design, thereby allowing them to become vested in the process.

Opposition may also come from outside interests not directly related to the school or community. Regional or national interest groups may attempt to curtail restructuring efforts to maintain the status quo. They may advocate that change is not needed for a system that has existed and served the public well for so long. Again, two-way communication about the constructs and objectives of systemic change is needed. If all those genuinely interested in quality education are included and their ideas incorporated, they too will come to support the proposed changes.

Old Paradigms of Professional Development

An additional problem may stem from the fact that professional development in systemic change is unlikely to follow the typical paradigm of staff development. Traditionally, educators are required to attend programs that may only be lecture based, with very little interaction required of participants. In systemic change, participants are the authors and owners of the process, with a facilitator to guide them as needed. Many systemic change programs also require longer periods of time than the brief programs usually offered for inservice development. Professional development in systemic change necessitates a time commitment and a level of involvement not generally expected during regular professional development programs.

Availability of Resources

Another issue that places constraints on systemic change is the availability of human and monetary resources. At this time there are few trained and experienced facilitators of systemic change. It is hoped that this number will grow with the creation of more inservice professional development programs, such as those under development at Indiana University's Department of Instructional Systems Technology, Pennsylvania State University's program in instructional systems, and Western Michigan's Department of Educational Leadership. Likewise, there are few professors in schools of education that have the knowledge base and experience or the support of their departments that is needed for teaching educational systems design to preservice or inservice educators.

Funding is also a problem issue. For a school to go through an effective systemic restructuring effort, a commitment of time and resources must be agreed upon at the onset. Released time for participating faculty and staff is very important. This obligates the hiring of an adequate number of substitute teachers and aids. Often, additional or reallocated funds are needed to design and implement the new system. But there are strong indications that the new system can be more cost effective than the current system once it is implemented and "debugged." As funding is always a major concern for schools, administrators must be committed to supporting change efforts and employing financial creativity in the design and implementation of systemic restructuring.

Political Factors

Another impact on restructuring efforts are political factors. These include legislative actions and mandates as well as personal political agendas. This reality underscores the need for stakeholders to become politically savvy in order to make the political arena work for them. Such political clout can result in waivers and changed state and local policies.

A good facilitator will quickly identify and mitigate personal political agendas of any stakeholder that might undermine the process. This may be difficult to do and can create potential obstacles for collaborative teams. Yet it is important for the team to recognize such problems and develop solutions to the extent possible. In the same manner, the agendas of local and state school board members must also be addressed. Additionally, it is important for design teams to take into consideration curriculum mandates before they put their designs in action.

Having discussed what systemic educational change is—its process and issues—we will now address the need for professional development in systemic change. In the same way that systemic change requires a new paradigm for school restructuring, it also requires a new paradigm for professional development. The following sections will discuss the rationale and purpose for professional development in systemic educational change and how and where it can occur.

RATIONALE FOR PROFESSIONAL DEVELOPMENT IN SYSTEMIC CHANGE

Despite opposition, schools continue to seek fundamental reform. Increasingly, educational leaders recognize the need for systemic versus piecemeal reforms of our outdated industrial age schools. Piecemeal reforms have not made large or lasting differences, nor have their corresponding, traditional professional development paradigms provided the knowledge and skills necessary to empower teachers and other stakeholders to create the schools they desire. Hence, there is a need for systemic change, which requires professional development that is systemic, sustained, and long term rather than brief and isolated.

During systemic change all components of a school's environment and functions should be examined by the school's own stakeholders and redesigned in order to better meet the immediate and future needs of learners. This emphasizes the need for teachers, administrators, and other educational professionals to provide leadership in systemic educational reform. They must learn to assist parents, community members, business representatives, and other stakeholders in the process of creating our future schools. In order to do this, educational professionals must acquire the attitudes, knowledge, and skills needed to act as instigators, participants, or facilitators of systemic

change. Professional development in systemic educational change is crucial to educators gaining the skills of "user-designers" (Banathy 1991). User-designers are stakeholders in a system who take the initiative to identify areas of need and then create action plans and solutions to answer those needs.

As user-designers of systemic change, educators within a particular educational system are empowered to create and maintain needed change. Relevant, permanent change is best initiated by those within the system, which is more appropriate than waiting for outside forces to instigate and dictate it. This type of professional development also supports the current movement toward increased professionalism in the field. Systemic change allows educators to move from being end users of reform efforts initiated by others to becoming developers and managers of changes that they, along with other stakeholders, identify as needed for their respective schools. The need for educators to take leadership positions in systemic restructuring efforts, create needed changes, and increase professionalism is the basic rationale for a truly new paradigm of professional development, which we refer to as *systemic professional development*.

PURPOSE OF SYSTEMIC PROFESSIONAL DEVELOPMENT

The purpose of systemic professional development is to prepare educators to instigate, participate in, facilitate, and maintain this urgently needed change process. Each role is critical to the success of systemic change.

As instigators, educators help others within the school system become aware of how learners' needs are rapidly changing in the information age. This awareness is initiated by comparing what should be and what really is occurring within their own classrooms and schools. Comparing what is needed to what is currently provided leads to an instigation for change. This is a more effective method for initiating change than having problems and solutions identified by outside interests. Initiating change can also lead to participation in the design phase.

Teachers, administrators, and other educational professionals act as key stakeholders on the design team during the systemic change process. Their participation is vital to the success of the process and the educational design it generates. Their prior understanding of systemic change and its objectives strengthens the quality of the process, and they come to the process with an understanding of the underlying theories and phases that it goes through. Most importantly, the participants gain a better idea of what will be expected of them, and they have opportunities to develop and practice skills that lead to a successful process. They can also assist other stakeholders in developing the mindset necessary for effective participation in systemic change.

Process facilitation is one of the most important roles that educators experienced in systemic educational change can assume. There is a great need for facilitators who can assist stakeholders making the "design journey" through systemic change (Banathy 1991). Experienced facilitators can be used to support collaborative school teams through the change process. Their purpose is not to supply predetermined solutions, but to help each school create their own unique design solution that answers their particular mix of educational needs. They need a variety of skills and knowledge, including an understanding of the stages of facilitation, considerations that impact the process, and content to be learned (Salisbury, Reigeluth, and Soulier 1994). Facilitators must also develop the ability to gradually relinquish influence and withdraw support as design team members master the process.

Once the new system is designed, developed, and implemented, it is critical that it be maintained and sustained. After implementation of the system design, educators must be ready and able to debug the system and make needed adjustments to their design in order to continue to meet the changing needs of learners and society. For the design to remain viable, it must have the ability to continue to adapt and coevolve with society. This requires insight and flexibility on the part of the design team as they continue to assess the changing societal environment within which the school system is embedded.

ATTITUDES, KNOWLEDGE, AND SKILLS

There is much to be learned and many skills to be acquired before engaging in a successful systemic change process. This is where effective professional development becomes critical. It is through systemic professional development that educators first learn about the phases of the systemic change process. This knowledge is essential for participation as stakeholders, change instigators, or process facilitators. After gaining an understanding of the overall process, specific attitudes, knowledge, and skills must be developed for effective participation in systemic change. These skills are needed for each participant to maximize his or her contribution to the change process.

Attitudes That Support Systemic Change

Attitudes must be developed that assist educators in being open to change and participating effectively in the dynamic, collaborative environment of a systemic change process. An openness to using this new paradigm of school restructuring is the most important attitude one needs. Professionals must be able to take risks and think creatively while shaping innovative educational systems. They must also be self-reflective, cooperative, and encouraging. With the wide variety of stakeholders that must be involved in a systemic effort, a supportive attitude can facilitate not only one's own design process, but also that of others.

Necessary Knowledge and Skills

One of the most important functions of systemic professional development is direct teaching, not only of attitudes, but also of the necessary knowledge base and skills required for participation. Effective systemic professional development imparts these elements in a timely, logical manner and assists educators in developing a concept of systemic change that they can use either to change their own schools or to act as facilitators for other teams.

As discussed in the section describing systemic change, the most important knowledge and skills to be acquired revolve around an understanding of evolutionary change, systems thinking, and design theory. These are the most integral constructs of systemic change and should be followed by a supporting repertoire of communication, collaboration, group processing, and managerial and interpersonal skills that underwrite the change process. Communication, collaboration, and group processing skills are especially important for participants to exercise effectively. Experiential-based programs that provide direct instruction in these areas can give participants practical experience in developing these skills. This is often needed, as many people may not have experience with team-building skills.

Managerial skills are used extensively during systemic change, particularly by facilitators. Donahoe (1993) gives a good description of how an experienced educator can function as a facilitator or change agent to prepare a school for change and coordinate its restructuring efforts. The role of facilitators in systemic change is similar to that of change agents in diffusion and adoption theory. Diffusion theory is built upon research that has examined the way in which change agents and organizations can interact effectively during diffusion and adoption of an innovation (Burkman 1987; Dormant 1986, 1992). Some of the most useful elements from diffusion theory that can be utilized in systemic change include recommendations for change agents, descriptions of adopter groups, analysis of adoption issues, identification of adoption stages and corresponding diffusion strategies, and determination of organizational readiness.

Because they support an open, safe environment for collaboration, effective interpersonal skills are imperative for educators planning to become process facilitators. These skills help the facilitator gradually relinquish control and ownership of the process to participants. A strong program also informs managers of change about ways to efficiently bring additional stakeholders on board over the lifetime of the process.

The depth and breadth of what must be learned highlights the need for the creation of systemic professional development programs. How these programs are conducted is very important.

HOW AND WHERE SYSTEMIC PROFESSIONAL DEVELOPMENT OCCURS

Of primary importance to systemic professional development programs is a sense of community and a cohesive design culture. Programs that promote these two ideas are usually sponsored by schools. Professional conferences provide another avenue for professional investigation and discussion of systemic change.

Prepare Educational Practitioners in Concert

One of the goals of systemic professional development programs is to prepare educators and other stakeholders in concert with each other. It is critical for stakeholders to be brought online together. This is one of the primary differences between the traditional professional development paradigm and the one integral to systemic change. The importance of training all stakeholders, not just school personnel, is acknowledged. Everyone on the design team is encouraged to participate in systemic professional development opportunities.

This also invites an equalitarian atmosphere in which all ideas are given equal weight and consideration. Starting at the same time and receiving the training together supports the development of a group identity, which is an important element for building a strong design culture (Banathy 1991). The ideal design culture or community fosters (1) participation by all; (2) integrated efforts that create an atmosphere of cooperation; (3) output in the form of relevant insights, ideas, and values; and (4) quality design decisions (Frantz 1994). The goal is to build, through effective team processing, a highly collaborative environment and process. Site-based programs in the schools often provide the training and support for this to occur.

School-Sponsored Programs

Site-based systemic professional development programs include seminars and workshops that prepare and support stakeholders for participation in systemic change. Participants should include not only educators, but also parents and community members and, where appropriate, learners. Other programs sponsored by the school may take place away from the school site. These may also be seminars and workshops as well as retreats. Retreats can be especially effective in building collaborative and group processing skills. Often, when participants are in a neutral environment, hindrances created by the prominence of their professional roles can be reduced and personal reservations can be mitigated. While most systemic professional development is sponsored by the schools, institutions of higher education are beginning to provide increasing numbers of programs to support school restructuring efforts. Examples of these include the Coalition for Essential Schools at Brown University, NCREST at Columbia University's Teachers College, the School Restructuring Consortium at Indiana University, and the Instructional Systems program at Pennsylvania State University.

College and University Settings

Colleges and universities are another appropriate setting for systemic professional development opportunities. They can provide regular and continuing education classes in systemic educational change within programs such as that described by Salisbury, Reigeluth, and Soulier (1994). As well as offering courses, colleges and universities can also engage in collaborative efforts with public schools. These can be the backbone for many systemic restructuring efforts. The number of graduate programs that are researching and developing applications related to systemic change is increasing. These departments are also a source for trained facilitators and systemic professional development workshops and seminars for schools to utilize (see Lee and Reigeluth 1994). Often these programs can be customized to meet the unique needs of a particular school. Additionally, some universities are now offering services similar to the restructuring support service at Indiana University, which is staffed by professors and graduate students who provide workshops for schools undergoing restructuring efforts. These types of services also provide collaborative teams that can support the stakeholder team based at the school. Collaborative efforts provide an important

complement to more formal systemic professional development programs.

Professional Conferences

Conferences and conventions of various professional organizations offer opportunities for systemic professional development. These organizations include the Division for Systemic Change in Education in the Association for Educational Communications and Technology (AECT), the Association for Supervision and Curriculum Development (ASCD), and Phi Delta Kappa (PDK). They offer lecture sessions, workshops, and discussion groups that engage in dialogues intended to further the research of systemic educational change and encourage the development of practical applications. The activities in these organizations allow professionals not only to learn more about systemic change, but also to disseminate their findings and experiences from their own restructuring processes.

THE PROFESSIONAL DEVELOPMENT CONTINUUM

All these structured opportunities can and should occur throughout an educator's career. Professional development in systemic change can be viewed in relation to a career continuum. It can occur during each of the three phases of an educator's career: preservice, inservice, and postservice. Each phase has unique needs and requires a differentiated approach.

Preservice Development

Education in systemic restructuring is particularly important for preservice educators. During preservice professional development, systemic change education should become part of the curricula for teacher education, curriculum and instruction, and educational leadership. Instruction and experience with systems thinking, design theory, and the change process are appropriate disciplines for preservice educators because they are forming many of the approaches and methods of instruction and management that will be incorporated into their classrooms and schools. While they may not initially have the clout needed to instigate change, their knowledge of systemic change will be reflected in their personal philosophy and approach to learning and learners. This will also prepare them to provide support and leadership for any restructuring efforts that may be initiated in the schools where they are employed. Moreover, they will be better prepared to participate in any inservice programs that become available.

Inservice Development

Most efforts for systemic professional development are currently being applied to inservice development. In this career phase, educational professionals have the greatest potential for becoming active participants in and facilitators of change. Therefore, it is important to empower teachers for their new roles in a systemically restructured school (Lee and Reigeluth 1994). This can be accomplished through workshops, retreats, and other experiential activities that build the necessary foundations of knowledge, skill, and attitude. Professional educators should also be encouraged to build collaborative networks with other schools undergoing restructuring and with those at institutes of higher education that are investigating systemic change. Involvement in professional organizations interested in systemic change can provide additional opportunities for systemic professional development.

Postservice Development

Postservice professionals can be especially valuable participants in systemic change as experienced facilitators and mentors to other educational professionals. These educators are an underutilized or unrealized source of support for systemic change. These mature professionals can provide the following: (1) experience and support, as well as insights into the complex nature of the change process; (2) insights into participation in restructuring efforts that support new efforts; and (3) identification of proven methods, probable obstacles, and viable solutions for teams just beginning their change processes.

CONCLUSION

Systemic educational change offers the most viable type of restructuring for schools. However, educators need to have access to appropriate, well-constructed systemic professional development opportunities. There are a variety of settings and ways to meet these needs, from site-based programs to higher-education classes. The most important goal is for systemic professional development programs to actually be developed and implemented. As of yet, no large-scale opportunities are available. But as more research in this area is done and ways to apply it are formulated, programs will increase. This is evidenced by the ever-increasing interest that educational graduate programs and professional organizations are showing in systemic educational change.

REFERENCES

Banathy, B. H. 1991. *Systems design of education: A journey to create the future.* Englewood Cliffs, N.J.: Educational Technology.

———. 1992. *A systems view of education: Concepts and principles for effective practice.* Englewood Cliffs, N.J.: Educational Technology.

Branson, R. K. 1987. Why the schools can't improve: The upper limit hypothesis. *Journal of Instructional Development* 10 (4): 15–26.

Burkman, E. 1987. Factors affecting utilization. In *Instructional technology: Foundations,* edited by R. M. Gagné. Hillsdale, N.J.: Erlbaum.

Checkland, P. 1984. *Systems thinking, systems practice.* New York: John Wiley & Sons.

Cross, N. 1990. The nature and nurture of design ability. *Design Studies* 11 (3): 127–40.

Donahoe, T. 1993. Finding the way: Structure, time, and culture in school improvement. *Phi Delta Kappan*, December, 298–305.

Dormant, D. 1986. The ABCDs of managing change. In *Introduction to performance technology.* Washington, D.C.: National Society for Performance and Instruction.

———. 1992. Implementing human performance technology in organizations. In *Handbook of human performance technology: a comprehensive guide for analyzing and solving performance problems in organizations,* edited by H. D. Stolovitch and E. J. Keeps. San Francisco: Jossey-Bass.

Eason, K. 1988. *Information technology and organizational change.* New York: Taylor & Francis.

Frantz, T. G. 1994. Systems for design learning: Evolving perspectives. *Educational Technology* 34 (1): 54–61.

Kaufman, R. 1993. Beyond tinkering: Educational restructuring that will work. *International Journal of Educational Reform* 2 (2): 154–65.

Lee, I., and C. M. Reigeluth. 1994. Empowering teachers for new roles in a new educational system. *Educational Technology* 34 (1): 61–72.

Nelson, H. G. 1994. Learning systems design. *Educational Technology* 34 (1): 51–54.

Peck, K. 1994. Systemic restructuring and educational technology, 3: Promising starts (Session #532). Paper presented at the annual conference of the Association for Educational Communications and Technology, Nashville, Tenn.

Reich, R. B. 1991. *The work of nations: Preparing ourselves for 21st-century capitalism.* New York: Alfred A. Knopf.

Reigeluth, C. M. 1994. The imperative for systemic change. In *Systemic change in education,* edited by C. M. Reigeluth and R. J. Garfinkle. Englewood Cliffs, N.J.: Educational Technology.

Rogers, E. M. 1983. *Diffusion of innovations.* 3rd ed. New York: The Free Press.

Salisbury, D. F., C. M. Reigeluth, and J. S. Soulier. 1994. A professional development program in education systems design. *Educational Technology* 34 (1): 73–80.

Secretary's Commission on Achieving Necessary Skills. 1991. *What work requires of schools: A SCANS report for America 2000.* Washington, D.C.: U.S. Department of Labor.

Toffler, A. 1980. *The third wave.* New York: Bantam Books.

INSTRUCTIONAL INFORMATION MANAGEMENT SYSTEMS AND SYSTEMIC CHANGE

Michael L. Burger

The ultimate impact that information systems can have on organizations, people, and processes can be profound, so the motivation driving their design, implementation, and evaluation is important. In this chapter, the proposition is forwarded that the primary reason to implement information systems in educational organizations should be to deepen practitioners' vision and understanding of instruction and instructional processes, not simply to alleviate pressures for change, nor to automate instruction in order to increase its "efficiency."[1]

When the need to change takes precedence over the need to understand what is being changed and what it is being changed into, information systems are likely to be considered only as adjunct, usually optional, assistants. In such contexts, if information systems are used, they are operationalized in the context of the need to help solve the specific problems that precipitated the change. They tend to be implemented without the aid of systemic thinking about the nature of the information that they will be managing and the impact they (and the information they manage) will have on the organization and its employees and clients.

In education agencies, information systems are typically designed to help practitioners improve such things as the scores of third graders on a standardized exam. The change is justified if that occurs, because change is both the ends and the means. However, the information systems are effective only if they (1) help empower professionals and their clients as decision makers; (2) help practitioners understand things like how the structure of the organization affects inherent instructional processes; and (3) help practitioners understand how instructor skills in different program areas impact each other and the learning in the organization. Generally, information systems are designed to help answer questions like, How can we fix what we are doing wrong and how do we know when it has been fixed? Information systems that are designed with a systemic focus will help answer questions like, What are we really trying to accomplish and how can we best go about accomplishing it?

There is evidence that the use of information systems in schools will continue to increase. The role that these systems will play in school systems is not yet understood, but it is certain that whatever that role is, it will dramatically affect both the nature of change processes and the characteristics and capacity of the resulting organization.

Of course, the implementation of information systems cannot be systemic unless the psychosocial dimensions of schools are incorporated into the design and implementation processes. If the goal for their use is to better understand education and to learn how to optimize learning in the context of formal social systems, then their value to education will not be realized, and their implementation will be of little value unless educators appreciate the value of information and understand how it can function as an organizational resource and as a means to leverage productivity and the worth of work. That is, educators (administrators and teachers) must want to know how to continually perform better from both a personal and an organizational perspective. They must be willing to collaborate and share ideas and information (including performance results). Moreover, they must value feedback and seek it out as a method of effecting improvements.[2]

In this chapter, it is contended that information systems planning must be contemplated primarily in the context of the instructional mission and purpose of schools. It must also be within a framework for conceptualizing information associated with the instructional functions. Cursorily addressed here is the fact that information systems must permeate the support and administrative functions of schooling and integrate information across functions and organizational boundaries. If instructional systems are not well understood or well informed, there is no hope for meaningful and sustainable (i.e., systemic) change, regardless of what other technology is in place.

THE IMPORTANCE OF MANAGING INFORMATION IN THE CONTEXT OF EDUCATIONAL CHANGE

A quick review of the history of American education or educational literature more than thirty years old will reveal that not much of the modern reform movement is new. Most of what is being tried at the close of the twentieth century in the name of transforming education has been tried al-

ready. This is because good educators have existed in every generation and good educators have always wanted to create quality learning opportunities and environments for their clients.

The extremely powerful and affordable information technologies that have become available at the end of the twentieth century may be the key that enables educators to finally effect systemic change rather than only tinker with subsystems in their organizations. If these technologies are used well, they can be used to help educators establish a referent perspective for change; obtain insights into complex organizations such as schools; challenge the programmatic, organizational, and political barriers that heretofore have kept information dissociated and impotent; and develop a knowledge base that emanates directly from and therefore informs practice.[3]

In spite of the talk about the need to improve education, and despite the fact that by the early 1990s billions of dollars had already been spent on bringing computers into schools, the new technologies have not seriously challenged mass-production oriented schooling. In fact, the argument could be made that, rather than enabling and encouraging systemic change, such technologies have largely been used to further crystallize existing paradigms.[4]

But many students are getting turned off by a plethora of sessions with computers that drill them, test them, and "program" them. Teachers are in danger of becoming separated from the learning process as more and more schools depend on increasingly sophisticated technology to deliver and manage instruction (especially for "low achievers") and make available more and more learning opportunities that transcend (or bypass) traditional classrooms. To illustrate, in the 1990s it is not difficult to give children more access to worldwide information and sophisticated learning systems in their homes than in a typical classroom. Of course, this raises at least two very important questions: (1) Who or what group determines what should be learned? and (2) What happens to children whose families cannot or will not obtain these technologies? Regardless of whether these questions are answered, the American public is continuing to gain confidence that there are viable alternatives to traditional public education.

That teachers do and should continue to play a powerful role in designing, delivering, and assessing instruction at the local level is an assumption underlying much of the thinking in this chapter. If this assumption is rejected, the nature of information systems and how they can be used to make instructional systems better can be much different than what is described here. This assumption is coupled with the contention that it is the lack of information about instruction that is the bottleneck preventing systemic change from occurring in schools. Progress is not hindered by a lack of good ideas, the absence of capable educators, or insufficient funds. In order for systemic change to occur, teachers who play such an important, personal, and pervasive role in establishing the quality of instruction on a daily basis need immediate and timely access to all the information that contributes to the quality of the decisions they make. As a beginning step, educators need to understand how these new tools can enhance their own productivity, empower learning at all levels, and alter the organization of schools.

But teachers have been largely ignored in the process of implementing "high tech" in the schools, and the important role that information technologies can play in leveraging sustainable, desirable, and defensible change continues to be underestimated. Not a few restructuring efforts are planned and initiated without contemplating the importance of an information infrastructure and accompanying technologies.

When systemic change is discussed in the context of education agencies, very few educators seriously examine the evolving nature of information technologies and the symbiotic relationship between them and what is possible in redefining formal education. There is, on the other hand, a general awareness of how technology can make distance learning and sophisticated simulations integral parts of instruction, and some general understanding of terms such as local area networks, fiber optics, and multiuser operating systems. But what good is plumbing if water is not available, or if the water coming through the pipes is contaminated? Is the tacit expectation that, once the plumbing (hardware and software) is in place, pure, life-sustaining water (information) will begin flowing automatically?

In addition to establishing and communicating vision and initiating change, leaders who are interested in systemic solutions also need to understand the climate and processes that characterize their organizations, the complex interplay between major subsystems, how current practice (and structure) leverages or inhibits the organization's mission, and what changes are most likely to produce the outcomes they desire. Leaders would be hard pressed to understand these data in the absence of powerful information management systems. In short, leaders (and teachers) are problem solvers, and very few problems are solved in an information vacuum.

There are two broad strategies that leaders can use if they want to lead from an informed base. The first strategy ignores the power of information systems technology. In this scenario, leaders must require all subordinates to follow standard practice, because without standard practices and procedures they are unable to determine and report on the nature of the organization for which they are responsible. Alternatively, the second strategy allows leaders to encourage diversity, exploration, and discovery because they expect to rely on information systems to help them understand the resultant complex characteristics of their organization. Good information systems allow leaders to discover patterns (among a diversity of practices) and determine the state of the organization and its quality by examining information generated as the organization functions.

Determining What Information Is Important to Manage

Upon what information should reform and transformation occur? What should be the basis for determining the appropriateness and effectiveness of instructional programs or the strategies or media that characterize them? Who should be the primary decision maker(s) empowered with information to help guide change?

What information do practitioners, clients, patrons, and administrators need in order to accomplish the mission the public is willing to pay for? How do requirements for information change as schools themselves change? In an era of declining public resources, should information systems be implemented to help automate existing practices, or should they supply critical information in transformational contexts and inform practitioners how to implement and manage quality instructional programs in continually changing environments? The attractiveness of changing schools away from labor-intensive and toward capital-intensive organizations drives a considerable amount of design and development of instructional technology.

The questions beg Zuboff's contra examples of "informating" vs. automating technologies (Zuboff 1988). Should these decisions be made and/or driven by vendors? National standards? New technologies? Or the skills and expertise of professional educators attempting to use their skills, training, and insights to meet the needs of learners in each community in America? An interesting exercise to propose to educators follows.

Establish a framework wherein practicing educators understand some of the dramatic power of information technologies and how (both now and in the next few years) these technologies are transforming the home, the workplace, and society. In that context (including how formal learning opportunities are becoming more viable in nontraditional settings) explore what value educators will add to society in 2010 and how that value will be expressed, evaluated, and supported.

One reason that effective, meaningful school reform has not occurred is that, at the practitioner level, there has been only a minimum focus on answering these questions, identifying and understanding the information critical to the nature and business of quality education, and identifying the information needs of each person and process associated with quality education. That is, the education profession is not yet fully committed to finding out what happens (in real schools on an ongoing basis in the context of change) as teachers make instructional decisions and students and others respond to those decisions.

Practicing professionals have not yet recognized how to leverage information associated with in-

structional processes as an organizational resource to build a learning organization via an integrated set of information tools. At this point in time, educators and vendors do not seem nearly as interested in learning about instructional processes as they are in automating them. If we are willing to tackle the complex issues associated with systemic change, we surely must at least be willing to look at the consequences of adding technology to complex social systems in the absence of informational planning.

INTERPLAY BETWEEN TECHNOLOGY AND PROCESS IN THE CONTEXT OF CHANGE

One of the most difficult tasks in designing new schools is shedding existing paradigms, which are clothed in technique. The shedding process is difficult because of the interplay between technique and our inability to understand the process it is designed to enhance. Technique is not just a collection of tools that help people manage and execute processes reliably, consistently, and with a measure of quality. It is also a mediator, standing between the actor and the processes acted upon. Once technique has been applied to a process, it assumes the foreground and veils the process. The more the technique is utilized, the more obvious it becomes and the more difficult it is to recognize the underlying process in its unmediated state. Change soon comes to mean improving the technique rather than the process. When understanding technique (the means) becomes more valuable than understanding the process (the ends), true change becomes difficult if not impossible. A couple of examples are in order.

Example 1: The report card is a technique developed to communicate information about children's performance to their parents and guardians and establish a basis for dialogue between teachers and parents or guardians. They are a necessary compromise between providing information that is really useful and information that can be easily obtained, communicated, and interpreted in the context of the mass production, assembly-line model of education that has evolved in this nation. Some information systems are designed to generate report cards more quickly than they can be generated by hand. If these information systems were designed to communicate information about children's performance (the underlying process) instead of generating report cards (the technique), they would be designed to provide much more meaningful information than grade point averages and course codes and would create interaction and feedback between teachers and parents that would clearly impact instructional quality. (Actually, a more powerful example would explore the technique of grades themselves, because they have become both the means and ends of education in many schools. The example would, however, be more complex and difficult to present than the one presented here.)

Example 2: Individualized education plans (IEPs) are generally required for special needs children. Their purpose is to (a) involve people with varying expertise in a planning process with others who have a vested interest in the children's education; (b) generate doable instructional goals; and (c) help assure that specific needs are being met in the context of formal schooling. Some information systems are designed to generate IEPs, which are, in turn, placed in students' files as evidence that planning occurred. If they were designed to help bring people together, establish instructional goals, and help assure quality, they would be more of a communication and planning support system (the process) than a document generator (the technique), and would be used in the context of general education as well.

Such examples are not limited to education. They occur everywhere. The company that built the first railroad, for example, was initially interested in transporting goods and people. Though in the transportation business, they ignored the Wright Brothers' experiments because, by that time, they considered themselves to be in the railroad business. Similarly, the minds and dedication that built the first transcontinental telegraph system did so to facilitate communication among people across great distances. But the same minds ignored Bell's invention because they were focused on the telegraph

business. The relevant question for educators is whether it is education or schooling that defines practice and serves as the referent for systemic change.

Conceptualize an information system that is designed to support instruction in technique-bound schools (e.g., those designed to reinforce lecture-based instruction, segmented learning controlled by bells, age-based grouping, and dependency on school-based resources). Now conceptualize another one that is designed to support an instructional model that encourages open-access curriculum, access to worldwide resources, continuous progress, student-initiated learning, and grouping based on interests and instructional needs. The requirements for an instructional information management system (IIMS)[5] will be much different for one system than they will be for the other.

The techniques of schooling must be separated from the purposes and nature of education as a first step in information systems planning. The next step is to identify the critical processes associated with education (not schooling) and determine information interrelationships and dependencies among the different processes. The critical processes that have been identified by groups involved with our information resources planning work have been generalized and are identified in the following text. They serve as a reference point for the later discussion on instructional information systems design and implementation.

Critical Processes

The business of education involves several critical processes, each of which needs to involve a mix between professionals, learners, environment, and technique. Taken together, these processes offer a systems approach to the design of instructional programs. In formal education, each requires some ongoing interaction between humans (e.g., teachers and learners) and should involve collaboration between and among multiple groups. None of them stands alone, nor can any one of them be completely understood by itself. All must be understood if systemic change is to occur.

The quality of information input and output associated with each process affects the quality of the other processes. Furthermore, the information requirements of each must be defined in context of that which is provided and consumed by various people interacting with them. The complexity of each process urges the use of information tools in order to help practitioners and researchers understand, manage, and optimize the interplay among the processes.

No attempt is offered here to quantify the information requirements associated with each process. Those are best determined via local activities. The critical processes listed are general and suggestive and are extrapolated from planning and needs assessment activities conducted in context of designing an IIMS, IMSeries.[6]

Curriculum Processes

A major dilemma faced by curriculum designers is that it is impossible to capture in documents the richness of knowledge and information that accurately defines, characterizes, and provides reference for the formal instruction that occurs in schools. Curriculum guides tend to be noninteractive, static documents like dictionaries or reference encyclopedia. Like those documents, they are difficult to change and are updated only every three, five, or seven years to reflect new knowledge.

In many schools, "successful" instruction occurs without referencing curriculum guides and without the following:

1. common frameworks, formats, or terms to guide instructional design and development of learning across the entire instructional program;

2. identification of gaps, overlaps, or omissions in the instructional program;

3. clear and mutually agreed-upon frameworks (especially across disciplines) for concept and skill development;

4. a way to determine the extent to which, and the nature with which, curriculum and standards actually guide and inform instruction.

People continue to pay their taxes, students still learn (and graduate), teachers still negotiate for

pay increases, and the overall environment is satisfactory (at least in many suburban schools). Success, thusly defined, occurs even where there is very little support (time, staff, technology, institutional reinforcement) to overcome the weaknesses in the curriculum design processes that almost everyone recognizes occurs in most school systems. What results is (1) educators are unable to demonstrate clear benefits from the resources invested in the curriculum process; (2) textbooks remain as the default curriculum; (3) curriculum revision cycles keep curriculum significantly behind real world change; (4) curriculum documents are often placed on shelves and in drawers and are not consulted when instruction is planned, conducted, and evaluated; and (5) revision processes are often decoupled from processes associated with the selection, use, and evaluation of instructional strategies and resources and from those processes associated with assessing, interpreting, and reporting student performance.

In this context, it is obvious that educators do not have the information or processes in place to manage quality, and many see no need to change. Practitioners tend to yield instructional design decisions to textbook publishers and developers of other instructional media (e.g., computer-assisted and computer-managed instruction programs). But one of the primary reasons that these materials are attractive is because extensive resources and skill are invested in their design (or so we trust). For example, it often takes from three hundred to eight hundred hours to design a single twenty-minute lesson that will be delivered via computer.

Another dynamic that often goes unnoticed is that the sophistication and complexity of high-tech instructional systems grows at least geometrically if not logarithmically with the power and flexibility of hardware, operating systems, and development environments. This suggests that, if nothing else changes, the practitioner's understanding of the tools he or she uses will continue to decline. This is not bad in itself, but it does establish a precedent for the future of schools and for teachers' roles within them. If teachers are not leveraged as instructional designers in their local schools and for their own clients, teaching as a profession will be doomed, and they and their clients will increasingly become servants of technology designed by someone else.

Requirements

If information technologies are used only to change the way curriculum information is stored while the underlying curriculum processes and information modeling go unchanged, the old paradigm will remain entrenched at a critical reference point and transformational thinking will not impact instruction at the classroom level. The following requirements are offered for consideration in the context of information systems planning for curriculum.

- Curriculum development should be a local process and should occur in the context of explicit societal expectations (i.e., standards and outcomes). This is the only way a district can capitalize on the strengths, training, and special insights of its faculty, and it is the only way practitioners can incorporate local nuances and adapt instruction to their clients while capitalizing on local facilities and resources and remaining accountable to the broader community.

- Curriculum must continually reflect the standards, interests, and expectations of the local community, professional and regulatory bodies, and the larger society as a whole.

- Curriculum should be revised on a continual and ongoing basis to reflect changes in the world, research findings, and insights and discoveries of practicing educators.

- The primary function of curriculum information is to empower teachers and learners as designers and planners. However, curriculum information must also be able to be used (a) as a research base to explore what works, what doesn't work, and why; and (b) as a reference for providing accountability information to clients, patrons, governing bodies, and regulatory agencies.

- Those who teach and assess should be actively involved in the curriculum process. With broad involvement, the curriculum is likely to be dynamic and relevant.

- Curriculum processes should be tightly coupled with all other aspects of the instructional program.

- Two-dimensional, linear models cannot adequately represent complex knowledge structures inherent in good curriculum models. Design, analyses, and reporting must be able to cross boundaries in curricular structures and hierarchies.

- It is necessary to be able to obtain a holistic perspective of curriculum for analysis and discussion and to be able to understand and describe the plethora of component parts that define its essence.

Understanding the big picture is necessary in order to determine and discuss the overall quality and integration of instructional processes as they relate to the mission and goals of the instructional program. It is important to be able to grasp the component parts in order to increase the understanding of when, under what conditions, and for whom specific processes do or do not work. Understanding the nature of each subsystem and process and how they fit together and affect each other gives rise to learning organizations.

Implications for IIMS Design

Clearly, the above requirements suggest a powerful, interactive, multiuser information database that is accessible to all people who hold a vested interest in the quality of the instructional program.

The word *powerful* implies that collaborative and ongoing design of curriculum should be facilitated and common definition of terms and specificity of language encouraged. The definition of curriculum should be made explicit and should be agreed upon by the practitioners and incorporated into the design of the IIMS. If total quality management and an understanding of the entire instructional process are primary goals, then curriculum would seem to be best defined as "all the experiences a learner has under the aegis of the school." The more traditional definition of curriculum —"a set of intentions for the instructional program"—is more appropriate to help establish sets of standards or cross references against which the curricula are designed and aligned. (The definition, of course, should be a product of the information systems planning process.)

The design of the IIMS does not have to be such that only one curriculum model can be managed. Indeed, provisions can be made for the management of several alternative approaches to curriculum design (e.g., discipline oriented vs. problem based). However, if multiple approaches are incorporated into the design of curriculum, practitioners must be able to conceptualize and manage them in juxtaposition. Flexibility and diversity should be encouraged, but such should be tempered with consensual decision making and disciplined, clear thinking. The underlying design should facilitate inquiry into and the understanding of interrelationships among the various types of data as well as among the various informational categories. Information modeling should enable practitioners, clients, administrators, and patrons to obtain the answer to any question they may have about the nature of curriculum and its components.

Interactivity suggests that those who consume online curriculum information can also modify that information (by suggesting improvements, adding new ideas, or establishing new links between data). Because curriculum is a system resource (rather than a personal one), appropriate security features should be incorporated to help assure that only those who have the requisite skills or needs can modify the curriculum or that established procedures are followed in its modification.

The term *multiuser* implies that interactions between several people and the database can occur simultaneously. *Accessibility* means that the information and, therefore, the technology that serves as its carrier and interface are brought to the information workers in the context of the settings in which they practice.

Alignment

The process of alignment involves two bodies of information. One body, the sets of standards or outcomes, are ideally antecedents to the development of curriculum and are contemplated as curriculum is designed. The sets of standards provide the rationale for the sustenance of, and a powerful reference point for the determination of quality for, the instructional program. They represent the perspectives of various groups as to what should occur as a result of formal instruction and for what the public is willing to pay.

The curriculum attempts to define and establish a reference to guide the instructional vehicle, which carries teacher and learner toward the expected outcomes by providing learning opportunities. Curriculum should be the purview of the local educator (as mentioned above), while the cross references are determined by groups largely external to any given school system.

Requirements

- Societies and states have a right and obligation to establish standards for public schools, and educators have an obligation to demonstrate accountability to those standards.

- Professional organizations also establish standards to guide instructional design and quality within special areas of expertise.

- Standards for curriculum and instruction do not imply a standard curriculum or standard instruction. For example, the many standards for automobiles have not forced the design and development of a standard automobile. Likewise, there can be standards for curriculum without requiring a standard curriculum. (Society should determine the *what* of public schools, professionals should determine the *how*.)

- Any given standard or outcome transcends the discrete components (e.g., content area, instructional strategy, or resource) in any curriculum structure.

- It is likely that the content contained in two sets of standards (developed by two different groups) will overlap. However, it is unlikely that two sets of standards will be organized around the same constructs or have the same levels of specificity.

- Standards (if they are truly standards) tend to be stable, whereas curriculum is dynamic because information about content and process is constantly changing.

- It is highly probable that every standard is addressed in multiple places in a well-designed curriculum. Likewise, it is highly probable that every component in a curriculum addresses multiple standards.

- When students move from one school system to another, common reference points should be accessible to both schools. These reference points can serve as a basis for making decisions about their placement in the new system and the methods, strategies, and resources that might be most useful to them. (A common set of standards, or a method of translating across standards, would seem to be more appropriate than insisting that standardized methods and content characterize instruction in all schools).

Implications for IIMS Design

A good IIMS will help local practitioners manage multiple sets of standards and engage in continual curriculum development activities, while enabling them to perform analyses on how the standards and curriculum interact. Revision and maintenance of curriculum should be able to be performed independently of revision and maintenance of the sets of standards, but both should be coupled so as to encourage and enable alignment between them and the analysis of their relationships. Furthermore, the information system should enable educators to establish multiple points of alignment between the curriculum and standards and should enable alignment to occur across content boundaries that define each set.

PLANNING AND DELIVERING INSTRUCTION

The quality of instruction depends at least in part on the quality of the planning process. In turn, the quality of the planning process is dependent on how thorough, timely, and accurate the information is that "feeds" the planning process. As teachers plan instruction and instructional sequences, they need to be able to access critical information about students; curriculum; national, state, and local guidelines and standards (outcomes); and decisions they and their colleagues and students have made that have impacted previous learnings.

Lesson plans may be the most important documents in organizations that have education and training as their primary purpose. Lesson plans should capture examples of the intelligence, training, insights, guesses, and experience of those who are designing them, just as blueprints or project plans capture similar attributes in other contexts. Good plans show how students, instructors, resources, facilities, strategies, and time are combined to help bring about (facilitate or enhance) learning and help further the organization's mission. Whereas assessment data often capture the "what" of instruction, plans (when complete) can capture the "how." Therefore, lesson plans (in addition to assessment data) must serve as a pivotal and critical source of information if educators are to understand the nature and dimensions of instructional quality.

Poorly designed plans, incomplete plans, or plans that inaccurately reflect instructional processes serve as barriers to an organization's ability to understand its instructional program and prevent it from learning how to improve. Furthermore, teachers who cannot consult each others' plans are not able to truly ply their professional skills, systematically test their insights against those of their colleagues, or craft the most effective instruction for their students.

If Locke (1992) is right, that the challenge is not to increase efficiency, as in the heyday of mass production, but to deepen vision, and Senge (1990) is right that interrelationships, not linear cause-effect chains, are important, then recording and analyzing lesson plans is essential, especially for those who are interested in developing professional skills and assuring instructional quality. This is consonant with Eisner's (1975) contemplated contemplated notion that curriculum is never really definable until after the learner has experienced the instructional program. Hosford (1973) has argued similarly.

Requirements

- Teachers must be able to incorporate new knowledge, professional judgment, intimate knowledge of the changing learner, and their own creativity and spontaneity as they design and deliver instruction. These data must be shared with the broader educational community in order to provide a basis for continual school improvement.

- Information systems should not be used to control instruction, but rather as a tool to help educators ascertain the nature of their instruction and the extent to which it is effective in meeting the agency's goals and standards. Curricular validity cannot be defined a priori but must be ascertained in context of practice.

- Teachers should be able to obtain the instructional history on any of their students to analyze what has been tried and its relationship to the student's performance and/or understanding and skills.

- Collaborative planning (including clients and parents in the process and leveraging of professional skills of teachers across content and program boundaries) should be supported (even if all cannot meet at the same time and place). The concept of collaborative planning could be extended to include any person who is working with the learner in the process (e.g., physicians, nurses, social workers, counselors, clergy, representatives of the legal system, etc.) But someone will have to assume primary responsibility for instructional planning and quality. It seems reasonable that that person should be the teacher until the responsibility can be yielded to the learner.

- Teachers should be able to ascertain the extent to which their instruction contemplates the goals and mission of the district, the extent to which their instruction addresses the sets of standards and outcomes for which they will be accountable, and the extent to which their instruction complements or overlaps that of their colleagues.

Implications for IIMS Design

To facilitate planning and capture information about instructional plans, a good IIMS must meet all the criteria established above. In addition, a good IIMS must be able to deliver to the teacher the information he or she needs in order to generate and test hypotheses, examine the needs and characteristics of his or her clients, explore alternative approaches to instruction, understand broad instructional contexts, and assure compliance with standards and other requirements. Through one interface and one integrated information system, teachers should be able to access and interact with a complex information system that includes information about curriculum, instruction, assessment, demographics, and standards.

The IIMS should filter the information so as to provide the most relevant and timely data immediately, and it should enable inquiries into other data of all types. Various functions should be included to encourage students and parents to participate in the planning process, but protections should enable teachers to exercise professional judgment and practice their diagnostic, evaluative, and prescriptive skills to guide and monitor planning processes. The IIMS must enable teachers to extend instructional alternatives for their lessons and the curriculum, and they must be able to record reflections and insights about the effectiveness and appropriateness of the curriculum they use. The technology should be as unobtrusive as possible (encouraging quality planning and gathering information about the plans and planning process without interrupting or interfering with them).

ASSESSING PROGRAMS AND PERFORMANCE

Most districts depend exclusively on averages when describing student performance to external audiences. However, these data cannot describe what a student really knows, nor can they describe student progress very well. Although grade point averages are often computed to the nearest .001 point to determine which students are the best, few people would argue that learning can be assessed at that level of precision. Averages are not very useful to educators when attempting to understand how student performance relates to decisions made in designing and delivering instruction. They tell nothing about the relevance, effectiveness, or appropriateness of the instructional program.

Again, educators are caught in the middle. Many recognize that performance profiles and portfolios give a more accurate and authentic picture of student performance and progress and are more useful than averages in determining relationships between performance and instruction. Yet teachers have no access to information systems that can help them generate and manage those data.

Requirements

- A better picture of what students know, can do, and are like can be obtained by reducing emphasis on averages and on a few precise measurements and increasing emphasis on many, varied, and (perhaps) less precise assessments.

- "Mastery" should be inferred by analyzing patterns of performance over time and in various contexts, not by examining averages or by interpreting data from a single assessment.

- Progress must be interpreted by combining professional judgment and actual samples of student work, both gathered over time.

- Assessment data that cannot be linked to instructional decisions that influenced them are not useful in managing instructional quality or in improving practice. However, they are useful in labeling students.

Implications for IIMS Design

A good IIMS should enable educators to:

- assure that assessment instrumentation and methodologies align to and are consonant with instruction, curriculum, and standards;

- encourage and facilitate diversity in methodology, instrumentation, recording of student performance, and evaluation of student performance;

- enable standards to be implemented across program boundaries;

- permit analysis and reporting of performance data for any skill, construct, concept, or content knowledge (from simple to complex), independent of (and across) program, time, and organizational boundaries;

- encourage multiple, diverse assessments in different contexts with different assessors and at different times for similar skills, knowledge, and attitudes;

- facilitate the analysis of performance data in terms of patterns rather than events; and

- manage actual samples of student work in context of (a) the judgment of that work, (b) the instructional context from which the work was generated, and (c) the standards and options that were used to frame the instructional context.

Validating Programs

Where change is more pervasive in society than in the schools that serve it, there is a high probability that, as time passes, increasing numbers of students who graduate will do so with skills and knowledge that no one needs. At the close of the twentieth century, not only are there large numbers of adults who are considered "functionally illiterate," but there is an increasing number who are "nonfunctionally literate." To keep education relevant and schools coupled with society, feedback loops between school systems and external agencies are needed. Not only do educators need to establish reliable ways to report student performance, skills, and attitudes to outside agencies, they also need methods of examining how on-the-job performance (or other performance outside of school) relates to skills, knowledge, and attitudes that they have previously certified.

Requirements

- External agencies need to know what school graduates know, can do, and are like. They do not need to know how the graduates were taught, how the school was organized, the sequences in which the courses were taken, the number of Carnegie Units earned, or the graduates' grade point averages.

- The importance of ongoing validation increases with the rapidity and pervasiveness of change in the external environment.

- Data must be relevant in the context of the external environment. Since it is impossible to predict what data will be needed after graduation to validate the skills, knowledge, and attitudes of a student who is not yet in high school, the information system must be designed to permit ad hoc inquiries, analyses, and reporting based on those inquiries across program, content, and organizational boundaries.

- Data obtained from on-the-job performance evaluations and other sources should be incorporated into the decision processes associated with curriculum design, alignment, delivery, and assessment. Where there is a sufficient difference between what external agencies and educators report about the skills and performance of graduates, educators need to reconcile the difference.

- The differences between anticipated performance and actual performance must not only be significant in degree, but must also occur for a reasonable number of graduates in order to warrant action. Of course, the decision to intervene is a judgment based on several factors besides degree and number.

Implications for IIMS Design

Predictions about how students will perform in the "real world" after they graduate need to be based on data obtained from assessing students within formal instructional contexts. The reliability of performance predictions will increase as do the number of judgments, especially if those judg-

ments are made by a series of assessors observing the student in a variety of circumstances at different times. In addition to the implications listed for curriculum, delivery, and assessment, the information system must be useful in helping educators triangulate across different time frames, instructional contexts, and assessors as they generate inferences about student abilities, knowledge, and attitudes.

Educators and their clients and patrons must be able to specify the skills, knowledge, and attitudes about which inferences can be made on a post hoc basis. That is, they need to be able to wait until after instruction has occurred to define which data they want to examine and how to conduct their analyses. Methods for translating data among systems are required in order to coordinate instructional programming and enhance effectiveness across separate agencies.

PLANNING AND IMPLEMENTING INFORMATION SYSTEMS

Implementing a comprehensive IIMS in K–12 schools is difficult at best. It requires continual systemic support at several levels over a period of several years and must be preceded and accompanied by a commitment to the belief that information is both a critical need and an important asset to the organization and its people. An IIMS designed around the principles and assumptions stated in this text requires most practitioners to rethink instructional processes, and it challenges the heretofore "private" and ad hoc nature of instruction. The best environments for IIMSs will be those where the IIMS is not the innovation; rather, they will be those wherein the IIMS is used to help implement the innovation and to help people understand both the innovation and the organization it is helping transform.

If the assumptions in this chapter are valid, then no one will be able to implement a well-designed IIMS and maintain the same school system that existed prior to its implementation. Indeed, the implementation of an IIMS should commit the organization to continual change. If that commitment is not there or is supported insufficiently, the IIMS will be tossed out because its value will not be realized. The work invested therein will be seen as extra, invasive, and unnecessarily obtuse. This is not to imply that all IIMSs are well designed or all school systems who throw them out are not committed to change.

But well-designed IIMSs are very complex, and their use requires the rethinking of educational possibilities. A complication stems from the fact that the process of designing information systems is iterative and intertwined because of the changing demands placed on it by the organizations they are designed to informate. It is possible, therefore, that the IIMS may not keep pace with the organization in transition. Winograd and Flores (1987) have written an excellent and powerful book that addresses these issues.

To begin addressing these concerns, four main themes have evolved around implementing IMSeries in schools and training environments. To provide a context for the discussion of the four themes, the following assumptions, which guided the design of IMSeries and are now guiding its implementation, are included first. The assumptions are the following:

1. Teachers and teacher supervisors are primarily professionals, not technicians.

2. Technology should be designed to meet people where they are while enabling them to do things that could not be done without it.

3. Technology should not drive or define change. Rather, it should provide information about, and support for, change.

4. Educational reform doesn't occur unless it occurs in the environment and at the levels at which the practitioners work.

5. Information is the key to educational reform. Practitioners' inability to access, manage, and interpret information is the bottleneck that prevents reform.

6. Data that are important to inform practice must be gathered unobtrusively, automatically, and continually as the processes that they are to inform are being conducted.

7. Technology must not replace human intelligence and decision making. Rather, it should enhance them.

Four Themes as a Framework for Implementing an IIMS

Information

This dimension of the planning and implementation framework challenges personnel to think about what information is essential in order to do their jobs well and how decisions they make relate to decisions made by others. Once hidden information is made explicit, it changes the way people think; the questions they ask; and the expectations they place on themselves, their colleagues, and their organization. Educators contemplating the acquisition and implementation of an IIMS would be wise to continually ask and record the answers to the following questions:

1. What information is needed to do our jobs well, to report how well we did them, and to learn how to do them better?

2. How should these data be gathered and stored? Who should gather these data? How will their accuracy be assured?

3. How should these data be used? What standards and methodologies should guide their interpretation?

4. Who should have access to this information and for what purpose?

5. How are our information needs going to change as we change the organizational structure, develop collaborative alliances with others who are working to develop learners, change staff roles and required skills, and change the role of students?

6. What policies should be effected at the local, state, or national levels to protect individuals (teachers, students, and administrators) from misuse and misinterpretation of data? What policies should protect against unauthorized access to sensitive instructional information?

What instructional information is sensitive and requires protection?

7. What new staff positions are required (or how can staff be reallocated) to take maximum advantage of the information an IIMS can provide. Who will be in charge of obtaining and communicating a deep understanding of what the data, gathered as the IIMS is being used, is telling about the organization and how it operates?

Technology

The nature of the technology infrastructure in an organization can dramatically influence what transformation is possible. This aspect of the planning framework urges a thorough examination of technologies in context of informational and functional needs as they are continually defined in the context of the transformation. Unfortunately, technology infrastructures are disjointed or nonexistent. When given a choice between two competing systems, school personnel (who have not typically performed thorough analyses of their long-term needs) will usually choose the cheapest, rather than the most functional. This is due partly to the fact that the functional specifications they require have not been formulated and because they do not understand the technology, its potential, or the trends and standards guiding its evolution.

Once functional specifications have been defined and articulated, a systems integrator (one who has no vested interest in a particular hardware or software solution) can be an invaluable aid to educators as they struggle to define what the technology infrastructure might look like. All requirements for the technology to support a good IIMS cannot be predefined, of course. But a district that doesn't adequately plan for technology in the context of the requirements of an IIMS and its relationship to other technologies that leverage its value and that are leveraged by it may find itself trapped and unable to effect the transformation it wants.

Planning for and acquiring technology should itself be done in context of a transformational model. Due to organizational dynamics, local politics, social concerns, and resource limitations, the implementation of the IIMS needs to be phased in over several (five to seven) years, and the purchasing and implementation of technology should parallel the transformation. Finally, substantial consideration should be given to continual support and maintenance of the technology before it is acquired.

Staff Development

Of the four dimensions to the framework proposed here, staff development has traditionally received the most attention. However, in order to implement an IIMS, staff development must be more systemic and systematic than commonly conceptualized. Staff development, in this framework, extends far beyond developing the staff's skills in operating the IIMS and interpreting data it manages. The staff development program must be as transformational as is the innovation and the organization. That is, the staff must understand and value the vision guiding the transformation, and they must realize (at least to some extent) the implications the transformation, and their commitment to it, has for them and their clients.

In the context of a dramatically changing external environment and in the context of the rapidly increasing potential of technology to redefine teachers' work roles for them, they must be confronted with questions about what skills they will need and what roles they must assume in order to remain an asset to the organization in five to ten years (especially in the face of transformation). They will need to understand the value the information they generate has to themselves, their colleagues, their clients, and their organization.

If the organization is to become a learning organization, educators, too, must be learners and contributors to the learning community. Because learning very seldom occurs without dither, uncertainty, and confusion, educators must be willing to invite those aspects into their jobs. At the same time, they need to be assured that they can influence the quality of the school system, the nature of their jobs, and the direction in which the organization is headed. They must certainly be supported in as many ways as possible as they commit to the vision.

Organizational Dynamics

The nature of the organization, its climate, its leadership, and the processes that it supports and rewards is another dimension of the planning framework. The organization, its technology infrastructure, information flow, people, and the interaction among these components and subsystems are important considerations in planning for an IIMS.

Teachers who share the vision and are willing to take risks and invest extra effort in learning how to use information technologies cannot be trapped by the same expectations and techniques that are imposed on them before an IIMS is implemented. Decision makers who purchase IIMSs must be willing to make a long-term organizational commitment (hopefully in context of systems thinking) to implementing the IIMS and supporting the people who use it. Decision makers who are not willing or able to modify the organization based on new capabilities and better understanding of the underlying processes of education engendered by IIMS users will be wasting their time, a considerable amount of system resources, and the goodwill of their staff by purchasing an IIMS.

There are profound implications engendered by the interaction of information systems and the organizations in which they are implemented. Informating technologies can help practitioners and researchers understand the underlying processes that serve as the organization's raison d'être and increase the flexibility and interactiveness of the techniques used to help manage them. If the IIMS is designed to promote and effect systemic change, but is expected to succeed within the existing structure, it will not be used. But, if it is perceived to be one aspect of a larger, transformational plan for the organization, it can help leverage that plan and help assure its success.

SUMMARY

Improving education is a function of educators' abilities both to understand and to ply their practice. Lack of information is as big a barrier to improved practice as are inappropriate organizational structures, staffing practices, and facilities. Changing a structure will not, in itself, produce sustainable, desirable change. Change often elicits excitement and proffers an image of movement and action. Innovators hope that in the new environment, all learners will succeed. But what if the learners don't succeed? What if there are problems?

Too many innovations are attempted without giving thought to what information is needed to (1) determine how effective they are systemically or (2) solve problems without causing negative ramifications on other subsystems both now and later. Even where some thought is given to the information needed to guide future decisions, inadequate technologies and resources are allocated to the acquisition, management, and evaluation of that information. Therefore, in most cases, when problems arise as change occurs, the solution is to return to previous practice where the problems and landscape were familiar.

If educators are not able to access, interpret, and use information requisite to their own practice; if they do not understand the intimacies and complexities of data they (and their clients) generate as a matter of course; and if they fail to use and develop professional skills because their actions do not germinate or mature in informed environments, what good can evolve for the profession and its clients and patrons even in the most "dynamic" school systems? Passion, verbiage, and resources to support reform are not sufficient. If there is a lack of information and an inability to use it to support and improve decisions, there is no hope for any type of reform other than that characterized by just trying new things endlessly.

But society has changed and continues to change at an ever-increasing pace. The changes are largely due to increased ability to access, manage, and interpret complex and intricate bodies of data. A dissonance between America's schools and the society they serve will probably always exist, but it most assuredly will increase, perhaps to a critical breaking point as society's expectations of what schools can and should accomplish continue to change and educators' expectations do not.

None of the strategies or items listed herein can be meaningfully pursued or developed until educators recognize the need to integrate a comprehensive information system into their work environment and have learned how to use information technologies as productive, informational tools. That is, educational reform will never occur until educators find some way to effectively gather, manage, analyze, and evaluate (in a systematic and systemic way) the information associated with the practice of education.

Heretofore, educators have not had the luxury of such powerful information tools to help them meet the high expectations and difficult instructional tasks they face each day. How these tools are used will be the legacy left to the next generation, who will, in turn, continue to struggle to make education more effective, relevant, personalized, and flexible.

In order for educational reform to have a chance, educators must do the following:

1. design instructional technologies to empower practitioners as professional decision makers, evaluators, and researchers, and implement information technologies to inform them about the practice of education (at each of the instructional design points);

2. implement information technologies in ways that help dissolve traditional boundaries that prevent the free flow of information among people who have vested interests in the quality of education as well as its continued evolution;

3. consider an information infrastructure as a requisite to any and all other efforts to effect systemic change;

4. commit to an ongoing, systematic, and systemic gathering, analysis, and dissemination of information associated with the processes of education as it occurs in each classroom, and build the technical capability (equipment and human resources) to support that effort.

A commitment to less will not prevent the increased incorporation of technology into the schools, but it will prevent systemic change from occurring.

NOTES

1. The word *efficiency* is placed in quotes here because much of the impetus driving educational reform is the notion that increased efficiency means getting more students to master more objectives in a shorter amount of time with fewer resources. If learning to learn is the goal, the word would probably imply something entirely different. The following example illustrates the difference. In the West, the most efficient journey is usually one where the traveler gets to his or her destination in the shortest distance, with the least expenditure of time, fuel, and discomfort. On the other hand, from a Sufi's perspective, the most efficient journey is one that, when taken, enables the traveler to help the most people and do the most good.

2. The feedback must be meaningful, systemic, and systematic, and the organization must be structured so as to reward and encourage the collaborative use of feedback in defining, defending, and altering practice.

3. In fact, much of the discussion about learning organizations, complex systems, and distributed decision making, which is contributing to awareness of how schools might be changed, originates from knowledge generated by those who have worked with information processing and information systems in business and industry. The effects that information technologies have had on business and industry should motivate educators to consider their potency in education, especially when combined with a commitment to systems thinking and change.

4. One reason this occurs is that selling technology is difficult (if not impossible) if those for whom it is designed have to change the way they think about what they do in order to use it. The most successfully marketed technologies are those that enable their purchasers to enhance existing practice. So, where technologies have impacted instruction, they have merely enabled it to occur more rapidly and (to some extent) with individualized pacing.

5. I make a distinction between an instructional management system and an instructional information management system. One is designed to manage instruction, the other is designed to help others manage instruction by focusing on managing the information.

6. IMSeries is a software package designed to help educators manage all information associated with instruction. It was developed through a joint effort between the colleges of education and engineering at Texas A&M University in a project directed by the author of this chapter. It was transferred out of Texas A&M University in 1991 to a company called Learning Technology Systems, Incorporated (LTS), and later purchased by Campus America. Since being transferred out of the university, the software has undergone extensive redesign to capitalize on capabilities of newer technologies and what was learned in the earlier research. Educators in around two hundred districts were working to implement IMSeries at the time this text was written.

REFERENCES

Eisner, E. 1985. *The art of educational evaluation.* Philadelphia: The Falmer Press.

Hosford, P. L. 1973. *An instructional theory: A beginning.* Englewood Cliffs: Prentice-Hall.

Locke, C. 1992. Making knowledge pay. *Byte,* June, 245–52.

Senge, P.M. 1990. *The fifth discipline: The art and practice of the learning organization.* New York: Doubleday.

Winograd, T., and F. Flores. 1987. *Understanding computers and cognition: A new foundation for design.* Reading, Mass.: Addison-Wesley.

Zuboff, S. 1988. *In the age of the smart machine: The future of work and power.* New York: Basic Books.

ENABLING SCHOOLS FOR SELF-RENEWAL

A principle that is fundamental to all self-organizing systems [is] that of self-reference. . . . the system changes in a way that remains consistent with itself in that environment. The system is autopoietic, focusing its activities on what is required to maintain its own integrity and self-renewal. As it changes, it does so by referring to itself; whatever future form it takes will be consistent with its already established identity. Changes do not occur randomly in any direction. . . .

Self-reference is what facilitates orderly change in turbulent environments. In human organizations, a clear sense of identity—of the values, traditions, aspirations, competencies, and culture that guide the operation—is the real source of independence from the environment. When the environment demands a new response, there is a reference point for change.
—*Margaret J. Wheatley*

Real learning gets to the heart of what it means to be human. Through learning we re-create ourselves. Through learning we become able to do something we never were able to do. Through learning we reperceive the world and our relationship to it. Through learning we extend our capacity to create, to be a part of the generative process of life. . . .

This, then, is the basic meaning of a "learning organization"—an organization that is continually expanding its capacity to create its future. For such an organization, it is not enough merely to survive. . . . for a learning organization, "adaptive learning" must be jointed by "generative learning," learning that enhances our capacity to create.
—*Peter M. Senge*

Educational systems design, systemic change, is not just about designing the new learning system, it is also about designing and changing existing support systems that currently enable the school organization to carry out its various functions. Educational systems design is also about creating entities that are self-directing and self-correcting, as they engage in self-design through a "stakeholder approach." Stakeholders become designer-learners, engaged in learning that is generative and oriented toward creating the future educational system and schools. Stakeholders will not only learn what to learn, they will learn *how* to learn, entering a level of meaning and understanding about design while simultaneously creating their own self-renewing learning system. They become learning communities, learning forward to the future.

Where self-renewal is an implicit part of any community and school that engages in design, new dynamics are required for how people work together. As individuals connect to become teams, it will be necessary for schools and stakeholders to begin to change existing mindsets about the roles of managing and evaluating in the context of systemic change. Managing people and projects will necessarily change to managing knowledge and process. New relationships will emerge that are collaborative and focused on learning as a collective process that serves the larger community. Likewise, we will see an evolution in the mindsets about evaluation, where the evaluator becomes facilitator for organizational learning rather than for providing information about the compliance-driven requirements of the organization. In educational systems design, evaluation enables the stakeholders engaged in the design and implementation process that serves in directing systemic change. Evaluation as learning moves from the form of *adaptive mechanisms* to *generative processes* that support design and change through dynamic positive feedback loops.

This section furthers our understanding of systems design and systemic change by introducing touchstones for future schools that enable the process of designing, implementing, and evaluating the systemic change process. Future schools, as they engage stakeholders and assume responsibility for their own destiny, will necessarily look to enablers of design and change to sustain their efforts over time.

The first chapter in this section further establishes the need for systemic change and encourages the reader to examine the ideal of self-managing schools. The second contribution examines the role of evaluation in the school as learning organization, contrasting the traditional school organization and its use of evaluation to a future "learning organization" model of schools and the new role evaluation will take. Next follows an article that informs the reader about building collaborations and teams while considering a TQM philosophy. The fourth chapter suggests that their is an important role for an assessment subsystem in providing vital information to the larger collective system. The final chapter in this section offers readers insight into how to manage change and improvement within schools undertaking systemic change. Here the authors reconsider conventional project management within the systemic change context, providing the reader with tools and strategies that help to manage the complexities of changing the whole system.

SYSTEMIC CHANGE TO TRANSFORM EDUCATION

—

Patricia Cloud Duttweiler

f we know what to do to improve education, why hasn't anything changed?" This question was asked during a session at the 1993 annual conference of the American Educational Research Association. Unfortunately, the answer is both lengthy and complex, and no one was willing to tackle it at the time. In a way, this book, and in particular this chapter, provides a response to that question. Many changes have taken place in our society, but, unfortunately, educational policymakers have attempted to meet the challenges presented by these changes with fragmented efforts rather than with systemic change. The reasons for this lie in the characteristics of the traditional structure, the paradigms that shape our approach to organization, and the barriers that have to be hurdled when trying to change organizational structures. Yet we *do* have the knowledge to change the system—its structure, governance, culture, curricula, and instruction—and some educators have changed their paradigms, surmounted the barriers, and created a self-renewing structure, transforming the system to ensure quality educational experiences for all students.

ADOPTING NEW PARADIGMS FOR SYSTEMIC CHANGE

Dependence on Old Paradigms

Implementing systemic change requires fundamental changes in deeply held beliefs. To go beyond the rhetoric of change and embrace new ways of thinking about schooling, those in education must engage in "second-order changes" that address the level of basic assumptions—those beliefs which are taken for granted and are invisible or preconscious (Schein 1985). These second-order changes must alter the fundamental ways in which the system supports the needs of its teaching and learning functions if we are to solve persistent educational problems (Cuban 1988). Such changes, however, are constrained by the paradigms that shape our thinking.

The *paradigms* of a society are the patterns of basic concepts that form the map of reality which guides our perceptions. Our paradigms tell us what is real, what may be false, and what to pay attention to; they dictate the methods we use to solve problems. Paradigms act as screens that filter what enters the mind. The better incoming information fits a paradigm, the easier it is to accept. The less expected or more unusual the information, the harder it is to accept. In some cases, when information is so out of sync with the reality shaped by our paradigms, we fail to perceive the information at all (Schwartz and Ogilvy 1979).

Paradigms encompass a society's fundamental view of the structure of knowledge, its view of how things are ordered, and its view of causality (Schwartz and Ogilvy 1979). Paradigms are so powerful because they are implicit. They tend to surface—to become explicit—when they are changing and the old paradigms are no longer adequate for solving the problems created by changes in the world around us. As Schwartz and Ogilvy (1979) pointed out, such shifts occur infrequently:

> Until the seventeenth century, the Aristotelian model of organic growth provided for Western civilization an internally consistent world view or paradigm. It finally began to crumble under the onslaught of new ideas. (p. 5)

During the Enlightenment, the common understandings of the nature of things were drastically changed across the natural sciences and humanities. In time, the new understandings were reflected by changes in the human, social, psychological, religious, political, and economic arenas. "The era shattered and reformulated Western civilization's shared patterns of belief" (Schwartz and Ogilvy 1979, 5).

Paradigm Shifts

Evidence from a broad range of human inquiry suggests that, again, major shifts are occurring in the paradigms of Western society. Schwartz and Ogilvy (1979) identified three common threads in the new paradigms: a shift from seeking an ultimate truth to exploring multiple perspectives, a shift from linear causality to a model of multiple causation and interdependence, and a shift from hierarchical control to heterarchy. These paradigm shifts have important implications for the philosophy undergirding the educational subsystem and for practices within the larger system.

The shift to multiple perspectives is a shift from assuming there is "a universal truth" in a field of

knowledge and that rational, objective reasoning can uncover "the right way" to solve a problem, to an understanding that in any human endeavor the collective knowledge of the group is greater than the knowledge of any subset. This shift suggests the need for changes in the larger system's governance and policymaking procedures and in the educational subsystem's authority structure, decision-making processes, curriculum, and classroom instructional practices—perhaps a change in the concept of the classroom itself.

The shift in our model of causality provides a rationale on which to base comprehensive, systemic change. This paradigm shift is from linear/mechanical, probabilistic, and cybernetic explanations of why and how things change in any environment, to a model that incorporates the concepts of positive feedback, multiple causation, and mutual adaptation. This paradigm shift recognizes that there is interdependence among the various factors within an environment and that change comes about through a complex interaction of these factors. Systemic change in education requires the realization that in order to facilitate effective changes in teaching and learning, the relationships between the educational subsystem and other subsystems—such as the political, economic, and health and social services—must be taken into account along with changes at all levels of the educational subsystem itself.

The shift in our understanding of order involves moving from models of hierarchical control to "heterarchical" sharing of knowledge and influence. Again, this paradigm shift requires a change in our view of the proper structure and functioning of the educational subsystem. A system that survives, adapts, and renews itself cannot have a rigid, hierarchical structure and communication process. The concept of heterarchy implies many different forms of leadership or government, using whichever form is appropriate for the situation or problem. It also implies a communication structure resembling that of a DNA molecule or hologram, that is, a structure where all the information necessary for the system to function is available to all segments.

The effectiveness of educational changes based on the old paradigms has been equated with efforts to rearrange the deck chairs on the Titanic as it was sinking. The traditional educational subsystem has been unable to address effectively a set of "impossible problems [that have] accumulated on the shelf," unsolvable by the current paradigms we use to structure our schools (Barker 1989, 23).

In order to design a more effective, more responsive educational subsystem, we must change the paradigms that currently guide its structure and functions—our beliefs and values must be re-examined and new paradigms articulated. As it is currently structured, the educational subsystem lacks resilience to adapt to societal changes. The public school system, like a biological system, will either evolve to a new state or, like the dinosaur, become extinct. If public education is to survive, a self-renewing system must be created based on multiple perspectives, interdependence, and different forms of leadership and shared information.

SELF-MANAGING SCHOOLS
Learning from Business and Industry

Having argued that systemic change must take into consideration components of both the subsystem to be changed and the larger system within which it is embedded, I would like to violate my own exhortations and focus on a specific change in the educational subsystem—the change to self-management in education.

Most early attempts at school-based management in the United States focused on local-site management of finances. Many current efforts incorporate some type of decision-making component but restrict the shared aspect to the school site and to a limited range of issues. Fully functioning, effective school-based management, however, involves focusing the entire resources of the system at the school level and allowing important decisions to take place at this level (Dade County Public Schools 1987). The ability to redefine, adjust, and renew can only be achieved if schools have the authority to identify changing priorities and special needs and the resources needed to implement decisions.

American businesses have been forced by competition abroad and changes in the society at home to experiment with less hierarchical, less authoritarian organizational structures. The focus of this experimentation has been to increase productivity, to accommodate an accelerated rate of technological change, to make increasingly complex decisions, and to foster innovation and creativity (Heller 1985). The educational subsystem is being forced by these same pressures to search for alternative organizational structures by examining the lessons learned by the business sector.

Well-run, successful companies do not create processes of control to compensate for the weaknesses or limitations of their personnel. Instead, successful companies develop management styles aimed at empowering people (Levine 1986). Elmore (1983) pointed out that

> when it becomes necessary to rely mainly on hierarchical control, regulation, and compliance to achieve results, the game is essentially lost. Moving from delegated control to hierarchical control means moving from reliance on existing capacity, ingenuity, and judgment . . . to reliance on rules, surveillance, and enforcement procedures. Regulation increases complexity and invites subversion; it diverts attention from accomplishing the task to understanding and manipulating rules. (p. 358)

Many businesses have adopted a new shared leadership and information paradigm that restructures the organization to incorporate self-managed work units where administrative authority is shared more broadly, the pyramid of organizational power is flatter, and more work is done by consensus, teamwork, consultation, and networking. Self-managed units are viewed as the most effective entity for allocating resources and delegating tasks to deal with unique work conditions. In a self-managing unit, the members have the responsibility for executing the task, defining how the task will be structured, controlling the resources needed to accomplish it, and monitoring and supervising their own performance.

Self-Managing Units

The following four different functions must be performed in an organization (Hackman 1986):

1. Set direction for the organization.

2. Structure tasks, decide who will perform them, establish norms of conduct in the work setting, and arrange for needed organizational supports for the work, making sure people have the resources and supports they need to carry out the work.

3. Monitor and supervise the performance of the workers and the work process.

4. Apply the energy required (physical or mental) to accomplish tasks.

The distribution of authority for these four functions determines the degree of self-management in an organization. For example, in an authoritarian bureaucracy, the administrator has the authority for carrying out the first three functions and the workers have responsibility only for executing the task. In this type of organization, the administrator monitors and supervises performance, structures the work of the unit and its context, and sets overall directions.

The rationale for self-managed units is based on the belief that the most effective level for allocating resources and delegating tasks to deal with unique work conditions is the working group. In organizations that have self-managing units, the workers have the responsibility not only for executing the task, but also for defining how the task will be structured, the resources needed to accomplish it, and the authority for monitoring and supervising their own performance. Rather than competing individually for rewards or recognition, members of a self-managing unit define their work roles in terms of their value as contributors to the group's primary task (Manz and Sims 1987).

Well-functioning, self-managing units can achieve a level of synergy and flexibility that cannot be mandated, enforced, or preprogrammed by administrators. Properly designed and supported self-managing units have the following characteristics (Hackman 1986):

- Members take personal responsibility for the outcomes of their work and show in their behavior that they feel personally accountable for the results of what they do.

- Members monitor their own performance continuously, actively seeking data and feedback to learn how well they are accomplishing their tasks.

- Members supervise their own performance, taking corrective action on their own initiative to improve their performance.

- When members do not have what they need to perform well, they actively and constructively seek from the organization the guidance, help, or resources they need for excellent performance.

- While members make sure that their own responsibilities are being met, they also have a vested interest in reaching out to help others. They are willing to make the effort to help members in other areas improve their performance, thereby strengthening the performance of the organization as a whole.

The effectiveness of a self-managing unit can be evaluated by the degree to which it achieves success on the following three criterion dimensions (Hackman 1986):

1. The unit's productive output meets the standards of quantity, quality, and timeliness of the clients who receive, review, or use that output.

2. The process of carrying out the work enhances the capability of organization members to work together interdependently in the future.

3. Work experiences contribute to the growth and personal well-being of unit members.

Developing Self-Managed Schools

Successful schools are distinguished from not-so-successful schools by the organizational norms and belief systems that characterize the individual school (Lotto 1982). Each school has a different mix of students and staff, is surrounded by a different community culture, faces special problems, and has a different history of efforts at improvement. The complexity and professional discretion involved in running schools and in teaching require an approach that maximizes the ability of staff and builds their problem-solving capacity. Attempts to improve student learning will be successful only to the extent that changes throughout the system give schools sufficient latitude to adapt new policies or practices to their unique circumstances and to develop their own solutions to problems.

Effective self-managing schools are not created by a state or district-office decree that "henceforth there will be school-based management." Certain conditions must be in place for a school to have a real chance of achieving a high standing on the three criterion dimensions discussed previously. If schools are to be effective self-managing units, they must have the following characteristics:

- clear and engaging direction
- an enabling school structure
- a supportive organizational context
- expert coaching and consultation
- adequate material resources
  (Hackman 1986)

In other words, the organizational structure must support the school's efforts.

Clear, Engaging Direction

Effective self-management is not possible unless there are clearly established goals that orient school staff toward common objectives, energize staff by adding to the meaning and purpose they find in their work, and provide criteria for staff to use in testing and comparing alternatives for their behavior.

An Enabling School Structure

For self-managing schools to be effective, they must (1) exert sufficient effort to get tasks accomplished at acceptable levels of performance, (2) bring adequate levels of knowledge and skill to bear on the tasks, and (3) employ performance strategies that are appropriate to the work and to the setting in which it is being performed. In order to accomplish this, schools must have a task design that creates internal motivation, freedom to select personnel committed to the task, and an obligation to monitor and adjust the working of the school.

A task design that creates the *internal motivation* to sustain a focused effort in the absence of external controls and direct supervision requires that (a) tasks are meaningful, (b) school staff know the results of their performance, and (c) school staff accept personal responsibility for the outcomes of their work.

When individuals are being selected for positions in a self-managing school, several factors need to be considered. The internal leader—principal—of the self-managing school should be firmly committed to participatory management. Since what members know (and know how to do) has a significant effect on school outcomes, and since some people are more responsive to opportunities for self-management than others, staff should be selected based on the school's need.

An enabling structure communicates the expectations to school staff that they are responsible for regulating their own behavior, continuously assessing the situation (with particular attention to changes in the environment), and actively planning how they will proceed with the work of the school based on those assessments.

A Supportive Organizational Context

The imperative for systemic change becomes clear when considering the support needed for effective self-managing schools. Three specific features of the organizational context are particularly significant in supporting self-managing schools: (1) the reward system, (2) the professional development system, and (3) the information system.

The reward system should recognize and reinforce excellent school performance rather than individual performance. The professional development system should develop and build on the school staff's knowledge and skill. The information system should provide school staff with information about (a) task requirements, constraints, and opportunities that may limit or channel strategic options; (b) the resources that are available for use; and (c) the characteristics of the students.

Expert Coaching and Consultation

Staff of self-managing schools need coaching on learning self-management skills, working collaboratively together, and adjusting to often uncertain working situations. A leader or consultant can do much to promote team effectiveness by helping members learn how to work together as self-managers.

Adequate Material Resources

Insufficient material resources are a major constraint on the effectiveness of self-managing schools. Even with all the other elements in place, schools eventually will fail if they do not have (and cannot get) the resources they need to do their work.

Leadership for Self-Managing Schools

The assumption underlying self-management practices is quite different from that of more traditional organizations with a top-down philosophy of control. The assumption is that subordinates can perform leadership functions for themselves, and the external leader's job is to teach and encourage subordinates to manage themselves effectively. In a system with self-managing units, organizing, directing, and monitoring functions—all functions of traditional management—are located within the group (Manz and Sims 1987).

What, then, is the role of district office personnel or state department of education staff when schools are self-managing? Manz and Sims (1987) investigated the role of leaders in business organizations with self-managing groups. The researchers used the term "coordinator" to indicate the external leader of the group and "support team" to identify the upper-level managers of the organization.

The coordinator's role was originally ill-defined and emerged largely through trial and error. At the time of the study there was still some degree of ambiguity about what coordinators were actually contributing and ought to be doing. The emerging leadership practice, however, was to encourage and support the group so that the members would be able to do things themselves. There was a notable absence of direct commands or instructions from the coordinators to the team. Rather than allow the dependence that is fostered in more traditional work groups, the coordinators made a deliberate and calculated effort to encourage independence. The uniqueness of the coordinator's

role lay in the commitment to the philosophy that the groups should successfully carry out the leadership functions for themselves. The dominant role of the external leader was to lead others to lead themselves (Manz and Sims 1987).

The teams were trained in conducting meetings and group problem solving. While the elected team leader usually organized and conducted the meetings, other team members had the opportunity to speak freely. The teams engaged in various problem-solving activities during weekly scheduled meetings that were characterized by a relatively sophisticated level of discussion and problem solving. There was a persistent focus on reaching a solution, on improving performance, and on various concerns of individual team members (Manz and Sims 1987).

Examples of Systemic Change

When schools are self-managing, there is a comprehensive approach to school management that links goal setting, needs identification, policy making, planning, budgeting, learning and teaching, and evaluating (Caldwell and Spinks 1988). In such an organizational framework, each school has the authority to make decisions related to curriculum; to the technology of teaching and learning; to the acquisition of materials and the use of facilities and equipment; to the allocation of people in matters associated with teaching and learning; to those aspects of administration, scheduling, teaching, learning, and staff professional development that deal with time; and to the allocation of money (Manz and Sims 1987).

Following are examples of *systemic* educational change in Australia and the United States and *subsystem* change in a U.S. school district.

Collaborative School Management Model

Caldwell and Spinks (1988) described a system for school-based management developed in two states in Australia (Tasmania and South Australia). The Collaborative School Management Model integrates goal setting, needs identification, policy making, planning, budgeting, implementing, and evaluating. The focus of the model is on the central functions of schools—learning and teaching—and organizes the management of the school around the preferred patterns of work in the school. The model calls for the appropriate involvement of staff, students, and the community in "policy groups" and "program teams."

The policy group has responsibility for goal setting and needs identification, policy making, approving the budget, and evaluating the extent to which goals and policies are being achieved and needs are being satisfied. The program teams, which consist of teachers working within a framework of policies and priorities set by the policy group, prepare plans for the implementation of policy and identify the resources required to support those plans. The program teams also are concerned with implementing and evaluating programs. While these responsibilities are clearly designated, some people may be members of the policy group as well as of one or more of the program teams, and members of program teams frequently provide information for the policy group.

Kentucky

Kentucky is the only state implementing statewide educational reform that also addresses health and family needs, and, therefore, the only example that comes close to true systemic change. In April of 1990, the Kentucky Education Reform Act (KERA) took effect. Spurred by inequities in school funding, the Kentucky Supreme Court abolished the state's public school system. The Kentucky General Assembly replaced it with one radically different in form and philosophy. The goal of the resulting change was nothing less than the complete transformation of Kentucky schools by 1996.

This transformation included the Kentucky Department of Education. KERA provided for an appointed commissioner of education (to replace the elected superintendent of public instruction) under whom the department of education was reorganized into a professional service center to support education reform in local schools and districts. A Professional Standards Board was established to develop new standards for teacher training and certification.

The following initiatives are part of the state's campaign to help all children succeed in school:

- **School-Based Decision Making** empowers a council of three teachers, two parents, and the principal in each school to adopt policies based on what is best for the school's students. Councils make decisions about instructional materials, school staff, curriculum, extracurricular activities, and other issues.

- **Curriculum and Assessment** focus on linking knowledge and skills across the curriculum, with students learning to use knowledge in real-world applications and assessing what students are able to do with what they have learned.

- **Technology** is being used to link 150,000 student workstations, 35,000 teacher workstations, 1,400 school management systems, 176 district administrative systems, higher education campuses, educational television, the state library system, and state agencies in a communications, instructional, and administrative network.

- **Regional Service Centers/Professional Development** make expertise and technical assistance more accessible to districts and schools.

- **Extended School Services** provide additional instruction and support before or after school, on Saturdays, or during the summer for students who are at risk of falling behind in school.

- **Pre-/Primary Schools** use a developmentally appropriate curriculum and related services to prepare at-risk students for learning. Preschool is available for all four-year-olds from low-income families and for three- and four-year-olds with disabilities. Primary schools place five- through eight-year-olds in multi-age, multiability classrooms so they can learn and progress at their individual paces. Children are assessed on a continuous basis and advanced to fourth grade when they are ready.

- **Family Resource and Youth Services Centers** provide health, social, justice, and education services for students and families. Centers are located in or near schools in which at least 20 percent of the students qualify for free school meals.

Lake Washington School District

In 1991, the Lake Washington School District in Kirkland, Washington, reorganized its central office staff, building administrators, and support personnel into three regional teams and a support team (Scarr 1992). The regional teams—each includes one high school and the schools that feed into it—focus on supporting the operations and restructuring efforts of their area schools. The support team provides services to the schools such as business, facilities, and personnel.

The teams engage people at all levels of the organization and include teachers, other staff, students, parents, and business people. In addition to the area teams, individual buildings operate as work teams. Building principals and their staffs develop processes and decision-making models to harness the creativity and participation of teachers and staff.

Each area team is self-regulating and has developed its own organizational structure and processes including budget allocation, communications, and decision making. Each team is responsible for working with staff and the community to make changes in the schools' organizational structures so that all students will obtain the skills, knowledge, and attitudes they need to be successful.

Lake Washington Superintendent L. E. Scarr wrote that the compelling reason for making the radical departure from the traditional structure was that work teams transformed a narrow, compartmentalized system into one with broad perspectives. He pointed out that bureaucracies break work down into a series of discrete tasks, whereas educating students is a set of integrated steps and responsibilities. The system as a whole—kindergarten through twelfth grade and the entire curriculum—rather than fragmented segments has become the focus of change efforts. Each team is responsible for every student until the student demonstrates the required skills, knowledge, and abilities.

RECOMMENDATIONS

The overarching goal of systemic change in education is to provide an organizational structure that allows each school to design a learning environment that ensures quality education for all of its students. The assumption is that greater decision-making authority at the site level will enable the group to respond to changing conditions or problems more efficiently, effectively, and flexibly. To accomplish this goal, the following four recommendations are offered (adapted from Duttweiler and Mutchler 1990b):

1. School sites, districts, and states should effect a transformation of authority. A transformation of authority may be understood best as a change in the definition of leadership and as new expectations for all participants in the educational subsystem. Authority is the currency with which people influence what goes on in an organization. Within a framework provided by policy and law, it is the freedom to make decisions within an area of professional expertise. The experience of those involved in implementing change strategies suggests there is a much greater likelihood for the success of a change effort when the entire system—including state department of education staff and district staff—practices what is preached.

2. For systemic change to be successful, long-term, systemwide commitment to the concept should be built and maintained. Such commitment is reflected by clearly defined goals and outcomes, continuity and stability, protection from external constraints, and the necessary resources for successful implementation. School and district staffs, parents, and communities must be empowered to maximize the educational experience for students, and whole-system commitment must be built and maintained to support change that directly responds to the needs of all children.

3. A systemwide culture should be developed that supports norms of collegiality and collaboration. Effective implementation of systemic change means finding ways to create a collaborative mode of work to replace the existing isolation and powerlessness under authoritarian bureaucracy. Collegial norms must be established for group problem solving in

which ideas are shared and alternative solutions to problems are explored. A first priority must be the development of mutual respect and trust throughout the system; otherwise, suspicion, competitiveness, and inflexibility will defeat any attempt to establish collegial relationships.

4. Professional development should be provided so staff at all levels can acquire new knowledge, skills, and attitudes. Professional development should focus appropriate training to develop the knowledge, skills, and attitudes required to carry out new roles. Participants at all levels need to receive professional development that addresses personal and interpersonal needs and includes experiences in group processes, team building, and conflict resolution. In addition, staff and other participants must be prepared to deal with the substantive and technical aspects of the issues about which decisions must be made.

CONCLUSION

School systems across the country are antiquated bureaucratic and technical structures, "highly complex, surprisingly similar, and very resistant to change" (Holzman 1993). Sparks (1993) asserted that "examining trends, anticipating new paradigms, and successfully managing change in turbulent times are the challenges educational leaders face in the 1990s." Scarr (1992) summed up the need for systemic change: "As educators, we must accept that constant change and flexibility are the norm, not the exception. Organizational structures in education must change. The youth and the future of our country require no less."

REFERENCES

Barker, J. A. 1989. *Discovering the future: The business of paradigms.* St. Paul, Minn.: ILI Press.

Berman, P., and M. W. McLaughlin. 1978. *Federal programs supporting educational change, vol. VIII: Implementing and sustaining innovations.* (R-1589/8-HEW). Santa Monica, Calif.: The Rand Corporation.

Bonstingl, J. J. 1992. *Schools of quality: An introduction to Total Quality Management in education.* Alexandria, Va.: Association for Supervision and Curriculum Development.

Bradford, D. L., and A. R. Cohen. 1984. *Managing for excellence: The guide to developing high performance in contemporary organizations.* New York: John Wiley & Sons.

Caldwell, B. J., and J. M. Spinks. 1988. *The self-managing school.* London: The Falmer Press.

Carnegie Task Force on Teaching as a Profession. 1986, May. *The report of the task force on teaching as a profession of the Carnegie Forum on Education and the Economy.* Hyattsville, Md.: Carnegie Forum on Education and the Economy.

Cetron, M. J., W. Rocha, and R. Luckins. 1988. Into the 21st century: Long-term trends affecting the United States. *The Futurist* 22 (4): 29–42.

Cook, W. J., Jr. 1988. *Strategic planning for America's schools.* Arlington, Va.: American Association of School Administrators.

Cornbleth, C. 1986. Ritual and rationality in teacher education reform. *Educational Researcher* 15 (4): 5–14.

Covington, M. V. 1992. *Making the grade: A self-worth perspective on motivation and school reform.* New York: Cambridge University Press.

Cuban, L. 1988. A fundamental puzzle of school reform. *Phi Delta Kappan* 69 (5): 341–44.

Dade County Public Schools. 1987. *School-based management/shared decision making.* Miami, Fla.: Dade County Public Schools.

Duttweiler, P. C., and S. E. Mutchler. 1990a. *Weaving a new paradigm: Steps to organizational excellence.* Austin, Tex.: Southwest Educational Development Laboratory.

———. 1990b. *Organizing the educational system for excellence: Harnessing the energy of people.* Austin, Tex.: Southwest Educational Development Laboratory.

Education Deficit, The. 1988. A staff report summarizing the hearings on "competitiveness and the quality of the work force" prepared for the use of the Subcommittee on Education and Health of the Joint Economic Committee, Congress of the United States, December 14.

Elmore, R. F. 1983. Complexity and control: What legislators and administrators can do about implementing public policy. In *Handbook of teaching and policy,* edited by L. S. Shulman and G. Sykes. New York: Longman.

Firestone, W. A., and B. L. Wilson. 1985. Invited perspective: Using bureaucratic and cultural linkages to improve instruction: The principal's contribution. *Educational Administration Quarterly* 21 (Spring): 7–30.

Frymier, J. 1987. Bureaucracy and the neutering of teachers. *Phi Delta Kappan* 69 (1): 9–14.

Hackman, J. R. 1986. The psychology of self-management in organizations. In *Psychology and work: Productivity, change, and employment,* edited by M. Pallak and R. Perloff. Washington, D.C.: American Psychological Association.

Heller, R. 1985. Changing authority patterns: A cultural perspective. *Academy of Management Review* 10 (3): 488–95.

Hodgkinson, H. 1989. *The same client: The demographics of education and service delivery systems.* Washington, D.C.: Institute for Educational Leadership, Inc., and the Center for Demographic Policy.

Holzman, M. 1993. What is systemic change? *Educational Leadership* 51 (1): 18.

Hutchins, C. L. 1988. Design as the missing piece in education. In *The redesign of education: A collection of papers concerned with comprehensive educational reform,* December, 47–49. San Francisco: Far West Laboratory.

Kearns, D. T., and D. P. Doyle. 1988. *Winning the brain race.* New York: Kampmann and Company.

Levine, M. 1986. Excellence in education: Lessons from America's best-run companies and schools. *Peabody Journal of Education* 63 (2): 150–86.

Lotto, L. S. 1982. Revisiting the role of organizational effectiveness in educational evaluation. Paper presented at the annual meeting of the American Educational Research Association, March, New York.

Mann, D. 1988. The honeymoon is over. *Phi Delta Kappan* 69 (8): 573–75.

Manz, C. C., and H. P. Sims Jr. 1987. Leading workers to lead themselves: The external leadership of self-managing work teams. *Administrative Science Quarterly* 32 (1): 106–29.

NCES. 1992. *Dropout rates in the United States: 1991.* U.S. Department of Education, Office of Educational Research and Improvement, National Center for Education Statistics.

O'Neil, J. 1993. Turning the system on its head. *Educational Leadership* 51 (1): 8–13.

Scarr, L. E. 1992. Using self-regulating work teams. *Educational Leadership* 50 (3): 68–70.

Schein, E. H. 1985. *Organizational culture and leadership.* San Francisco: Jossey-Bass.

Schwartz, P., and J. Ogilvy. 1979. *The emergent paradigm: Changing patterns of thought and belief.* Menlo Park, Calif.: Values and Lifestyles Program.

Shanker, A. 1990. The end of the traditional model of schooling—and a proposal for using incentives to restructure public schools. *Phi Delta Kappan* 71 (5): 345–57.

Sparks, D. 1993. 13 tips for managing change in schools. *The Education Digest* 58 (6): 13–15.

Vaughan, R. J., and S. E. Berryman. 1989. Employer-sponsored training: Current status, future possibilities. In *Education and the economy: Hard questions, hard answers.* New York: The Institute on Education and the Economy, Teachers College, Columbia University.

THE ROLE OF EVALUATION IN SCHOOLS AS LEARNING ORGANIZATIONS

Patrick M. Jenlink and Rosalie T. Torres

Renewal, restructuring, transformation: familiar words that have educational scholars and practitioners abuzz with their efforts to meet unrelenting demands that our educational systems change. The call for change comes amidst increasing movement away from long-held traditions in American society and its institutions. Thus, in the face of challenges to the values and mores most mainstream Americans grew up with, educators are roused further to upstage business as usual. And there is no end in sight—nothing to suggest that we will find again the 1950s prosperity and tranquillity, certainty in our approach, or little apparent need to question. What is now required is to accept a constant state of learning.

> A learning culture is one where collaborative creativity in all contexts, relationships, and experiences is a basic purpose of the culture. It is a culture where the measure of success is the combined wisdom of groups and the synergy, leadership, and service of the organization as a whole. Up to now, individuals have done the learning, but in a learning culture with multiple interactions among learning groups, the whole culture learns in a self-aware, self-reflective, and creative way.

> The groups become cells in the body of an organization, which itself becomes a new learning individual in the emergent global culture. (Jaccaci 1989, 50)

The learning organization concept has its origin with pioneers of organizational development such as Kurt Lewin (1947), W. Edwards Deming (1981), and Chris Argyris (1977), among a few, who first began to understand the importance of not only framing what individual learning was, but also of viewing organizational learning as a complex process by which the organization adjusts to external and internal forces. More recently others, primarily in organizational psychology and management (see Kline and Saunders 1993; Senge 1990; Stata 1989; Watkins and Marsick 1993), have elaborated on the concept. Operating as a self-renewing system, the learning organization does the following:

- Provides a framework within which continuous learning takes place for all participants, adults and children alike.

- Depends upon explicit acknowledgment of our social and moral responsibility for learning and renewal in the context of individual, organizational, and societal roles.

- Thrives on the basis of individual motivation, conviction, and commitment; the values women, men, and children live by; and the experiences that give meaning to our lives.

- Creates an atmosphere that at once encourages effort, striving, vigorous performance, and change in a context of love, hope, acceptance, and forgiveness.

- Compels individuals to see themselves in relation to others as well as the whole.

- Considers continuity as well as change, carrying forth artifacts of prior successes as building blocks for the future.

- Recognizes that the purpose of knowledge is to create and maintain environments conducive to individual fulfillment.

- Negotiates its destiny in the broader societal environment, rather than the broader environment determining its destiny.

Learning organizations create settings that enable participants to reach beyond basic needs and begin to attain higher aspirations (Senge 1990). Jaccaci (1989) explains that, contrary to what we might think, schools and universities are not true learning organizations:

> It is also important to realize that schools and universities are not learning cultures as the concept is now emerging. Although learning goes on in our schools and universities, it is primarily replicative learning aimed at passing along the intellectual and social agreements of the day to students. A learning culture, by contrast, is a new challenge, a radically different step in the evolutionary process. It is not just an organization or institution full of people placing emphasis on individual learning and more time at it. (p. 50)

Moreover, for the most part school districts are not characterized by collaborative cultures where growth and renewal are shared endeavors. Schools within districts often operate as separate closed systems, competing for resources and not learning from their individual or collective past experiences. Nor are they typically engaged in meaningful ways with the community or the larger sociopolitical environment. Overloaded with the demands and expectations of the day, schools are characterized by episodic improvement projects and fragmented efforts at change (Fullan 1993). The bureaucratic structures that currently organize schools typically prevent them from learning, change, and renewal.

Fullan (1993) notes two basic reasons why much educational reform has been unsuccessful. The first is the complex and intractable nature of problems in schools, a point that Sarason (1990) has emphasized for years. Failing to see schools as systems and to understand the dynamic relationship between the school and the community has contributed heavily to past and existing failings of reform or change. Communities themselves often exert significant constraints on schools' capacity to change. These constraints are applied through (a) adherence to out-of-date perspectives on schooling, (b) expectations that all children now in schools can learn successfully through the pedagogical methods through which adults in the community themselves learned, (c) apathy with respect to involvement in schools, and (d) resistance to increase funding for schools.

The second reason why reform is failing is because it has attempted to change structures without paying attention to the culture that sustains them. Miles and Fullan (1992) emphasize that change must be systemic, focusing on the culture as well as the functional or structural elements of the school. The culture or deep structure of America's schools has been in the making for generations now. How school organizations learn, make decisions, approach productivity, and operate, as well as the kinds of the people who work in schools, are all manifestations of their deep structure, which now must be explored.

In the remainder of this chapter we undertake that exploration by contrasting schools as traditional and learning organizations on these dimensions (see table 1). Second, we explore program evaluation as a means of learning in schools. Third, following the framework of table 1, we contrast evaluation in traditional and learning organizations on a variety of dimensions. The chapter concludes with practical steps for transitioning from a tradi-

DIMENSION OF SCHOOLS	TRADITIONAL ORGANIZATIONS	LEARNING ORGANIZATIONS
Learning	Episodic Taking in of Information	Continuously Building the Capacity to Create
Productivity	Individual Achievement	Collaborative Creativity
Means for Decision Making	Nonparticipatory Rational Analysis	Contextually Sensitive Examination of Issues; Intuition; Collaboration
Mode of Operation	Fragmented	Systemic
Characteristics of Individuals	Technically Competent	Reflective, Open, Self-Aware

Table 1   Characteristics of Schools as Traditional and Learning Organizations

tional school to a school which functions as a learning organization.

LEARNING

School organizations today learn in much the same manner as their counterparts of decades ago. Solving problems in isolation while adapting to external demands, schools have changed little over the years. Like most organizations, schools strive to maintain business as usual. They react to change by modifying organizational and individual behavior in order to do so. That is, teachers and administrators typically respond to changes in the internal and external environment of the school by detecting perceived errors, which they correct so as to maintain the basic structures of the school.

This approach results in *episodic taking in of information* and fragmentary learning. Consider staff development as an example. Teachers or administrators engage in intermittent and often uncoordinated development activities that respond more to the demands of outdated policy than to real needs. Rather than challenge norms, schools react by adapting to traditional demands and expectations. As a result, they experience little significant change or growth. This isolated and episodic learning represents the lowest order of learning. It has

been referred to as single-loop learning (Argyris and Schon 1978) or adaptive learning (Senge 1990). Although this type of learning in schools is important to basic functioning, if not survival, it is insufficient to current demands for significant change. Energies are expended in maintaining the status quo at the expense of opportunities for more substantive change.

"'Adaptive learning' must be joined by 'generative learning,' learning that enhances our capacity to create." This then is the "basic meaning of a 'learning organization'—an organization that is continually expanding its capacity to create its future . . . it is not enough to survive" (Senge 1990, 14). This type of learning requires new ways of looking at the world; it requires discernment of the underlying systems that control events. When we fail to grasp the systemic source, we fall back into a coping mode where we tend to the symptoms rather than addressing underlying causes.

Our greatest challenge in shifting from traditional, resource-based organizations to knowledge-based learning organizations is in finding and keeping a "dynamic imbalance" (Waterman 1988, 232). This imbalance enables organizations to *continuously build the capacity to create*, rather than maintain a level of homeostasis through routine behaviors. There is a kind of rhythm to the process:

first, a constant questioning of standard ways of doing things and then deliberate breaking of old rules, familiar patterns, and past practices. Thus the only way to respond to change is to treat it as a learning process—for both individuals and the organization.

The central tenet behind the concept of a learning organization is that every change requires a new participative experiment (Weisbord 1987, 95). Enabling organizational participants to experience and understand the process in motion creates the learning dynamic essential to change, growth, and constant renewal.

> Members reflect on and inquire into previous contexts for learning, previous episodes of organizational learning, or failure to learn. They discover what they did that facilitated or inhibited learning, they invent new strategies for learning, they produce these strategies, and they evaluate and generalize what they have produced. (Argyris and Schon 1978, 26–27)

Thus, organizational learning is dependent upon a collective of learning by individuals within the organization. Drawing on Vygotsky's (1978) constructivist theory of individual learning helps our understanding of learning as continuously building the capacity to create. Vygotsky's zone of proximal development encompasses the context in which learning takes place. Viewing classroom teachers as learners, this context consists of (a) their perceptions of the settings in which they work—their pupils, other teachers, the school and its community—as well as (b) their perceptions of learning and teaching (Mayher and Brause 1991). Concomitant with changing circumstances, this context is in constant flux.

Learning within the zone of proximal development consist of four stages. These stages define the difference between actual and potential learning at any given point in time and within any given context. The stages are as follows:

Stage One. Learning and performance is assisted by more capable others. A teacher, facilitator, or expert designs learning experiences, creates appropriate settings for learning, and gives cognitive support as required. This stage represents the most traditional means of learning for adults and children in our society. Learning might also be facilitated by peers, a strategy used by classroom teachers and adult trainers when they engage students/participants in cooperative learning (Brown and Pilincsar 1989; Hill 1992; Johnson and Johnson 1992; Kolb 1984; Matthews 1993; Slavin 1991).

Stage Two. Learning and performance is self-assisted. Learners take over responsibility for their participation and carry out learning tasks without assistance or prompting from others. As learners internalize new knowledge and mature in their application of it, there is less need for assistance from others. For example, classroom teachers become reflective inquirers of their own practice by examining the outcomes of their work (i.e., student learning) in terms of self-generated (i.e., teacher-generated) questions about its effectiveness.

Stage Three. Based on the self-directed learning processes of stage two, the learning process and subsequent performance are now fully developed and routinized. That is, self-directed behaviors with respect to learning and subsequent performance have become tacit due to skill maturity in a given area. They occur as a matter of course.

Stage Four. Finally, deautomatization of performance leads to recursion back through the first three stages. For example, what has become tacit knowledge for a teacher in his or her classroom is periodically analyzed for its appropriateness given changing circumstances. At this point, reengagement with and assistance from more capable others is needed to enhance performance in a given area. This ability to constantly monitor and improve enhances the individual's and organization's capacity to create. A recursive path back through stages one, two, and three provides the cycle of opportunity for continuous renewal. Waterman (1988) describes the nature of leadership in learning organizations that fosters this kind of self-determination:

> We used to look primarily to the top of the organization for both the energy and the leadership. The leadership still has to come from the top, but it's a kind of leadership that creates the environment for renewal. It's the kind of leadership that encourages,

nurtures, nudges, supports, and inspires people everywhere in the organization. It's a leadership that offers direction, but doesn't pretend to know all the answers. At some very important level it is counting on the totality of individual initiative to be a lot smarter. (p. 105–06)

This theory of learning and development and others which emphasize self-directed learning is based on the assumption that "genuine change—like all kinds of genuine learning—must spring from the learner's defining the question to be answered and/or the problem to be solved" (Mayher and Brause 1991, 25).

PRODUCTIVITY

Individual achievement is the hallmark of schools as traditional organizations. Often immersed in competitive climates and reinforced through culture and behaviors, individuals are discouraged from collective or team efforts. Performance and productivity are assessed on an individual level, giving little incentive for collaboration and team efforts. This is true whether we speak to student and/or professional educator productivity.

Schools are guided by implicit and deep underlying assumptions (Senge 1990) held by individuals who people the schools—internal pictures that people continually use to interpret and make sense out of the world. In traditional schools these assumptions are often outdated or inconsistent with the demands of a rapidly changing environment. Individuals within traditional schools and, in turn, schools time-bound by traditional assumptions have learned to avoid making mistakes at all costs and to protect themselves out of fear of loss. Monitored by managers and assessed individually, workers' assumptions and interpretations of the world are continuously reinforced by the culture and bureaucracy of the organization. Traditional authoritarian organizations are dominated by internal politics, game playing, fear, and self-protection (Senge and Lannon-Kim 1991). Immersed in this environment, an individual's behavior is driven by precedent and organizational expectations.

Further, our focus on individual student achievement does not appear to have served us well. In terms of student exit outcomes, American schools have failed consistently during the last decade (Murphy 1990). Murphy reports a set of indices of school failure which explain declining U.S. productivity. These indices include historical and cross-national comparisons of student achievement, basic literacy, preparation for employment; holding power (schools' ability to hold children from dropping out); knowledge of specific subject areas (i.e., geography, economics, history, literature, science and mathematics); mastery of higher-order skills; initiative; responsibility; and citizenship.

These indices alone serve as a warning cry, echoing the need to change old organizational patterns, to consider creating new schools. We must overcome the old guards of tradition, the mechanisms that temper our actions. We have, over time, instilled the need for a win/lose competitiveness coupled with individualistic focus to the point of self-destruction, both for our children in their learning environments and for many organizations in a global market. We do not learn in isolation nor can we survive in a global economy that demands a systemic view of the world. Achievement, growth, or change in isolation from the whole will not redirect the successes of the organization or enable the self-renewal process essential to exist in a global economy. Whether it is the school, the university, or the corporation, competition must be replaced with collaboration. Our core values and practices must be realigned with current demands and expectations for an effective work force.

On the other hand, learning organizations demonstrate *collaborative creativity*. Increasingly, these organizations use systems thinking to see interrelationships within their broader environment—not isolated bits of events and processes representing only snapshots of the scenario. Collaboration, including advances in the use of team and group dynamics (see Orsburn et al. 1990; Bonstingl 1992), provides the infrastructure through which all dimensions of the organization interface. In the context of a learning organization, competition is reduced to only that within ourselves—driven by an intrinsic value to continuously improve—as opposed to the more destructive force of a win/lose view of life.

In the learning organization, shared visions and commonly constructed mental models induce higher levels of achievement from the combined energy and synergy of an organization thinking as a system. Productivity increases as resources are reallocated for constant experimentation and focused on new levels of understanding around organizational learning—constantly increasing our capacity to create.

MEANS FOR MAKING DECISIONS

Decision making is a process pervasive throughout the workings of any organization. Schools, like many organizations emerging from the industrial era, have traditionally been characterized as top-down, autocratic, and even dictatorial (Brown 1990; Hill and Bonan 1991). Given that all those in schools—from individual students to teachers and the principal—make decisions daily, how those decisions are made and who is involved determines the structure, social architecture, and culture of the school.

In a centralized, top-down model of decision making, the worker—the person who often has the most direct contact with the broad stakeholder base—is left to implement a decision without being involved in the process of making it. Such decision making is based upon *nonparticipatory rational analysis.* For example, teachers typically must carry out decisions made by principals, superintendents, and legislators far removed from the realities of what it takes to make their ideas or visions operational. As a result many decisions, while well-intended, further strain an already taxed system. Consider, for example, the current national emphasis on alternative assessment led by the assessment community consisting primarily of university scholars (see Linn, Baker, and Dunbar 1991; Wiggins 1989; Worthen 1993), state departments of education (see Hewitt 1993; Kahl 1992) and central office administrators of large districts (see Carriedo 1992; Hansen and Hathaway 1993; Lemahieu 1992a, 1992b). In Colorado the use of alternative assessment in classrooms has been legislated. If working properly, it requires significant change in (a) delivery of instruction, (b) curriculum, and (c) daily practice for teachers. The substance of decisions about alternative assessment is not so much in question as are the means through which the decisions have been made—typically without the involvement, support, or readiness of those who must now execute them.

In schools where bureaucracy is a strong influence, rational models of the world are applied to often irrational situations by individuals ill-informed about the work and context of teachers and students. Often, school officials react to the demands of the environment and attempt to adapt accordingly, thus maintaining organizational norms. For instance, local district interpretations of state accountability requirements typically result in minimal compliance without even marginally actualizing the spirit or intent of the improvement initiative.

The business world has provided examples of participative decision making and site-based management emulated by schools in their attempts to change (Brown 1990; Shedd and Bacharach 1991). Yet both business and school organizations have met with relatively little success in these endeavors (Cuban 1990; Fullan 1993; Sarason 1990, 1993; Kendrick 1992). Where the business world has failed in their attempts to change a hierarchical decision-making structure, schools have similarly failed. This failure is a result of our inadequate understanding of the deep structure of power relationships in schools (Sarason 1990). Traditionally, schools approach problem solving by breaking problems apart and by focusing on symptoms rather than underlying causes.

Decision-making behavior comes from deeply rooted habits of thinking and interacting. Mental models, constructed through interactions in bureaucratic settings, serve as strong forces to govern how we see and understand the world. Rational models of the world are applied to a rapidly evolving and irrational organizational context. Reliance on rational analysis, in an often ambiguous, uncertain, and rapidly changing context, produces confusion, alienation, and disenchantment. The lack of sharing in authority, information, and responsibility are characteristic of an organization built upon centralized decision making. At the same time that schools suffer under the weight of previously made top-down decisions, existing mental models continue to reinforce this same framework that ill-serves schools' purposes.

The learning organization exemplifies a decentralized structure, one premised on cooperation, collaboration, and a collective team dynamic. Rather than decisions governed by rational analysis and directed unilaterally from the top, the learning organization is the consummate relational dynamic. In place of singularly made decisions, we find a synergistic power that speaks to the combined intellect of the whole in the decision-making process. Such synergism is based upon "decision makers acting in good faith on the basis of knowledge about themselves and their environments" (Torres 1991, 196). Indeed,

> The most threatening risks are those unknown to decision makers who, as a result, have not anticipated resolutions should a negative outcome ensue. Moreover, when negative outcomes do develop, uninformed decision makers are unlikely to see the cause-effect relationship between their decisions and the outcome. Often these situations address long-term impacts, such as high employee turnover due to insufficient consideration of employee perspectives, experiences, and motivations. (Torres 1991, 194)

Changing power relationships, that is, how schools make decisions, has an impact on the ways a school and its members learn. We must understand that creating a learning organization necessitates change in existing structures like decision making. A key element of this transformation is to build an enabling structure for students, teachers, and administrators to break clear of existing organizational norms. Such a structure empowers all those in schools within an environment supportive of freedom and creativity. Most importantly, it requires a voice in decision making that is also a voice in determining what changes and how we learn. A new intellectual connectedness emerges when power relationships no longer perpetuate the distance between a learner (student or adult) and his or her work. In effect, changing how we make decisions provides an enabling structure that allows those in schools to change how they learn.

In the learning organization, collaboration, which combines individual strengths, knowledge, and intelligences, is at work and the organization is constantly learning to adapt when necessary—but more importantly to increase its capacity to create through generative learning. Decision making at any one point is premised upon input, a *contextually sensitive analysis of issues and perspectives*, and understanding of previous decision-making processes and outcomes. The objective is to learn forward for continuous improvement.

MODE OF OPERATION

Most schools continue to struggle in a rapidly changing world, attempting to operate without a fluent and constant reminder that change is the order of things. They structure plans to maintain business as usual. The tendency is toward adaptation and survival rather than growth and evolution. Schools exemplify this in their hierarchical structure, a structure that attempts to maintain organizational norms, values, and beliefs—thereby protecting what is familiar and comfortable.

In traditional schools, principals manage staff and staff in turn manage students. These distinct boundaries are constraining and distancing in their effect. Roles and relationships are defined by rules and procedure. Disconnected from peers and constrained by job definitions, staff and administration often work in adversarial ways. Murphy's (1990) analysis of research on schools reports that the basic operating structure of schools is inadequate. Management was found to be wanting, especially in providing leadership. Curriculum, instruction, and materials (textbooks) were implicated as well. While most students were allowed to drift through school unchallenged and uneducated, it was even worse for disadvantaged and minority pupils. Finally, he found intellectual softness and a lack of expectations, standards, and accountability.

These findings reflect issues that haven't developed overnight. Rather, the symptoms presented suggest a long-developing and endemic problem brought to surface by an educational system that is misaligned with the needs of a rapidly changing global community. It suggests that schools view their work and their worlds mechanistically. Highly centralized in nature, work is segmented and specialized, contributing to the complexity and inefficiency of the schooling process. The mode of operation is typified by *fragmented* and sporadic activities, resulting in increasing chaos and disequilibrium. Individuals see the organization in parts rather than *systemically*. When one part is broken it is fixed without consideration of the larger whole. If a new policy is passed that implicates curriculum, frequently other aspects of the schooling process are not considered (i.e., instruction, assessment, etc.), resulting in further inefficiency and fragmentation.

Administrators fight to stabilize the organization in ways that further distance the school from the community. Failing to see the connectedness of one action to another, individuals within schools and schools within districts tend to struggle against change rather than embracing it. Incomplete or inappropriate ways of learning ensure that schools will stay much the same. Modes of operation change little or in only superficial ways. Failure to engage in new types of learning will send schools down the same path of failure and frustration.

On the other hand, those organizations that are learning, that are renewing, constantly remind themselves to expect change. Their willingness to understand and exploit change is a powerful competitive weapon. Learning organizations understand the importance of customer demand and expectation; they have both the technical structure and social architecture for continuously using feedback to realign their scope, structure, and purpose. Learning organizations incorporate what Weisbord (1987) terms

> third-wave management and consultation. It is based on an open-systems thinking that includes economic realities, technological change, and democratic values—the dignity of each person and the responsibilities of each for the common good. It is first and always a broad learning strategy, one that includes self-awareness, interpersonal, group, and technical skills, economic knowledge, and social responsibility. (p. 257)

According to Waterman (1988) such "companies . . . are able continuously to renew; the management system is best described as consistency with constant experimentation" (p. 232). Core values, core beliefs, and core ideals all are the stabilizing force for the motion that surrounds the learning organization. Renewing organizations, according to Waterman (1988), "lay a stable foundation. They build it from sets of core beliefs, constant reminders that change is the norm, and policies that furnish security of employment without promising security of position. They find and manage a delicate balance: enough security so that people will take risks, enough uncertainty so that people will strive" (p. 233). For Weisbord (1987) this "new arena for action is networks of people learning and deciding together what to do next, based on open-systems maps, freely available information, and the evidence of their senses" (p. 257).

CHARACTERISTICS OF ORGANIZATIONAL MEMBERS

In summary, traditional school organizations have been characterized as places where learning is replicative (Jaccaci 1989) rather than creative, where competitive rather than collaborative behavior is reinforced, where management and decision making are centralized rather than participatory or shared, and where the use of scientific management principles dominates over more philosophical or humanistic perspectives. There is less attention to change in the substantive areas of identity, purpose, and meaning, and continued attention to change in policy and structure. Most importantly, the school is not understood as a complex interconnected system, intertwined with the community and broader environment. Certain characteristics of how individuals work in schools support this picture:

- Typically, individuals are hired and retain their positions based more upon technical competence than their capacity for inquiry and the creation of new knowledge.

- People work within role-specific boundaries, infrequently confronting them or questioning authority.

- Those who create visions and make decisions are expected to be from higher levels of management.

- Learning is an individual activity directed toward maintaining technical ability of individuals and existing norms of the school. It is adaptive rather than generative in purpose.

- Immersed in a political climate that individuals often find threatening and unforgiving, their behavior tends to be survival oriented.

Teachers, administrators, and other practitioners who work in schools that are learning organizations hold a different set of beliefs about their work. First, they have redefined the work of schools and the individuals within them as *learning*. Second, they believe that we must move from a resource-based orientation to a knowledge-based orientation. In order to do so teachers and administrators in schools must be seen and perceive themselves as knowledge workers (Drucker 1993). The value of school, as well as the quality of experience for students in the school, resides in the centrality of knowledge to all aspects of the school's work. This means that the most important tool educators bring to their work is the knowledge they hold individually. This knowledge includes, but is not limited to, specific content knowledge an educator attempts to impart to students. Even more importantly, it includes the ability to create meaningful learning environments, authentically assess students' learning in those environments, and engage in reflective inquiry of one's own practice. In the learning organization the productivity of students and adults does not depend on resources allocated, but rather on the allocation and management of knowledge. Knowledge of students, administrators, and teachers must all be viewed as the critical resource—the medium for exchange in the learning relationship that connects the various actors and their environment into a learning community. What individuals think and do, particularly how they use feedback to improve performance, is critical to the success of a learning organization (Torres 1994a).

Thus, in contrast to the hyperscientism that pervades traditional organizations, a need is developing for the persistent use of philosophical and other humanistic perspectives as the bases for hiring, retaining, and promoting individuals. These perspectives about individuals as knowledge workers include the following:

- People are curious, intellectually able, and inventive.

- At the heart of the work of the learning organization is learners' ability and willingness to transcend conventional work-life boundaries.

- Knowledge workers can and should be partners in determining their own learning—they must be both co-producers and co-consumers of their learning as their work.

- Knowledge workers are professionals who have sufficient knowledge, skill, and experience in common to promote important collegial learning.

- Knowledge workers' life interests are comprehensive and integrated with their work—even when those interests may appear to be distinct from the content of their work. Further, knowledge workers make life-work connections as a matter of course, not because they are stimulated by outsiders to do so.

We live in an information age with knowledge-based organizations immersed in what Drucker (1992) has termed a "society of organizations" (p. 95). The self-renewing organization is one that understands this new coinage of knowledge. Such organizations embrace and enable change as a central value of their existence. These learning organizations constitute thinking systems peopled by systems thinkers. They will carry forward new mental models that constantly embrace alternative futures for the individual and the organization. They seek quality in their work-life environment through a new learning paradigm.

EVALUATION IN SCHOOLS AS TRADITIONAL AND LEARNING ORGANIZATIONS

By now it should be clear that the central tenet of a learning organization is self-renewal through continuous learning. Feedback is used in a dynamic, collaborative fashion to inform the organization so as to facilitate change in organizational norms and enable new behaviors to evolve. Argyris and Schon (1978) termed this type of learning *double-loop learning.*

One means through which traditional schools have sought feedback and improvement is program evaluation. Yet, often in traditional schools renewal is minimal and evaluation is practiced in such a way that it enables organizational norms to remain intact. That is, evaluations typically examine programs as distinct entities without consideration for how they relate to other programs and the organization as a whole. Further, evaluations often assess programs in terms of stated goals and objectives without examining the assumptions underlying them. These assumptions are typically rooted in organizational norms and long-standing expectations about how the organization ought to operate. The provision of feedback exclusive to such goals often serves to maintain them.

On the other hand, based on new assumptions about the nature of organizations and organizational learning, evaluation might be seen as an opportunity for learning—always formative in purpose, it facilitates and mediates social constructions that can help dismantle organizational norms

and familiar modes of coping. Table 2 contrasts six dimensions of evaluation in schools as traditional and learning organizations: source of motivation for evaluation, scope, focus, purpose, role of evaluator, and methods. Each is discussed here in separate sections.

Source of Motivation

Historically, the source of motivation for evaluation has been *external and compliance driven.* This circumstance is rooted in evaluation's beginnings, where evaluation of federally sponsored educational programs served a social auditing function (Hamilton 1977). That is, funding agencies required summative, external evaluations to provide what was seen to be credible, objective evidence of program effectiveness.

Since that time many organizations, large school districts in particular, have developed their own internal evaluation departments. These units often effectively function, however, as though they were conducting external evaluations. That is, they are seen as threatening by other members of the organization who are directed by superiors to cooperate with evaluation activities. Moreover, in traditional organizations, research, development,

DIMENSION OF EVALUATION	TRADITIONAL SCHOOLS	LEARNING ORGANIZATIONS
Source of Motivation	External, Compliance-Driven (i.e., Peripheral, Expendable if Necessary)	Internal, Ownership-Driven (i.e., Integral, Required for Continuous Learning)
Scope	Program/Project	System/Organization as a Whole
Focus	Product/Outcomes	Process/Implementation
Purpose	Reduce Uncertainty/Anxiety, Simplify	Stimulate Creative Tension, Construct Meaning
Role of Evaluator	Expert-Authority	Consultant, Mediator, Facilitator
Methods	Quantitative	Quantitative and Qualitative

Table 2   Evaluation in Schools as Traditional and Learning Organizations

and evaluation efforts are the first to be considered for elimination under circumstances of diminishing resources. The relationship between these activities and the organization's raison d'être—whether it be student achievement or sales—is unconvincing in the minds of administrators or managers.

Failing to adequately support, but at the same time requiring, evaluation activities is another characteristic of evaluation in traditional organizations. Consider, for instance, educational accountability mandates from state legislatures. While most parents, educators, and evaluators find the demands for educational accountability reasonable on the face of it, these mandates are now recognized as fundamentally defective because they provide no technical or financial support for the implementation of the evaluation activities they require. In addition to meeting the needs of an increasingly complex constituency, school personnel are now being compelled to document measurable outcomes, an activity for which they have neither the time, nor—as they readily admit—the expertise.

In the learning organization the impetus for evaluation lies within the persons responsible for implementation of programs, organizational functions, or services. Evaluation is seen as an essential means for understanding oneself as well as the organization and, on that basis, making self-correcting changes. Thus reviews of progress, success, failures, and the like are routine rather than threatening. Evaluators working with organizations so inclined (see Fetterman 1994; Mathison 1994; Preskill 1994) are doing so because of the "organization's interest in and commitment to becoming a learning organization" (Torres 1994b).

Further, support for evaluation activities is provided because *self-renewal is a requirement for the governing value of continuous learning* which the organization holds. No more products are produced or services are provided than can be successfully evaluated. This view holds that we should set in motion less and evaluate more.

Scope

Traditionally, the objects of evaluation are discrete entities—*programs, projects, or materials*—with defined boundaries of staff, funding sources, purposes, etc. As evaluators we are cautioned to delimit the scope of evaluation to ensure its manageability and to do so by identifying evaluation questions relevant to program managers (see Joint Committee for Standards on Educational Evaluation 1994). At a minimum these questions seek to assess program outcomes and, sometimes, program implementation. Sticking to these questions during the course of the evaluation then facilitates the delivery of a recognizable product to evaluation clients. This course of action further helps us adhere to typical advice not to present surprises at the time of the final report. That is, we only address issues or aspects of the organization the client is prepared to allow as pertinent to or within the domain of the evaluation.

In the learning organization a wider purview is apropos for the evaluative lens (Mathison 1994; Torres 1994b). The traditional questions of "Was the program implemented as specified?" and "What gains in student achievement did the treatment and control groups make?" are reframed as "Was the program implemented as specified? If not, what circumstances contributed to changes in implementation?" and "What unanticipated impacts of the program, positive or negative, have occurred?" Addressing the later questions immediately gives the evaluation warrant to access information, issues, and perspectives beyond the customary boundaries of a program, project, or set of materials. The evaluator is concerned with the *school and district as a whole*, including long-standing cultural elements that mediate action and decision making. This perspective involves moving away from narrowly focusing on problems to instead seeking connections among whole sets of problems—the values, beliefs, and assumptions that support them. Further, it speaks to the empowerment of all actors in the organization as decision makers, not just the program managers and administrators.

Focus

Again, historically, program evaluation has focused more on *outcomes* than on *implementation*. Recently, however, evaluators have begun to stress the value of assessing program implementation in order to explain program outcomes (see Conrad and Roberts-Gray 1988; Patton 1986, 1988; Scheirer 1986). That is, while program outcomes are important in terms of their relationship to the learning organization's governing values and goals, they are seen as unachievable without full attention to the implementation of activities and processes designed to accomplish those outcomes.

In education, it is not the theoretical integrity of programs that accounts for their failure, but rather the lack of focus on and understanding of issues of implementation. In the real-world settings of schools, it is unlikely that we can unequivocally prove cause-effect relationships between instructional programs and student achievement. However, we can work to understand issues of program implementation, for example, the poor morale, resistance to change, and patriarchy that are deeply rooted in school structure. Such issues serve to constrain implementation of new programs or initiatives and likely account more for their failure than do issues of theoretical soundness of the programs. "By expanding evaluation beyond the mere measure of outcomes to cover the causes of the consequences observed, we can use such knowledge to alter programs or their mode of implementation" (Browne and Wildavsky 1983, 101).

Purpose

Traditionally, the purpose of evaluation—and social science research in general—has been to *reduce uncertainty* around alternatives in decision making. And this view of evaluation is still popular among many evaluators today. Love (1991) describes two successful roles for internal evaluators: management consultants and decision support specialists. In the former role, evaluators "consult with managers on the use of data-based approaches to solving managerial problems" (p. 10). The latter evaluators "assist managers in their functions of planning and controlling and in their decision-making roles" (p. 10). The press here is to decrease complexity, and thereby reduce anxiety.

Another purpose for evaluation, perhaps more promising, is to *increase complexity and stimulate creative tension*. Creative tension comes not so much from the understanding of others, as from the understanding of self in relation to others. In this view, evaluation's purpose is to promote insight which will lead to action (Torres 1991). In learning organizations, this insight is a product of generative learning where shared meanings are constructed through dialogue (see Guba and Lincoln 1989). Rather than between managers and evaluators, such a dialogue is held among participants from all levels of an organization. The evaluator's role is to facilitate an emergent process whereby various stakeholders identify relevant problems and issues through inquiry and reflection. This process of identifying and framing problems then almost unconsciously moves to generating solutions. Iterated cycles of data generated through dialogue and analysis leads to a transformation of the system (Hazen 1986).

Role of Evaluator

In traditional organizations an evaluator functioning as an *expert-authority* is charged with analyzing and presenting viable solutions to programmatic or organizational problems. If things are working properly, managers then implement these solutions. As many concerned with evaluation use have long disparaged, this rarely happens.

An alternative role for evaluators is that of consultant, but also facilitator and mediator. In the school as a learning organization, the purpose of the evaluator is to facilitate a learning climate, not to dispense solutions. In this role the evaluator enables the construction of a collective perception of what is real, teasing out the nuances of particular organizational contexts and creating a socially mediated environment conducive and necessary to learning. It is essential that we do nothing that would reinforce the idea "that people cannot make sense of their own experience" (Emery 1983, 4). Viable solutions then emerge from facilitated dialogue among organizational members. In this dialogue the evaluator moves beyond the role of interpreter to that of integrator.

Whereas in the traditional organization decision makers are those in authority with responsibility for policy and fiduciary management, in the learning organization decision makers are all those persons responsible for any aspect of its implementation: teachers, administrators, community members, and students. These decision makers are facilitated in their efforts toward growth, change, and continuous self-renewal by an evaluator who (a) facilitates contextual understanding, (b) helps to expose deep underlying assumptions, (c) mediates meaning as well as individual and collective views, and (d) facilitates reflective practice across the organization (Jenlink 1994).

Methods

Traditional organizations focus on easily assimilated, measurable outcomes that are characterized by a sense of objective neutrality. In some senses, a focus on *quantifiable outcomes* helps individuals in the organization remain disengaged from understanding and resolving issues that mediate their daily activities and choices in the implementation of programs and services. Such issues are usually not best represented with quantifiable data.

On the other hand, *qualitative approaches* (observations, interviews, case studies) can be used to probe meaning in the learning organization. The perspectives of and meanings experienced by individuals in the organization arbitrate how they function, what motivates them, and how they "invest their time, talent, and energy" (Maehr and Braskamp 1986). For organizations undertaking the kind of innovation and change called for in America's educational system, these issues are critical to self-understanding and development. In the learning organization both quantitative and qualitative data are seen as a basis for discussion and interpretation (see Fetterman 1994; Reichardt and Rallis 1994)—the objective of which is to increase awareness and readiness to evolve.

GUIDELINES FOR TRANSFORMING SCHOOLS INTO LEARNING ORGANIZATIONS

Creating schools as learning organizations, as self-renewing systems with a capacity for generative learning, first requires that we identify the existing nature of school organization. This chapter has undertaken the exploration of schools in the traditional sense and as learning organizations by contrasting the kinds of people who work in schools with how school organizations learn, make decisions, approach productivity, and operate. Secondly, the chapter has explored program evaluation as a means of learning in schools. Third, the chapter has contrasted evaluation in traditional and learning organizations based on what motivates organizations to evaluate: the scope, focus, and purpose of the evaluation; the role of the evaluator; and the methods the evaluator uses.

Traditional school structures that are rigid and fragmented must give way to a more fluid, dynamic infrastructure. Changes in the culture of schools will include collaborative networks while engaged in generative and creative activities, as well as shared visions and team learning. Building on self-reflection, inquiry, new modes of individual and organizational learning, and new perspectives for evaluation, the traditional school organization can collectively transform itself into a self-renewing learning organization.

What we know and what we believe about schools is grounded in a long tradition of the American school and the deeply embedded structures of the American schooling processes. Building schools as learning organizations will require new vistas of not only the school organization but of how it uses evaluation to enable learning. It will also require evaluators to think and practice their craft from a more systemic perspective.

To this end, building a new kind of school organization requires a new focus on self-renewal through continuous learning. Where traditional program evaluation tended to focus on product and outcomes, evaluation in the learning organization redirects its focus to continuous learning about implementation processes. Simultaneously, the scope of evaluation will expand from programs or projects to the entire system.

Transforming schools into learning organizations with a capacity for self-renewal will require engaging in a systemic change initiative. In doing so at least four main areas should be considered: communication across and integration of efforts; self-renewal/evaluation; resistance to change; and time/resource intensiveness. Each of these areas is discussed here along with general guidelines that practitioners should consider as they set out to build a learning organization.

Communication across Groups and Integration of Efforts

Communications is the process by which a common language of systemic change evolves and contributes to the success of the initiative. Without a well-designed and continuously improving system of communication, participants are unable to create the network essential to sharing and learning—two critical elements of systemic change. Equally important is the integrative power of communication to connect discrete activities and efforts to create a whole perspective of the school organizaiton. Generative learning relies heavily on the use of conversation and dialogue to mediate meaning and create common understandings. Toward this end, school can do the following:

- Develop an organizational chart of teams highlighting their purposes, areas of overlap, and shared responsibilities. Disseminate and discuss the chart with all groups/participants to give them a "big picture" perspective. Stimulate discussion around questions such as: What does the school improvement team have to do with the math curriculum team? How does the work of the language arts curriculum team relate to the overall systemic change initiative? And more generally: How do the missions/goals articulated in other teams, stakeholder groups, and the community at large fit in with systemic change?

- Activate ongoing and open exchange of activities and progress reports across major groups (school improvement teams, curriculum teams, design or core teams, etc.). Encourage feedback across various task forces, teams, etc., created as part of the systemic initiative. Emphasize areas of overlap and encourage exchange of information between teams.

- Track linkage of all professional development and learning events, workshops, and inservices to the systemic change initiative. Clearly identify how each training workshop,

inservice session, curriculum team speaker, etc., fits into and/or expands the overall purposes of the initiative.

Self-Renewal/Evaluation

Self-renewal through continuous learning is the central tenet of a learning organization. When school organizations engage in systemic change focused on creating learning organizations, a new emphasis on the role of evaluation as it relates to organizational learning emerges. The following recommendations are provided as beginning steps to creating schools as self-renewing systems:

- Initiate and maintain a focus on formative feedback that drives continuous integrated reflection on (a) the purposes, goals, beliefs, and values behind the systemic change initiative, and (b) how each committee, team, or stakeholder can contribute to this change initiative.

- Include as part of each committee or team responsibility and as a part of its regular meetings periodic review of (a) accomplishments/activities to date, (b) what part they play in the overall systemic change process, (c) the future focus of the committee or team (short and long term), and (d) any changes an adaptations that need to take place.

- Each team or committee could produce bimonthly reports documentng their tasks/activities and documenting their evaluation activities. These reports could be presented at quarterly/yearly "conferences" within the district so that each team or committee could present its accomplishments, as well as its suggestions for future goals and improvements.

- Reduce reliance on outside consultants or grant/funding requirements to drive and guide evaluation efforts. In order to become more self-evaluating, begin discussing (a) the responsibilities that could be assumed within prestanding committees/teams, and (b) the possible development of new committees/teams in connection with reflective evaluation.

Resistance to Change

Resistance to change is a natural phenomenon that occurs in any organization. The complexity of systemic change requires particular attention to the endemic nature of such resistance. How the school stakeholders have responded to change in past efforts often determines patterns of behavior that must be considered when undertaking new and more complex efforts. Similarly, individuals as well as the school organization often engage in self-defeating behaviors that set up defensive resistance to change. The following strategies engage the school organization and stakeholders in understanding the presence of resistances to change:

- Engage stakeholders in inquiry and reflection on past and current change efforts to determine existing barriers and constraints to change within the school or community.

- Explore the degree to which fragmentation contributes to resistance, whether relationships and linkages exist, and at what level of integrity.

- Investigate the extent to which resistance and opposition to the change process can be utilized for positive results.

- Identify self-defeating behaviors and existing negative energies at the individual and organizational levels. Address strategies for overcoming these behaviors and create a collective reflection and inquiry process that will serve to mitigate the deleterious effect these behaviors have on the system.

- Monitor membership of various teams and existing committee structures like school improvement teams and curriculum teams, as well as parent groups, etc. Look for growth/change vs. deterioration. Monitor the varying perspectives/needs of the members and plot out both long-term and short-term goals, as well as individual and organizational responsibilities.

Time/Resource Intensiveness

Finally, it should be recognized from the outset that systemic change initiatives are complex undertakings. Practitioners who undertake an initiative to create a learning organization must understand the time and resource intensiveness of the process. Embarking on the journey of systemic change ill-equipped to commit adequate resources will likely result in frustration and stress on the participants and a devolution from a systems perspective of change to a traditional fragmented perspective of change. The following recommendations are offered to assist in the design, planning, and implementation of a systemic change initiative:

- Routinize work associated with the systemic change inititative (i.e., make this work part of key participants' job descriptions and provide for regularly scheduled meeting times to implement it).

- Set up mechanisms for regular communication with all levels of participants so they are aware of progress being made and the value of their roles in the systemic change initiative.

- Make specific budget allocations or reallocations for the work of the initiative. Base budgetary decisions on the achievement of specific goals related to systemic change.

- Make full utilization of existing resources, such as those afforded through state departments of education, area intermediate school districts, local businesses, and community stakeholders.

- Strive to create internal capacity for sustaining the initiative and reduce reliance on outside consultants who may be engaged initially to support it.

CONCLUSION

Creating schools as self-renewing systems where continuous learning is the central tenet will require school practitioners and consultants to begin to think and act systemically. Building a learning organization engages the active participants in new levels of complexity with respect to a systemwide effort of this type. The pivotal role of evaluation in the self-renewal process carries with it new understandings and responsibilities for the evaluator and the members of the school organization. School organizations will become learning organizations in direct relationship to how individuals change and transform their own understanding and learning within the organization.

The nature of organizations must be rethought along lines that embrace a sense of dignity, meaning, and community (Weisbord 1987). Dignity, meaning, and community in the workplace are the anchor points for economic success in democratic societies. We need to preserve, enhance, and enact these values for reasons at once pragmatic, moral, humanistic, economic, technical, and social—the choice is ours.

REFERENCES

Argyris, C. 1977. Double loop learning in organizations. *Harvard Business Review* 55 (5): 115–25.

Argyris, C., and D. A. Schon. 1978. *Organizational learning: A theory of action perspective.* Reading, Mass.: Addison-Wesley.

Bonstingl, J. J. 1992. *Schools of quality: An introduction to total management in education.* Alexandria, Va.: Association for Supervision and Curriculum Development.

Brown, A., and A. Pilinscar. 1989. Guided, cooperative learning and individual knowledge acquisition. In *Knowing, learning and instruction: Essays in honor of Robert Glaser,* edited by L. Resnick. Hillsdale, N.J.: Lawrence Erlbaum.

Brown, D. J. 1990. *Decentralization and school-based management.* New York: The Falmer Press.

Browne, A., and A. Wildavsky. 1983. Should evaluation become implementation? In *Developing effective internal evaluation,* edited by A. J. Love. New Directions for Program Evaluation, No. 20. San Francisco: Jossey-Bass.

Carriedo, R. 1992. From no. 2 pencils to multiple solutions. *School Administrator* 49 (11): 20–21.

Conrad, K. J., and C. Roberts-Gray, eds. 1988. *Evaluating program environments.* New Directions for Program Evaluation, No. 39. San Francisco: Jossey-Bass.

Cuban, L. 1990. Reforming again, again, and again. *Educational Researcher* 19 (1): 3–13.

Deming, W. E. 1981. *Out of crisis.* Cambridge, Mass.: Massachusetts Institute of Technology, Center for Advanced Engineering Study.

Drucker, P. 1992. The new society of organizations. *Harvard Business Review* 70 (5): 95–104.

———. 1993. *Post-capitalist society.* New York: HarperCollins Publishers.

Emery, M. 1983. Learning and the quality of working life. *QWL Focus* 3 (1): 1–7.

Fetterman, D. 1994. Steps of empowerment evaluation: From California to Cape Town. *Evaluation and Program Planning* 17 (3): 305–13.

Fullan, M. G. 1993. *Change forces: Probing the depths of educational reform.* New York: The Falmer Press.

Fullan, M. G., and M. B. Miles. 1992. Getting reform right: What works and what doesn't. *Phi Delta Kappan* 73 (10): 745–52.

Guba, E. G., and Y. S. Lincoln. 1989. *Fourth generation evaluation.* Newbury Park, Calif.: Sage.

Hamilton, D. 1977. Making sense of curriculum evaluation: Continuities and discontinuities in an educational idea. *Review of Research Education* 5:318–48.

Hansen, J. B., and W. E. Hathaway. 1993. *A survey of more authentic assessment practices.* Washington, D.C.: ERIC Clearinghouse on Test, Measurement, and Evaluation, American Institute for Research.

Hazen, M. A. 1986, August. *Dialogue: Its importance to organizational development and to management education.* Paper presented at the annual meeting of the Academy of Management, Chicago.

Hewitt, G. 1993. Vermont's portfolio-based writing assessment program: A brief history. *Teachers and Writers* 24 (5): 1–6.

Hill, M. H. 1992. Strategies for encouraging collaborative learning with traditional classroom. *Contemporary Education* 63:213–15.

Hill, P. T., and J. Bonan. 1991. *Decentralization and accountability in public education.* Santa Monica, Calif.: RAND.

Jaccaci, A. T. 1989. The social architecture of a learning culture. *Training and Development Journal* 50:49–51.

Jenlink, P. M. 1994. Using evaluation to understand the learning architecture of an organization. *Evaluation and Program Planning* 17(3): 315–25.

Johnson, D. W., and R. T. Johnson. 1992. Implementing cooperative learning. *Contemporary Education,* 63:173–80.

Joint Committee for Standards on Educational Evaluation. 1994. *The program evaluation standards.* Newbury Park, Calif.: Sage.

Kahl, S. R. 1992. *Alternative assessment in mathematics: Insights from Massachusetts, Maine, Vermont and Kentucky.* Paper presented at the annual meeting of the American Educational Research Association, April, San Francisco. (ED 346 132)

Kendrick, J. J. 1992. Companies continue to embrace quality programs—but has TQ generated more enthusiasm than results? *Quality* 31 (5): 13.

Kline, P., and B. Saunders. 1993. *Ten steps to a learning organization.* Arlington, Va.: Great Ocean Publishers.

Kolb, D. A. *Experiential learning.* 1984. Englewood Cliffs, N.J.: Prentice-Hall.

Lemahieu, P. G. 1992a. Defining, developing a well-crafted assessment program. *NASSP Bulletin* 76 (545): 50–56.

———. 1992b. Using student portfolios for a public accounting. *School Administrator* 49 (11): 8–15.

Lewin, K. 1947. Frontiers in group dynamics, part 2: Channels of group life: Social planning and action research. *Human Relations* 1:143–53.

Linn, R. L., B. L. Baker, and S. B. Dunbar. 1991. Complex, performance-based assessment: Expectations and validation criteria. *Educational Researcher* 20 (8): 15–21.

Love, A. J. 1983. The organizational context and the development of internal evaluation. In *Developing effective internal evaluation,* edited by A. J. Love. New Directions for Program Evaluation, No. 20. San Francisco: Jossey-Bass.

Maehr, M. L. and L. A. Braskamp. 1986. *The motivation factor: A theory of personal investment.* Lexington, Mass.: Lexington Books.

Mathison, S. 1994. Rethinking evaluation's role: Partnerships between organizations and evaluators. *Evaluation and Program Planning* 17(3): 299–304.

Matthews, M. 1993. Meaningful cooperative learning is key. *Educational Leadership* 50 (6): 64.

Mayher, J. S., and R. S. Brause. 1991. The never-ending cycle of teacher growth. In *Search and research: What the inquiring teacher needs to know,* edited by R. S. Brause and J. S. Mayher. London: The Falmer Press.

Murphy, J. 1990. *The reform of American public education in the 1980s: Perspectives and cases.* Berkeley, Calif.: McCutchan.

Orsburn, J. D., L. Moran, E. Musselwhite, and J. H. Zenger. 1990. *Self-directed work teams: The new American challenge.* Homewood, Ill.: Business One Irwin.

Patton, M. Q. 1986. *Utilization-focused evaluation.* 2d ed. Newbury Park, Calif.: Sage.

———. 1988. Integrating evaluation into a program for increased utility and cost effectiveness. In *Evaluation Utilization*, edited by J. A. McLaughlin, L. J. Weber, R. W. Covert, and R. B. Ingle. New Directions for Program Evaluation, No. 40. San Francisco: Jossey-Bass.

Preskill, H. 1994. Evaluation's role in facilitating organizational learning: A model for practice. *Evaluation and Program Planning* 17 (3): 291–97.

Reichardt, C. S., and S. F. Rallis. 1994. *The qualitative-quantitative debate: New perspectives.* New Directions for Program Evaluation, No. 61. San Francisco: Jossey-Bass.

Sarason, S. B. 1990. *The predictable failure of educational reform.* San Francisco: Jossey-Bass.

———. 1993. *The case for change: Rethinking the preparation of educators.* San Francisco: Jossey-Bass.

Scheirer, M. A. 1986. Managing innovation: A framework for measuring implementation. In *Performance and credibility: Developing excellence in public and nonprofit organizations.*, edited by J. S. Wholey, M. A. Abrahamson, and C. Bellavita. Lexington, Mass.: Lexington Books.

Senge, P. M. 1990. *The fifth discipline: The art and practice of the learning organization.* New York: Doubleday.

Senge, P. M., and C. Lannon-Kim. 1991. Recapturing the spirit of learning through a systems approach. *The School Administrator* 9 (48): 8–13.

Shedd, J. B., and S. B. Bacharach. 1991. *Tangled hierarchies: Teachers as professionals and the management of schools.* San Francisco: Jossey-Bass.

Slavin, R. E. 1991. Synthesis of research on cooperative learning. *Educational Leadership* 48 (5): 71–82.

Stata, R. 1989. Organizational learning—The key to management innovation. *Sloan Management Review* 30 (3): 63–74.

Torres, R. T. 1991. Improving the quality of internal evaluation: The evaluator as consultant-mediator. *Evaluation and Program Planning* 14:189–98.

———. 1994a. Linking individual and organizational learning: The internalization and externalization of evaluation. *Evaluation and Program Planning* 17 (3): 339–40.

———. 1994b. Evaluation and learning organizations: Where do we go from here? *Evaluation and Program Planning* 17 (3): 327–37.

Vygotsky, L. S. 1978. *Mind in society.* Cambridge, Mass.: Harvard University Press.

Waterman, R. H. 1988. *The renewal factor.* New York: Bantam Books.

Watkins, K. E., and V. J. Marsick. 1993. *Sculpting the learning organization: Lessons in the art and science of systemic change.* San Francisco: Jossey-Bass.

Weisbord, M. 1987. *Productive workplaces: Organizing and managing for dignity, meaning, and community.* San Francisco: Jossey-Bass.

Wiggins, G. 1989. Teaching to the authentic test. *Educational Leadership* 46 (7): 41–49.

Worthen, B. R. 1993. Critical issues that will determine the future of alternative assessment. *Phi Delta Kappan* 74:444–85.

COLLABORATION, TEAM BUILDING, AND TOTAL QUALITY PHILOSOPHY FOR SYSTEMIC CHANGE IN EDUCATION

—

Edward W. Chance

Reform. Redesign. Restructuring. Rebuilding. All are methods and approaches designed to provide and achieve quality and systemic change in education. All four have adopted different approaches and mechanisms to bring about positive change. Although the concepts differ, the desire to improve the educational process and achieve quality is a common link. An additional common link is the realization that nothing of substance can be achieved without people committed to the actualization of established organizational goals. However, individuals, albeit in significant numbers, can accomplish little unless they share a common vision and approach to change (Chance 1992).

In point of fact, the key to any attempt at bringing quality to an organization through a change process rests in the degree of commitment and collaboration between those within such an organization. This means that a team approach to change is the only method by which success can be guaranteed. A quality organization, as Scholtes (1988) stated, "fosters teamwork and partnerships with the work force and their representatives" (p. 1–13). An involvement of all within the organization is further supported by Wellins, Byham, and Wilson (1991), who indicated that those involved in the daily operations of the job are the ones who know best how to improve the job. They further identified teams as the mechanism for empowerment for all employees.

The team-building concept is not necessarily new but is of more relevance and use to schools than ever before. Although schools often talk about teams and collaboration, it is the reality that more often than not the predominant leadership approach has been one of top-down management with very little employee input. However, as the quest for quality has increased and as the educational reform movement has remained on the political agenda, true efforts at building functional educational teams have taken place. Such team-building efforts can result in an increased sense of team spirit; better process skills for educators; a focus on intellectual discussions relevant to the organization's goals; a new level of self-esteem for teachers; and collaborative relationships with businesses and higher education (Maeroff 1993).

Team success does not simply happen. It requires a planned, well-designed effort on the part of the organization's leadership. It also mandates a commitment to the collaborative process by those involved. Change theory indicates that significant programmatic innovations take time but that a well-focused team effort can create an atmosphere of attainment. In order to be successful in the team-building effort, it is imperative that knowledge of group developmental theories, group parameters, teaming activities, group roles, and consensus building be understood and utilized in the effort. The remainder of this chapter will discuss such areas.

GROUP DEVELOPMENTAL THEORIES

As the team-building process begins, it is important to create groups with diverse membership. It is as important to remember that any person's involvement in the team should be voluntary. Maeroff (1993) recommended involving the total faculty in any team selection process. This ensures that everyone has an opportunity to participate, if desired, while providing "those who end up on the team some advance knowledge of the attitudes of the entire faculty . . . " (p. 516). A rich diversity of team members can be an asset as the team strives to collaboratively move toward quality concepts and change. Creating a homogeneous group that accepts and supports everything suggested establishes an opportunity for those who are left out of the team process to feel no ownership and destroy what has been developed. The initial involvement of a diverse population also creates a stronger foundation for community support. Certainly, a variegated group may be more difficult to work with, but it is better to accept and recognize this from the inception so that the team-building process may succeed.

A leader will also find it necessary to decide how various teams will be utilized in the development of a quality-oriented agenda. The larger the team, the more aggregate is the knowledge, but it becomes harder to accomplish tasks and maintain the team's focus. It is best to initially have a large, het-erogeneous team and break this team into smaller ones with specific subtasks. The ability to design successful teams becomes easier to accomplish once one accepts the concept that as groups of individuals they may evolve somewhat differently, yet comparably. Teams and groups develop in a sequential, predictable order. It may be useful to think of groups as living organisms that evolve, change, and mature as a result of experiences, knowledge, and opportunities.

Any developmental process of groups must also be viewed in light of the sociological differences of each team or group member. Group members' sex, ethnicity, age, socioeconomic status, and educational background contribute to the success or failure of each group. Additional elements that may influence group development and group success are personal and community aspirations; the nature of the school as an organization; the degree of ruralness or urbanness of the community; and the ability of the school's leader to work with a broad spectrum of people. It is necessary to remember that although the formal group structure may be quite specific, the informal group is often more powerful. The informal group, just as the formal one, will have its own norms, roles, and expectations. It is also important to remember that all change-oriented teams will experience stages of concern similar to those described in the work of Hord et al. in *Taking Charge of Change* (1987). These concerns will focus initially on personal issues and then on management issues. Eventually the concerns will address the change impact on students and the need for further collaboration with other professionals. These stages of concern coincide with the group developmental activities.

Although there are a multitude of group developmental theories, for the purpose of the chapter it is not necessary to discuss every theory in detail. Only two of the several theoretical approaches to group development will be presented. Tuckman and Jensen (1977) espoused a group developmental theory that is relevant to a group leader. They concluded that all groups progress through five stages of development.

Tuckman and Jensen's stages of group processes are forming, storming, norming, performing, and adjourning. All five of these stages should be viewed by looking at both task orientation and a concern for the advancement of interpersonal relationships. The first stage, forming, refers to the formation of a new group and the sense of uneasiness that can result from such a situation. This initial period of apprehension and caution is often followed by a period of storming. Storming represents a stretching of group boundaries as members assert themselves in establishing their personal realm of influence and power. Conflict often results that can destroy any productivity of the group if the next stage is not achieved.

The third stage is called norming. This is a time when group and individual, implicit and explicit, norms are firmly established. The increased sense of order results in a greater focus on the task and leads to the fourth stage. Performing finds an intense focus by the group on the task at hand. The group is well solidified in its membership, its roles, and group norms. Productivity is extremely high as a sense of camaraderie increases. The final stage, adjourning, comes about as the group nears the completion of its task and either prepares for new tasks or group dissolution. Once the initial task is completed, groups need new challenges. If these are not forthcoming, then the group's function is over and the group should disband. To remain together as a group but without purpose or function is both ineffective and inefficient.

Napier and Gershenfeld (1985) developed a composite theory representing various theoretical approaches. They identified a five-stage process through which all groups progress. The five stages are (1) the beginning, (2) movement toward confrontation, (3) compromise and harmony, (4) reassessment, and (5) resolution and recycling (p. 459–66). The basic theoretical tenets advanced by Napier and Gershenfeld represent an important synthesis of various theories.

The beginning represents the stage of group development where people tend to observe and gather as much information as possible about the group task and about other group members. Each group member joins a group with certain life experiences and personal expectations that may impact his or her ability to function in the group. The beginning represents a time of inhibition as well as a time of testing of group limits as norms and expectations are established by the group. This first stage of group development also represents a time when members are more security minded. This concern for security in the group guides each member into seeking to establish a role in which they will be comfortable. It is essential that the group not be pushed too quickly or group members will never fully adjust to the group and its task.

The second stage, a movement toward confrontation, is a normal result of group members becoming more comfortable and beginning to seek their individual areas of influence. Gaining power and recognition becomes important at this stage. Group roles become more entrenched and members begin to develop alliances and garner support for their personal agendas. The result of this newly found need for power and assertiveness is the creation of an air of caution, suspicion, and mistrust which can cripple the ability of a group to effectively function. Ideas and issues often become polarized as each member tests his or her influence to the limit. Some members become frustrated with the power needs of others and either lash out or withdraw in anger or disappointment. It is imperative that the focus on quality and the need for a productive team be maintained at this critical time. A few team members recognize the destructive bent of the group and by utilizing a variety of methods move the group to a third developmental stage. Some groups never move past the confrontation stage and continue to exist as a group but in actuality cease to function. One should not be afraid to step in when necessary to guide and assist a group so it may move forward. This requires a degree of skill and timing on the part of a leader.

The third stage as identified by Napier and Gershenfeld represents compromise and harmony. This stage is generally arrived at as group members recognize that a failure to compromise will result in a collapse of the group. Movement to this stage is often accomplished by members who serve as intermediaries between polarized members. Some utilize humor in dealing with the hostility that has been generated in previous group stages. Some members develop new alliances and effectively block those who have become overtly hostile and unproductive. Some team members model the behavior they desire from their colleagues (Maeroff 1993). Whatever method is chosen, this third stage finds the easing of group dissension with a greater acceptance of either individual or group deviation.

Group members actively collaborate with each other in this third stage. There is an overriding sense of caution as members overtly avoid any type of hostility. The group still seeks an open, honest atmosphere but couples this with concern for the whole group. Because there still may be a degree of underlying tension between some members, the group may fail to address important issues. Harmony for the sake of harmony can paralyze the group and hamper its effectiveness. A leader needs to be able to recognize any group inertia. This can be successfully accomplished by narrowing and restating the group charge as well as group parameters.

The fourth stage, reassessment, recognizes the group's establishment of new organizational and operational restrictions. If the organizational restraints are too tightly structured, overall problems of the group may continue to exist and multiply. Certainly, group decisions may be more efficiently formed with the new limitations, but underlying group interpersonal problems may continue to exist. There is frequently a level of fear that group conflict will begin anew. If conflict can be avoided, the group generally begins to accept and support concepts such as individual accountability, shared responsibility, and a more formalized division of labor.

The final stage as advanced by Napier and Gershenfeld (1985) is called resolution and recycling. The group is fairly mature, having survived the first four stages, and has an ability to resolve group problems. The level of productivity in the final stage is quite high. There generally is a positive feeling among group members toward both the task and each other. If conflict comes, the group is now better equipped to resolve it.

Whichever theory one accepts is not as important as the knowledge that groups are not static entities. A basic understanding of group development provides one with a sense of comprehension that is necessary if an organization is to adopt a total quality philosophy. This knowledge of group processes remains important as the group eventually develops strategies that communicate the quality concept. One who does not understand group developmental processes will often become frustrated and resort to coercive behavior in order to elicit quality. Coercion on the part of a leader inevitably results in group alienation, not the quality-oriented focus desired. A leader understands this and uses his or her knowledge of group theories as the means by which the organization can better be served.

ESTABLISHING GROUP PERFORMANCE PARAMETERS

A leader must be able to effectively utilize teams in order to develop a plan by which a total-quality, change-oriented approach can become a reality. He or she must also understand group development and how the various developmental stages of groups directly impacts the functioning of every team. A leader is obligated to guide the team in a collaborative quality-oriented approach. Yet, too often the area that creates the most difficulty for the productive functioning of a team is the inability to establish necessary team parameters or to develop an effective charge for the team.

A team should develop, with the assistance of all group members, a few ground rules that facilitate team development and task completion. These rules can include concepts such as attendance, promptness, participation, agendas, group behavior, and even group breaks. Once established, these should be clearly explained to all members of the team. These explicit rules (norms) coexist with other explicit and implicit norms that the team may also establish. The following are examples of group norms that can be useful:

- People should be listened to and recognized.

- Feelings are important. Team member *ideas* may be criticized, but not individual group members.

- Feelings, behaviors, and concerns of everyone in the group can be freely acknowledged and discussed.

- It is safe to say what you think in the team. Honesty is valued.

- Objectivity is encouraged and supported by all.

- The group learns from doing things, deciding on issues, and analyzing ideas.

A leader is well prepared for each group meeting. If he or she is not, this sends a strong message to group members that the task is not really an important one and that change does not matter. The use of a premeeting checklist can facilitate success of the team. Following are things that a leader can do to prepare for a group meeting:

- Focus on what specifically needs to be accomplished at each meeting.

- Remind all team members of the time, place, and purpose of the meeting as well as what members need to bring with them to the meeting.

- Reserve the meeting room; arrange it appropriately for the meeting.

- Prepare and distribute an agenda.

- Prepare the opening comments as well as the group charge.

- Develop a repertoire of ways and means to initiate participation, stimulate thinking, and create interest and support for vision development.

- Plan carefully and provide adequate time for the task.

- Gather any data that may be needed by the group as it begins working on the task at hand.

In addition to being thoroughly prepared for each meeting, all tasks must be clearly articulated to the team. Too often groups are established without an appropriate group charge and the group either creates its own or disintegrates as it attempts to do so. Group fragmentation can result when the group task has not been well formulated. The result of failing to provide clear organizational parameters for the group or an appropriate group charge is intense disillusionment by group members as they begin to perceive they are not really part of an improvement process. The group charge should specifically address what the group is to accomplish, develop, or design.

Scholtes (1988) provided an example, with some adaptation, of various components of a group charge, or mission. He indicated that a group charge should include the following:

- What is the process or problem to be studied by the team?

- What are the group's boundaries and limitations, especially as it pertains to time, money, and information (data) that can be provided?

- What type of quality improvements are to be made by the team, and to what degree?

- What levels of authority does the team possess in regards to coworkers, outside experts, information, and equipment?

- What outcomes or standards should result from the team's work, and how should they be focused?

- What decision-making authority will the team possess?

- How often will the team meet and when should the task be completed?

The group charge is structured so that no misunderstanding of purpose or task can later arise. It is best to reiterate the charge at each subsequent meeting so that every group member remains focused on the task. Even when the group charge is clearly stated, some members may still have difficulty in understanding or accepting the parameters and guidelines set by the charge. Questions should be asked of the team so that one may judge whether or not the group charge is understood. Clarity of purpose by the group guarantees success.

TEAM-BUILDING ACTIVITIES/ COLLABORATION

Team-building activities may be found from a multitude of sources, especially from the human resource development literature. It is not so much the activity selected but the intent of such an activity. A central goal of all team-building activities is to develop a sense of cohesiveness and esprit among the various team members. Team-building activities provide an opportunity for the team to grow stronger because the various members begin to recognize their diverse strengths and abilities. Team members begin to understand that united their strength and abilities far outweigh any individual efforts. This understanding and recognition is the true beginning of productive collaboration. Productive collaboration is the result of bonding between team members.

Team-building activities may be focused on several team-oriented attributes. Phillips and Elledge (1989) identified several objectives for team building. Some of the objectives include:

- Improving the effectiveness of a group in which members must work together to achieve results.

- Helping the work unit engage in a continuous process of self-examination.

- Developing a model of team effectiveness specifically designed to help the work unit.

- Providing an opportunity for the group, as a whole, to analyze its functioning, performance, strengths, and weaknesses.

- Identifying problem areas of team behavior and corrective actions to be taken.

- Developing a continuous process of team building. (p. 8)

Maeroff (1993) indicated that team building must be a first step in any schoolwide change process. Activities that build collaborative teams create a common language, a sense of cohesion and camaraderie that allows a team to be successful.

A repertory of warm-up activities and team-building exercises are useful because they provide several different ways to improve a team's productivity. Increased productivity is the result of a cohesive, collaborative team working toward a total-quality agenda.

GROUP ROLES: TOWARD COLLABORATION

Each group has its own personality and typically develops along the lines of one of the group theories previously identified. Within each team, individuals often choose a particular role. These roles often relate to the task or to the individual personalities and needs of a group member. It is important to recognize the types of roles that may exist in a group (see table 1). It is also important that a leader facilitate and support those roles that lend themselves to group productivity and task completion. Conversely, one needs to recognize those roles which may hinder the group. A set of strategies should be developed that may lessen the impact of negative roles on the group.

Table 1 lists only a portion of roles which may develop in a team. Team members may change roles and could project a more positive image at one time and a more negative one at a different time. One needs to understand that various roles may be exhibited in the team. It remains incumbent on the team leader to maintain focus on the group charge while nurturing those roles that assist the group to become productive. Understanding group roles allows one to successfully work with all team members to achieve organizational goals. A team leader should be able to maintain the focus of the team on the task at hand.

There are several methods which can be utilized by the leader in supporting the team's actions. The first, and foremost, method is to be prepared for each meeting. A second strategy is to utilize questions that will keep the team on task. An example of the type of questions that may be used are listed below. These questions can be used directly in conjunction with one's knowledge of team roles.

- **Factual Questions** gather needed information: "How many students. . . ?" and "Who are the. . . ?"

- **Leading Questions** are useful in getting opinions from the group: "What if. . . ?" and "How about. . . ?"

- **Alternative Questions** often elicit a yes or no answer that can then be followed up by

ROLES THAT FACILITATE TEAM BUILDING

The Gate-Keeper	Keeps communications open; encourages participation.
The Encourager	Praises and supports others; friendly; encouraging.
The Harmonizer	Mediates differences; reconciles points of view.
The Compromiser	Willing to yield when necessary for progress.
The Tension Reliever	Uses humor or calls for breaks at appropriate times to reduce negative activities.
The Summarizer	Reviews discussion, pulls it together.
The Tester	Raises questions to "test out" whether the team is ready to come to a decision.
The Clarifier	Gives relevant examples; offers rationale; probes for meaning; restates problems.
The Elaborator	Builds on suggestions of others.
The Opinion Giver	States pertinent beliefs about discussion and others' suggestions.
The Initiator	Suggests new or different ideas for discussion and approaches to problems.
The Opinion Seeker	Carefully seeks ideas and encourages the participation of all the team.
The Evaluator	Dispassionately views group ideas and logically utilizes them without negatively impacting team members.
The Procedural Expert	Understands how the organization functions and understands various rules and regulations.
The Energizer	Provides energy, motivation, and drive to the team.

ROLES THAT HINDER TEAM BUILDING

The Devil's Advocate	More devil than advocate; takes the team off task.
The Self-Confessor	Talks irrelevantly about his or her own feelings.
The Playboy or Playgirl	Wastes group's time showing off; storyteller; nonchalant; cynical.
The Special-Interest Pleader	Uses group's time to plead his or her own case.
The Dominator	Tries to assert authority, manipulate group.
The Topic Jumper	Keeps changing the subject and focus of the team.
The Recognition Seeker	Boasts; talks excessively; conscious of his or her status; seeks to be the center of attention.
The Withdrawer	Won't participate; "wool gatherer"; converses privately; self-appointed note-taker.
The Blocker	Stubbornly disagrees; rejects others' views; returns to topics already resolved.
The Aggressor	Criticizes others; disagrees with others aggressively.
The Sympathizer	Attempts to garner the team's sympathy by complaining, confessing, or condemning certain activities of the organization.

Table 1   Common Group Roles

"Why?" or "What?" or "How?" Examples: "Do you agree. . . ?" and "Do you think this. . . ?"

- **Ambiguous Questions** often have more than one meaning: "Could we. . . ?" and "Would it be possible to. . . ?"

- **Provocative/Controversial Questions** are designed to get a reaction from the members of the group that often provides the leader with insight into their values and beliefs: "You know that. . . ?" and "What if we did not. . . ?

Questions may also be asked in a variety of ways to group members. They may be "nebulous" and not asked of any particular person within the team. Questions may also be "front end" loaded. This type of question typically begins with a person's name and then a question. These questions can be useful in refocusing an individual or in helping him or her get on task. A problem with this type of question is that some members automatically stop listening once they hear the person's name called and realize that the question is not intended for them. Questions also may be "rear end" loaded. This type of question places the name of the recipient of the question at the end. A rear end loaded question is useful because it maintains the whole group's attention to the question since no one knows who is going to be called upon until the name is spoken. The usefulness of such tactics is that they assist in keeping the team focused and on task.

BUILDING CONSENSUS AND HANDLING CONFLICT

All groups eventually experience conflict. That conflict may come early in the development of the group or it may happen when the group is highly productive. Conflict in itself is neither good or bad. It does have the potential to be destructive or constructive, and that is what is important. One should recognize that conflict is normal and diligently attempt to keep any conflict constructive. An effective leader realizes that organizations, groups, and individuals mature when conflict is successfully addressed and resolved.

Constructive conflict provides an opportunity for team growth. Constructive conflict often cen-

ters around disagreements on goals, methods to achieve goals, values, and group focus. It may result when there is an unequal distribution of information between group members or because of disagreements on how to meet individual needs in the group. Constructive conflict can be resolved by utilizing open group discussions and compromise. One should never mandate that constructive conflict cease. If this is done, it only allows for disagreements to remain suppressed, which may eventually erupt into destructive conflict.

Destructive conflict has little or no potential for improving the team, its members, or the organization. Destructive conflict can be the result of feelings such as pettiness, jealousy, immaturity, uncertainty, or indefensible feelings of injustice. Symptoms include heightened tension, frustration, threats, withdrawal by group members, verbal attacks, and intense anger. Conflicts that can destroy the team's capability to effectively function must be handled swiftly by the leader and resolved so the group can continue to function.

When conflict arises one may respond in several ways. He or she may ignore it and hope that the conflict will eventually extinguish itself. This rarely succeeds, especially if it is destructive conflict. The second, more viable, choice is to confront the conflict. The steps for resolving a conflict are quite simple but do require a degree of patience and tenacity on the part of all involved. First, the conflict must be openly acknowledged. It must then be examined by the team. One must be able to accurately state the nature of the conflict to the group. This is where team members can also be extremely helpful. They may possess an insight into the problem that a leader may not have. Once the nature of the conflict has been clarified, it is then necessary to determine if there are any areas of agreement between those in conflict. All points of disagreement must also be recognized at this time. The next step is to generate as many alternatives as possible to resolve the conflict and then reach an agreement as to which alternative can best be utilized to resolve the situation. The goal is to compromise as necessary and establish a win-win situation so that there are no real losers in the conflict. An action plan is developed using the chosen alternative. The plan is then summarized to the team and a firm commitment from group members to implement the resolution strategy is solicited. The plan is implemented and the conflict hopefully resolved. The team may then move on to future challenges as it fulfills its responsibilities as established in its charge. Resolving a conflict should not be seen as a power play by anyone, but rather a means to maintain team productivity.

A leader must possess the skills of listening, conceptualizing, interpreting, responding, and synthesizing in order to successfully resolve conflict. He or she must also have a sense of timing and communication abilities. It is important to know when to introduce structure, use authority, defer or ignore, seek consensus, and show concern. A leader needs the ability to be descriptive, forthright, and patient throughout the resolution process.

One must be able to recognize some of the typical problems that can lead to conflict. Some of these potential problems can be avoided if the team understands its task and how it is to accomplish it. Table 2 lists typical problems that can generate conflict.

If a conflict is not resolved, the group may eventually cease to function. The ability to recognize

---

PROBLEMS THAT CAN GENERATE CONFLICT

Personality conflicts	Lack of openness and trust, underlying tension, racism, and sexism.
Poor meeting environments	Can't hear, can't see, too stuffy.
Communication problems	Not listening to or understanding what others are saying, or making faulty assumptions.
General negativity and lack of challenge	There is nothing we can do about it, so why try?
Problem avoidance	Everything is fine. There are no problems around here.
Unresolved questions of power and authority	Do we have the authority to make this decision?
Confused objectives and expectations	Why did you call the meeting and what is the team supposed to be doing? Hidden agendas.
Win/lose approaches to decision-making	Partial solutions, compromises, polarization, and low commitment.
Repetition and wheel-spinning	Going over same old ideas.
Data overload	Holding on to too many ideas in your head at one time.
Unclear roles and responsibilities	Who is supposed to be doing what?
Traffic problem	Difficulty in leaping into the conversational flow and getting a chance to participate.
Personal attack	Attacking individuals rather than their ideas.
Confusion between process and content	Are we talking about how to discuss the topic or what topic to discuss?
Multiheaded animal syndrome	Everybody going off in different directions at the same time.

Table 2   Typical Problems That Can Lead to Conflict in Groups

whether the conflict is constructive or destructive is vital. It is just as important that one know how to effectively mediate a destructive situation so that the group can continue to grow and be productive. A good leader recognizes situations that have the potential to develop into conflicts and seeks to resolve such problems before they escalate. One does not seek conflict nor does one shy away from it. Indeed, conflict is inevitable, but the appropriate use of consensus-building activities can diminish the number of conflict situations that may take place.

It is important that all team members understand the concept of consensus building. One may have to instruct the team members in how to develop a consensus. It is important that some degree of consensus be reached by the team. Some basic guidelines for developing consensus may be useful. Consensus is often difficult to reach and is time consuming. Not every decision will meet with everyone's complete approval. Consensus helps identify those areas on which team members can at least partially agree. To reach consensus, team members should keep the following in mind:

- Avoid arguing blindly for your own opinions. Present your position as clearly and logically as possible, but listen to other members' reactions and consider them carefully before you press your point.

- Discuss underlying assumptions, listen carefully to one another, and encourage the participation of all members.

- Seek out differences of opinion. They are natural and expected. Try to involve everyone in the decision process. Disagreements can improve the group's decision because a wide range of information and opinions improves the chances of the group hitting upon more adequate solutions.

- Do not assume that someone must win and someone must lose when discussion reaches a stalemate. Instead, look for the next most acceptable alternative for all members.

- Avoid changing your mind just to reach agreement and avoid conflict. Support only solutions you are able to agree with to at least

some degree. Yield only to positions that have objective and logically sound foundations.

- Avoid conflict-reducing procedures such as majority voting, tossing a coin, averaging, and bargaining.

Consensus building is not easy, but it is an important element for all teams to seek to achieve. Consensus strengthens a team's focus and facilitates a quality approach.

CONCLUSION

The quality paradigm is rapidly becoming an essential component of the reform movement in education. As it becomes obvious that a total quality philosophy is a key to true school improvement, it becomes imperative that collaborative activities and team building become a priority for school personnel. Teams, if productive, provide an opportunity for educators to unite in creating an atmosphere for positive change. It is important to remember that Hall and Hord, in their book *Change in Schools: Facilitating the Process* (1984), determined that after a year-long attempt at implementing a new program that required systematic change, 65 percent were at a mechanical-use level and only 5 percent were at a refinement level of the program. This illustrates the difficulty in bringing about change and achieving quality. Effective teams are part of the solution to a difficult task.

Maeroff (1993) identified several ways for teams to contribute to school change and quality. According to him, teams can assist in establishing priorities; can model quality-oriented behaviors; can "spread ownership throughout the school community"; can be a positive influence; and can react appropriately to negative reactions (p. 517–18). Appropriate team-building efforts create a climate of collaboration and a commitment to organizational goals.

Effective collaborative teams are able to achieve positive change in the workplace. The effort to build such teams is worth it when one considers the result. That result—a quality education for all children—is mandatory for the United States to survive in the twenty-first century.

REFERENCES

Chance, E. W. 1992. *Visionary leadership in schools: Successful strategies for developing and implementing an educational vision.* Springfield, Ill.: Charles C. Thomas.

Cohen, A. M., and R. D. Smith. 1976. *Critical incidents in growth groups: Theory and technique.* La Jolla, Calif.: University Associates.

Hall, G. E., and S. M. Hord. 1984. *Change in schools: Facilitating the process.* Albany: State University of New York Press.

Hord, S. M., W. L. Rutherford, L. Huling-Austin, and G. E. Hall. 1987. *Taking charge of change.* Alexandria, Va.: Association for Supervision and Curriculum Development.

Maeroff, G. I. 1993. Building teams to rebuild schools. *Phi Delta Kappan* 74 (7): 512–19.

Napier, R. W., and M. K. Gershenfeld. 1985. *Groups: Theory and experience.* Boston: Houghton-Mifflin.

Phillips, S. L., and R. L. Elledge. 1989. *The team-building source book.* San Diego, Calif.: University Associates.

Scholtes, P. R. 1988. *The team handbook: How to use teams to improve quality.* Madison, Wis.: Joiner Associates.

Tuckman, B. W., and M. A. C. Jensen. 1977. Stages of small group development revisited. *Groups and Organizational Studies* 2 (4): 419–27.

Wellins, R. S., W. C. Byham, and J. M. Wilson. 1991. *Empowered teams.* San Francisco: Jossey-Bass.

THE ROLE OF ASSESSMENT IN EDUCATION SYSTEMS

—

Joe B. Hansen

Inherent in the general assessment standards is an assumption that all evaluation processes should use multiple assessment techniques that are aligned with the curriculum and consider the purpose of an assessment.

—*NCTM Standards*

Just as all true *systems* need a regulatory mechanism to provide a cybernetic feedback loop that helps maintain their dynamic equilibrium, all educational systems have a need for an assessment subsystem to provide timely and appropriate feedback on the extent to which students are attaining the system's desired learning and skill outcomes. An assessment subsystem must have a clear purpose within the educational suprasystem it serves or it will fail to provide the vital information needed for the suprasystem to successfully accomplish its purpose. If the assessment subsystem is operating within a hierarchical system, as most educational suprasystems currently are, it must provide all the assessment data required by the suprasystem at each of the levels of the hierarchy, and it must provide these data in a timely manner. Furthermore, the information derived from these data must be capable of being interpreted at the level of detail required by the decision-making functions at each level of the hierarchy within the suprasystem, and it must satisfy the purposes for which it is needed at each given level. An assess-

ment subsystem designed to satisfy these requirements is an essential consideration for any systemic educational restructuring effort. Without one, the system being restructured will be unable to gauge the effects of the restructuring effort on student performance and may drift far off its intended course. In this sense, the assessment subsystem can serve as a navigational compass for the system.

A PURPOSE-DRIVEN ASSESSMENT MODEL

In this chapter I will describe a conceptual model for an assessment subsystem that is based on recognizing the purposes of assessment data at each level of an education system. There are many purposes for assessment, from screening and selecting students for special programs to summative program evaluation. The model presented here is derived from an analysis of assessment purposes and a partitioning of all assessments into three basic categories: norm-referenced tests (NRTs), goal-referenced tests (GRTs),[1] and performance-based assessments

(PBAs). I refer to this as the Purpose-Driven Assessment Model (PDAM) (Hansen 1992). The PDAM is illustrated in figure 1.

The PDAM is based on the philosophy that multiple assessments are essential in any assessment subsystem in order to ensure that there is an appropriate assessment tool available to meet each of the diverse purposes for which assessment may be needed. Additionally, multiple assessments provide a means of cross-checking for validity. Ideally, no decision should be made regarding the achievement or skill level of any student on the basis of a single assessment. This is especially true if the decision bears great consequences for the life of the student. A decision that has serious consequences is said to be a "high-stakes decision." High-stakes decisions involve determinations such as passage to the next grade or graduation from one level of

school to the next. Generally speaking, the greater the stakes in any student-focused decision, the greater the need for multiple measures. This view is shared by the National Council on Educational Standards and Testing (NCEST).

The NCEST endorses the establishment of high national standards for student performance and a system of assessments to measure performance against those standards. The recommended system of assessments should have two components—individual student assessments and a large-scale sample assessment (such as the National Assessment of Educational Progress). Further, the system of assessments should have

> multiple methods of measuring progress, not a single test; the system must be voluntary, not mandatory; and the system must be developmental, not static. (NCEST, p. 4)

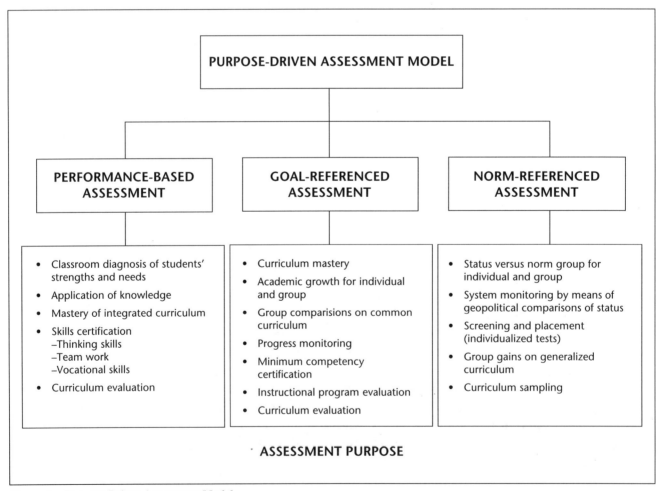

Figure 1   Purpose-Driven Assessment Model

The NCEST has taken a leadership role in advocating multiple methods of assessment, voluntarily applied in a dynamic and responsible manner. The philosophy expressed by the NCEST recommendations is highly similar to that which underlies the PDAM.

The PDAM is based on an analysis of assessment type by purpose patterned after Stiggins and Bridgeford (1985), Stiggins (1987), and Airasian (1984). This analysis lists common purposes of assessment and examines each of the three basic types of assessments in the model in terms of their appropriateness for each purpose, resulting in an analytic framework as shown in table 1.

Table 1 illustrates typical uses of each of a number of different types of assessments. A more detailed analysis of the types of information needed for each purpose and the characteristics of each type of assessment will verify that this table depicts appropriate usage. Obviously, the issue of purpose of assessment is complex and cannot be dealt with in a quick or superficial manner without substantial risk of oversimplification. Nonetheless, any analysis of assessment applications that begins with the question of purpose is likely to lead to more appropriate and effective uses of assessment than one that does not take purpose into account. Therefore, I view the PDAM not as the ultimate answer, but as a necessary foundation upon which a comprehensive assessment subsystem can be constructed.

GOAL-REFERENCED TESTING

The centerpiece of the PDAM is an item-bank-based, Rasch-calibrated[2] GRT subsystem, developed and marketed by the Northwest Education Association (NWEA). This computer-managed item bank contains more than ten thousand calibrated items. It has been used in numerous school systems to develop a series of overlapping levels of tests in selected content areas (reading, language arts, and mathematics) that measure the most significant outcomes, as determined by a group of master teachers. The levels tests, illustrated in figure 2, are suitable for students in grades three through nine. Because these tests follow a curricu-

PURPOSE OF ASSESSMENT	TYPE OF ASSESSMENT		
	Performance-Based	Goal-Referenced	Norm-Referenced
Pupil selection and placement	X	X	X
Grouping for instruction	X	X	X
Diagnosis of instructional need	X	X	
Evaluation of achievement or growth			
• Group		X	X
• Individual	X	X	
Instructional program evaluation			
• Program efficacy	X	X	
• Identify strengths and weaknesses		X	X
Curriculum evaluation			
• Fidelity of instruction	X	X	
• Efficacy	X	X	
• Strengths and weaknesses		X	X
Certification of skills or knowledge	X	X	
Geopolitical comparisons with other schools, districts, states, or nations			X

Table 1   Analytic Framework for Assessment Type by Purpose of Assessment

lar continuum on which the degree of difficulty varies as you move to higher levels, one can, theoretically, predict whether a student's future performance will be at, above, or below a predetermined standard. This is a highly desirable feature for a proficiency assessment in the core curricular areas because it allows for an early-warning system for students in danger of not meeting predefined proficiency standards. Many states have now mandated that local school systems implement performance standards or a proficiency-based approach to education, including a system of proficiency assessment.

The levels testing system is operational in major school systems, including those of Alameda, California, and Portland, Oregon; the Colorado Springs Public Schools; and the Thompson Valley

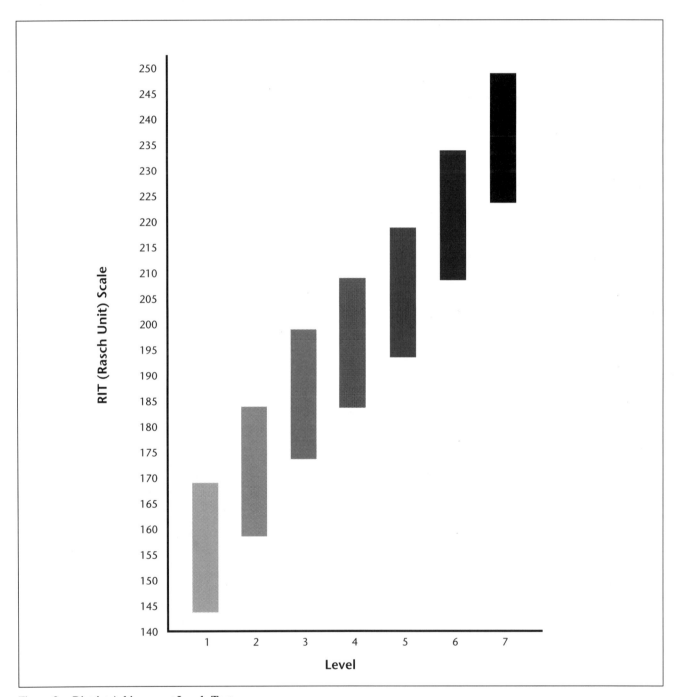

Figure 2   District Achievement Levels Tests

School District in Colorado. In the two Colorado districts, the levels tests are the primary means of assessing proficiencies and certifying that students have met predetermined content standards, as required by state law. Benchmark scores on the levels tests are established by using key points that correspond to expert teacher judgments about what students should know and be able to do at grades four, eight, and ten in the key disciplines of mathematics, reading, and language arts. The law requires that by January 1, 1997, districts establish content standards in six primary disciplines—reading, mathematics, language arts, history, geography, and science. It also requires that they have an assessment system for certifying attainment of those standards by January 1, 1999.

Purpose of the Levels Tests

The levels-test approach provides direct measures of knowledge acquisition and skill attainment based on the goals of the curriculum. The fundamental purpose of levels tests is to provide data on goal attainment by individual pupil, class, grade, and school groups. They are used for the following testing situations:

- accountability pre- and posttesting for state-mandated school improvement programs

- program and instructional effectiveness evaluation

- assessment of student proficiencies at designated grade levels as required by state law

Assessment techniques can also be evaluated by their information yield, validity, reliability, cost-per-pupil use, ease of use, and instructional value. My analysis of the three major assessment types based on these criteria has led me to conclude that, overall, GRTs have the best balance. This may be due, in part, to the relative dearth of experience we have with PBAs in the educational assessment world. Perhaps as we gain experience we will find satisfactory ways to improve reliability, generalizability, fairness, verification of validity assumptions, and reduction of costs, while sustaining high information yields and driving instruction toward more complex, integrated curriculum and higher cognitive levels.

PERFORMANCE-BASED ASSESSMENTS

Since the current wave of educational reform began with the publication of *A Nation at Risk* in 1983, there has been a clamor in education for changes in the way student achievement is assessed. This clamor for change is characterized by the criticisms of Cannell (1989), Neill and Medina (1989), and others of the inadequacies of standardized multiple-choice tests. These criticisms have led to a major movement toward performance-based assessments as the ultimate solution to many, if not all, of education's ills, either real or imagined. This trend toward PBAs and away from more-traditional forms of assessment is a powerful influence on the current wave of school reform.

Performance-based assessments are not new. Indeed, they have been with us for generations in one form or another. However, in recent years, the call for more-authentic approaches to assessment (Wiggins 1989, 1990) has led to a proliferation of PBAs. More-authentic assessment means that the assessments should simulate the conditions that students would experience in applying their knowledge or skills in the real world. Many advocates of PBAs claim that they are better suited for assessing more complex, cognitive processes, or so-called higher-order thinking skills.

As defined by Archibald and Newmann (1988), authentic assessments must meet three criteria: production of discourses, things, or performances; flexible use of time; and collaboration. These authors also indicate that an authentic-assessment task should be worthwhile, significant, and meaningful and should provide substantive information. These assessments require students to demonstrate what they know and can do rather than just select a "correct" answer from a list of alternatives. Therefore, these assessments are performance based. They have diverse, varied formats dictated by the skill or knowledge being tested (Hansen and Hathaway 1993).

Performance assessment was defined by Berk (1986) in the following manner: "Performance assessment is the process of gathering data by systematic observation for making decisions about an individual." This definition contains five key elements that distinguish performance assessment from other types of assessment:

- It is a *process*.

- Its focus is on *data gathering*.

- Data are collected by *systematic observation*.

- Data are used for *making decisions*.

- Decisions are about an *individual*.

Stiggins (1993) identifies two separate disciplines of assessment: "trickle-up" assessment, which begins at the classroom level and focuses on the individual student's progress in attaining the outcomes established by the teacher, and "trickle-down" assessment, which serves the information needs of policy makers and administrators. Trickle-down assessments tend to be used for higher-stakes decisions than the trickle-up variety; therefore, they should be subjected to more rigorous technical standards. In the classroom setting a teacher has many opportunities to assess an individual student, collect assessment data, and form judgments; therefore, each individual assessment carries less weight. Errors in judgment will occur, but they are more likely to be ameliorated by the multiple-assessment opportunities in the classroom than if they were made in a high-stakes assessment, such as that of proficiency or diploma certification.

Performance-based assessments come in many varieties, and an analysis that accurately depicts one may not exactly fit another, depending on the specific characteristics of the assessment tool in question. For example, given the purpose of summative program evaluation and three types of PBAs—portfolio assessment, direct-writing assessment using an analytic trait model, and oral presentation—it would be easier to obtain results that meet specific criteria of validity, reliability, and aggregability using the analytic trait model than with either of the other two approaches. (This is illustrated in table 2.) Thus, another dimension of analysis is needed, that of criteria for judging the quality of the PBAs. Arter (1990) and Linn, Baker, and Dunbar (1991) have addressed this issue from different perspectives. Arter deals with "metarubrics" for determining the desired characteristics of a scoring rubric. Linn et al. propose eight appropriate criteria for determining the validity of performance assessments: consequences, fairness, transfer and generalizability, cognitive complexity, content quality, content coverage, meaningfulness, and cost and efficiency. This issue of quality standards for PBAs is crucial to the long-term viability of the trend away from the traditional forms of assessment and toward these alternative approaches. This trend is rooted in discontentment with traditional assessments and is based on unverified assumptions that PBAs will automatically result in higher-quality assessment that will, in turn, drive higher-quality instruction. Potentially disastrous consequences could result from replacing valid and reliable traditional measures with poorly designed performance measures deficient in reliability, validity, generalizability, and fairness. Far more research is needed to assure that these assessment techniques meet the highest possible standards of technical quality and rigor.

Under the PDAM, performance-based assessments are viewed as being most useful and effective at the classroom level. Here, the teacher, interacting with the student, can benefit from the greater depth of detail in the information produced and can have access to multiple opportunities for assessment. As the assessment of individual pupil performance moves toward larger-scale group assessments, a number of issues arise that pose difficulties in the use of certain PBAs, such as portfolios. These issues include aggregation of data and the managing and reporting of data. In my experience in working with teachers on the development of such assessments, teachers tend to have little concern for these problems because their focus is, quite appropriately, on helping individual students. This problem stems in part from the fact that the teachers themselves have little or no formal assessment training; therefore, they lack a fundamental understanding of the need for technical quality in assessments they use.

I strongly advocate three key elements as essential components of PBAs: (1) complex, challenging assessment tasks that engage students' interests; (2) well-defined scoring rubrics; and (3) careful

	PORTFOLIO ASSESSMENT	ANALYTIC TRAIT WRITING ASSESSMENT	DEMONSTRATION BY ORAL PRESENTATION
STRENGTH	Provides rich, detailed picture of student development Drives instruction in a positive manner consistent with adopted curriculum Encourages teacher-student interaction	Provides quantitative data on multiple traits Drives instruction in positive manner, based on writing process Relatively high reliability, compared to other performance assessments Easily aggregated data	Corresponds more closely to real-life situation Encourages integration of skills and knowledge across disciplines
WEAKNESS	Difficult to quantify or aggregate without compromising the holistic-qualitative concept of portfolio Reliability questionable Can be very subjective if standards are not present and used Reliability can be a problem Validity is assumed, but not readily measurable	Some educators may find it too reductionistic Some may find it too structured or rigid instructionally	Interrater reliability is questionable unless a well-defined scoring rubric exists and judges are well trained Data can be difficult to aggregate Predictive validity is assumed, but not known Construct validity is assumed, but not known

Table 2   Analysis of Three Performance-Based Assessments as Tools for Summative Program Evaluation

training of raters in the use of rubrics. These are essential features for maintaining minimally acceptable levels of cognitive complexity, objectivity, reliability, and facilitation of validity. The type of PBA with which educators have the most experience and familiarity is direct-writing assessment (DWA).

DWA is a means of assessing student writing performance by obtaining writing samples produced in response to a common writing prompt given to all students. The most common forms of DWA, based on the methods used for scoring the samples, are holistic, primary trait, and analytic trait.

Holistic scoring is based on the precept that the whole is greater than the sum of its parts and that good writing cannot be decomposed into specific and discrete components for the purposes of scor-

ing. Instead, a piece of writing must be judged based on the total impression it gives the reader. Scoring may be done on a multipoint scale, but the entire piece is to be judged as a whole. Technical issues and mechanics such as spelling and punctuation are taken into account as they affect the overall impression of the rater. Raters are trained using anchor papers that represent points on the scale (e.g., this paper is a "1," this is a "3," and so on).

Primary-trait scoring is focused on the single most important trait or characteristic of the paper. For example, the purpose of the paper might be to persuade someone to vote for a certain candidate. The persuasiveness of the paper is therefore the primary trait. Scoring is done in a similar fashion to the holistic approach, but raters may be instructed not to rate on mechanical and technical errors such as punctuation, spelling, or even minor grammatical errors.

Analytic-trait scoring is multidimensional. A paper may be rated on several traits. Analytic-trait models vary in the number of specific traits they define. Some may use as few as four, others as many as ten. Regardless of the type of scoring system used, each paper should be scored separately for each of the traits by at least two raters. In cases of wide disparity between the two raters, a third rater is usually asked to rate the paper.

An excellent example of the DWA model is the six-trait analytic model (Spandel and Stiggins 1990). The traits of the model are

- ideas/content
- organization
- voice
- word choice
- sentence fluency
- writing conventions

The model also embodies four writing modes: descriptive, persuasive, expository, and poetry. Modes are selected based on the curriculum and the developmental level of students. A paper is written in response to a standard prompt for a specific mode and then scored on each trait. The DWA six-trait analytic model has been in use in many school districts in the Pacific Northwest for more than a decade.

CURRICULUM-BASED ASSESSMENT

Occasionally, there is a need for a short, easy-to-administer assessment that will provide a teacher with accurate information on a student's degree of fluency in reading, mathematical computation, or spelling. Specific application of such an assessment includes the special-education child-study process, Chapter 1 compensatory education, and any situation that might require remedial instruction in the basic skills. For these purposes, the PDAM employs curriculum-based assessments (CBAs). Using CBAs, a teacher can obtain data on how well a student is

doing in reaching specific skill-level targets that have been set for him or her. The focal point of interest here is the number of errors within a specific unit of time, such as three minutes. For example, a reduction in miscalled words while reading aloud for three minutes would indicate progress in word recognition. The CBA's value is limited to use with special populations and remedial instruction, but within those parameters it can be a very useful assessment device for teachers to use in monitoring student progress on a continuous basis.

PORTFOLIO ASSESSMENT

Portfolio assessment is less well defined at the present time than is DWA. A portfolio may take on many different forms, from a cumulative folder of student work to a videotape containing segments of student performances and work samples selected to demonstrate the student's best work or to illustrate progress. Computerized portfolios are also beginning to appear, some using CD-ROM and other advanced technology. Such technological sophistication is still beyond the reach of most school districts because of its high cost.

The NWEA has developed a portfolio model based on the following definition:

> A portfolio is a purposeful collection of student work that exhibits the student's efforts, progress, and achievements in one or more areas. The collection must include student participation in
> - selecting the contents
> - determining the criteria for selection
> - determining the criteria for judging merit
> - evidence of student self-reflection (Paulson, Paulson, and Meyer 1991)

This model is based on the belief that assessment should be an interactive process between teacher and student and that student involvement in the selection of pieces to include in the portfolio is crucial to the student's motivation. Teachers using this model are encouraged to conduct review sessions with students, individually, to dialogue about the portfolio and reflect "metacognitively" on its contents. Students may be expected to write a metacognitive letter in which they explain why they selected a particular piece for their portfolio and what the piece means to them personally.

NORM-REFERENCED TESTING

NRTs have been subjected to much criticism in recent years and I will not repeat that criticism here, but it seems appropriate to cite some of NRT's more commonly identified strengths and weaknesses. Their most frequently cited weaknesses include a focus on lower-order cognitive skills, such as memorization, factual recall, and lower-order reasoning skills, and a tendency to influence teachers to teach to these skills rather than to focus on more-challenging, cognitively complex curriculum. In spite of these purported deficiencies, NRTs remain a highly cost-effective way to obtain data on the performance of a large group of students on a broad range of curriculum outcomes, where the standard of comparison is the performance of the [national] norming group. Such information has an important role in an assessment subsystem because it provides a reference point for determining whether or not a particular group of students is performing at a level commensurate with their peers on commonly accepted outcomes. Changes in recent editions of NRTs produced by major test publishers have resulted in an increased emphasis on measuring more-complex cognitive skills, such as analysis, interpretation, and integration.

Many states have recently enacted legislation or accreditation regulations that require the annual testing of students, if only on a sampling basis. They use a norm-referenced test in order to facilitate comparisons between schools and districts within the state and between that state's students and the national norming population. Although the use of test data in this manner is inherently political and fails to take into account myriad input and context variables that may affect students' scores, it serves a commonly perceived need of policy makers and the general public. GRTs and PBAs are not well understood by legislators, business people, and the general public; therefore, it may take several years before those groups recog-

nize these types of assessment as legitimate indicators of student skills and knowledge. Thus, there is a strong need to train teachers and educate parents and the rest of the public on the uses and limitations of various assessment types. In the meantime, NRTs will continue to be used to satisfy the need for making these geopolitical comparisons. The PDAM recognizes this need and includes NRTs as one of the three major types of assessments.

In summary, the PDAM is a model assessment subsystem that comprises three different types of assessment—norm referenced, goal referenced, and performance based—each of which has a specific role to perform in providing data on students' knowledge and skills for decision making based on the purpose for which the data are needed. Examples of specific assessment purposes and types of assessments used for each purpose are summarized in table 3. The decision regarding which type of assessment to use for a particular purpose should be based on the following: the depth versus the breadth of information required; the time and cost involved in developing and using the assessment technique; the degree of accuracy required in the assessment results; and the consequences of the decision(s) to be made from the data.

The data collected under the PDAM are differentiated by level, from the individual student in the classroom setting to districtwide data. At the classroom level there is a need for rich, detailed data on what individual students know and are able to do; therefore, PBAs are most useful in the everyday instructional process of making decisions about whether a student has adequately mastered more-complex cognitive tasks and content. As you zoom out of the classroom to view the decision-making needs of the school and the district, the need for aggregated data becomes more important. Therefore, the PBAs are decreasingly useful and cost effective, while GRTs and NRTs are increasingly useful. GRTs provide useful data for both individual students and groups of students on attainment of specific outcomes that are inherent to the curriculum. They can be used for proficiency certification in those situations where the proficiencies are measurable by means of the multiple-choice format. As the need for data on more-

ASSESSMENT PURPOSE	PURPOSE-DRIVEN ASSESSMENT
Assessing student proficiencies in mathematics, reading, and language arts	District achievement levels tests, grades 3 through 9 Performance-based assessments at grades 4, 8, and 12
Assessing student proficiencies in general science and social sciences	Performance-based assessments at grades 4, 8, and 12
Evaluating student mastery of course-level subject matter for grades 10–12 in mathematics, humanities, science, and social sciences	Districtwide course-level tests and performance-based assessments
Selection and placement of students for special education and compensatory education, grades 2–9	Curriculum-based measurement
Monitoring progress of special education and remedial students in mathematics, reading, and writing, grades 2–9	Curriculum-based measurement, portfolio assessment
Assessing student growth across subjects, primary (K–3) level	District-level tests Portfolio assessment
Assessing student growth in writing, grades 3–9	Direct-writing assessment—six-trait analytical model
Evaluating language arts curriculum, grades 3–9	DWA–six-trait model
Certified diploma, assessing student attainment of exit outcomes, and content standards	Written expression: DWA–six-trait model Mathematics: levels tests, specific course content in mathematics, science, social sciences Course-level tests to be developed
Evaluation of Javits Vocational Education Grant Program	Employability and literacy skills: Portfolio system to be developed for grades 9–12
Meeting state and federal requirements for comparing performance of schools and programs against publisher norms	Norm-referenced tests

Table 3   Summary of Purposes for Assessment and Corresponding Types of Assessments Used in the PDAM

complex cognitive tasks increases, GRTs diminish in their usefulness and must be supplemented with PBAs. NRTs remain most useful for comparing group performance against that of a national sample of students. This serves a commonly perceived accountability need.

SUMMARY

In this chapter, I have introduced a model assessment subsystem and discussed the vital role of assessment in an education system that is striving to become more open and responsible toward its environment and the needs of its clients. An assessment subsystem is a critical component of an education system and it should be designed to provide valid, reliable, and timely information for decision makers at all levels of the system, as well as for the broader educational community served by the system. There is a strong need for an understanding of the role of assessment in an education system and the relationship between the characteristics of a particular assessment type and the purposes for which assessment data are being collected. A well-designed assessment subsystem based on multiple assessments can serve as a navigational compass for keeping the educational ship on course.

All too often in education there is a tendency for a bandwagon effect to develop, wherein practically everyone flocks to become involved with the latest innovative practice, regardless of its appropriateness for their situation. Performance-based assessment is such a phenomenon. We must temper our zeal for this phenomenon or face the risk of turning it into one more educational fad that will pass from the scene as so many before it have. More research is needed to guide the development of quality control standards for PBAs before they become widely relied upon for high-stakes decisions. The PDAM is an assessment subsystem based on multiple assessments that help guarantee all decisions based on its use are well grounded in valid, reliable data.

Understanding an education system in systems-theory terms and recognizing the role of an assessment subsystem as an essential tool for obtaining feedback on student performance with respect to important learning outcomes can help educational reformers make the most appropriate use of this innovation and avoid the pitfall of faddism.

NOTES

1. I have chosen to use the term *goal-referenced* rather than the more traditional term *criterion-referenced* because it has been my observation that many so-called criterion-referenced tests are goal- or objective-referenced tests that are not used in conjunction with any particular criterion of performance. Therefore, they are misnamed.

2. Rasch calibration—sometimes referred to as the single-parameter, item-response model—takes its name from the Danish mathematician George Rasch, who developed the method of scaling test items based on their log-item easiness. This method of scaling assigns a value to an item based on its position on a continuum of difficulty on the underlying educational trait, such as reading skill.

REFERENCES

Airasian, P. 1984. Classroom assessment and educational improvement. Keynote address for conference, Classroom Assessment: A Key to Educational Excellence, at Northwest Regional Educational Laboratory, Portland, Oreg.

Archibald, D., and F. Newmann. 1988. *Beyond standardized testing: Assessing authentic academic achievement in the secondary school.* Reston, Va.: National Association of Secondary School Principals.

Arter, J. 1990. Developing a scoring guide (Meta-rubric). Working paper, Northwest Regional Educational Laboratory, Portland, Oreg.

Berk, R. 1986. *Performance assessment: Methods and applications.* Baltimore: Johns Hopkins University Press.

Cannell, J. 1989. *How public educators cheat on standardized tests.* Albuquerque, N. Mex.: Friends for Education.

Hansen, J. B. 1992. Purpose-driven assessment. Presentation at symposium, Multidimensional Assessment Models, at the annual meeting of American Educational Research Association, San Francisco.

Hansen, J. B., and W. E. Hathaway. 1993. *A survey of more authentic assessment practices.* Washington, D.C.: American Institutes for Research.

Hermann, J. J. 1992. Total quality management basics: TQM comes to school. *School Business Affairs,* April, 20–28.

Linn, R., E. Baker, and S. Dunbar. 1991. Complex, performance-based assessment: Expectations and validation criteria. *Educational Researcher* 20 (8): 15–21.

Neill, M., and N. Medina. 1989. Standardized testing: Harmful to educational health. *Phi Delta Kappan,* May, 688–97.

National Council on Educational Standards and Testing (NCEST). 1992. *Raising standards for American education.* Washington, D.C.: GPO.

Paulson, L., P. Paulson, and C. Meyer. 1991. What makes a portfolio a portfolio. *Educational Leadership,* February, 60–63.

Spandel, V., and R. Stiggins. *Creating writers: Linking assessment and writing instruction.* New York: Longman.

Stiggins, R. 1987. Profiling classroom assessment environments. Paper presented at annual meeting of National Council on Measurement in Education, Washington, D.C.

———. 1993. The two disciplines of assessment. *Measurement in Educational Counseling and Development,* April, 93–104.

Stiggins, R., and N. Bridgeford. 1985. The ecology of classroom assessment. *Journal of Educational Measurement* 22 (4): 271–86.

Wiggins, G. 1989. Teaching to the (authentic) test. *Educational Leadership* 46:41–49.

Wiggins, G. 1990. Reconsidering standards and assessment. *Education Week,* 24 January, 25.

MANAGING IMPROVEMENT PROJECTS

—

Robert O. Brinkerhoff and Alison A. Carr

Project management is about getting things done. The science and tools of project management have evolved over many decades as humans have developed. Some efforts are extraordinary, like building cathedrals or launching astronauts into space; some are mundane, like packing for children's camping trips. Whether projects are large or small, project management procedures are always needed. It's important, however, to point out that project management does not equate with systemic change. Systemic change is a process in and of itself which can be aided by project management tools.

A project is, by definition, a complex set of interconnected tasks aimed at accomplishing one or more specific objectives. Erecting a building, planning and writing a curriculum guide, moving a family from one house to another, and organizing an overnight field trip for students are all examples of projects. Each has specific desired outcomes, a complex set of interconnected tasks, differing roles and responsibilities for people engaged in the project, a time line, and planned activities with interconnected results (dependencies). Each of these examples represents the defining characteristics of a project whose work is "special": it is outside the normal work routine; it brings different people together; and when the project is done, people move on to their routine work or other projects.

Change efforts in schools and other organizations can be aided by project management; for example, a curriculum redesign effort might entail such projects as (1) selecting new textbooks; (2) conducting a pilot test of a new instructional component; (3) training teachers and principals; and (4) constructing a technology lab. Each of these components of the curriculum change can be seen as interrelated projects. They are not separate from or parallel to the school organization; instead, they represent the integration of many interconnected task structures. Managing the entire curriculum changeover, coordinating the work of three or four (and probably more) projects, and interfacing them with other school activities can be seen as an overarching project that may be well served by project management techniques.

In this respect, organizational change necessitates project management. Even where all aspects of the change process have gone exceedingly well, and participants are eager to begin and supportive of the change, poor project management can derail the larger change effort, or fatally cripple it. Well-managed change projects will make clear progress, letting people see results, building a positive environment, and creating the conditions upon which more success can be built. On the other hand, if change projects do not go well, a negative environment builds. The natural and latent forces mitigating against change will be activated as projects are perceived to, or actually do, run afoul. Momentum is lost, and time that could be spent moving ahead is instead spent putting projects back on track. Worse yet, participants in the change process begin to spend their valuable time worrying and talking to one another about how badly things are going.

In a nutshell, school organizations and staff may find project management tools very helpful if they are to implement and sustain positive change efforts. This chapter provides an overview of project management: what it is, how it works, and the sorts of tools and procedures it incorporates. The chapter has three major sections. The first and most lengthy section describes and discusses the nature of projects and project management, paying particular attention to the characteristics of projects that make them so difficult, yet so important, to manage well. The second section overviews and summarizes the basic tools, technology, and procedures involved in effective project management. These tools have evolved over the past decades, are extremely powerful, and are amply defined in an abundant literature on project management. Therefore, this section is a sort of consumer's guide and overview. It is not intended to provide the reader with all the information needed to use the tools; rather, it aims to inform readers as to what is available and enable them to determine how much they do, or do not, know about this vital topic. In the final portion of the chapter, the authors discuss strategies that school staffs can use to build the competence required to conduct effective projects, and to create, nurture, and sustain the organizational climate needed for project management skills to grow and flourish.

THE CONTEXT AND PURPOSES OF PROJECT MANAGEMENT

Project management was born in the very earliest attempts of humans to accomplish tasks that re-

quired the efforts of a group of people, such as hunting in groups. Imagine a clan of cave dwellers dissatisfied with their boring diet of gathered roots and berries. One day, they come upon a woolly mammoth struck down and roasted in a forest fire started by (from the cave dwellers' perspective) a fortunate lightning strike. Imagine further their frustration, after many lusty meals, when the last of the windfall food is eaten. Now, some of them may have thought, couldn't we organize the death of one of these mammoth beasts? Must we wait for another find such as the first? Now imagine that some among them are persuasive enough to encourage a group to go for it: hunt down, kill, and cook a woolly mammoth. And thus, perhaps, was project management born.

Consider the following example.

Project Mammoth

A good plan was needed. The group might wait, sharpened spears at hand, in the brush surrounding the local mammoth watering hole. Then, when a mammoth appears, one will run forward, screaming and yelling, and generally behaving in such a way as to distract the beast while the others lunge with torches and hurl rocks at the beast's backside to drive it toward a handy, nearby closed-ended canyon along whose topmost walls another group is ready with huge boulders poised to topple down on the critter. The dazed and battered mammoth can then be dispatched with stabs to vital organs by a group of the strongest spear wielders.

If the plan sounds good to the others, and if the local cave-dweller chieftain can be persuaded to release the resources needed (torch stock, live coals, spears, etc.), the project may be a "go." At this point, we see how attaining approval may require a solid proposal, clear goals, a feasible plan, adequate leadership, and so forth. The next planning element will be, of course, to figure out who will staff the venture. Which fleet-of-foot and loud-voiced cave person, for instance, will be best suited (and willing) to leap out in front of an unsuspecting but very large and burly woolly mammoth, who will undoubtedly not feel good about having its morning drink disturbed? Who, likewise, will be best and willing to form the brigade that drives the beast to the canyon? How will the canyon wall positions, coveted perhaps for their safety, be allocated? Who will sharpen spears? Make torches? To what specifications? At this point, many staffing and organizing issues will arise. Will canyon wall boulder pushers need training in order to hit the mammoth and not the mammoth drivers? Will the mammoth drivers require a group leader? Can the torch makers work unsupervised? Will spear specifications be sufficiently clear?

Assuming that once these organizational issues are resolved such that the cave dwellers are able and motivated to do their jobs, and that all understand the roles they must play, the objectives for their jobs, to whom they report, and so forth, they still have to pull the whole thing off. Here, a leader well versed in the details of the plan, with the cooperation and respect of not just the staff but also the local cave denizens and leadership (after all, the project manager and staff want to be assured that, in their absence, their caves will not be looted and their spouses violated by the rest of the stay-behinds!), must be capable of keeping staff motivated and attentive to their tasks. Likewise, the leader may need to make on-the-spot changes to the plan, as things may not go as hoped. In this respect, the goals of the project are everything, and the leader and staff may need to abandon one planned task for another, if it serves their overall goal of dispatching the mammoth. Of course, the overarching goal is survival and freedom from unnecessary pain and maiming. If at some point it becomes clear that the mammoth has gained the upper hand (hoof, paw, whatever), then this larger goal may indicate a need to scrap it all and retreat to more berries and roots.

Finally, if all goes well, undoubtedly some parts of the plan worked better than others. The cave dwellers, in homage to the need for evolution, must now debrief their efforts and discuss how the next such hunt could be improved.

Fundamental Characteristics of Projects

In this brief imaginary sojourn, the reader will see most of the issues and problems facing those who aim to conduct projects in modern-day settings.

We can identify and summarize these, then go on to discuss their importance to the context and process of managing school improvement projects.

Basic Management Tasks

Once design has progressed to the implementation phase, basic project management tasks can be addressed. Projects of any scope or purpose have the same essential management tasks; these tasks are interrelated and are normally conducted in a continuing cycle. These tasks are depicted in figure 1, then briefly discussed following the figure. The terms for these tasks (defining, planning, directing, controlling) are defined and used as they are typically found in project management literature and texts. While these terms may have somewhat varying meanings to some readers ("directing," for instance, may be more familiar as "supervising"), the project-management-specific usage is employed in order to facilitate cross-referencing with other project management articles and books. Very useful and time-tested tools and technologies have been developed to help project leaders carry out these project management tasks; these will be overviewed in the second major section of this chapter.

Task 1: Defining the Project. During the defining stage, project leaders work to clarify the purposes, goals, and factors bearing on the shape and direction of the intended project so that they, and other project stakeholders, are absolutely clear and in agreement as to the "what" and "why" of the project. In the cave-people project, this stage would have culminated in agreement as to such determinations as how many mammoths are to be killed, who will participate, and who will share in the meat captured by the project.

In a school improvement project, this stage should be conducted so that the project leader(s) and other stakeholders, such as the school board and administration, external funders (if any), affected teachers, pupils and their parents, and so forth, are clear about and have had collaborative input about the project's goals, scope, and rationale. Because there are inevitably several stakeholder groups—and because their interests are

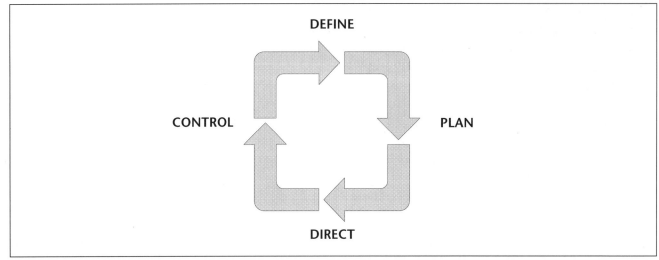

Figure 1   Project Management Cycle

often diverse, value-laden, and sometimes in conflict—project leaders must expect to identify, confront, and resolve political and other value conflicts during the definition stage. This is akin to the painful process of gaining a common set of core values and a unified vision for education in a diverse community.

Task 2: Planning the Project. Project leaders during this stage work to operationalize the definition into a detailed plan of action. This plan includes information about project organization (a staffing and management plan), who is to be in charge of which parts of the project, what their specific accountabilities are, to whom they report, and what is the nature and scope of their authority (what decisions they can make, and what clearances they must seek).

The plan also includes a schedule of tasks and milestones. In the cave-people project, for example, the plan may have specified that Oog (the person in charge of rock hurling) will commence hurling stones (task) as soon as the mammoth's head is in view above the bushes (schedule) and will continue hurling stones until the mammoth has stopped all forward progress (milestone event). The project plan is intended to direct action, and thus it must be very clear, concrete, and specific so that all staff understand what they are responsible for achieving and when they must produce their re-

sults. The plan is developed through participatory processes so that all stakeholders have a chance to provide their expertise and to shape the plan. Frequent meetings are conducted to review progress and revise the plan as the project moves ahead.

Task 3: Directing the Project. Directing the project consists of communicating "directions" to project staff so that they are clear as to what they need to do, then providing ongoing supervision to assure that they remain motivated, involved, and certain as to what their role and tasks are as the project proceeds. Project direction is accomplished through individual and group meetings with staff members, and through other communications media, such as memoranda, verbal coaching, telephone contact, and so forth. In many respects, project direction is similar in meaning to the term "supervision." But, in a project management context, the term "direction" is preferred because it is consistent with commonly used project management terminology and, more importantly, because it stresses the need in project contexts to continuously communicate and affirm the "direction" (as in compass reading and map usage) of the project with and to the project staff.

Task 4: Controlling the Project. In project management, the "control" task is characterized by measurement, not by power or authority. To "control" the project is to measure progress and compare what has been achieved to what was planned, in order to determine whether decisions need to be made to revise plans or to correct operations. The cave people may have assessed (measured), for example, whether the initial harassment with yelling and poking had turned the mammoth adequately toward the canyon, where the rock hurlers awaited. Had the harassment not yielded the planned-for results, the cave people may then have enacted a contingency plan of having more people rush forward with additional torches and prods.

In any large and complex project, like a school improvement effort, the project leader must plan for a variety of interim and final measures to assess progress and achievement of revision goals. Project control includes identifying key progress milestones (such as parent creation of a curriculum revision), defining and designing ways to measure progress toward milestones, and a system of data collection, analysis, and reporting procedures that will keep staff informed of the project's progress.

Control efforts inevitably result in the need for decisions, as no project ever works just the way it was planned. As progress measures indicate the need, the project staff and leader intervene to revise plans and operations to keep the project headed toward success.

In practice, all of the four essential project management tasks run and blend together. Project control leads to decisions to revise the project, and thus the project manager may frequently revisit the project definition task, meeting with project stakeholders to inform them about needs for change, and perhaps to renegotiate expectations. As new directions and project tasks are necessitated by decisions made to keep the project on course toward success, new plans are formulated, and thus new demands for direction and further control are created.

The "Iron Triangle" of Project Constraints

All projects, be they cave people hunting mammoths or school personnel hunting for better learning environments, have three essential parameters: quality, cost, and schedule. The aim of the project manager is misleadingly simple: to complete his or her project on time, within budget, and up to expectations for quality.

- Quality: The project must achieve results that meet quality criteria and expectations. These criteria and expectations vary, of course, depending on the nature of the project, but must always be identified, clarified, and defined such that agreement on them can be reached by all key stakeholders.

- Cost: All projects have a budget that defines the amount of resources available; a budget that the project is expected to consume. The budget may be more or less concrete and specific. Also, it may specify costs in other than dollar terms. Costs may be defined, for example, in terms of time of key personnel, or amounts of resources consumed (e.g., materials or supplies). But whatever the terminology of the budget or how explicitly and concretely it is defined, all projects have a budget, and the project leader is expected to control costs so that budget is not exceeded.

- Schedule: All projects are time bound and have a more or less explicit deadline by which project goals must be achieved or beyond which project resources may not be spent.

Together, the three project constraints of quality, cost, and time form a "triangle," such that if a change in one dimension occurs, there must be a change in another, as the sides of a triangle are rigid (see figure 2). If, for example, project stakeholders decide that they want a project's goal accomplished sooner than initially planned, then either costs will go up or quality must be diminished. As another example, if a project's resources are diminished, then quality or schedule will suffer. A project manager's role thus becomes one of constantly assessing implications for quality, cost, and schedule as project conditions change over the period of the project. At the beginning of a project, great care must be taken to define the quality, cost, and schedule constraints that will bind a project, for, once established, these expectations guide specific project plans.

When we combine the project management cycle (fig. 1) with project parameters such as cost and quality, figure 2 emerges to illustrate the complexity of managing large-scale organizational change. Figure 2 also includes design processes as the foundation, and implementation as the ultimate goal.

Matrix Organization

Most projects are characterized by a matrix organization in which the project roles and responsibilities of project staff are not their regular full-time jobs. In a school, for instance, there is a standing organizational structure with assigned roles and reporting responsibilities. Teachers, for example, are accountable for classroom management, instruction, planning, and so forth and report to the principal in carrying out these duties. Or, a central office curriculum coordinator has specific responsibilities and reports to, for example, an associate superintendent. When a project is created, staff from different parts of the school district may be assembled, with a part-time and "extra" responsibility to fulfill specific project responsibilities. When the project is over with, these project staff return to their regular full-time assignment, and the project organization is dissolved.

The matrix organization (sometimes called the "functional" organization) is so called because the project staff reports in two dimensions. Along the vertical axis, they continue to fulfill responsibilities to the permanent organization and its hierarchy. That is, they maintain responsibilities to their regular supervisor. Along the horizontal axis, project staff selected from across the organization report to a project manager in fulfillment of their specific project responsibilities.

A matrix organization has specific advantages, such as the removal of anxiety about job loss, since project staff simply return to their normal duties when the project is over, versus lose their job; likewise, because staff come from the organization,

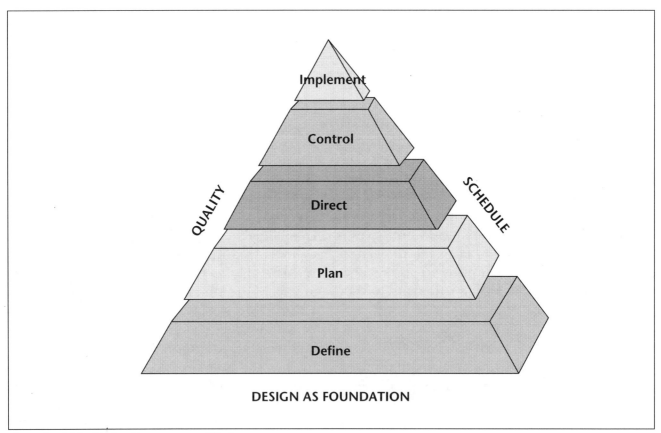

Figure 2   Major Project Parameters and Tasks

they also know how the school works and are already a part of the culture, thus knowing the formal and informal organization that helps get work accomplished. On the negative side, a matrix organization can create confusion about roles and responsibilities ("Am I working today on my regular duties, or the textbook project?") and create conflict as to priorities, since both project and regular team members expect that their work will receive attention. The key is to *not* view matrix organizational structures as opportunities to create wholly independent suborganizations which operate parallel to the parent organization. Instead, the matrix should be seen as an opportunity to create increased coordination among subcomponents emphasizing integration rather than stratification.

Another key feature of a matrix organization is that project managers (or submanagers) typically have little or no authority and power. This is particularly problematic for those managing large numbers of volunteers such as parents or community members. Change efforts are often staffed heavily by volunteers, and it is for this reason that project managers must seek alternative sources of power and influence to get the project accomplished.

The Project "Life Cycle"

Projects have a sort of biological cycle of birth, growth, and death that can have a strong influence on the achievement of success, and thus make special demands on project staff and managers.

At the beginning of a project there is a high degree of uncertainty and confusion as to what the project will really entail, what it will mean for others, what it will be accountable for, what it may threaten or displace, what others will expect from it, and so forth. The nature of the systemic change process itself exacerbates this difficulty. Systemic change tries to attend to the broad interconnections and global complexities of school organizations. In addition, what is easily agreed to during visioning phases can be seen very differently at the project stage when implementation issues begin to clarify precisely what form the vision will take. At the same time, there may be feelings of excitement and enthusiasm, particularly for those who champion the aims and activities of the project, and perhaps an

equal amount of threat and anxiety among those who are opposed to the project or left out of it.

The resolution of the confusion and the dispelling of uncertainty comes with more specific and detailed planning. At this time, project plans are made more concrete and expectations are clarified as project staff and managers work with other stakeholders to define objectives and parameters. Typically, this period of early planning and implementation is characterized by the project staff's high energy, commitment, enthusiasm, and excitement. Staff members often feel part of a special team, and bond to one another and the goals of the project. This period of high energy and enthusiasm may also begin to separate the project staff from other school staff who remain just a part of the regular, status quo work.

As the project matures and becomes more institutionalized, the early high energy begins to subside, as the staff start to view the project as just a regular part of their workaday life. At the same time, the initially high expectations for the project, which are often unrealistic and fanciful, become tempered by reality. Things don't always work as well as we hope, and the more usual problems and issues that are indigenous to the school's culture continue to crop up, just as they did before the project. There may be disillusionment at this stage in the midlife of the project, among the staff, participants, and other stakeholders.

As the project nears completion, another stage of uncertainty sets in. Staff and stakeholders begin to wonder what will become of the project results. Often, funding for the project expires, and unless alternative sources (such as the district operating budget) can be accessed, any follow-up portions of the project or other efforts to refine and continue the project are at risk. Further, staff who have been assigned to the project face the impending end of their project roles and a return to their regular, preproject assignments. Staff who have been hired for and are employed solely by the project (such as an additional instructor or a secretary) face termination of their jobs. This endgame period of the project may be characterized by staff drawing away from the project; staff members with regular and secure jobs may begin to prepare for their re-entry to their regular jobs, and full-time project staff may begin to search for other work. In either case, there is often a decreasing commitment to the project, and staff may pay less attention to their project jobs.

Project managers should anticipate these several phases of project life and the attendant waxing and waning of enthusiasm and energy among the staff and stakeholders. Early in the project, for example, the project manager may want to work hard to keep expectations for the project realistic and not let overenthusiasm inflate expectations to the point that major disappointment is inevitable. During the mid-life of the project, similar efforts may be necessary to rekindle energy and enthusiasm and to take quick action to resolve emerging issues and problems. During the latter portion of the project, the manager must plan to counter the inevitable reduction in staff energy, both by enthusiastic supervision and by initially planning less work during the latter portion of the project cycle.

THE FUNCTION AND ROLE OF PROJECT MANAGEMENT

In a nutshell, the role of project management is to make the project work: to accomplish its purposes with high quality, on time, and within the budget set for the project. But this is, of course, not an easy task. There are many forces operating against the success of a project, and projects operate in a complex political, organizational, and social environment. Thus the project management task is complex and often difficult.

At the core of the complexity and difficulty of the project management role is the fact that projects are, by their nature, unmanageable. Projects consist of a complex set of interdependent tasks. They represent more work than one person can do, thus requiring the work of others. The project manager's job is not to do the project, but to see that it gets done. But, because projects consist of many tasks and because several people are involved in carrying out these tasks, it is not possible for any one person (i.e., the project manager) to accomplish all the tasks required for the entire project. The project is more than can be seen at

one time. While the cave leader is, for instance, checking on the activities of the rock hurlers, and perhaps providing a little coaching, the spear carriers are meanwhile advancing, and preparations to cook the captured beast are underway back at the cave (or so the plan says). Thus the project manager must rely on only piecemeal news of what is really happening and choose to pay closer attention to those parts of the project that seem to require closer scrutiny or intervention. The project manager never deals with all of the project at one time (it's too big to do so); instead, he or she must rely on partial, sampled information about progress and problems.

If the whole thing could be run firsthand by one person, it would not be a project. But because it's bigger than that, it requires some sort of system of sampling and indirect control to help make everything happen the way it is supposed to. All such systems are imperfect, as all contain some error. Thus the role of project management requires tools and procedures that can help bring order and control over what is, in essence, a process that always escapes complete control.

The function of project management has been described by many different authors and management theorists, and each has a slightly different slant on the task. Many of the differences are dependent on and responsive to the differing contexts of the projects. For example, industrial engineering projects are viewed differently from social action projects. For a school setting, most of these different conceptions of the role and function can, however, be captured in four essential functions: creating and managing a vision; reducing risks and uncertainty; steering the project; and interfacing the project within and outside of the organization.

Creating and Managing a Vision

The overall vision for a changed system should be coordinated within the organization and across various projects. The creation of a *project* vision is accomplished in most part during the project definition task. The project vision is not a tangible product, though it may be that various documents and graphic devices have been produced to represent the vision. Rather, the vision is a mental picture of the project that exists in the minds of all those involved in the project. This vision includes both what the project will do (its components, tasks, and participants, for example) and what the project will accomplish (its goals, achievements, and lasting impact).

In the earliest life of the project, the vision may be very sketchy and incomplete, being little more than a vague dream of possibilities. As the first dreamers shares the dream, others may ask questions and contribute ideas, and the vision takes on more shape and detail. Planning proceeds, additional people participate, and the vision becomes even more specific.

The vision keeps everyone pointed in the same direction, striving toward the same goals. To the extent that the vision is the same in each participant's mind, the project is more likely to succeed and less energy has to be spent in conflict resolution. Further, a strong shared vision strengthens resolve and helps the project stakeholders remain committed during the inevitably stressful instances when they encounter obstacles or others challenge the project's plan or direction. However, when participants hold different visions or agreement is weak, the project is likely to become derailed. Then, unfortunately, even the slightest obstacle can precipitate a diversion, during which stakeholders question the vision and much energy must be spent simply to get people back on board.

The project manager's basic function is to first create a shared vision, then to manage that vision so people continue to share and strongly commit to it. The project manager accomplishes this by communications: talking about the vision, conducting meetings, discussing the vision with others, persuading doubters, listening to challenges, incorporating recommendations, and so forth. The key to managing the vision is frequent and open communication, keeping the vision in the forefront of all stakeholders' minds.

Initially, the vision may be readily compelling, especially before the project is actually implemented. Nothing is easier than professing allegiance and interest in an idea that, thus far,

requires no effort or action. Then, as the project becomes implemented, reality sets in. People discover that effort is required and that they must give their time and energy. When everything goes well, it may be easy for everyone to stay committed to the vision. Later, as obstacles are encountered and failures, however small, occur, project staff find themselves under fire. At these times, the vision is at risk, and staff may find themselves tempted to abandon the initial vision and return to the relative safety of the status quo. During these stressful times, the project manager must work harder than ever to remind others of the vision and encourage them to stay strong and unified.

It is important that the vision be perceived as a legitimate topic for discourse. On the one hand, questioning the vision may seem to run counter to the need for common commitment. To some extent, this is true, and the vision should be viewed as "sacred," thus retaining its vital force. On the other hand, if people think that questioning the vision is heresy, that it can only be discussed by the "high priests" of the project, then their commitment may be weakened, since they have no real input, impact, or voice. The healthiest and most vital vision is one that is held in high esteem yet is available to challenge at all levels of the project. Again, it is the function of the project manager to encourage discussion and review of the vision, remind staff of it when the going gets tough, and initiate changes to the vision when reality dictates that such changes are inevitable.

Reducing Risks and Uncertainty

Project management is, to a large extent, risk management. A project is a collection of risks, since each and every project task can possibly fail, and the whole project can likewise fail. For example, a new reading curriculum to help at-risk students contains many risks. Proponents of the old, less effective curriculum may implement the old curriculum even more vigorously than before as they perceive a challenge to the status quo; teachers unfamiliar with the new techniques may misapply them, creating less rather than more learning; parents of children not in the new program may be angry at the diversion; pupils spending more time on reading may slip in their other subjects; teachers, textbook salespeople, central office administrators, aides, and anyone else with a vested interest in the previous curriculum may work to undermine the new effort; inservice programs may not be effectively run, so that teachers in the new methods may be less than competent to implement the new techniques; materials may be late in delivery; budgets may be unexpectedly cut; and the list goes on.

A major task for the project manager is to forecast the risks to the project, then to intervene as necessary when the probability of a risk becoming fact runs high. The project manager accomplishes this task first by analyzing the plan for high-risk elements and designing procedures to reduce the risk. If, for example, it appears likely that a new inservice coordinator may have serious difficulty in getting teachers to the necessary level of competence, then the project manager may build detailed evaluation procedures into the inservice plan. The second way to reduce risk and uncertainty is by carefully monitoring the project to detect trouble early. This is accomplished by measuring activities frequently, staying in close touch with project staff and stakeholders, and keeping open communication channels with all project staff. Project staff must be encouraged to bring bad news to the project manager early so that something can be done before things get worse. If staff are afraid to communicate failure, then they will hide bad news until it is too late, thus ensuring the worst possible outcome.

Steering the Project

Project steering is accomplished by using what project management experts refer to as "control" systems. Control in project management involves measurement, wherein actual project progress and results are assessed, then compared to expectations (often referred to as milestones) to determine whether action is needed to redirect the project. Consider, for example, a school restructuring project. A part of this example project involves the formation of a community advisory committee. According to the plan the project director and staff had agreed to, the committee was to (a) have been fully formed and operational by August 5th, and

(b) representative of the school community, socioeconomically and ethnically. The schedule milestone in this example is "operational by August 5th," and there is also a quality milestone, that the committee be representative.

The project manager is making a steering effort when he or she meets with the staff member in charge of the community board portion of the project, say in mid-July, to review the names and backgrounds of potential board members and, together with the staff member, assess whether it is likely that the board will in fact be operational by August 5th and contain enough of the right sorts of members to be truly representative. If the progress seems adequate—all is on track for meeting the milestones successfully—then they may decide to take no action. If, on the other hand, it appears that they may be unlikely (for sake of example) to locate enough Hispanic volunteers, then the project manager and staff member may decide that an extra effort, beyond the initial plan, is needed. At this point, the project manager must review other elements of the project and, hopefully, find some portion that is doing better than expected. He or she should then borrow resources from this other portion to put the community board element back on track toward success.

Steering the project is a major and continuing responsibility of the project manager. This involves reviewing plans and establishing challenging but reasonable milestones, then working with staff to be sure that they understand and are committed to achieving these milestones. Then the manager must design a system of measures, and set in place review mechanisms (meetings, data analyses, checklists) to ensure a continuing flow of accurate and timely information about progress. As data are collected and the project progresses, the manager and staff meet frequently to review results and determine whether progress is satisfactory or action is needed. The steering cycle is completed when, as in the example, decisions are made to redirect resources and efforts to shore up project elements that are falling behind. Occasionally, the project manager may need to steer more drastically, abandoning initial plans or aborting parts—sometimes even all—of the project.

Interfacing the Project

The author once, while visiting in Australia, discussed the interfacing function with a new project manager who, many years before, had been a sheep rancher in Australia's expansive outback. "Oh," the former rancher said, "you mean ridin' fences." When he explained the details of riding fences—checking all of the perimeters of the ranch to look for fences broken by rampaging emus, or spots weakened by erosion, or even a branch that might fall in a strong wind and break a fence wire—I agreed. A project manager must indeed "ride fences."

Riding fences in project management means that the project manager must regularly meet with external project stakeholders to determine whether there are any current or looming issues and problems that threaten the well-being of the project. The manager of a school curriculum project might, for example, meet with teachers from other buildings to learn from them what they are hearing and feeling about the project, whether, for instance, they are satisfied with the amount of input they have in decision making, and whether they understand and agree with decisions made thus far. Interfacing meetings such as these must occur likewise with parent groups, funding agents, state department committees, and so forth.

The smart project manager will carefully analyze the context of the project and identify all stakeholders, being sure to understand what their interests, fears, hopes, values, and concerns are. Then a plan can be made to communicate regularly with these parties to be sure that they are positive, or at worst neutral, toward the project.

Similarly, the project manager must interface external concerns to the internal staff. The internal staff should be primarily concerned with getting project tasks done. They can work best when they know that their project manager is taking care of the external concerns and faithfully letting them know what concerns they must address. In this manner, a project manager provides "downfield blocking" for the project staff, so that when their work arrives at a critical juncture a smooth path is ready for them.

PROJECT MANAGEMENT TOOLS AND TECHNOLOGIES: A SAMPLER

When considering project management tools it is useful to reflect on the root meaning of the word "project." Consider a "projectile": something cast ahead of oneself. Consider a "projector": a device that casts an image ahead and outward. The function of project management and of a projector or projectile are profoundly alike, in that project management involves an initial then continuing projection of an image. In the case of project management, the image projected is of the future of the project, be it a future one year from the present, a month, a day, or even an hour.

A successful project manager (and thus a useful project management tool) will cast an image of what the project will look like in the future if it is going the way we want it to. Consider, for example, the short schedule depicted in figure 3.

This schedule projects the planned (desired) future, indicating that we intend to hold a brainstorming meeting on Monday, create a plan on Tuesday and Wednesday, then identify systemic impacts on Thursday and Friday. (The graphic device in fig. 3 is a Gantt chart, to be discussed shortly.) The utility of this, and most other, project management tools springs from their function of clearly depicting a desired future condition or action. Project staff can then use the projection in several critical ways:

1. They can assess the projected plan. Is Monday the best day to meet with stakeholders; do we already have a scheduled meeting that day anyway? Won't the stakeholders have additional changes to the plan that they'll share during the second Monday meeting; should we put off involvement until we have a plan to present rather than brainstorming all the possibilities early in the schedule?

2. They can use the schedule to plan ahead and allocate resources. Mondays are stakeholder meeting days; let's be sure the revised plan is available by the second Monday meeting time. Let's get some stakeholders from the

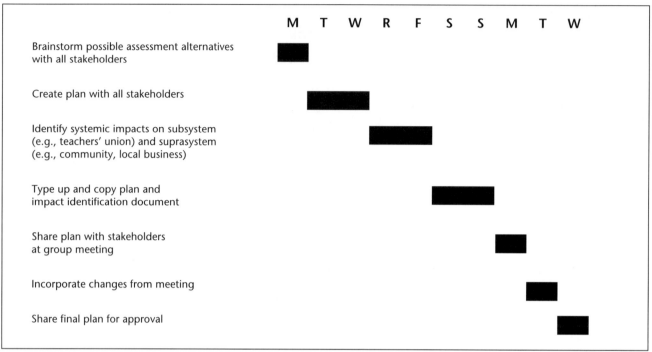

Figure 3   An Example Schedule/Gantt Chart

second meeting to volunteer to help incorporate the changes on Tuesday.

3. They can use the schedule to assess progress. Tomorrow is Friday: Will the plan and the systemic impacts be clearly identified for typing and copying?

While there is a considerable variety of project management tools and technologies, they are almost all alike in the function they serve of "projecting," so that all parties involved in the project can more clearly see what is planned and expected. Consider how even the most basic of tools—a written objective: "Have a final plan typed and copied for distribution to stakeholders by 6:00 p.m."—serves this function. It projects a future state and thus serves to clarify expectation for performance, inform planning, guide action, and enable assessment of results.

Virtually all project management tools are graphic and reductionistic. Graphic tools such as the Gantt chart in figure 3 reduce complexity (the chart doesn't provide detail about how to incorporate needed changes, for example) and show visually how things are expected to be. By using graphic images, project management tools capitalize on

the power of visualization; if we can clearly see how things will be if they are going the way we want them to, they are more likely to, in fact, go that way. It is no accident that most project management tools are graphic, and project managers are advised to use graphic images wherever possible.

In the following pages, the author reviews a small sample of the many tools available. There is an abundant literature for both novice and expert project managers, written at all levels of sophistication. The tools are powerful, have stood the test of time, and have proven themselves invaluable in planning, conducting, and evaluating projects. No one should try to manage a project without gaining a working knowledge of these useful devices.

Input-Process-Output (IPO) Charts

The IPO chart breaks down a complex project function into its related inputs (resources), processes (activities), and outputs (goals, objectives, products, results), and it illustrates the interconnections among these three components of systemic change. It is used during project definition as a shorthand way of explaining and designing major work activities and is useful in that it helps people see what results are expected from which activities and what resources will be needed to support those activities. Table 1 depicts a typical IPO chart for a stakeholder gap analysis to assess community readiness for change.

Network Diagrams

Network diagrams depict activities of a project in "chunks," showing what work is to be performed and in what sequence. Figure 4 represents the planned work to organize a community center at a school site.

The network diagram in figure 4 shows each component of the project as a box; the arrows connecting the boxes depict sequence. Component 1.0 (Assess Community Needs), for example, follows the Component 2.0 (Align Resources).

Network diagrams are used to provide a clear overview of complex activities. A network diagram (as do many other tools) breaks down work into chunks. This "chunking" feature is especially helpful, since it makes little, manageable things out of what would otherwise be large, unmanageable things.

Network diagrams are sometimes referred to as work breakdown structures, or WBS. They are most often used during the project definition stage of a project.

Dependency Charts

Dependency charts are similar to network diagrams in that each shows work as chunks and, again, lines or arrows show the flow of activities. However, a dependency chart is used strictly to depict dependencies among the several functions contained in a project or within a given project component. Consider the simple dependency chart pictured in figure 5.

The function "implement new scheduling system" is dependent upon the function "gain union and state legislature approval," in that the *output* of gaining approval (an approved policy without legal conflict) is needed as an *input* to the implement function.

Figure 5 also depicts a more complex dependency chart for a new scheduling system. Here the task is complicated by the need to consult research, gain approval, secure input, and select the best alternative scheduling system.

Dependency charts are important for planning schedules because they depict all of the critical dependencies among project tasks. They facilitate scheduling, since certain tasks must occur after the tasks on which they are dependent. In complex projects involving hundreds of tasks, dependency charting is absolutely necessary, for without such a tool it is impossible to comprehend and incorporate the myriad dependencies.

PERT and Critical Path Method

PERT (Program Evaluation and Review Technique) and Critical Path Method (CPM) are technologies devised for very complex projects where

INPUT	PROCESS	OUTPUT
• Interested school district • Willing principal • Secretarial assistance	Meet with principal to identify stakeholder groups	Initial list of stakeholder groups identified and vision of desired state of stakeholder participation from school's perspective
• Initial list of stakeholder groups • Stakeholder phone numbers • Interview personnel	Contact stakeholder groups and schedule appointments	Stakeholder interview schedule
• Completed interview schedule • Vision from school • Taping equipment • Interview facilities	Interview stakeholders re: interest in school, needs, and other stakeholders to be included, and compare to school perceptions	Initial report of stakeholder array, blank holding cells for newly identified stakeholders, comparison of school and stakeholder perceptions/visions

Table 1   Stakeholder Gap Analysis IPO Chart

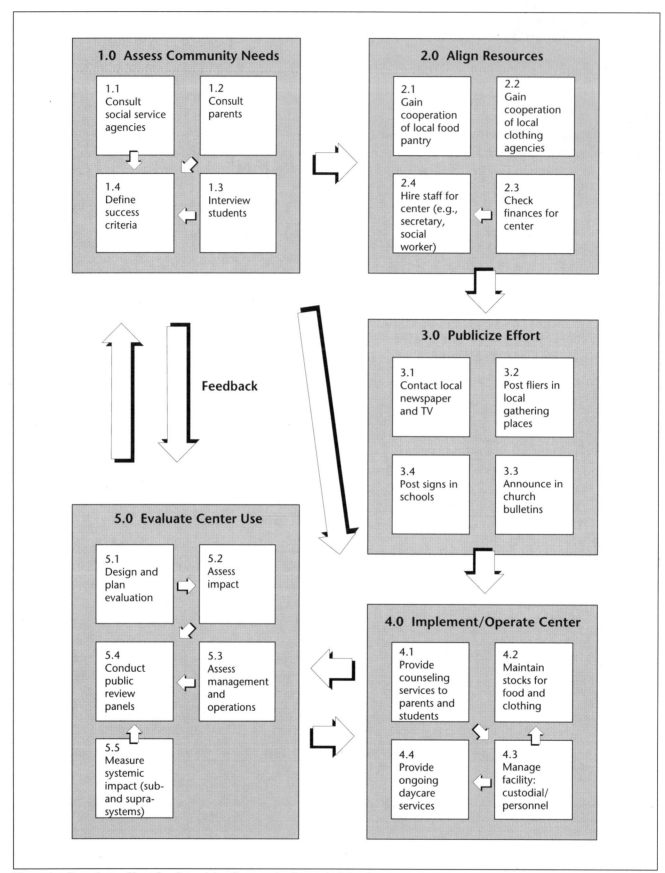

Figure 4   Depndency Chart for Organizing Community Center in School

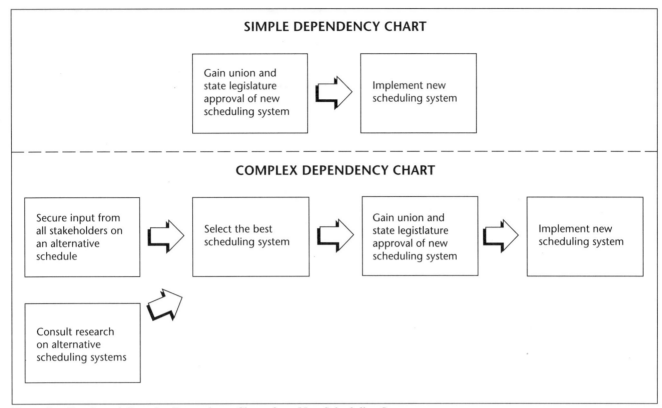

SIMPLE DEPENDENCY CHART

Gain union and state legislature approval of new scheduling system → Implement new scheduling system

COMPLEX DEPENDENCY CHART

Secure input from all stakeholders on an alternative schedule → Select the best scheduling system → Gain union and state legistlature approval of new scheduling system → Implement new scheduling system

Consult research on alternative scheduling systems →

Figure 5 Simple and Complex Dependency Charts for a New Scheduling System

dozens (or even hundreds or thousands) of interdependent tasks must be coordinated and monitored. Both PERT and CPM are variants of dependency charting. In PERT and CPM, a critical path represents the sequence of activities that consumes the most time. In this respect it is "critical," in that a delay in a critical path task will automatically cause a delay in the achievement of the project goal. Noncritical path activities, on the other hand, contain "slack," in that they can be finished later than planned without necessarily causing a delay in the final goal.

Both PERT and CPM enable a range of sophisticated analysis and forecasting activities. They are extremely powerful tools for use in complex projects and enable project managers to determine delay probabilities, schedule resource allocations so that daily expenditures are equal (or "level"), calculate minimum and maximum allowable slack periods, and so forth. Project managers assigned to complex projects are well advised to learn more about and use these powerful tools.

Matrix Budget Charts

The matrix budget enables a project manager to plan and monitor a budget for each of any number of project components. In this manner, greater control over costs is provided, since each project component is separately budgeted and tracked.

Table 2 shows an example of a matrix budget for the "Select New Textbook" project. Project components are shown in columns, and the rows represent cost categories (travel, personnel, etc.).

Goal/Risk Analyses, Stakeholder Analyses, Other Lists and Worksheets

Tables 3 and 4 show the worksheet formats, with hypothetical entries, for both a goal/risk analysis and a stakeholder analysis chart for the implementation of constructivist curriculum changes. These charts are typical of the dozens of such charts and worksheets that project managers can use to simply and clearly plan and communicate elements of projects. Such charts are very helpful in surfacing

Project Components	Establish Selection Criteria	Review Potential Textbooks	Make Final Selections	Totals
Personnel Teachers Administrators	8 days @ $60 = $480 8 days @ $100 = $800	20 days @ $60 = $1200 20 days @ $100 = $2000	3 days @ $60 = $180 3 days @ $100 = $300	$1860 $3100
Mileage (for parents)	$150	$300	$150	$600
Mail and Phone	–0–	$300	–0–	$300
Clerical Support	1 day @ $50 = $50	–0–	1 day @ $50 = $50	$100
TOTALS	**$1480**	**$3800**	**$680**	—
			TOTAL PROJECT COST	**$5960**

Table 2   Example of Matrix Budget for the "Select New Textbook" Project

critical issues and making project managers and others aware of those project elements that require attention.

The goal and risk analysis is used to specify the project goals and define measures for them, so that all project participants can agree and be clear about what the project is accountable for producing. "Risks" are potential negative outcomes that are to be avoided or managed by the project manager. Knowing what the risks are beforehand is a great help, since it enables the project manager to plan risk avoidance and reduction activities.

A "stakeholder" is any person or group that stands to gain or lose from a project. Because stakeholders may be affected either positively or negatively by the project, it is important for the manager to know who the stakeholders are and take specific actions to protect their interests.

These, and other worksheets, help make the planning process more systematic. They also make the planning process more visible and "public," thus inviting greater participation and enabling others to critically assess the thinking that has gone into the project plan.

Computer Software

There are many software packages that have been created to assist with project management. Some software programs help only with particular aspects of project management, such as course scheduling, or budgeting and cost control (such as spreadsheet software). Other software packages have been created to assist with the entire project planning and management process and are identified as project management programs. These programs can be extremely useful in large projects but are often too complex and sophisticated for smaller projects. For smaller projects, the author's experience has shown that "lower" technology tools, such as Post-it notes and hand-drawn graphics, may be all that are needed. Readers interested in software packages should consult a local software dealer.

This section of the chapter has only very briefly and superficially overviewed some of the many tools and techniques available to assist project management. There are many books, from complex and lengthy to brief and simple, available for readers interested in learning more. No one who must manage a school improvement project should attempt to do so without reference to such books or without otherwise learning project management methods, such as from a self-learning program or by attending a workshop or taking a course in project management. The tools are simply too useful, and the stakes in being successful are too high, to let such proven and effective tools go unused. Project manager: Teach thyself!

BUILDING PROJECT MANAGEMENT EXPERTISE AND CAPACITY

Successful project management is a matter of both individual and organizational expertise. A very

GOAL	MEASURES	RISK
Improved student learning	Parents of students report improved learning Improved ability of student work (reports, oral presentations, etc.) Improved student attitudes toward school and learning	Test scores may drop
More student control over learning	Teachers do more guiding versus didactic presentation Students display choice-making behaviors in classrooms	Teachers may revert to old, high-control behavior Students will reject self-control Parents will not support new student and teacher roles

Table 3   Example Goal/Risk Analysis Worksheet

STAKEHOLDER (Who?)	STAKE (What is their stake, interest, value?)	ACTION (What will you do to involve them?)
Parents	Best education for their children	Advisory board/design team representative(s) Send home periodic updates
Teachers	Professionalism, goals for positive learning for all kids	Advisory board/design team representative(s) Maintain union contact
Administration	Professionalism, strong school image . . .	Advisory board/design team representative(s) Periodic progress reports circulated
Students	Best education for personal fulfillment of goals	Advisory board/design team representative(s) Inform students of progress during homeroom
Social Service Agents	Linkage with strong agent of change in children's lives	Advisory board/design team representative(s)
Business and Industry	Outstanding employees appropriately prepared	Advisory board/design team representative(s)
Religious Factions	Representatation of adequate character development	Advisory board/design team representative(s)
University	Strong students seeking higher education	Advisory board/design team representative(s) Send periodic updates by e-mail
Political Representatives	Educated electorate, positive perceptions of constituents	Advisory board/design team representative(s)

Table 4   Example of Stakeholder Analysis Worksheet

skilled project manager can be successful at getting a project done in a hostile organization, but usually only once. Consistently excellent performance requires that the organization build, nurture, sustain, and reward good project management. This final section contains some guidelines and suggestions that schools or other organizations can follow to create this positive environment for project management.

Training and Staff Development

In general, there are two kinds of training that help build project management expertise. The first is training in project management tools and techniques, such as planning, scheduling, dependency analysis, and so forth. These are the technical skills particular to project management, and are typically identified specifically as "project management" training.

The second sort of training is in the more general human relations skills needed by managers and leaders of all types. Included in this category are supervision and coaching skills, communications, interpersonal relations, conflict resolution, and so forth. These more general skills are crucial, and a manager lacking in these skills will most surely fail despite the best technical expertise in tools and techniques.

A third type of training, not as basic as the first two discussed, is knowledge of the specific rules, policies, and operating procedures (such as selection and hiring, performance appraisal, resource acquisition, and budgeting) of the particular school system in which the project will be conducted. Good project managers have to know how to get the system to give them the things they need: where to get copies made, whom to see for maintenance work, which secretaries know financial routines the best, and so on.

There are a number of avenues through which individuals can receive training in project management skills. Universities may have formal classes, commercial training providers offer courses, professional associations (such as the American Management Association) offer workshops and correspondence courses, and school districts them-

selves can hire experts to offer seminars. The more general human relations and management skills can also be acquired through universities and commercial providers. Knowledge of the specific rules and procedures of the school district may best be learned from other, seasoned, managers or through a special school-sponsored workshop.

Other Staff Development

Individuals may build their skills through other staff development avenues in addition to training. For example, new or potential project managers could "intern" where they work for a brief but regular release period (e.g., every Friday afternoon) with an experienced project manager. Project management jobs can be rotated regularly among staff, so that more individuals have a chance to try out and build skills. Teachers and others can be encouraged to take courses to build project management skills as a part of their continuing graduate education; such courses are especially helpful when they have been selected on the basis of a skill review or individual needs diagnosis. These are just a few of a broader range of staff development strategies.

Performance Appraisal and Feedback

As in any organization, people tend to stay focused on the things that count and *are* counted. If people are expected to conduct projects as part of their jobs, then project management performance should be part of what is measured and reported on performance appraisals. The feedback itself is likely to improve performance and later capacities, and the discussion that precedes, including project management variables in the appraisal process, will help focus what is important. If the performance appraisal process is taken seriously and is positive, then including project management performance will help build capacity.

Rewards and Incentives

An issue related to performance appraisal is whether there is anything to be gained by one becoming involved in a project. In school settings especially, project involvement typically means work over and above the regular assignment. Often, of course, the project represents a change from the routine or otherwise entails intrinsically rewarding activities. But such intrinsic rewards may not be consistent or sustaining and should not be relied on to motivate people to take the inevitable risks involved in being a project manager. There should be some formal and consistent reward and incentive system.

Rewards may be tangible, such as monetary increases, comp time, release time, travel credits for conference attendance, and so on. Or rewards and incentives can be intangible, such as public recognition, formal praise, and the like. In any case, the rewards and incentives must work—they must be perceived by the staff to be rewards and thus worth striving to earn. If all a project manager gets as a reward is another project assignment, the system will not last.

Project Evaluation

Perhaps the greatest leverage for improved project performance can be achieved through project evaluation. At a minimum, the evaluation should include whether and how well the project has performed to meet its objectives. But beyond this, a formal and systematic review of the project management process itself is recommended. This review (sometimes called, rather morbidly, a project "postmortem") should focus on identifying the strengths and weaknesses of the management process: what worked, what didn't, and why.

It is important that the project management review process be entirely separated from performance review, so that it in no way intends to nor results in making judgments of any individual's competence or performance. In this way the process stays positive and results in recommendations and decisions to modify project management policies and procedures. If, for example, the review showed that some project customers were unclear about what was expected from them, and as a result later withdrew support from the project, then a procedure for later projects might be designed to conduct a preproject orientation to make customers clear about what to expect.

Review processes might include a group discussion among staff after the project, interviews with

some project customers and clients, an audit of budget performance, and so forth.

Time for Project Management

As simple as it may sound, some projects don't work, and people avoid project management assignments because time to manage the project is never officially allocated. Time is always needed, and almost always allotted, to carry out the work steps and procedures of a project. Time to manage the project may, however, be ignored. When this is the case, projects managers try to cut corners and may necessarily let key management tasks slide. This not only endangers the immediate project, but results in an environment that punishes management and keeps skills from growing.

A Risk-Tolerant Climate

This final guideline for building project management capacity is the most difficult to define and implement. But it may also be the most important. All projects involve risk; things can, and probably will, go wrong. Further, growth and learning involve risk. The greatest project and individual growth will occur where it is considered okay to make an error.

School district administrators should expect high quality but at the same time should encourage project staff to learn, try new approaches, and take reasonable risks. This is the first, and easier, half of the process. Then, as managers make mistakes, school administrators must be careful not to blame, criticize, or punish those who took the risk. Rather, they should celebrate the error because it represents a learning opportunity, thank the person who erred for having the guts to try something new, and seek mutually with project staff to understand what went wrong. This is, of course, easier to explain than to implement. Because it is hard to implement, the creation and maintenance of a risk-tolerant climate should be a specific point in the project evaluation and review process described earlier. Project staff and higher administration should review what errors were made, how the analysis and understanding process was implemented, and whether undue criticism and blame were leveled at anyone.

SUMMARY

The school improvement process is typically comprisd of onc, and usually many more, projects. When the other tenets of systemic design are held to and when these projects go well, school improvement has a chance to succeed. On the other hand, some excellent school improvement ideas can be rejected or receive an unfair trial when they don't work, not because they were bad ideas, but because the failed projects were not managed effectively. Project management capacity and performance is, therefore, a key ingredient in school improvement. But readers should avoid devolving systemic change into a series of projects where *planning* is primary, not *design*.

Project management is a time-tested, proven, and powerful technology. The tools and procedures of effective project management are logical, practical, and easy to learn. But they must be learned. Further, they must be practiced and nurtured through a positive project management climate that encourages risk and growth and provides training and continuing development along with self-reflective practice.

REFERENCES

Case, C. M. 1969. *The application of PERT to large-scale educational research and evaluation studies.* Princeton, N.J.: Educational Testing Service.

Earle, R. S. 1990. Performance technology: A new perspective for the public schools. *Performance Improvement Quarterly* 3 (4): 3–11.

Greer, M. 1988. Project management: An overview. *Performance and Instruction* 27 (4): 1–5.

Jackson, S. F. 1992. Planning and managing projects. In *Handbook of human performance technology,* edited by H. D. Stolovitch and E. J. Kups. San Francisco: Jossey-Bass.

Neroda, E. 1990. Uses and benefits of microcomputer project management software. *Cause/Effect* 13 (3): 43–49.

Sayles, L. R., and M. K. Chandler. 1971. *Managing large systems, organizations for the future.* New York: Harper and Row.

Shrock, S. A. 1990. School reform and restructuring: Does performance technology have a role? *Performance Improvement Quarterly* 3 (4): 12–33.

Stilian, G. N., et al. 1962. *PERT, a new management planning and control technique.* Edited by J. W. Blood. New York: American Management Association.

Tessmer, Martin. 1991. Back to the future: The environment analysis stage of front end analysis. *Performance and instruction* 30 (1): 9–12.

TRANSFORMING SCHOOLS FOR THE FUTURE

The trouble with our times is that the future is not what it used to be.
—*Paul Valery*

Those who look through the lens of the previous era see their own reality very differently from those who use the lens that the new era crafted. This change between two world views is often called a "paradigm" shift.
—*Bela H. Banathy*

We are on the threshold of the twenty-first century and the promise of a dramatically different future. Students crossing that threshold over the next few years must be prepared to shoulder the responsibility of what they find on the other side. What we know, what we understand, and what we believe about the current educational system is that to prepare students and society for crossing that threshold, we need fundamental change in schools, schooling, and education.

If we are to understand what designing schools, engaging in systemic change, and preparing for the future are about, it seems important to share in real-world experiences of practitioners involved in change. As a fundamental shift in our paradigm about educational change brings to light new perspectives through systems thinking, practice, and design, it creates a new vision of change as a design process for creating, rather than a problem-solving process for perpetuating. Obviously, we will all approach the new paradigm of change with different levels of understanding and capacity. Likewise, as those who have the major investments in our educational system begin to "leap out" of their existing paradigms of school and schooling, they will do so with a diversity of designs guiding their efforts.

The touchstones for future schools provided in this section represent a collection of real-world experiences with systemic change. While philosophy and theory are important in understanding the fundamental nature of systemic change, as stakeholders we need to connect with schools and people who are doing what we are exploring. The reader will note that the examples of systemic change selected represent, in large part, schools across the country. They exemplify small-scale systemic change at the school or district level. One example of large-scale systemic change is also provided for those interested in statewide systemic initiatives. Additionally, two distinct perspectives of systemic change are provided from an evaluator's and an external consultant's experience in working with schools undergoing change.

The first article in this section highlights the Saturn School's experiences in systemic change and connects the reader to a long-term venture that has received national attention. The second contribution takes the reader to British Columbia to examine, through the superintendent's perspective, the salient and critical factors important to fundamental change. Systemic change in Chilliwack School District has embraced the idea of a broad focusing effort to change the system. The third chapter shares the experience of an RJR-Nabisco Next Century School that selected the TQM philosophy as a core ideal for designing their future school. Following are two articles that bring the consultant and evaluator perspectives of working with systemic change. From the evaluation perspective, the reader is sensitized to the evolving role of evaluation. Here the evaluator suggests the learning organization concept as an appropriate metaphor for understanding evaluation in the context of systemic change. From the consultant's perspective, we see their focus of beginning systemic change with the leadership of a system. The final contribution to this section brings to the reader a large-scale systemic change perspective. Focusing on a math and science statewide initiative, the authors create a portrait of bringing about systemic change, contributing to our understanding of the complexity often associated with large-scale change efforts.

SCHOOLING SUCCESS AND PERSONAL CHANGE
Some Lessons Learned

—

D. Thomas King

Most of us have heard the story of the Garden of Eden, the biblical tale of Adam and Eve, created and placed in a perfect world, a paradise of no pain, no sickness, great understanding, even communication with all the creatures of this unique Garden. It was delightful, but always *delightful. A world of no change. Maybe even boring? So, they ask God, during one of their daily walks, if "changes" to their idyllic existence might be possible. "Yes, my children," God replied, "but not without the loss of what you have now. You will risk failures, become aware of your new ignorance as well as your new knowledge. Some things you will cause to be worse, as well as better. You will have much to learn and toil long hours of hard work to get it. If you really want 'change,' just eat an apple from my Special Tree, you know the one. It's in the middle of the garden." Not pausing very long, they say, "No thanks, God. That's hardly a bargain. We'd be giving up a lot for who knows what." That night, the serpent slithers in and tempts Eve: "God is lying to you. If you eat the apple, you will instantly have perfect and complete knowledge. You will be able to change all things the way you want them to be, instantly. You will be as great as God. . . ."*

> *The rest has become the history of education,*
> *. . . here is where we are,*
> *. . . this is a story about more of the toil,*
> *. . . and more of the change.*

Before I launch off to a look at the reinvented, renowned Saturn School in St. Paul, Minnesota, it is important for the reader to understand that school change is a highly personal experience. Saturn School happened because of what happened to me, as an early learner and a later learner: as a teacher, husband, parent, reader, thinker, dialoguer, wonderer, tinkerer, negotiator—the many roles that make us what we are and what we can become. Many paths are not taken in education and life, some for very good reasons and others by chance. Whatever we choose to do and not do, the sum total of these life and learning experiences accumulate, enabling or disabling or redirecting later learning. As my mother used to remind me, "As the twig is bent, so grows even the mighty oak."

EARLY EXPERIENCES OF LEARNING

My own earliest recollection of school is wanting to go home. This aversion came from a five-year-old filled with high expectations on his first school day. The expectations were a gift from my grandfather. My grandpa would stop by our house every Sunday morning, put me on his knee and read me the funny papers. "One day soon you'll be off to school," he would remind me, "and then you'll be able to read this to *me!*" But when I showed up, I found that reading wasn't even on the kindergarten agenda, and I could play just fine in my own sandbox, thank you. So, I found a propitious time to sneak out the door and home I went. I would wait till reading was on the agenda.

A little direct encouragement from my parents and grandpa convinced me that reading would happen soon enough. I decided to give it a second chance. I'll be forever grateful that I did. Reading, writing, and a lot of other good things happened to me in schools for the rest of my life, both as student and teacher. And, like nearly everyone else, some not so very good things happened too: being called on for questions I couldn't answer stands out the most, followed by tests that were handed back in descending order of marks, or being found out for just not understanding what was going on. I was lucky, though, there weren't many such days. I wanted to be a learner. But, for many early learners, the bad experiences drive out the good. Over time, the bad school experiences can drive out the good learning; they can eventually drive out the students too. For this loss, everyone pays.

School and learning are often such intense and personal experiences that everyone remembers at least some of them. Good memories usually surround our "Eurekas!" and "Ahas!" It's a great thrill to discover something we didn't know before, to be proud of our newly found, newly owned learning—but not the memories associated with failing to learn, or being found out when we don't know. Someone once remarked that there is no real learning without accompanying emotion. But emotion can also accompany *not* learning. If you are reading this book, though, chances are you will remember more success in school than failures. If not, then you have been, at the very least, persistent. So, for you readers, the following question shouldn't be too hard to answer in a personal way: What makes for learning success?

WHAT IS "SUCCESS" IN SCHOOL?

What do you think the American public believes constitutes "success" in school? A grade of "A"? A diploma? Getting to school on time? Not getting thrown out of class? Being able to get a job? Or is it the satisfaction of solving a tough math problem; finishing a knotty research project; giving an extemporaneous talk to your peers; working effectively in a group? It depends on who and where you are and your needs, doesn't it? And what you know and what you don't know. It depends a lot on your perception of yourself as an able learner or one of the real "losers" who leave school early, first in mind, later in body. Lost learners lose future opportunities, monetary gain, access to higher education; and society loses too. One definition of learning success is figuring out how to get through the school system successfully and coming out a bonafide graduate.

Most would agree that although there are many different definitions of school "success," far too many students who pass through our schools have not been very successful learners, even those who have received a diploma. Many things may have been learned while in school, but the skills that school or society or business has wanted students to master may not be among them. Perhaps we need to know more before we can offer a definition of what learning success is. Teachers often try to figure out a workable definition as they practice their craft. At least, I did.

LEARNING FROM TEACHING

Several stories from my early days as a high school mathematics teacher come to mind. They serve to illustrate my belief that our current system of learning is not designed to produce real success with many students. More importantly, these students, both the "winners" and the "losers," can teach us something about learning and failure to learn.

Learning from Harry

Harry was a quiet student in my algebra class during my first year of teaching. In our teacher preparation courses we were told we must reach all our students. But it became very clear early on that such reach too often exceeds a young teacher's grasp. I could tell by Harry's eyes (good teachers must become good "eyeball readers") that I wasn't reaching him. One bright October day, Harry came up after class and announced that he wanted to drop algebra. When I reminded him that we had hardly begun the course and pressed him further he solemnly announced: "Mr. King, this is really as much about algebra as I care to know!"

Personal lesson: students are given very little choice. I don't know if Harry was unable or unwilling to learn algebra, or just wanted to wait awhile; it didn't matter either way. Everyone but Harry understood he had to stay in the course for the rest of the year. So, Harry had learned about as much algebra as he was going to know, my best efforts notwithstanding. Who knows what might have happened if I had been able to say, "Look, Harry, why don't you stop back when you're more ready to learn?" Or, "Let's see what we can do to help. Maybe there's a learning style problem here. Let me ask my associate to sit down with you and run a few tests. There's more than one way to learn algebra." But I wasn't there yet in my understanding and neither was the system.

Learning from William

My next lesson was taught by William. He was one of those bright kids you discover once in a while, so bright that they have a hard time hiding it. When goaded, he might just snap off an elegant answer to a complex problem. His sarcasm, if I pressed too much, could show real wit. He knew how to handle language, and that's usually a dead giveaway that you've got a live mind. What a waste, I thought to myself on more than one occasion. Here's this William kid with plenty of brains and who could care

less. Others in my class, who actually seemed to be trying, needed more time and help than the school calendar or my energy allowed. One day I noted that the Kenny Scholarship was going to be awarded again in the spring to one of our school's deserving students. A chance to attend Harvard or Yale! And all expenses paid! A ticket to a promising future!

William was bright enough, and if I could motivate him to work for this award, he might even have a chance to win it. One afternoon after class I told him that I thought he might have a real shot at winning the scholarship. A chance to change his life, leave the project he came from and his family's welfare checks behind. But his brightness and laziness did him in. With all the logic of an Aristotelian scholar lost in irrelevancies, he asked me why he should head off to four years of school, and probably a lifetime of hard work, when the welfare system met all his basic needs just fine. And he didn't have to work to get it. Remember the novice scholar who approached Plato and asked what all this commitment to learning was really "worth" to him. Plato made it instantly worthwhile by tossing him a coin. Our tossing William a scholarship was met with the same response Plato got. Neither student really got it: Learning throughout life is what humans are designed to do. One's personal growth and societal gain depend on it. If you don't get it you won't get much. Next lesson: Being smart or prudent or wise are different, and not necessarily highly correlated. William had been given a great gift, but he refused to "invest" it, make it grow, and share his gift with others.

I taught secondary school mathematics for nearly a decade. After four or five years and more "lessons," my initial enthusiasm for teaching gave way to a growing despair. What author Jon Hassler has called the "Belikov Syndrome," in honor of one of Chekov's characters, seemed to describe my symptoms: burnout, depression, looking for different work. To succeed in a system that denies systemic success, you either continue to struggle with the commitment and energy of a superperson burning a two-ended candle or, like survivors everywhere, you learn to cope and aim for lesser goals. Though the rewards are not as great, the risk is reduced and you are less likely to fail.

My first reaction to this stress was that I didn't know enough about teaching to be able to do enough as a teacher. Off I went to get a couple of advanced degrees in mathematics education, believing that I just didn't have the theoretical knowledge. But newly learned theories didn't really help my teaching much either. In a way, it made teaching more depressing, though I began to view the causes of these same old problems in different ways. As before, I felt that I learned more from my students than I taught them. Not about mathematics, but about why they weren't learning it. Two more short stories will illustrate more lessons learned.

Learning from MaryAnne

MaryAnne came to my advanced geometry class full of misgivings. She seemed a very bright student in this young teacher's dream of a math class—small size, able students, motivated learners. After a day or two of pre-Euclidean musings, she announced her intention to drop the course. Oblivious, I asked why. Wide-eyed, she said, "Mr. King, haven't you noticed that I'm the only girl in this class?" If I did, I surely hadn't made any efforts to accommodate her uncomfortable isolation. Somehow, I was able to persuade her to stay. I made every effort to make her comfortable in class. Years later, I learned she had earned an advanced degree in biology; I had advanced a degree in my sensitivity to the need for more young women in science and mathematics and a supportive environment to make it happen. That was my next lesson on learning: A good teacher is like an orchestra conductor, drawing out the excellence of the voices of all the players. I was beginning to discover that my lessons had as much to do with learning as they did with teaching.

Learning from Joe

Joe taught me my greatest lessons. If truth be told, he was more the teacher and I the student. Joe taught me two great truths about learning. I took his class in my General Math II course in my fourth year of teaching. You found two kinds of students in this twelfth grade course: those taking basic arithmetic for the tenth time (and still unable to master it when such intricacies as long division or fractions came up), and those more able learners who had to satisfy the math requirement and were "escaping" the harder work of algebra. Joe was atypical even in the former group. My first great revelation about Joe came while reviewing the topic of long division of large numbers. I was explaining what the students and I whimsically called "guzintos" (that is, the algorithm or process for how 127 "goes into," say, 4,872). It's a tricky algorithmic skill, being able to estimate how many divisors are contained in the first part of the dividend, multiplying back, subtracting, bringing down a next digit, and repeating this process until a remainder less than the divisor appeared. As I wandered the room one day watching students doing "guzintos," I looked down at Joe's paper. That he was doing it "all wrong" didn't surprise me, it was his getting the "right answer" that stopped me in my tracks! Joe, sensing my confusion, explained, "You see, Mr. King, my sixth grade teacher showed me this other method because she saw I was having trouble with the "hard way" (so much for my sensitivity to the needs of special learners). She told me to keep subtracting the divisor from the dividend until my remainder is smaller that the divisor. I then count up the number of times I subtracted, put the remainder along side of it and that's the answer!" And so it was, and so it is. A longer method, perhaps, and one in fact used by computer programmers, but he had showed me an elegantly simple one that we had never learned in our college math classes.

His greatest teaching was yet to come. To address the needs of two very diverse groups in Joe's class, I often brought in mathematics puzzles and other challenges to keep students engaged after they finished the assignment. This was my only way of challenging the students who had the assignment done right away, the ones who really should have been in algebra instead of General Math II. One day I came across an issue of *Scientific American* with an article on a puzzle called the "Soma Cube." These mindbogglers were the precursors of the more recent Rubik's Cube. The big difference was that the Soma Cube could be taken apart and, if you were lucky and careful, you *might* be able to put it back together again. If you were very lucky and very imaginative, you might even be able to build another shape, like a "pyramid" or a "throne." It was a great challenge. So, the night before I brought it into class, I practiced one of several thousand correct solutions among a billion or so ways to go wrong.

One of the great fears teachers have is appearing ignorant in front of the class, not knowing an answer or even having to call on one of the more able students in class for help. With a fair amount of earlier practice, I began to demonstrate this challenging "extra credit" assignment. "It's easy!" I said. "You just pull it apart and then you put it back together, like this." Try as I might, face flushing, I could not get the cube back together. So, I set the pieces down on the desk alongside me and began to explain the handout materials I had brought, fervently hoping that this extra time would restore the solution to mind. As I stumbled on, a small hand came up alongside my peripheral view, the cube now intact. A voice belonging to Joe meekly asked if there were any other cube puzzles he might help me with. It turned out that Joe was a spatial genius of sorts and, though my memory has dimmed, I think he ultimately solved many of the most difficult Soma Cube puzzles in addition to the many others I brought him. A great personal lesson was taught me that day: *Everyone is gifted in some way.* The lesson for the teacher is to help *each* learner develop and share his unique gifts with others. All students are gifted and talented in some way or other. The teacher's job is to help them soar with their unique strengths.

MORE LESSONS

My education as a teacher was coming too slowly. I was learning a lot from my students, but what else? What could academia contribute, I wondered, that I hadn't already found? In the mid-60s it was much easier to find out. The federal government was more enlightened about education in those days. There were numerous and generous programs to help educators learn more and, hopefully, teach better.

With some good letters of reference identifying me as a teacher who definitely had more to learn, I

was selected for an NSF Academic Year. A full tuition grant with a monthly stipend to attend a math-education program for a full year at the University of Wisconsin. Great teachers, great ideas, and a great opportunity to learn how to make changes in education. Leading thinkers and researchers: Herb Klausmeier in cognitive learning and systems thinking; Henry Van Engen, M. Vere DeVault, Tom Romberg (my advisor), who saw the power of manipulatives and "doing" in mathematics learning (what is now called "constructivist" theory); wonderful instructors in education, mathematics and computer science. Fate helped too. The second year, after the fellowship ended, I needed a job if I wanted to continue my doctoral studies. Madison Public Schools was opening a brand new, flexible, modularly scheduled school with all the best equipment that money could buy and powerful new strategies for learning. A dynamic, brainy principal hired me largely because I happened to know who Stanford logician-psychologist Patrick Suppes was. Suppes's work was current research, exciting to me and applicable to what we were trying to do at this new school. We had a generous budget and the principal's encouragement to try anything that seemed sensibly connected to the modular scheduling concept. And we did.

The young staff worked long hours designing powerful learning systems in large group, small group, tutorial, and independent study modes. We bought state-of-the-art equipment, computer telephone links, even the first portable video system. Students had a rich learning environment and, given encouragement from us teachers, many succeeded remarkably well. They learned and showed evidence of their learning in products we called Independent Study projects. Of course, many were kids who always succeed, no matter the system. But some were turned on to the power of learning who were otherwise disempowered. Where the new model didn't work so well was the greater amount of unscheduled time it gave students for planning and independent study. We assumed that given this new freedom, students would also assume the greater responsibility. Many did, but many didn't. We weren't able to "fix" it fast enough. This turned out to be the flaw that compromised the other good changes we brought to that new learning community. The system failed to hold onto the learners in direct proportion to the help they needed on their way to becoming "independent, self-reliant learners," as our mission statement read. Another lesson learned: The new system must be responsive to the needs of each learner. We were not responsive quickly enough in the early stages of development, so the school regressed to the traditional.

All of these "lessons" began to teach me something. Successful learning was not what I thought it had been. It was not "one right answer," or "never making a mistake," or "doing it the way we were taught." Success depends on the learner and his or her goals, unique gifts, diverse motivations, a timetable and a host of other factors that make each one of us uniquely us. It also depends on finding and putting in place a system that not only allows, but assures these goals. If we want students to learn differently, the place for the learning to happen must be different too.

It began to occur to me, at last, in this accumulation of personal experiences and dialogues and reflection about schooling, that there was no way this clumsy system of education, designed more than a hundred years ago, can meet each student's learning needs. While the current system was well designed, conceptually at least, to provide *educational opportunity for all* (through a factory-like model), it fails to secure the success of *each* child. This group-based, assembly line, industrially modeled system, which held time-to-learn constant for all (regardless of aptitude or readiness), which treated all learning styles alike, which held virtually no one to appropriate and demanding standards of performance, could not work. To me it made more sense to try to build a new model of personalized learning success and, equally important, to invent a new schooling environment to ensure it.

TOWARD ANOTHER DEFINITION OF LEARNING SUCCESS

School just doesn't work for most students. Teachers know this. Our students know it too. All you have to do is watch a movie like *Ferris Bueller's Day*

Off or *Teachers* to get some sense of how irrelevant school is to most students, even for many of the good ones. The employers of our high school graduates know it too. They're often forced to re-teach skills that should have been learned in school.

Most parents and much of the general public don't seem to know it, though. Few believe this tragedy is happening, at least in their school. Witness the annual Gallup poll. Parents think their child's school is just fine, thank you. It's the other schools that are having the problems. A classic case of greener grass in your own schoolyard. The fact is that it's the rare school that well meets most learners' needs.

What we have here, to paraphrase the warden in the movie classic *Cool Hand Luke,* is a real "failure to communicate" and a failure to disclose the real failures. Daily, students face diversions, disenchantment, and growing detachment and disillusionment. The result of all this failure to communicate is that too many students know too little to become good citizens, good workers, good parents, and good lifelong learners. Most parents don't realize how off-target K–12 education really is. Nostalgia seems to repaint their own schooling as a relatively successful experience. Even if that were true, the world is a very different place in this generation. The employers seem to realize that most school graduates don't have requisite job skills, but their critique usually stops there. It makes a thoughtful educator wonder if we are educating the right public. It seems impossible to make broad changes in a "broken" educational system if our constituencies don't think it is broken.

We humans are gifted with the higher-order ability to learn and adapt. Education, both formal and informal, heightens these needed behaviors. For two centuries, our educational system did a good job of passing on the needed skills for an agricultural and industrial revolution. It isn't working for the current information revolution, though. Futurists tell us that today's students will likely see several careers in their lifetime, not just different jobs. If they don't learn the process of learning (the "how to learn" approach to new problems), students will be learning-locked into yesterday's world, full of solutions that just don't work any-more. As Eric Hoffer put it: "In times of change, learners will inherit the earth, while the learned find themselves beautifully equipped to deal with a world that no longer exists."[1] This self-educated New York longshoreman was a true learner. So much for those who claim to be "learned." Perhaps a better definition of learning success is one that addresses both content and process. We have to become a learner to become more learned. Learning can't stop at fourth grade, dropout age, high school, or even postdoctoral studies. Our species requires constant learning of us, for our whole learning lives.

When I visit schools on opening day in the fall, it's always interesting to note the different response to my question, "Are you glad to be back?" Invariably the answer from the primary kids (K–3) is positive; they love their teachers, their friends, and learning new things. But intermediate grades and beyond, that's not the response. Students, mostly boys, find the question itself incredulous. And it's not just a matter of being "cool." They'd rather be hanging out with their friends, their teachers don't care about them personally, and school gives them al-most nothing of what they need *now* in their lives: acceptance, security, money, caring friends, under-standing parents and adults, and so on. From the teacher's side it is equally disconcerting. By fourth grade, individual differences in learning styles and learning rates have become so great that the teacher is unable to address each student's needs very well. Schooling also has changed from the ex-periential to the didactic, from projects and assess-ment to objective tests and letter grades. The desperate teacher, given a fixed time to learn for all students (regardless of their learning skills and needs) and meager resources, aims at the mythical mean, no longer able to meet each student's needs. The result is another example of chaos theory in the learning universe.

UNSUCCESSFUL STUDENTS AND MORAL OUTRAGE

Let's suppose you get to define learning "success" anyway you please. AFT President Al Shanker maintains that only one in five students are highly successful. Four out of five students are not success-ful learners! Twenty percent drop out and three-fifths go through school by the "seat of their pants." If you can sit still and avoid hassles, you'll likely get a diploma certifying that you know some-thing, when you really don't know very much of anything. In quality performance terminology, we have a quality-free system.

An 80 percent learner rejection rate, by anybody's definition, is more than a disaster—it is a societal tragedy. Those with spiritual leanings would call it a moral outrage. If schools were busi-nesses and turned out gizmos or widgets with the same quality assurance level as their students, they wouldn't be in business very long. Human learners are far more valuable commodities. But most stu-dents, even those who stay to graduate, are often unable to fill the new, increasingly complex jobs that are being created daily. There is no way our society can continue to tolerate this personal loss, nor what this loss is costing all of us.

There seems to be no great rush to remedy this fundamental failing of our schools. Most changes that have occurred are cosmetic. We try to tweak a single, promising factor and fail to find significant positive change. We tinker with the symptoms and not the cause. Larger, systemic failings, because of their complexity, are often ignored, and the "sys-tem" seems to swallow up singular, minimal change efforts. Those who study systemic change tell us we must look deeper and further. Over a decade ago, educational change agent Ted Sizer reminded us that the system itself must be a part of the change process:

> Most of the problems that beset education are obvious and long-standing. Educators and their critics have been rhetorically ham-mering away at them for several decades. It is the remedies that seem problematic. None seems to stick. Why? Things remain the same because it is impossible to change very much without changing most of everything. The result is paralysis.[2]

One of the first mandates for successful learning to happen is for more students to change the schools they learn in. The old factory model of "one size education fits all" just doesn't work anymore. There was vocational room for the "rejects" in the past, but that's no longer true. Too many key and needed jobs go begging, while fewer workers bother to opt for the minimum wage or seek the new skills for the new jobs. Schools aren't helping make it any better.

The chaos on the streets has invaded many of our schools. School buildings are becoming increasingly unsafe, hostile environments, the curriculum irrelevant, and real learning a rarity. There is no curriculum to address the new issues of making prudent choices, developing moral character, building a sense of binding social ethics, finding a common spirituality, and fostering the communal bonds which lead to shared learning. Instead, these skills are considered by many to be "soft," or else irrelevant, outcomes. Experienced learners know that other learners help us to create and aid us in testing and revising our own learning. Without a community of learners, one's capacity to learn and to grow is stunted. It first takes a village to educate a learner; then the learner must provide the same service to the village. My growth depends on the growth of others. Newton reminded us that we need shoulders to stand on in order to see further. If competition and natural selection are at work in the world, so also is a community of learners. Competition and cooperation are dynamic, complementary forces. We need both. Today, perhaps, the latter more than the former.

CHANGE NEEDS CATALYSTS

Al Shanker came to visit our city in February 1986 to speak to a group of business leaders. When I saw the headlines the next day, I was amazed that this union leader didn't talk about more money or better terms and conditions of employment. He challenged educators to see the shortfalls in its current system and to design a new and more effective educational model. He cited General Motors's new Saturn automobile—a team-driven, customer-oriented, newly designed approach to building cars where the input of the line production workers was as valid, if not more so, than the engineers and bosses. Even more surprising was their emphasis on listening to the customer first. Why not use these same notions to create a "Saturn School," he prodded. Personally, I was thrilled to hear it. At last, a validity check which affirmed my own inclinations! At last, a renowned teacher-leader saying what I had been discovering for years.

As I heard and read more, I was more astonished that this AFT leader, who for years had been calling for higher teacher salaries and better working conditions, was now urging fundamental changes in schooling. Ironically, our school district had just hired a new superintendent who was open to new ideas and had a handful of his own. When I approached him with the suggestion that we be the first school district in the nation to respond to Shanker's call for a Saturn School, he challenged, "It's an intriguing idea, but let's see what kind of plan you can put together." Prudently, I took his use of "you" to be plural, and invited a team of teachers (including our local federation president), local technologists (from both the hardware and software industry), teacher trainers, community leaders, parents, and other experts to draft a proposal for a "Saturn School of Tomorrow Project." It was a good idea at the right time in our city, with the right people in place who were committed to making it happen. Timing is everything when it comes to change.

Our committee met regularly for more than two years, beginning in 1987, and crafted what I believe now was a truly visionary proposal for its time. After some initial funding disappointments, we eventually secured a grant of equipment from Apple Computer (thanks to our zealous Apple rep). Given that upfront nudge, the superintendent was able to sell our board on a pilot project. Five years later, while this truly unique school is still in the process of becoming, the Saturn School of Tomorrow remarkably has been endorsed as a needed and continuing research-and-development effort by our school board. They are pleased with what we have learned about school reform, and have endorsed a continuing search for new answers and new questions.

What makes this new school different from other attempts at change? What were the difficulties faced and why has the board's commitment remained after five years? I believe it begins with the rightness of our original vision. The vision we captured was to design a school where virtually *each child would become a successful learner*. More than educational opportunity for all, we wanted learning success for *each*. We spent our early planning on building a vision of what such a school would look like, sound like, feel like, be like. What would people do in this school? What kind of tools would you find? How would you know that this individual success was happening? Where's the evidence?

VISIONING AND THE FIVE CHARTER PRINCIPLES

We tried to work backward from the early vision to build a rough blueprint. It was my task to suggest ideas and guide the group forward. I served as a temporary project director, one who would help guide the school forward during its beginning phase. In some sense, I was the conceiver of the project, then moved to a "godfather" role, and now just visit occasionally and wish the risk takers well. At the beginning, I spent a lot of time trying to discover other efforts at "reinvention." There were a number of "restructured" schools, but Saturn was a bolder attempt to systemically start over. Try as I might, I could find no other, similar efforts anywhere. The only helpful notion I found, besides Shanker's sketchy urgings, was George Leonard's visionary "Jefferson Interactive School," as described in his book *Education and Ecstasy*. Out of all our individual and collective efforts came what we called the "Five Saturn Charter Principles." Each focused on assuring a new paradigm of learning success for each student.

The notion that makes the Saturn School a truly reinvented school are its five operational, charter premises:

First Charter Principle: *The personalization of learning for each child.* There is no more personal human experience than the learning experience. We believed that every learner is so important and unique, he or she deserves a *personal* learning plan. We began to lay out some early notions of what might constitute what we then called a personal growth plan (PGP). This new process involved first

and foremost the student, then the parents, then an advisor who becomes an advocate for the student as long as they are at the school. The ultimate goal for the PGP is that each student eventually learns to become responsible for his or her own plan and, thereby, for his or her own learning. If a school was to secure a commitment to lifelong learning, it made sense to create a process where each student would learn to use a personalized planning tool to set goals, find resources, and show evidence that successful learning was happening.

Second Charter Principle: *Teachers had to be truly empowered* to help craft this new process. Remember the wisdom of the Saturn automobile redesign: put greater control in the hands of those most knowledgeable about the product.

Third Charter Principle: *Parents had to be brought back into the PGP process* in a frequent and interactive way. Somehow, society has robbed us of broad parental involvement in this latter half of the twentieth century, and everyone knows the key role of parents in successful learning; we insisted on their rejoining us in this venture.

Fourth Charter Principle: *The community and its resources had to become more available to learners* who would one day work with and in it. It amazes me that we in school create these poor microcosms of the outside world for students to study when the real world itself is just outside the schoolroom door, waiting to be experienced.

Fifth Charter Principle: *Technology had to become a powerful, enabling tool* for learners and staff. Increasing numbers of students come into our schools and ask where the "tools" are. They know the world uses them; they even use them in some of the electronic games they play. We characterized this new school with its new Five-Point Charter as "high tech, high teach, and high touch."

DESIGNING A SYSTEM IN WHICH CHANGE CAN THRIVE

We wanted a school that was truly different, one in which the system does not get in the way of effective learning. We did not want to restructure a school, moving a few things here and a few things there; we wanted to reinvent it. As one pundit said:

"When Edison set out to invent the electric light, he didn't tinker with candles." Educators try to test a seemingly powerful educational idea and it is often swamped by the phenomenon of what I call the "chaos of the classroom." Student differences, teacher differences, rigid class schedules, erratic student attendance, and different learning styles and rates all make for a learning chaos, perturbing factors which can effectively block learning for many students. Recalling Ted Sizer's advice (cited earlier), we wanted to combine the most powerful ideas on educational change we could find and build a new concept of school around them. Systemic change addresses real R&D in education, where we might find more questions than answers. Long journeys, the proverb reminds us, must begin with the first steps.

EARLY DESIGN PROBLEMS

While we allowed ample time for the initial visioning process, the negotiation process between our school board and the teacher's union took so much time that the new staff had only several weeks before the students showed up to turn this radical new concept into reality. We hoped to find and hire able staff and give them up to a year to come up with an operational plan. Nearly 300 of our 2,500 teachers had attended an initial informational meeting. But only a dozen applied for the four key teacher positions. Reasons given were that good teachers were happy where they were and that the new positions required a master's degree and five years of teaching experience, thus excluding newer teachers. All these issues resulted in delays and placed great startup burdens on staff.

It also took time to get administration to let us involve parents in the staff interviewing process. But our logic of change prevailed. Staff were then hired and allocations were provided at the same ratio as other district schools. We chose to use two of the allocated teacher positions to convert to four graduate interns from a nearby college. Although eager and bright, these interns had no classroom experience. Miraculously, this new team was able to get a plan in place, agree on who was going to do what, given their commitment to not using text-

books, and Saturn school opened in temporary quarters in September 1989. Our new era had begun.

SOME FACTS ABOUT SATURN SCHOOL

Saturn School is a nongraded, middle magnet school which served 280 students in grades 4–8 during the 1992–93 school year. The magnet selection process allows parents to choose from over thirty magnet programs among forty of sixty schools in this capital city. Students are randomly selected from a waiting list by ethnic category only. Since St. Paul schools have 45 percent children of color, so did the student body at Saturn. No other criteria are used for selection. Interestingly, the school had nearly two-thirds boys, since the selection pool also had more boys. We think this is due to the fact that the extensive technologies attracted more boys and the school's personal learning plan attracted more male students with learning difficulties who were "counseled" into Saturn from other schools.

Parents are told that attendance at Saturn requires a greater involvement on their part. They must participate in the several Personal Growth Planning conferences held during the year. Virtually 100 percent of parents participate. Saturn is located downtown to draw on the many resources there. Students attend classes offsite at the Science Museum of Minnesota, the Minnesota Museum of Art, and the downtown library. Staff and students set up mentorship and apprenticeship experiences to help establish the relevance of schooling to the world of work. Community volunteer service is also encouraged.

To simplify the planning, we opened with grades four through six and added grades seven and eight in subsequent years. Primary grades K–3 in a downtown setting were a concern for our board. Since then the district has opened a downtown kindergarten. We find it difficult to attract fourth graders from other elementary schools to leave and come to Saturn. The board recently indicated Saturn may add the primary grades in 1994–95. Not only would this provide the school with a cohort, but it would also let more students start fresh with a new approach to learning, rather than unlearning and relearning a new schooling process.

SATURN DIFFERENCES

Saturn is a unique school. Even the mission statement is unique. While staff changed it some in recent years, it began as, "To bring together the best of what is known about effective learning research and powerful learning systems, to employ a PGP for each student, a curriculum for today and tomorrow and the assumption of learning success for each child." Staff believe their goals are truly unique.

Here are some of the other differences:

- comprehensive use of downtown resources such as the public library, the science and art museums, state and local government

- mentorships and apprenticeships with businesses and agencies

- differentiated staffing: a lead teacher, associate teachers for curriculum, generalist teachers, intern teachers

- a longer school year, student portfolios, ungraded classes, no report cards or textbooks

- a school council of staff, parents, and students

- a focus on process as well as content

We changed whatever traditions we thought would lead to more effective learning. After a very comprehensive evaluation process, staff are beginning to find some of the answers to the original questions. However, more questions continue to surface.

SHARING WHAT'S LEARNED: WHAT WORKS AND WHAT NEEDS WORK

Over five thousand visitors have come to Saturn to see this unique school program. Among them have been former President George Bush, who recognized Saturn as a site where "teachers are reinventing school" during the announcement of his *America 2000* plan. Students conduct most of the school tours. They explain best the intricacies and workings of the program. Most visitors are impressed by what they see and hear, especially from the students. Their positive comments have balanced some of the more local negative publicity. More will be said on the media's influential "counter-spin" later. Suffice it to say that bad news seems to sell more newspapers than good news.

The superintendent and board have remained supportive of the school in the face of opposition from other schools in the district and the tight budgetary constraints which limit resources at all sites. Saturn was expensive to renovate and equip in its new downtown building, and the board committed major dollars to fund it. Helpful, though, was the fact that one in seven dollars for the first two years of the project was raised from outside sources. While this outside help was considerable, the balance funded by the district was still a major investment for a local board to make in educational research and development. Funding local R&D is a politically "gutsy" commitment.

MORE LESSONS LEARNED AT SATURN

After four years, a lot has been learned at Saturn. The school has willingly participated in several major evaluation efforts. Staff, students, and even parents have been open to scrutiny by evaluators and visitors. The Saturn community has shared the belief that more is to be gained by openness. The observations and findings of others inform the school's continuing progress. A better product is more likely if we listen to the customers, the observers, and the "window-shoppers."

There are many things learned by trying, changing, listening, guessing, and sharing. Educational change, contrary to the opinion of some renowned educational researchers, is worth trying. It is incredible to those of us involved in school reform how few outside it, even skilled observers, realize that change is "messy," that mistakes will be made, setbacks will occur, and disagreements will be provoked within the entire community. They hold successful change up to high standards and short time lines. Saturn has found that the more major the change, the longer it takes. For change agents, this is a price worth paying.

Finding better ways for students to learn seems to us to be a cultural necessity. Many parents are reluctant, and understandably so, to try new approaches with their children, fearful that their futures may be compromised by untested methods. Experience teaches us, however, that promising, well-thought-out change excites students, rekindles their interest in learning, makes them partners in change, and causes no serious, lasting losses. At worst, we have the benefits of what researchers call the "Hawthorne effect": performance improves solely because the subjects think the changes are for their benefit.

Change is a worrisome process, especially for the participants. When a local reporter was queried about her frequent and negative reporting on Saturn School, she said, "I just can't imagine my daughter at a school like Saturn," and referring to the nongraded curriculum, added, "Why, she would miss the experience of the fourth grade!" She failed to understand the many reasons why Saturn was a nongraded school. If she did, she failed to tell us why "fourth grade" was more important than improved learning. Parents who have chosen to send their child to Saturn are the greatest "risk-takers," if risk is to be found.

Success does not happen overnight. It takes time to find out what works best. Mistakes will be made and, because of that, better ways will be found. The project's formative evaluator, Dr. Hallie Preskill, put it this way:

> We know from various educational historians and contemporary educational researchers that educational reform does not happen overnight and without much pain and sacrifice. *For real change to occur teachers, students, parents, administrators and community members must be willing to let the school experience the successes and near successes of their efforts.* (italics added)

She goes on to add that one of Saturn's greatest successes was that they did indeed continue to address the issues that faced them in the first two years. What worked they said they would keep, and what didn't work they would discontinue and search again for what would work. She cited the project's highlights: (1) a truly student-centered curriculum, (2) a successful response to concerns about standardized test performance, (3) an innovative and powerful Personal Growth Plan for each student, (4) the power given to teachers to design the program resulted in their persistent attempts to meet students' cognitive and affective needs, (5) teachers and students began to use technologies in new and productive ways, (6) virtually all parents participated in student personal growth planning and assessment, and (7) Saturn has not only informed local change, it has served the national and international reform communities.

ONGOING PLANNING

Planning is essential to the success of any project. Unfortunately, there is rarely enough time for it. At the higher-ed level, there is time for research, planning, and teaching. K–12 has no such flexibility. One hour for prep does not allow enough time for planning and training for new tasks, let alone meeting the standard classroom needs. Yet for change to happen, planning must be a high and continuing priority. Moreover, the planning process needs to be continually informed by what you are learning from change, both formally and informally. Planning time was a big problem; therefore, the school year and day were lengthened (and staff were compensated) so Saturn could have more planning time. Staff need to review and revisit the project's mission and goals, build new schedules, learn about new technologies, understand how to work effectively together in new roles, dialogue with evaluators and other observers, and discuss what's working and what needs working on. If you don't take adequate time to plan, events will take on a life and a resolution of their own. Planning is an entire school community issue. All participants need to be involved, both customers and providers. The single biggest obstacle to change is that there is rarely enough planning time in K–12 education, and certainly not where change is concerned.

TEAM BUILDING

Whenever something radically new and exciting is begun, it seems to attract very different personality types to it. These radical "creators" tend to be very bright, highly energetic, individualistic, and, therefore, strongly convinced that their ideas are the right ones. Staff who join at a later time may have great difficulty entering the "inner inventors" circle. Creators are often very different from "main-tainers" or "developers." Issues of working productively together must be raised and time spent on keeping the communication and trust channels open. Saturn was no exception. Staff spent considerable time with several capable organizational development consultants, and these sessions met with limited success in promoting more comprehensive teaming. At least, they did help define the issues of difference so discussion could continue.

Much of the difficulty, in hindsight, may be due to the fact that the new roles at Saturn were never sharply defined (new teacher positions, such as lead teacher, associate teachers, generalist teachers, and intern teachers, were all created by a memorandum of agreement between the school board and the teacher's union). At the outset it wasn't known with any certainty all of the responsibilities that these new positions had to take on. Regrettably, the leadership model at Saturn did not effectively invite broad staff participation or a team-based approach. More time should have been spent on effective teambuilding.

THE ISSUE OF UP-FRONT COSTS

Schools that are designed to be very different don't usually fit into existing school sites (without a lot of renovation). The learning environment is a major issue of school change. New technologies for staff and students cost a fair amount of money too. Cost will be among the first criticisms of your critics. In need of a new school site, the Saturn community found a languishing YWCA building, replete with gym, auditorium, and pool. No outside playground and little parking, but, nonetheless, the site was located right in the middle of the community resources Saturn wanted to use. In walking distance were the science museum, the art museum, and the downtown public library. So, ultimately the deal was made. Lease purchase and renovation

costs ran the levy outlay to $9 million, a fraction of the cost of building or leasing a new school downtown. The budget for technology was a major cost factor too. Nearly a million dollars was earmarked for various computers and other media. Even the furniture, though comparably priced to other typical school selections, was high-tech and futuristic looking. That "difference" invited criticism too.

Midway through the first year of operation, when a good part of the technology was in place, Saturn held a "grand opening" and invited the community to come and take a look. Not too surprisingly, only the technology and furniture, the more readily visible, seemed to catch the visitors and the critics' eyes. That this new school was an early R&D effort, or that the program was highly innovative, fell on deaf ears and blind eyes. The questions in many minds was, "How could the district approve such major expenditure of dollars on untried assumptions, and with resources so scarce?" Before the first year was over, the numerous naysayers were lobbying administration and board members to pull the plug. The local paper, which gave some encouraging coverage before the school opened, began to focus almost exclusively on the more visible program shortcomings and the other rumors and criticisms fed to them. Some even came from a couple of disgruntled Saturn staff who left early in the project. Before the end of the first-year evaluation period, Saturn was being held to more than the original outcomes of its five-year plan. To the staff it seemed they were entering a "you can't win no matter what" mode. Responding to those challenges also diverted too much attention from other pressing issues. Worse, the negative publicity made student recruitment to this magnet school all the harder.

EQUITY AND SUPPORT FOR CHANGE

The St. Paul School District serves nearly forty thousand students in more than sixty schools and programs. It is still highly centralized, although efforts have been underway to create several site-based schools. As in many schools across America, there are not nearly enough resources to address the broad array of services that schools attempt to provide. Change is not a process that makes most folks comfortable. Most seasoned educators have been led through their share of unsuccessful innovations and remain unconvinced. Their negativism is heightened by the shrinking resources in public schools. With supply budgets cut every year, there is less and less to go around. Equity is impossible. When a new program or idea gets funded, the "equity of resources" issue gets loudly raised by staff in other schools who have been waiting forever for their equipment or supplies. Their loss has clearly been your gain. Those are the complaints that go to the district office or board members and begin to work against the success of your change efforts. More and more, Saturn was not viewed positively in its own school district.

THE "NONPROFESSIONAL" REACTIONS OF OTHER PROFESSIONALS

It is ironic that educators work in a profession where change is not only difficult in and of itself, but is often actively subverted by education professionals. And this is a profession that is dedicated to change in behavior. Apparently, changes that are good for our students are not good for us educators. Virtually every district has concerted opposition to finding better ways for learning to happen. New learning models mean new roles for staff. Year-round teacher positions were negotiated between the bargaining agent and the board and compensated beyond the teacher contract. The lead team of teachers had salaries greater than some of the school administrators in the district. Originally we planned to re-create the role of "principal teacher," a half-time administrator and half-time teacher who would serve in a supervisory and leadership position. Once the principals caught wind of the proposal, protests were carried to the superintendent. So, we went with a half-time principal and a lead team of teachers who took up some of the new administrative roles. The good news was that we had a principal assigned to the school who, like us, was new to such demanding challenges and was open to new ideas.

THE LIMELIGHT

Being in the limelight shows your mistakes as well as your successes. Schools that are very different attract attention. It's not only prophets who have trouble with the hometown press. The press is in the business of selling newspapers. They seem afflicted by a great case of "the school grass is always greener somewhere else." Columnists often lament that schools have dysfunctional students, overpaid teachers, and inept school administrators. Even when the articles the press writes aren't all bad, whoever writes the headlines for major newspapers seems gifted with a bad case of cutesy humor laced with cynicism and pessimism. We saw such cleverness as "Has the Sun Set on Saturn?" or "Saturn Comes Crashing to Earth!" even when the test scores had improved! This was not the case for publications outside our hometown. Those stories were highly positive and encouraging. Unfortunately, they were not read by most of the families of the students we hoped to attract. Once a reputation is tarnished, deserved or not, it is hard to change.

Our local paper has been our most negative detractor. Rarely is positive news covered. Anything which seems to suggest that all is not well with this new school gets front-page coverage. A local columnist wrote about one of our students who nervously misspelled a word when he was entering information into a computer for President Bush during his visit to Saturn. This very bright fifth grader, who programs and repairs our computers, had spelled "college" as "colage." It was all we could do to keep the students from writing a letter to the editor when that same columnist misspelled a word in one of his stories a few weeks later. The important lesson here is: Never fight with folks who buy their ink by the barrel. You can't win and they always get the last word. Staff doesn't worry so much about spelling anyway. That's what spell-checkers are for. We focus more on getting students to write and worry about the paper's "cosmetics" later. Standardized test scores have not risen at Saturn. Other skills have been stressed. Staff and students concentrate more on the skills these tests really don't measure very well: problem solving, induction, deduction, group learning, brainstorming, project construction, videos, and Hyperstacks. Even though Saturn students built exhibits for the Science Museum of Minnesota (where they also take their science classes), painted a colorful downtown mural, and won the citywide mathematics league, the press ignored these significant achievements and chose to focus on their very average standardized test scores. Standardized tests are for standardized schools. Saturn is far from a standard school. Other coverage has been kinder and more encouraging, understanding the tremendous tasks this restructured school faces. Others seem to realize, unlike the local media, that change makers and risk takers need to be encouraged, not discouraged.

PUTTING ON YOUR OWN SPIN

The "trick" with telling your reform story is getting an agreement to be held to standards of your own choosing. Try to negotiate a set of project outcomes that align with the mission. Set the goals up front and get the district leadership to agree. Without a clear mission statement, a sensible set of objectives, and some agreed-upon milestones, you will spend energy wherever the critics turn you. If goals are unrealistic or unclear, milestones will become millstones and drag your efforts under. It's imperative to also have a clear, proactive program of current information. Better for you to release the good and the not-so-good news (and what you propose to do about it) than to answer a reporter's leading question about why there has been another screwup. You need an adept staff person in charge of this key area. It's better to let the sun shine brightly on what you do and haven't done. That's what R&D is all about anyway. Much of the criticism can be defused if you're the first to offer it along with a sensible solution to the problem at hand.

CHOOSING YOUR NOOSE AND YOUR RIBBONS

Saturn agreed to participate in the district's standardized testing program. Staff bartered for, and

won, other standards of performance to be measured against. They emphasized measures that seemed more sensible and appropriate to a reinvented school than standardized tests. These norm-based measures held us to standards our staff weren't spending very much time addressing. Besides, a new model like Saturn wasn't really ready to be compared to traditional schools. It was a legitimate question in the staff's minds if it ever should be, district requirements notwithstanding. From the beginning they focused on student performance outcomes, as measured by portfolios and directed by each student's Personal Growth Plan. While national norms may be helpful in comparing different schools with similar curriculums, they are nearly worthless when it comes to evaluating individual student performance and outcomes. If you have a very new, nonstandard, developing program, watch out for the standardized pitfalls. Truly experimental programs should be exempted from standardized test issues for their beginning years.

But sometimes that isn't possible. Restructured schools may be held to both new and old standards. So it was at Saturn. Faced with the dilemma, and given some bad advice, we counted on our new computer-based Integrated Learning Systems (ILS) to address the skills of reading, math, and language mechanics. It didn't work. These individualized, tutorial, drill-and-practice systems were designed to be helpful adjuncts to standardized, textbook-driven learning. Saturn had chosen to use no textbooks. With no connection back to a typical classroom environment, the ILS activities seemed to go in one ear and out the other. Many students progressed quickly through the lessons but were not learning the skills.

They were unable to apply what they had learned when the standardized tests came along. We found that there is a limited role for these systems. Students who had been below grade level did seem to benefit from ILS. But the better students often found the system boring and disliked the highly prescriptive learning and lack of choices. Until ILS is more flexible and addresses various learning styles and abilities more appropriately, it is a questionable tool from the standpoint of cost-effectiveness.

SETTING THE CURRICULUM COMMANDMENTS

Much of what happens in K–12 education gets dictated by higher education. Postsecondary admission standards are set and the faculty writes most of the textbooks K–12 uses; higher ed trains our teachers. If exit interviews were conducted with teacher training grads or after a year or two of teaching, the colleges would find that their own curriculum had missed the mark. Teachers spend not nearly enough time observing other good teachers, practicing teaching skills, using new learning technologies, teaming and working in multicultural environments, becoming skilled with project-based learning and cooperative learning strategies, and knowing how to be a facilitator or conductor of learning and not a purveyor or font of all knowledge. If teacher trainers aren't passing these skills on to our teachers, how can teachers pass them on to students? Until higher education is itself restructured, there is a tremendous burden placed on district inservice and training for staff. It makes better sense for teacher education to be a collaborative effort between higher ed and K–12 schools. The medical profession uses an intensive, hands-on training model; doctors even call their working years a "practice." We need a lot more practice in teacher training and teaching.

BEYOND ARCHITECTURE

Form needs to follow function. Too many school reform projects are located in settings that are not only unconducive to change, but change is effectively blocked. Moreover, just because a school may look different doesn't mean that it is. A lot of construction and renovation money can be spent poorly if the thinking about new purpose is also poor. Space and equipment changes alone don't mean restructured schooling. You can add Wide Area Networks and Local Area Networks and labs and modems and even complex Computer-Assisted Design and Drafting tools. But if students and teachers behave in the same old ways, nothing has really changed. It's often difficult for new behaviors to match the new visions if the surroundings don't allow or even encourage it. This early "visioning" process of what you want your new learning site to look like, sound like, and feel like is key to its actuality. Spend enough time with it.

It makes good sense to involve the school community in the early design phase. There's much greater ownership when those involved have input into what a building looks like and how it works. Students particularly need to be heard about what their school should be like. At Saturn they chose the colors of the walls and the carpets and had input to the design of the unique cooperative learning areas. The consulting architect we retained didn't come to the project with the "right answers" before the questions were asked. He was wide open to new thinking, encouraging visioning and discussion on the part of the school community. A school that claims to be very different probably ought to look very different too. Current school spaces are not conducive to innovation. Cooperative learning is hard to make happen when desks are aligned in rows. Classrooms are just not well designed for most student project activities, small group work, different uses of technology, independent reading or thinking, and so on. If evolution is to happen in schools, schools must evolve in the way they look and function.

GRANDMOTHER'S RULES FOR INNOVATORS

When I first started in school administration some twenty years ago, a colleague gave me a copy of some tips on rules to follow to be successful. One part was called "Grandmother's Rules." They were a lot more meaningful to me than the hard-line "Grandfather's Rules," which gave competitive tips on how to assure one's effective and competitive climb through a vertical organization. Grandmother's Rules serve as good rules for innovation too. Here's my top five from that list and a rejoinder:

1. "Everyone needs success and praise!" Decorate the "troops" for their heroism (staff, students, and parents); there will be plenty of it. Keep your eyes open for success and for extraordinary effort. Run off award certificates

or just say a public or private thanks now and then.

2. "Some days you just can't make it!" Every day may not be a good day, but every day you look for good, you'll find some. You can learn from the bad experiences too. Accept the balances in life.

3. "No one can do better than they can do!" Give it your best shot; if it still doesn't work, forget it and try something else. The list of workable solutions in this world is plenty long and it needs to be longer. No matter how many times someone hasn't done it right, there's always the next try. A quote I saw recently says, "Regardless of your past, the future is a clean slate." So you keep on trying.

4. "Everyone at every moment can be more than he or she is!" Encourage the best in others; you just might get it. Challenges can bring supreme and successful efforts that most folks thought they could never achieve. You have to think you can do it before you try it. We all possess skills and gifts that oftentimes we never knew we had. Create a community that brings out these superlative efforts.

5. "If you want happy people, hire happy people!" This works for more than happiness. It's critical that the right people be selected for the right job. Yes, you can often change people's behaviors. That's why we're in the profession we are. But sometimes you can't make people do what they can't or won't do. Hire the critical skills you want by first finding people who have them. Create an interview and selection process that will select the right person for the job. Help people soar with their strengths and manage their weaknesses.

BUILDING COMMITMENT FOR CHANGE

If you have ever been involved in a major change effort, it's not hard to understand why it's not a highly populated arena. Personal and professional reputations are put on the line; it is physically and psychologically demanding; support is often withdrawn over time; major goals may not be realized; friendships and professional associations may become strained; burnout and dropout are commonplace. Most true change agents I have known are a persistently disquieted and committed group. They are not satisfied with the way things are. They are the ones who see things as they might be and wonder, "Why not?" Major school changes do not occur overnight. Whatever major success that happens won't happen overnight either. The real test of success of school reform is in the learning lives of the students who experience it. Will they take the self-directed skills they learn with them into later learning, will they continue their commitment to question, to collaborate, to research, to construct, to test, to revise, to share?

The evaluators and the staff at Saturn don't know the answers to these questions yet. The former lead teacher is completing a doctoral thesis that examines these long-term issues and other questions. It is my belief in talking with staff that many of the students and their parents believe that new, self-directed learning is happening. Many former Saturn students lament the lack of an active learning environment in the schools to which they transfer. But they also know how to make their learning more active and productive. There seems to be reason to be cautiously confident that many Saturn students are learning how to learn and integrating a commitment to learning into their lives. Firmer conclusions as to the persistence of this desirable behavior won't be known for decades. We need to hear from these students when they become adult learners. Having received this new product, they can tell us more about their satisfactions and suggestions.

LESSONS FROM SATURN

I, too, continue my learning. Much of it still comes from students. My visits to Saturn have provided me with optimism and a couple of wonderful anecdotes with which to close this chapter. They are my "lessons from Saturn."

The first lesson occurred during the second year and not long after we had moved into our new downtown site. We have this marvelous learning space students call the "Coop." It's a student- and staff-designed space that encourages cooperative learning: tables, computers, reclining areas, even telephones to gather information. Students do a fair amount of research in the Coop. In fact, a course is taught on what goes into good and productive research, culminating in a paper the students must do and present.

One day I was touring the area and caught Nathan's expressive, seemingly troubled eyes staring out the third floor window, watching airplanes land at St. Paul's nearby downtown airport. "What's up?" I asked. "Oh, I got this paper I've got to do and I don't know what to do it on," he replied. Trying not to be too helpful, I said, "Well, it often makes sense to pick something you're really interested in." I thought no more of it until a couple of weeks later, when I passed him in the same area. This time he was busy writing notes on the Mac. "How's the paper going?" I asked. "Well, I haven't had time to write it yet," he said. "I've been too busy researching it." When I asked what that meant, he told me that he had always been interested in flight and the nearby air traffic led him to pick up the phone and call the airport. Saturn teaches students how to get information from many sources and that includes using the phone. That, in addition to his natural loquaciousness, got him an invitation to come down and visit. In fact, they said there was a civil air patrol meeting that weekend and he could come by. And so he did. Then he had lots of ideas, but wasn't sure yet what to write about. Another couple of weeks passed and my next inquiry brought a similar response: too busy. When I asked why he was so busy he told me that he had met a Northwest Airlines pilot and somehow had cajoled his way into their DC-10 and 747 simulators in the name of his "research." Well, I was clearly impressed, having had the same wish for years. "How was it?" I asked. "Oh, the DC-10 is no problem after a few tries, but that 747 is really tough!" When I pressed further, he allowed as how the cockpit on the 747 is so high it distorts the pilot's perception. The wheels hit the ground long before he or she thinks they will. This results in some awful hard landings. I was amazed. Further research on my

part from a pilot friend revealed that Nathan was absolutely right and was experiencing, precociously, what pilots in training had to learn. To make this long story short, Nathan eventually wrote up some parts of this marvelous learning experience. More importantly, he had found a passion. Wanting to become a navy pilot, and wanting to learn those skills as a part of a Naval Academy education, he now had a renewed interest in science and mathematics. I have no doubt that Nathan will "land" wherever he wants to. I recognize that this story could have happened in any school, but I like to believe that the Saturn environment made it more likely.

This last story is one that was very moving for me. Jeremiah came to Saturn in the second year as a seventh grader and a considerable challenge to those who worked with him. Tall and street smart, he just wasn't buying without trying. Getting him to try was no easy task. His mouth had him in occasional trouble, but the staff is accustomed to "students of challenge." Persistence matters most, and our lead teacher got him interested in Lego-Logo, a computer program that lets students create robotic devices and write the programs that make them do things. Most kids love it, and Jeremiah was no exception. In fact, he got so good that when our school was notified President Bush would be visiting us, Jeremiah was chosen as one of a few students who would demonstrate their projects to the President. Many of those selected were nervous about all this hoopla, but not Jeremiah. When I escorted President Bush to Jeremiah's table and stepped back, I could see that he had the President's full attention as he explained the intricacies of his apparatus. But, being some distance back, I couldn't hear what was said between them. When we moved on, the President allowed as how young Jeremiah was an impressive lad with a seemingly good future. The next day a local paper ran a remarkable photo of Jeremiah (in the classic pose of Rodin's "The Thinker") and the President asking what must have been a tough question. When I saw Jeremiah, I showed him the photo and commended him. I asked him what the question was. "Well, he asked me what I like about computers," he said. "I had to think awhile, because I like computers a lot. But I told him what I liked most was that they let me learn with my hands." He explained further to this important Washington visitor that learning from books or lectures was hard for him, but he loved learning by doing. That was a message the President really needed to hear about technology. Knowing I had the "teachable moment," I told Jeremiah that the President expected great things of him. He looked me squarely in the eye, smiled, and said quietly, "I know." We shall see. I remain optimistic that this presidential prophecy will be fulfilled.

The long-term answers about the success of school change aren't in yet. Some will be years in the finding. It has seemed to us to be a good idea to involve current students at Saturn in getting the answers from former students. As a part of their research course, they could contact our graduates and find out what worked and didn't, what they liked and didn't. This kind of research is what informs Saturn's progress. And former students get a chance to model what they learned for those who are learning it. Isn't that what real learning is all about, passing it on with whatever uniqueness we can add?

SUSTAINING CHANGE: THE IMPORTANT THING IS TO LAST . . . AND TO GET BETTER

To Ernest Hemingway's, "The important thing is to last," I would add Sam Snead's great quote, "The more I practice, the luckier I get." Then add Vince Lombardi's, "Perfect practice makes perfect," and you've got a formula that, over time, is bound to produce success. But change, if it is to happen, has got to be given a real chance. There is growing evidence to support that minor changes take three to five years to work. Major change probably needs five to ten years or more to become successful. After all, change in behavior is what educators are

committed to make happen. We must be willing to make the same commitments we would ask of our students. That's what is great about school reform: both students and teachers (and even parents) get a chance to learn together. The best learning happens in schools where everyone is a learner.

REINVENTING SCHOOLS, REINVENTING OURSELVES

There are many communities which affect our lives and may ask for our efforts. Worthy of our abiding commitment are those that encourage the continued personal growth of each member. Those who reflect on their learning know that it comes as a part of communal, interdependent experiences. Fairly, we would find ourselves both receiving and sharing learning with and from others. One reason that it is as important to give in learning as to receive is that the "teacher" grows just as the student. Whether teacher or student, we test and refine our knowledge in the sharing and the taking. We may see our knowledge complemented or expanded by others as they return their delvings and doings. The greatest achievement for a teacher is to find that our students have become teachers. They teach us too. What a wonderful compliment it is to a teacher to see what we taught remolded, expanded, rethought, and given to others. Paraphrasing Sir Isaac Newton, we become the shoulders that future giants stand on, as we once stood. That's how it's been for me.

And so I thank you Grandpa, for your gift of learning. It's a gift that truly keeps on giving.

NOTES

1. Hoffer, Eric. 1982. *Between the devil and the dragon.* New York: Harper and Row.

2. Sizer, Ted. 1983. High school reform: The need for engineering. *Phi Delta Kappan* 64 (June): 679–83.

REFERENCES

Bennett, D., and D. T. King. 1991. The Saturn school of tomorrow. *Educational Leadership,* May, 41–44.

King, D. T. 1992. The Saturn school of tomorrow: A reality of today. *T.H.E. Journal,* April, 66–68.

Hoffer, E. 1982. *Between the devil and the dragon.* New York: Harper and Row.

Hopkins, M. 1992. Technologies as tools for transforming learning environments. *The Computing Teacher,* April, 27–30.

Preskill, H., D. T. King, and J. M. Hopkins. 1992. Rings around Saturn. *The Executive Educator,* May, 43–46.

Sizer, Ted. 1983. High school reform: The need for engineering. *Phi Delta Kappan* 64 (June): 679–83.

SYSTEMIC CHANGE AND STAFF DEVELOPMENT

—

Ray Williams

Systemic change is necessary if schools are to be transformed into communities of learners. This change requires cultural norms that promote collective action toward common goals. As Joyce and Showers (1988) have asserted, systemic change is made by *communities* of people, not by individuals.

The literature on staff development has focused on the dynamic tension between the need to support individual professional growth and the need to support the organization's goals (Futrell 1991; Joyce 1990; Loucks-Horsley 1989; Nebgen 1990). Recent publications on successful organizational change have emphasized the importance of viewing organizations as systems and change strategies as systemic initiatives (Senge 1990).

Initiatives for systemic change in Chilliwack School District in British Columbia have dealt with the complex issue of integrating staff development with organizational development. These change initiatives were based on the proposition that individual growth must take place within the context of systemwide change.

SOCIETAL TRANSFORMATIONS

Lewis Mumford (1956) noted that every transformation has rested on new metaphysical and ideo-logical foundations. He proposed that we stand on the brink of a new age, an age of renewal and self-transformation. More recent authors such as Rozack (1970), Toffler (1980), Ferguson (1980), Curtis (1982), Capra (1982), Morgan (1986), Sculley (1989), Gleick (1987), and Nasbitt and Aburdine (1990) discuss different aspects of the common theme of rapid and massive changes in our lives that characterize the transformation of society. Harman (1988) suggests that the global problems we face today will be successfully resolved only through a change from the current paradigm. In essence, our society is experiencing a number of paradigm shifts. The term "paradigm shift" centers on a concept developed by Thomas Kuhn and has been further popularized by Joel Barker. A paradigm is a set of rules and regulations that defines boundaries and tells you what to do to be successful within those boundaries (see table 1).

SYSTEMIC THINKING

Over the past four or five decades, we have been faced with increasingly more complex and pressing societal and global problems. Through these problems we have learned to recognize the limitations of the traditional scientific approach that has reigned during the industrial age. Systems think-

• New paradigms are created/discovered while the old paradigms are still successful.	• When people change paradigms, their perception of the world changes significantly.
• The initiators of new paradigms are usually outsiders or insiders on the fringe.	• Leaders, not managers, are needed to facilitate paradigm shifts.

Kuhn, 1962; Barker, 1988

Table 1   Characteristics of a Paradigm Shift

ing has demonstrated a capability of dealing effectively with highly complex and large-scale issues.

In contrast to traditional scientific thinking, which emphasizes reductionism, cause and effect, and fragmentation, systems thinking uses a world view, manifested in integration, holistic thinking, and process-focused inquiry. Senge (1990) states that "the most successful organizations of the 1990s will be learning organizations, which have the ability to learn and change faster than their competitors" (p. 6).

Senge outlines the elements of the learning organization as the following:

- Systems Thinking—a conceptual framework, a body of knowledge and tools to make patterns, directions, and relationships clear. This is both analytical and intuitive.

- Personal Mastery—the process of continually clarifying and deepening our personal vision, focusing our energies, seeing reality.

- Mental Models—ingrained assumptions, generalizations, or images that influence how we see the world and how we take action.

- Building a Shared Vision—requires leadership and interaction.

- Team Learning—supporting the individual in a team environment with high expectations for continual learning.

A major inhibitor to improvement of systems is rooted in current assumptions and beliefs about cooperation and competition. Specifically, the biological model of competition and human behavior has been seriously questioned by scientists. The evidence for the Darwinian biological model as the natural state is no longer convincing. Competitive behavior is not a natural state of man or animals. Survival in nature is a cooperative and ecological system (Banathy 1990).

Fullan (1990) identified six essential themes for paradigms of change in the educational setting:

- from negative to positive politics

- from monolithic to alternative solutions

- from innovations to institutional development

- from going it alone to alliances

- from neglect to deeper appreciation of change process

- from "if only" to "if I" or "if we"

Still others would argue the need for greater stability and continuity in changes, suggesting that change and continuity represent complementary parts in both individual and organizational development. These proponents of continuity argue against the notion of change strategies that involve the destruction and replacement of the past. They argue for change strategies that honor the continuity of values and beliefs in the organization because these will be more readily acceptable to people (Srivasta and Fry 1992).

In either case, the need for significant change in social institutions that keep pace with society is compelling. What becomes difficult is the leader's task of structuring the necessary changes while being sensitive to the anxiety and discontinuity change causes.

WHAT KIND OF CHANGE IS NEEDED IN SCHOOL SYSTEMS?

In the past few years, observers have pointed out the need for new thinking and approaches that are very different from the first two waves of educational reform. These views effectively point to the need to look at the total system and to seek new designs.

In a proposed new design for achieving educational excellence, Hutchins (1990) suggests that what prevents us today from attaining excellence is the prevailing (old) design of schooling. Hutchins says in the 1830s employers wanted a work force that would meet the needs of industrial society; they wanted workers who would work long hours, follow orders without question, do repetitive work, and be on time. The old design worked well for the society it served; it brought schooling to millions of immigrants who were needed to make industrial society work. Today's society, however, no longer requires such a work force. We need people who can think creatively and solve problems using information and technology. We need people who can work together and act in an ethical, socially responsible manner.

For the transformation of school systems to be successful, a new image is needed, a vision quest that engages imagination and creativity, that is both individual and shared (Banathy 1990).

ORGANIZATIONAL CULTURE

Organizational structures and their capacity to change are directly linked to the organizational culture. Culture can be defined as the idea or habit pattern that forms the basis for action. It consists of all the values, attitudes, and behavior patterns that individuals, in their organizations, use in coping with their environments.

Culture is not innate; rather, it is learned through formal and informal experiences. Culture can be changed. Organizational structures and relationships among people in the organization can be changed if the cultural norms are changed (Ouchi 1981; Deal and Kennedy 1982). Peters and Waterman's *In Search of Excellence* (1982) identified eight organizational characteristics that tended to be a major feature in excellent companies. "Hands on–value driven" was the characteristic which most closely reflects the importance given to organizational culture.

Sarason (1974) has suggested that viewing schools as cultures is useful in determining issues of school change. Fullan (1991, 1992) and others emphasize the importance of covert processes in the creation of meaning for individuals who are experiencing change (Rutter et al. 1979; Murphy et al. 1982; Lezotte 1981; Purkey and Smith 1983; Ouchi 1981; Deal and Kennedy 1982).

Firestone and Wilson (1985) also recognize the importance of the school's culture in shaping its effectiveness by suggesting the importance of working with both bureaucratic and cultural linkages in the school. Greenfield (1986) and Dufour (1990) describe the principal as the culture builder.

The power of the school culture model lies in its recognition that school restructuring must begin with attention to the subtle, habitual regularities of behavior that make up the culture of the school district and schools. While changes in the overt organizational structure are an integral component of change, leadership strategies must attend to underlying values, norms, attitudes, and behavioral patterns of people.

ORGANIZATIONAL CULTURE OF SCHOOLS AND PROFESSIONAL COLLEGIALITY

Traditional schools have been characterized as loosely coupled systems. Weick (1982) has suggested that the matter of coupling was more complex than a simple "tight is terrific—loose is lousy." Loosely coupled systems tend to be more difficult to manage and less responsive to rapid, top-down changes, but they have advantages like adaptability to small changes, novel problem solving, and limited problem identification. Astuto and Clark (1985) have concluded that effective schools are more tightly coupled in key areas.

Simultaneous loose-tight properties, with loose properties of autonomy and innovation, are found in successful adaptive organizations (Peters and Waterman 1982). A strong culture develops where the tight properties of central values and beliefs are a powerful, cohesive force (Owens 1987).

A key to organizational change in schools and the development of conducive cultural norms is the issue of collaboration and professional collegiality in schools. Research reveals that one of the most enduring conditions of schools is that teachers and principals generally work in isolation and on different aspects of schools. When interaction does take place it is usually focused on administrative and managerial tasks rather than on issues of student learning and instruction (Cuban 1988; Johnson 1989; Rallis 1990; Berry and Ginsberg 1990; Manasse 1985; McEvoy 1987).

Research indicates that collaboration is associated with

- an increase in teachers' sense of efficacy and commitment to teaching (Newmann, Ruther, and Smith 1989; Rosenholtz 1989; McLaughlin and Yee 1988);

- improvement in student achievement (Little 1987; Rosenholtz 1989);

- more successful implementation of education innovations (McLaughlin 1976; Fullan 1982; Crandall, Iseman, and Louis 1986);

- more effective induction of beginning teachers (Huling-Austin 1990).

Table 2 outlines the district- and school-level factors associated with teacher-teacher collaboration.

Despite several years of research regarding professional collaboration of teachers, it is rare, superficial, or difficult to maintain (Bredo 1977; Cohen et al. 1989; Hargreaves 1991; Little 1987, 1990; Little and Bird 1986; Rosenholtz 1989). Recent work in this field seems to point to two factors which inhibit this collaboration:

- the difficulty of changing the cultural norms of schools;

- the difference in the work roles of teachers and principals (Hargreaves 1990; Jackson 1968; Lortie 1975; Mitchell, Ortiz, and Mitchell 1987; Barth 1986).

Leithwood and Janz (1990) concluded that new forms of collaboration are unlikely to last in the absence of educationally compelling changes that make collaboration worthwhile. They identify six strategies for administrators to establish cultural norms of collaboration in relation to school improvement:

- strengthen school culture through processes of shared vision, goals, participative decision making, team planning, and team teaching;

- use existing bureaucratic mechanisms to build norms of collaboration (resources/policies);

DISTRICT- AND SCHOOL-LEVEL FACTORS ASSOCIATED WITH TEACHER-TEACHER COLLABORATION

District	School
• Systems, policies, and support for school goal setting; strategic planning	• Principal's vision building
• Flexible staffing policies	• School-based shared decision making
• System program priorities and support for their implementation	• Alternative, nonhierarchical communication systems
• System support for joint staff development of all staff	• Training in collaboration
• System support for team planning	• Establishing norms of collegiality and collaboration
• Decentralization of implementation	

Anderson, 1992

Table 2 District- and School-Level Factors Associated with Teacher-Teacher Collaboration

- expand and use staff development that is focused on shared goals for change;

- use frequent and direct communication with staff regarding change;

- share power and responsibilities regarding improvement processes;

- use symbols and rituals to highlight values—public and private recognition of staff efforts that contribute to implementation of goals, encouragement for sharing.

THE MANAGEMENT OF CHANGE

The global challenges and changes of the current millennium compel the creation of both new forms of organization and new forms of leadership.

Despite the considerable evidence for the need for substantial organizational and structural changes to our school systems, and abundant literature regarding the aspects of societal change that can form a conceptual framework, resources that identify practical strategies for the management of change remain scarce. For example, the curriculum changes as reflected in the *Year 2000* curriculum for British Columbia represent a bold step forward in learner-centered instruction that is outcome driven and emphasizes greater success for all students. However, in the absence of structural and organizational changes and the development of new cultural norms in school systems, the *Year 2000* curriculum may remain yet another unfulfilled curriculum exercise. A paradigm shift in the organization and relationships in school systems must take place before changes promised by innovations such as the *Year 2000* curriculum will be realized. The challenge we now face is to find new tools, structures, and methods to accelerate organizational learning and build a consensus for change.

Work in organizations such as school districts has traditionally been seen as the development of individual learning. The new era requires organizational learning. This type of learning, like individual learning, entails new insights and behavior, but, unlike individual learning, organizational learning occurs through shared insights, knowledge, and concepts. As Fullan (1991) states, one of the most significant problems regarding educational change is the lack of shared, coherent sense of meaning regarding the changes that are necessary and how they should take place.

We need to develop a conceptual framework for change that determines whether change is incremental or strategic, reactive or anticipatory. What is needed if we are to control change is educational change that is anticipatory and strategic—in essence, a process of renewal.

Change is difficult and fraught with conflict and uncertainty. Figure 1 indicates that changing attitudes and values is much more difficult than changing actions or behavior. For this reason, leaders should focus on an action agenda, organizational structure, and management style changes, rather than emphasizing the need for attitude and belief changes by everyone before structural changes are implemented.

Change needs to occur by changing the way we change. The structure of school systems resists the changes needed. The challenge for educational leaders is to help the school systems build a social system that is self-renewing.

ORGANIZATIONAL CHANGE AND LEADERSHIP

There have been 2,500 years of research and 10,000 published articles on the topic of leadership. Few topics have been the focus of so much attention in the Western world. We have had a preoccupation with leaders as great heroes. As we have moved through the last decades of the twentieth century, the concept of the leader as a hero is waning. This decline has less to do with training, skills, or personal qualities of leaders than it has to do with societal and organizational changes. The leadership techniques developed by industry and the military, which are used still by many of our current leaders, are obsolete for leaders in a postindustrial society. These leaders achieved success with a work force that had little education, little mobility, and restricted rights. These conditions no longer exist.

In *Megatrends 2000,* John Naisbitt and Patricia Aburdene identified several trends that underpin

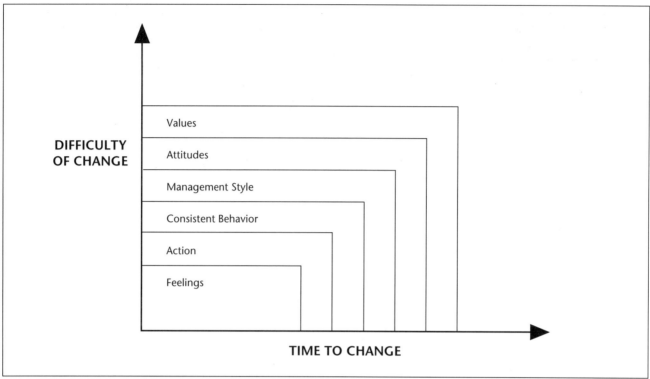

DIFFICULTY OF CHANGE

Values

Attitudes

Management Style

Consistent Behavior

Action

Feelings

TIME TO CHANGE

Figure 1   The Difficulty of Change

our new society and new conditions for work: centralization to decentralization; instructional help to self-help; representative democracy to participative democracy; and hierarchies to networking. All of these trends emphasize self-control and self-leadership.

During the 1990s a new quest has emerged—the pursuit of integration and balance. Individuals, families, organizations, and society are searching for greater harmony among work and personal relationships, worldly success, and fulfillment. There is now a clear need to integrate incremental change strategies with paradigm shifts, to combine change with continuity.

Many people in leadership positions are experiencing escalating conflict and schism between the managerial and leadership requirements of organizations. This is due, in part, to the existence of traditional bureaucratic organizational structures within which administrators work. Traditional organizational life assisted managers by supporting them with numerous policies, practices, and procedures that helped them control and check employee behavior. But organizations must become

more adaptive and flexible to keep pace with changes in society and survive. More than ever before, there is a need for understanding how organizations learn. A new type of leadership is required to develop adaptive learning organizations.

Our traditional view of leaders as special people who set the direction, make all the key decisions, and energize the "troops" is clearly rooted in an individualistic and nonsystemic world view (Senge 1991; Ferguson 1987; Capra 1982).

The most recent research on the nature of leadership in adaptive organizations points to a different purpose and structure of leadership as well as different kinds of characteristics of leaders. Leadership in learning organizations such as school systems centers on complexity and subtlety and assumes a nonbureaucratic, nonhierarchical organization. Leaders need to be designers, teachers, and stewards. These roles require new skills and the ability to build a shared vision, challenge prevailing mental models, and foster systemic thinking. Above all, leaders in learning organizations are responsible for building organizations where "people are continuously expanding their capabilities to shape their future" (Senge 1991).

The following are the essential elements for the focus of leadership for adaptive and learning organizations:

- building an organization's culture and shaping its evolution;

- stewardship of the organization's mission and vision;

- enabling others to lead themselves (teaching empowerment);

- moral/ethical leadership;

- alignment of people's interests with those of the organization;

- self-mastery and harmony.

If it is true that second-order change (i.e., fundamental changes in the organization) is required for school systems, then the use of consensual power rather than authoritarian or position power is needed. To use consensual power, a new kind of leadership style is necessary (Leithwood 1992). Change then becomes a negotiated process (Fullan 1991). The characteristics and elements of the new leadership, organizational structure, and the implementation of change strategies become inseparable.

One of the essential attributes and tasks of leaders is to develop a covenantal relationship with employees. People must develop a positive, complementary, continuous view of themselves as persons and as workers. Leadership becomes an "inside-out" process, beginning with self-mastery for the leader and ending with the self-mastery of others. Table 3 provides a summary of the major common elements of leadership as seen by contemporary experts.

LEADERSHIP ROLES

Recent research has indicated that teacher leadership has become a key element in the management of change in school systems (Berry and Linsberg 1990; Darling-Hammond and Berry 1988; Lieberman 1988; Little 1990; Fullan 1991). Teacher leadership may bring principals and teachers who assume

leadership roles into collaborative relationships because they are forced to interact in this way. Shared leadership will require principals and teachers to build new working relationships that are significantly different than the structural relationships occasioned by unionization. Shared leadership will also introduce elements of ambiguity for teachers and principals in their accountability for decision making and instruction (Rallis 1990). Finally, expanded leadership roles may alter teacher-leaders' positions as members of a socially and normatively defined collegium of teachers (Little 1990; Smylie and Denny 1990).

Table 4 summarizes from research the elements of new leadership and indicates the implications and applications to school systems.

STAFF DEVELOPMENT

Staff development can be defined as a collective activity for staff in a common direction, usually related to district or school goals, vision, or mission. Professional development, in contrast, is an individual activity that fosters the cultivation of uniqueness and skill development. Staff development has undergone a transition both in structure and acceptance. In the past, staff development activities were characterized by individual teachers and administrators attending courses or workshops outside of the school, based on

- their individual interests, and/or

- a district administrator's or university professor's perception of staff deficiencies.

State/provincial and district education authorities supported these activities within annual budget limitations and on a first-come, first-serve basis. The "one-shot" skill-based activities were rarely related to school or district needs and rarely required participants to share with peers knowledge, skills, or attitudes gained from such activities (Joyce 1990; Sparks and Loucks-Horsley 1990; Joyce and Showers 1988; Wood 1989; Diettweiler 1989; Fullan and Stigelbauer 1991).

In the late 1970s and early 1980s there was growing concern and dissatisfaction about the effective-

CHARACTERISTIC	Block	Bennis	Covey	Kouzes	Leithwood	Kelly/Greenleaf	DePree	Senge	Sevgiovanhi	Koestenbaum	Tichy/Dervanne	Kotter
Servant leadership (followership/service to others)						X		X	X			
Enablement/ empowerment of others	X	X	X	X	X	X		X	X	X		X
Inspiring a shared vision	X	X	X	X	X	X		X	X	X	X	X
Modeling the way		X	X			X			X		X	
Self-mastery/balanced life		X	X	X		X			X	X		
Challenge to status quo	X	X		X	X			X	X		X	
Exercises moral/ ethical leadership	X	X	X			X		X	X	X	X	X
Encourages the heart (celebrates success of others)	X		X	X		X		X		X	X	X
Structures teamwork	X	X	X	X	X	X	X	X	X		X	X
Builds a learning organization	X	X	X	X	X	X	X	X	X	X	X	X

Table 3   Elements of the New Leadership

THE NEW LEADERSHIP ELEMENTS	IMPLICATIONS/APPLICATIONS TO SCHOOL SYSTEMS
• Systems thinking	• Leadership should focus on schools/districts as systems.
• Stewardship/servant leadership	• Nonbureaucratic, nonhierarchical leadership. • Build structures and process for autonomous cross-role teamwork.
• Challenge the status quo	• Initiating creative dissonance, proactive behavior; search for opportunities to change; experimentation.
• Inspiring a shared vision	• Envisioning the future, strategic thinking, and planning through an interactive process with employees and other partners in education.
• Enabling/empowering others	• Build collaborative structures and processes; "flatten" organizational structures; cross-role teamwork; effective staff development; proactivity.
• Building learning organizations	• Inspiring trust; empowering and developing others; learning by doing; designing organization with others; staff development.
• Ethical/moral leadership	• Developing shared vision, mission, organizational values; negotiating trust; modeling behavior; structuring caring organizations.
• Structure teamwork	• Cross-role teamwork; decentralization; "flatten" organizational structure; participative decision making.
• Self-mastery; harmony	• Modeling; building organization that puts people's concerns first; focus on results; no judging people.

Table 4   Leadership Research Implications for School Systems

ness of staff development programs. At the same time, several major studies and reviews revealed a better understanding of the characteristics of effective staff development. The resulting list of effective practices, well known by now, included:

- programs conducted in school settings and linked to schoolwide efforts;

- teachers participating along with school administrators as peer coaches to each other and as planners of staff development activities;

- emphasis on self-instruction, with differentiated training opportunities;

- teachers in leadership roles;

- emphasis on demonstration, supervised trials, and feedback; training that is concrete and ongoing over time;

- ongoing assistance and support available upon request.

As Sparks and Loucks-Horsley contend, staff development "had come of age in the 1980s" (p. 5).

The professional growth of teachers, administrators, and other staff does not take place in a vacuum. The school district's cultural norms and organizational context has a significant influence on successful staff development activities.

In school districts where staff development is most successful, there is the following:

- common, coherent mission/vision and goals that staff have helped formulate;

- administrators who provide leadership by promoting and structuring a norm of collegiality and collaboration, and by facilitating communication and sharing;

- a connection between staff development and continuous school improvement;

- a focus on improving processes and collectively examining results rather than using data to make judgments regarding the competence of individuals;

- flexible arrangements and processes that facilitate the provision of time and resources for

staff development. (Sparks and Loucks-Horsley 1990)

STAFF DEVELOPMENT AND SYSTEMIC CHANGE

The consensus of "expert opinion" is that school district and school improvement should be "systemic" (Fullan 1982). This ecological approach recognizes that changes in one part of the system influence the other parts. Consequently, a staff development program both influences and is influenced by the changes in the school system. A careful integration of individual, school-based, and district-initiated staff development within the context of strategic planning and thinking will maximize the success of staff development programs (see fig. 2).

CHILLIWACK'S STAFF DEVELOPMENT MODEL

The staff development model developed in Chilliwack School District has relied extensively upon the research on systemic change and effective staff development practices.

A staff development task force representative of teachers, administrators, and nonteaching support staff was established to develop a model of staff development for all employee groups in the school district. From September through December 1991, the task force consulted with all employee groups regarding their views on staff development. In addition, a thorough examination of the research literature was conducted.

The task force recommended the following elements for a staff development model:

- collaboration of staff (administrators, teachers, and support staff) in the planning, design, and implementation of staff development;

- programs and activities that are continuous and long term;

- activities based on knowledge about adult learning and career stages of teachers and administrators;

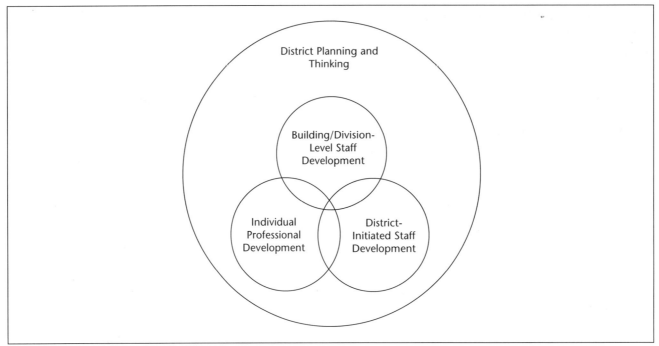

Figure 2   Integrated Model for Staff Development

- development of a school culture based on norms of collaboration, collegiality, and professional inquiry;

- a clear link between staff development and improvement in student learning;

- activities based on the assumption of staff efficacy rather than staff deficiency;

- a school-based focus.

The school district has acted upon these recommendations by doing the following:

- allocating significant funds and autonomy to individual schools to support staff development activities;

- creating a cadre of district facilitators to help school staffs with school-based strategic planning;

- expanding leadership roles to employees who are not administrators; and

- providing more staff development opportunities for support staff.

The task force recognized the importance of self-directed individual growth as a critical part of the staff development program. It also recognized, however, that a staff development program that is only skills based will not result in changes in the school's culture. Although individual growth is important, more tangible results occur where collective commitment is made to a shared vision.

STAFF DEVELOPMENT AND SYSTEMIC CHANGE IN CHILLIWACK

The effort to forge a staff development model appropriate for the school district was not a singular initiative independent of other parts of the school system. Simultaneously, along with the staff development initiative, the school district was initiating district- and school-based strategic planning and redefining the role of administrators by developing a new model for leadership preparation (see fig. 3). The school district saw strategic planning as leading to strategic thinking, a systems perspective. Chilliwack's strategic planning process emphasized participation of all the partners in learning; the school as the primary focus; and the identification of common beliefs, vision/mission, and goals. The school-based planning process was enhanced by the use of nonadministrative staff who were trained and given responsibility to be facilitators.

Another district initiative that became an integral part of the systemic change approach was the issue of leadership development. A task force comprising administrators, teachers, and support staff examined the role of administrators as it could and should be, and after an extensive interactive process both employee groups made a report that recognized the need for a new kind of leader.

The task force report concluded that the traditional role for administrators had been to manage, direct, control and monitor, distribute informa-tion, enforce rules, and evaluate personnel. A new leadership model that emphasizes the following was needed:

- building a culture or community of learners based on norms of collective work and shared values;

- developing a vision of the school through an interactive process with staff, parents, students, and community;

- enabling others to act in a purposeful, meaningful, and ethical manner;

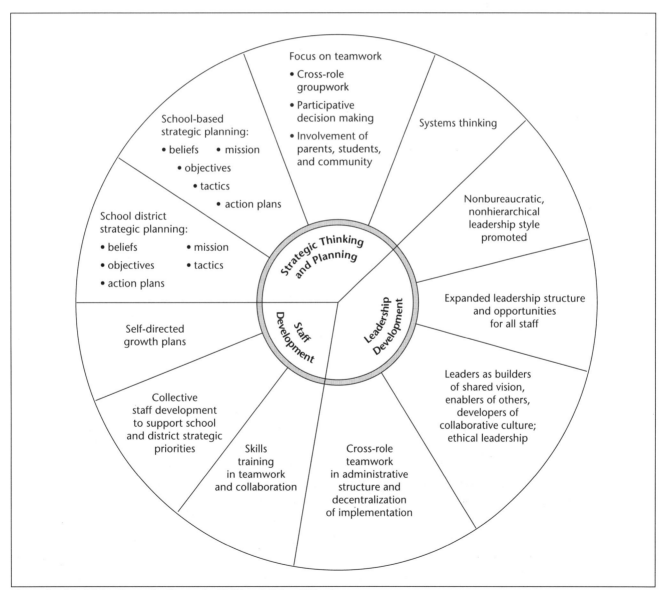

Figure 3   Model for Systemic Change in Chilliwack School District

- providing service to others;

- developing others as leaders;

- building teamwork.

Above all, the task force believed that leaders need to communicate a passion for learning and a belief in people.

The school district approved the report and has subsequently revised the role description for administrators as well as revising its leadership training program.

SUMMARY

The change strategies initiated by Chilliwack School District are consistent with research-based recommendations on change (Deal and Peterson 1990; Fullan and Stigelbauer 1991; Huberman 1983; Joyce and Murphy 1990; Miles 1983; Reaves and Griffith 1992; Tooney 1991). In particular, attention was paid to the following research-based recommendations:

- change is about people, not just policies;

- change requires a balance of top-down and bottom-up processes;

- change requires altering the culture and structure of schools;

- effective approaches to change combine and balance contradictory factors (e.g., simplicity and complexity, looseness and tightness, strong leadership and participation);

- change is a long-term, continuous process.

The school district was mindful of these research-based change principles as it pursued an integrated approach to change. As all three initiatives are discussed extensively by school staffs, parent advisory councils, and various district committees, employees throughout the system are becoming knowledgeable about the connections that were not readily apparent early in the process.

The Chilliwack initiatives have features which are consistent with change literature (Barth 1990; Edmonds 1982; Huberman 1983; Reaves and Griffith 1992; Shroyer 1990):

- the school is our focus for change;

- shared decision making and consensus building among staff, parents, students, and community is necessary;

- instructional and curricular reform that emphasizes desired student outcomes is needed;

- an emphasis on processes to develop shared values and collective action among staff, parents, and community is essential;

- a belief in the efficacy of all students and adults is critically important;

- the extensive involvement of hundreds of staff, parents, students, and community members produces greater support from—and a closer bond with—the community.

PROBLEMS ENCOUNTERED

As Fullan and Stigelbauer (1991) and Glickman, Hayes, and Hensley (1992) point out, successful change creates problems in the organization. Collaboration and participative decision making have produced interpersonal conflict in the school district, particularly concerning ways to bring plans or visions to life. While cognitive dissonance may be healthy for an organization, it is nevertheless stressful for individuals. When attempting systemic change, training is essential for all employees, students, and parents in areas such as group processes, decision making, team building, and leadership. Finally, the school board is establishing a new identity that requires extensive dialogue with various communities and parent groups.

Since the Chilliwack change initiatives are relatively new, a number of challenges still remain.

1. *The school district must provide sufficient resources to sustain the changes.* The initiatives are resource hungry. Critical decisions must be made regarding both resource allocation and reallocation. Selective abandonment of what is currently being done must accompany new visions and plans.

2. *A decision-making process must be delineated.* Extensive participation in the three projects has raised issues of what constitutes collaboration, consulta-

tion, shared decision making, and authority. The school board, administration, and employee groups will need to take an approach which would see school-based and district models of decision making develop based on a shared commitment to principles rather than imposing a uniform model in the system.

3. *New cultural norms need to be established.* Many of the new initiatives have no historical perspective, no veteran leaders to champion the cause. The tendency to revert to old ways is a powerful force. As a result, school system leaders must sustain the new initiatives until new cultural norms develop.

4. *Consistency between means and ends must be evident.* The management of schools should reflect the desired student learning experiences. The emphasis on cooperation, interdependency, and participation must apply to both adults and students in our school communities.

5. *There must be equal emphasis on the development of individuals within the organization and the organization itself.* The natural tension between the needs of the individual and of the organization is healthy.

6. *The role of leadership must be expanded to all employees in the school system.* Leadership is not naturally dispersed widely in organizations among all staff. Leadership cannot be the responsibility solely of administrators. A new leadership development program initiated by the district was necessary.

Individual and organizational renewal requires long-term personal and organizational commitment. Chilliwack recognizes that individual efforts for school improvement can bring localized and short-term success but that sustained change requires an integrated approach within a strategic context.

REFERENCES

Banathy, B. 1991. *Systems design of education: A journey to create the future.* Englewood Cliffs, N.J.: E. T. Press.

Barker, Joel. 1992. *Future edge.* New York: William Morrow.

Capra, Fritjof. 1982. *The turning point: Science, society and the rising culture.* New York: Bantam.

Curtis, R. 1982. *Evaluation or extinction.* New York: Pergamon Press.

Deal, T., and A. Kennedy. 1982. *Corporate cultures.* Reading, Mass.: Addison-Wesley.

Diettweiler, P. C. 1989. Components of an effective professional development program. *Journal of Staff Development* 10 (2): 2–6.

Dufour, R. 1990. *The principal as a staff developer.* Oxford, Ohio: NSDC.

Ferguson, M. 1988. *The Aquarian conspiracy.* Los Angeles, Calif.: J. P. Tarcher.

Firstone, W. A., and B. C. Wilson. 1985. Using bureaucratic and cultural linkages to improve instruction: The principal's contribution. *Educational Administration Quarterly* 21 (2): 7–30.

Fullan, M., and M. Miles. 1992. Getting educational reform right. *Phi Delta Kappan* 22 (6): 745–52.

Fullan, M., and S. Stigelbauer. 1991. *The new meaning of educational change.* New York: Teachers' College Press.

Futrell, M. D. 1991. Nine perceptions on the future of staff development. *Journal of Staff Development* 12 (1): 3–6.

Gleick, J. 1987. *Chaos.* New York: Vilroy.

Greenfield, W. D. 1986. Moral, social and technical dimensions of the principalship. *Peabody Journal of Education*, 130–49.

Harman, W. 1988. *Global mind change*. Indianapolis: Knowledge Systems, Inc.

Joyce, B., and Showers, B. 1988. *Student achievement through staff development*. New York: Longman.

Joyce, B. 1990. The self-educating teacher: Empowering teachers through research. In *Changing school culture through staff development*, edited by B. Joyce. Alexandria, Va.: ASCD Yearbook.

Kuhn, T. 1962. *The structure of scientific revolutions*. Chicago: University of Chicago Press.

Lezotte, L. W. 1981. Climate characteristics in instructionally effective schools. *Impact on Instructional Improvement* 4:29–32.

Loucks-Horsley, S. 1989. Managing change: An integrated part of staff development. In *School district staff development: A handbook of effective practices*, edited by S. Caldwell. Oxford, Ohio: NSDC.

Murphy, J., C. Evertson, and M. Radnofsky. 1984. Restructuring schools: Fourteen elementary and secondary teachers' perspectives on reform. *Elementary School Journal* 92 (2): 135–48.

Naisbitt, J., and P. Aburdene. 1990. *Megatrends 2000: Ten new directions for the 1990s*. New York: Morrow and Company.

Nebgen, Mary K. 1990. Strategic planning: Achieving the goals of organization development. *Journal of Staff Development* 11 (1): 28–31.

Ouchi, W. G. 1981. *Theory Z*. Reading, Mass.: Addison-Wesley.

Peters, T. J., and R. H. Waterman. 1982. *In search of excellence*. New York: Harper and Row.

Purkey, S. D., and M. D. Smith. 1983. Effective schools: A review. *Elementary School Journal* 83 (4): 427–52.

Rozack, T. 1977. *Person planet: The creative disintegration of the individual society*. New York: Doubleday.

Rutter, M., B. Maugham, P. Mortimer, J. Ouston, and A. Smith. 1979. *Fifteen thousand hours: Secondary schools and their effects on children*. Cambridge, Mass.: Harvard University Press.

Sarason, S. 1990. *The predictable future of educational reform: Can we change before it's too late?* San Francisco: Jossey-Bass.

Sculley, J. 1987. *Odyssey*. New York: Harper and Row.

Senge, P. 1990. *The fifth discipline: The art and practice of the learning organization*. New York: Doubleday.

Sparks, D., and Loucks-Horsley, S. 1990. *Five models of staff development*. Oxford, Ohio: NSDC.

Toffler, A. 1980. *The third wave*. New York: Bantam Books.

Williams, R. B. 1990. Teacher professional autonomy and collective bargaining: Conflict or compromise? *Education Canada* 30 (4): 4–7.

———. 1992. *The leadership edge: Strategies to transform school systems*. Vancouver: EduServ.

———. 1993. Initiatives for systemic change. *Journal of Staff Development* 14 (2): 16–21.

Wood, F. G. 1989. Organizing and managing school-based staff development. In *School district staff development: A handbook of effective practices*, edited by S. Caldwell. Oxford, Ohio: NSDC.

TOTAL QUALITY MANAGEMENT PHILOSOPHY AND AN RJR-NABISCO NEXT CENTURY SCHOOL

Robert Chappell and David Gangel

A Virginia public school district has been implementing Total Quality Management (TQM) since the fall of 1990. The Rappahannock County schools' top-level administrators got their baptism in quality training with a group of new Xerox Corporation employees. The district's superintendent, impressed with a new paradigm of schools' improving services to customers, aggressively sought and garnered a TQM employee training partnership with Xerox, the Virginia Department of Education, and the U.S. Department of Education.

As part of the school district's quality improvement effort, in 1992 it sought and obtained an RJR-Nabisco "Next Century Schools" grant. A cornerstone of the grant proposal was that the project use TQM strategies to systemically change instructional services for fourth grade students. Fourth grade teachers and grant-funded computer specialists designed core curriculum on interactive, multimedia software for fourth graders to use at individual workstations.

PUBLIC SCHOOLS TRY TQM

Increasing numbers of U.S. public school districts are looking to TQM to improve their services to "customers." Hailey, Horine, and Rubach conducted a survey in 1992 of school districts known to be interested in TQM. The results, reported in *Quality Progress,* showed that at least one hundred public school districts nationwide had implemented some form of TQM. It was found that 80 percent of the districts use quality tools to improve teaching methods, and 50 percent to increase student achievement (Hailey, Horine, and Rubach 1993).

There is great variation in the content and length of TQM training for educators. Some school systems provide as little as a memorandum or position paper on how their schools operationalize Deming's fourteen points (Deming 1986). Others offer a partial-day inservice titled "Introduction to Quality." The Rappahannock County schools provide up to four days of quality training for all employees on customer service, team problem solving, and quality improvement.

There is considerable variation in the way TQM is implemented in schools across the country. Some use the tools to try to improve all aspects of the system. Many rely on ad hoc teams to solve problems as they are detected (Horine 1993). The Rappahannock district mandates that all employees serve on problem solving/quality improvement teams to improve instructional and support services (Chappell 1993).

Evaluating TQM Efforts in Schools Is Difficult

A fair question to ask is, "How can we be certain that school districts that report implementing TQM are really doing TQM?" Corporations may vary in their approaches to implementing TQM, but those who wish to gain recognition for their efforts in quality must submit to a stringent evaluation. The Malcolm Baldrige Award process examines each corporate entrant on seven standardized criteria ranging from "management of process quality" to "customer focus and satisfaction" (U.S. Dept. of Commerce 1992). The Department of Commerce is piloting a Baldrige-like process to assess qualitatively TQM efforts in public schools. Until a standardized evaluation process is implemented, there can be no assurance that schools are really "doing" TQM.

From a cost-of-quality perspective, superintendents and principals cannot point to increases in corporate profits or to return-on-assets as evidence that quality makes a difference. However, a school district's annual market share may be an indicator of whether TQM is making a difference. Figure 1 depicts how market share in K–12 public education

can be measured as a percentage of the total resident student population being served by a school district (Chappell 1993). Parents who feel their childrens' needs are not being met in public schools may send them to private schools or elect to provide home instruction. Students who don't like school may drop out or purposely try to get expelled. When a district's average daily membership decreases, its share of state revenues shrinks.

From a strictly business perspective, if a school district's market share increases significantly over time, that is an indicator that the district may be improving its services to students. It also should generate more state revenues. Using the example in figure 1, if the district's market share increases from 79.8 percent to 85 percent, the number of additional students served would be 1,300. If the district receives $2,000 from the state for each student in membership, its state aid would increase by $2,600,000.

A School District Commits to TQM and Continuous Improvement

Once the Rappahannock schools' top-level administrators completed their initial TQM training at the Xerox Corporation Training Center, they felt that quality would not only have the potential for increasing the district's market share, but that

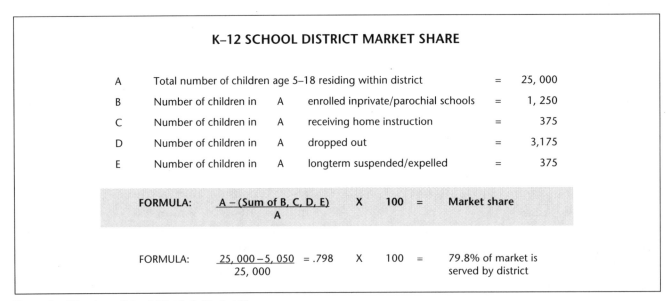

Figure 1   Figuring a School District's Market Share

CONTINUOUS IMPROVEMENT

Mission Statement

The Rappahannock County Public School Board and all associates (employees) are committed to education success and continuous improvement for all students, associates, the educational system, and society.

Policy

Continuous improvement of students, the system, and self is every associate's responsibility. The superintendent and all instructional leaders shall provide for ongoing planning, implementation, monitoring, and evaluation of improvement with periodic reports concerning the status of student, associate, and system continous improvement to the school board.

Figure 2   School Board's Policy on Continuous Improvement

TQM tools and processes held tremendous promise to systematically improve the educational system as a whole. To cement their convictions, they presented a Continuous Improvement policy and a Quality Mission Statement to the school board for approval (Rappahannock County Schools 1991). Figure 2 lists the mission statement and policy.

Quality Training

The next phase of implementing quality in Rappahannock County involved preparation for training. With funding from the partnership of Xerox, the Virginia Department of Education, and the U.S. Department of Education, four school division employees (associates)—the superintendent, the assistant superintendent, and two teachers—went through the equivalent of forty hours of advanced course work at the Xerox Training Center to become quality trainers. Each was credentialed to teach the thirty-two-hour training segment entitled "New Employee Quality Training."

Rappahannock's administration decided to make training in quality voluntary at the outset. Over 65 percent of Rappahannock school associates volunteered for the training, which began June 1991 under the cosponsorhip of Xerox and the Virginia Department of Education. In August 1992, the superintendent and assistant superintendent conducted training sessions with new hires and with returning associates who had not yet received the training. By the end of 1993, nearly 90 percent of all school division associates (classified and certified) had received the thirty-two-hour training.

The Xerox/Virginia Department of Education quality training program covers topics on quality, serving customers/meeting customer requirements, interactive skills, problem solving, and quality improvement. The training emphasizes use of quality tools such as cause-effect (fishbone) diagrams, Pareto charts, Gantt charts, flow charts, run charts, control charts, etc. (Xerox Corp. 1991)

Customer Satisfaction

Attention to customer concerns is a central focus of quality training. In an effort to detect and correct causes of client dissatisfaction, some school districts using TQM distribute customer satisfaction surveys (fig. 3). Surveys generate baseline data to help measure changes in attitudes toward school services (Rappahannock County Schools 1991).

In Rappahannock County, the Quality Steering Committee designed customer surveys for parents to fill out on "fee day" before the start of the school year. Responses are sought from parents on items concerning their perceptions of the effectiveness of the schools' instructional program, guidance services, administrative services, transportation services, fairness in handling discipline, cleanliness of restrooms, etc. The Steering Committee also seeks recommendations from associates about problems they would like to solve.

CUSTOMER SATISFACTION SURVEY

Please answer the following questions using the scale below. Any comments that you wish to add may be placed at the end of the form.

	5 Strongly Agree	4 Agree	3 No Opinion	2 Disagree	1 Strongly Disagree
1. The academic program provided by the Rapphannock County Public Schools will prepare my child/children for the world of work in the twenty-first century.	☐	☐	☐	☐	☐
2. The various programs (i.e., reading, math, science, etc.) of the Rappahannock County Public Schools meet the needs of my children.	☐	☐	☐	☐	☐
3. There is open communication between our childrens' teachers, adminstrators, and the family.	☐	☐	☐	☐	☐
4. The cleanliness of the school buildings and grounds is acceptable.	☐	☐	☐	☐	☐
5. Discipline in the Rapphannock County Public Schools is fair and consistent.	☐	☐	☐	☐	☐
6. The major emphasis of the Rappahannock County Public Schools is a strong academic education of its students.	☐	☐	☐	☐	☐
7. Parents and students are dealt with by school personnel in a friendly and respectful manner.	☐	☐	☐	☐	☐
8. The transportation services that are offered by the Rappahannock County School Board are excellent.	☐	☐	☐	☐	☐
9. Everything considered, I am satisfied with the Rappahannock County Public Schools.	☐	☐	☐	☐	☐
10. Extracurricular offerings (athletics, clubs, field trips, etc.) are adequate.	☐	☐	☐	☐	☐

11. Comments and suggestions: _____

_____

_____

_____

Figure 3   Sample Customer Satisfaction Survey

Voluntary Use of TQM

To address the problems identified by parents and associates, the Rappahannock County Quality Steering Committee established thirteen quality problem-solving project teams comprised of volunteer school associates, instructional leaders, parents, and some students. Over 60 percent of the district's associates volunteered for service on these teams. Excerpts of a few of the voluntary quality teams' work are found in table 1.

Quality Problem Solving Team	Problem Statement in As Is — — — — — — — — — — — — — *Desired-State Format*	Solutions Selected	Result
Parent satisfaction with transportation	34% elementary parents dissatisfied — — — — — — — — — — — — — *Fewer than 10% dissatisfied*	1–Revise and post rules on buses 2–Reduce overcrowding	11% Dissatisfied
The primary grades reporting instrument	Most teachers/parents dissatisfied — — — — — — — — — — — — — *Majority of parents satisfied*	Revise report card from graded to mastery format on a trial basis.	60% parents prefer new system
High school discipline	25% parents: discipline handled unfairly — — — — — — — — — — — — — *Increase percentage of parent satisfaction*	1–Preset steps 2–Stiffer penalties	Parents perceive fairer treatment
Elementary school building security	Unauthorized persons trying to pick up children from classes — — — — — — — — — — — — — *Only authorized will do so*	1–Personnel strictly enforce signout procedure 2–Place visible reminders at all entrances	Teachers report large reduction in violations
Student emergency procedures	Parents concerned about handling of injuries — — — — — — — — — — — — — *No complaints*	1–Preset process to follow 2–Individual signout records	Parents have been complimentary

Table 1   Results of Voluntary Quality Problem-Solving Teams

Problem-solving teams are asked to follow the problem-solving process learned in training. The process fosters a scientific-method-like approach to improvement. By identifying a problem in an "as-is" and "desired-state" format (fig. 4), a gap is identified (Chappell 1993). Whatever solutions the team selects are expected to help close the gap. The solution is, in a sense, a hypothesis of what it might take to close the gap. Once the solution is implemented and measures are taken to evaluate the outcome, a crude form of research to determine the effectiveness of the hypothesis has taken place.

Required TQM

During an administrative staff retreat at M.B.N.A., a financial institution that practices the TQM philosophy, the superintendent and other instructional leaders used the Baldrige Award criteria to conduct an informal quality audit of the school system. The most glaring weakness noted was the lack of a strategic process for continuous improvement in the organization. To correct the deficiency, the superintendent made use of quality processes mandatory. All Rappahannock associates, including those at Rappahannock Elementary, an RJR-Nabisco Next Century Schools site, used TQM within departments and grade levels to improve already solid instructional and support services.

Mandating use of TQM teams and improvement processes was a difficult decision, partially because "continuous improvement" processes are not institutionalized in public education. Senior management hypothesized that the only way to effect a paradigm shift, to facilitate systemic change, was to require all associates in the school district to use TQM to institutionalize "improvement." Mandated quality could help nearly 100 percent of the associates become fluent in quality improvement strategies. It was also seen as the only way to focus improvement efforts on the instructional process. The work of some of the thirty-three required quality teams is highlighted in table 2.

Required TQM teams used their solutions to reduce the gap between their "as is" and their "desired state." The fourth grade RJR-Nabisco quality team, for example, reduced numbers of students needing remedial math services from nineteen (as is) in September 1992 to fewer than eight (desired

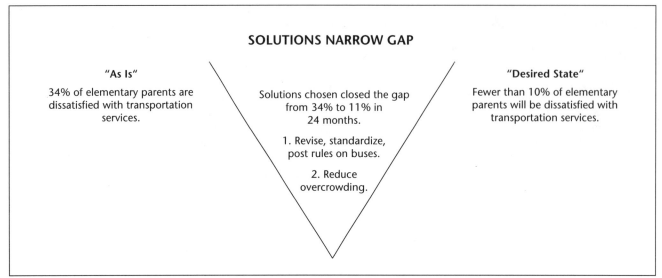

SOLUTIONS NARROW GAP

"As Is"

34% of elementary parents are dissatisfied with transportation services.

Solutions chosen closed the gap from 34% to 11% in 24 months.

1. Revise, standardize, post rules on buses.

2. Reduce overcrowding.

"Desired State"

Fewer than 10% of elementary parents will be dissatisfied with transportation services.

Figure 4   Narrowed Improvement Gap

Quality Team Examples	Targeted for Improvement	Solution
Elementary School		
RCES Cafeteria	Time it takes classes to go through line	Make special orders wait
	Lunch line runs late	Rotate worker assignments
Grade K	Remedial Math count	Practice bubble test format
Grade 4	Remedial Math count	RJR math on computer
Grade 6	Remedial Math count	Math drills in homeroom
RCES Custodial Services	Mowing reduces cleaning time	Revamp custodian schedule
RCES At-Risk Students	Too many students at risk	Teachers "adopt" students
High School		
RCHS Cafeteria	45% participation	Additional heat lamps, check supplies
RCHS Math	Curriculum for non–college bound	Team teach applied math
RCHS Social Studies	Increase students' graph/chart skills	3 graph/chart lessons/week
RCHS Spanish	Vocabulary retention averages 53%	Reintroduce vocabulary
RCHS Attendance	84% per-class attendance rate	Revised attendance process
Central Office		
Transportation Medical Emergency	No existing process to follow	Provide process and training
Transportation Lot Congestion	No existing process to follow	Assign drivers lanes by pumps
Transportation Safety	Motorists illegally pass buses	Radio in offender's tags
Transportation Bus Evacuation	Process lengthy, run by administration	Driver uses set process to evacuate
Central Office Customer Service	Telephone messages not seen	Message holders on doors

Table 2   Required Quality Improvement Teams Solve Problems

state) by March 1993. This was a 63 percent reduction in failure using the TQM change process.

With the exception of the elementary grade–level quality teams, which were asked to work on reducing numbers of students needing mathematics remediation, the required quality teams chose their own problem or process to improve. All selected their own solutions or methods of improvement. Because the teams had been asked to select for improvement things that were within their scope to improve, most team members were intimately involved in implementing improvement strategies.

Evaluation

During the fall of 1990, in the early stages of committing to TQM as an organizationwide modus operandi, the district's top-level management decided quality wouldn't be window dressing. The superintendent and his staff decided that systemic change of this public school district could be achieved by (a) learning strategies for continuous improvement; (b) using those strategies in a scientific-method format to improve already good instruction; and (c) expecting associates to treat one another, parents, and students as customers.

There are several evaluative efforts currently underway to determine if the implementation of TQM in the district is indeed changing the culture of the organization. The Virginia Department of Education is doing a study of the several districts involved in its partnership grant with the Xerox Corporation and the U.S. Department of Education. The federal government is conducting an independent audit.

A doctoral study on the effects of implementation of TQM in the Rappahannock County Public Schools found that over 50 percent of employees trained in TQM principles voluntarily used TQM to solve problems. Over 70 percent of employees surveyed responded that administrators increased efforts to meet their needs following the thirty-two-hour TQM training. Additionally, 66 percent of employees felt more empowered as a result of TQM implementation in the district (Chappell 1993).

In a market-share study of Virginia districts (including Rappahannock County) that started their TQM efforts in the Xerox partnership in 1990–91,

it was found that the seven districts increased their share of students served from 78.3 percent in 1989–90 to 84.7 percent in 1992–93. This market-share increase of 6.4 percent contrasted with an average increase of 2.8 percent for all Virginia districts during the same period (Chappell 1995).

Another TQM-related audit is scheduled for completion in 1996. Rappahannock County has an RJR-Nabisco grant at Rappahannock Elementary that incorporates TQM "quality improvement" strategies to change instructional delivery from the traditional mode to an interactive computer format. Achievement of that goal may bring about change not only in instructional processes, but also in the institutionalization of the process and concept of "continuous improvement" in public education. The RJR-Nabisco Foundation will help the school system evaluate the success of the revised instructional processes at the conclusion of the grant cycle.

RJR-NABISCO NEXT CENTURY SCHOOLS PROJECT

Vision of Education for the Twenty-First Century

The Rappahannock County Public School District has been recognized as a leader in educational technology in the Commonwealth of Virginia. Through a variety of partnerships with such corporations as Potomac Edison Power and Light, Apple Computer, IBM, and RJR-Nabisco, the Rappahannock County Public Schools have become the benchmark for the student-to-computer ratio in Virginia public schools at four students to one computer in grades kindergarten through twelve.

Rappahannock's vision for technology for the twenty-first century is the seamless application of all technologies. Technology is an ever-increasing part of our lives. Students must be able to effectively use technology as a tool in order to be productive in the next-century workplace. In order to meet the challenges of the next century, Rappahannock envisions a school system that models the use of technology as preparation for students. In addition, technology can change how educators provide instruction. Instead of a teacher repetitively providing instruction, technology can empower educators to be creators and improvers of instruction and share the learning process. Technology connected with the philosophy and practice of continuous improvement can help transform schools into learning institutions. A learning institution is one where students continually learn because educators continually learn how to improve instruction for students. The institution itself learns to improve by the collective efforts of all involved in improving the institution. Rappahannock holds a vision that by using technology and continually improving all school processes, we can obtain a high level of external and internal customer satisfaction measured in a variety of ways, including student achievement. We believe the answer isn't a new program or fad. We believe that we have the resources to improve education by using the physical and mental tools of the twenty-first century: technology and continuous quality improvement.

Rappahannock County Elementary School is developing a fourth grade instructional process (curriculum and delivery method) based on quality improvement and computerization that will revolutionize education. The instructional process is cooperatively developed by existing staff and grant-funded project staff through the use of the Xerox Corporation's Quality Improvement Process. The instructional process includes curriculum subject areas and delivery methods placed on computer through the use of multimedia authoring software. Once the instructional process is computerized, the instructional delivery is then individualized and interactive. The computerized instructional process contains much less variance than traditional instructional delivery. With less variance and a more stable environment, the entire instructional process can be continuously improved through a quality improvement process.

This project helps change the role of the teacher from one of repetitive instructional deliverer to one of delivery assistant and instructional process improver. The project will also improve student performance through quality improvement. As a result of this project, the concept of instructional quality control will have its birth.

Goals

The project will solve the problem of varying student achievement, which can range from extremely low to extremely high in a given subject at any given grade level. This project focuses on fourth grade. The specific goals for the project are the following:

1. Improvement of fourth grade student achievement as measured by growth scores in mathematics, social studies, science, and reading subtests on the Iowa Test of Basic Skills and on criterion-referenced tests matched to the instructional process to be developed.

2. Utilization of total quality management techniques to develop and improve a fourth grade instructional process (curriculum) that is completely documented and repeatable.

3. Control of as many instructional variables and learner variables as possible.

4. Utilization of computer technology as the instructional process delivery vehicle.

5. Training of classroom teachers to use a computer multimedia authoring system and off-the-shelf application software to transform a lesson plan into a computerized instructional process.

6. Training of students to use the computer as a learning tool.

7. Development of classroom furnishings to support the central medium of computerized instructional delivery process.

Strategy

Three new developments—in education, management and organizational practice, and technology—can be brought together to revolutionize public education. The project is aimed at taking advantage of the intersection of these three areas with public education (see fig. 5).

Education is at a crossroads. A national consensus exists that encourages educational reform and improvement. The current climate is ideal for exploring new instructional delivery methods.

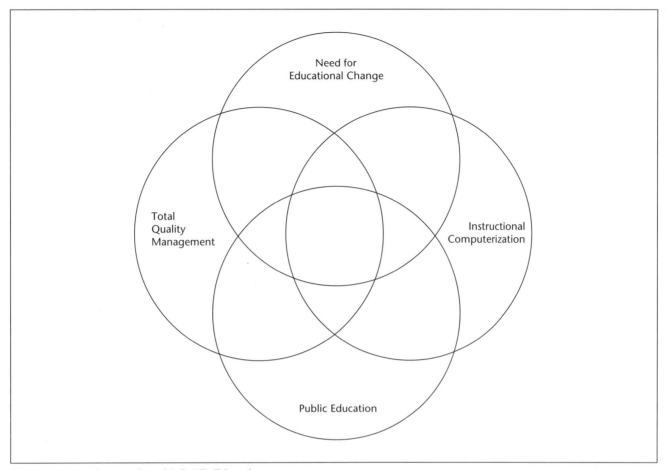

Figure 5   Areas Intersecting with Public Education

The concept of Quality or Total Quality Management is being discovered and applied to business, manufacturing, and service industries. Quality, as defined by Deming, Juran, Crosby, and others, can revolutionize education as it has other industries. Quality can be used on several levels in education. Its application to personnel or internal customers is obvious. However, its application to learning and its effect on student achievement is the real payoff.

The power of this project is in the intersection of the three areas with public education. The time is ripe for revolutionary change in education and for continued improvement based on a documented, repeatable, instructional process that is individually and interactively provided by the computer. Ultimately, the project holds the key to changing the role of the classroom teacher from a continuous curriculum presenter to a continuous curriculum process improver. By allowing the computer to

provide the "mechanical" repetition of instruction, the teacher is free for higher-order professional application (i.e., improving the instructional process, which will improve student achievement).

Computer technology has evolved to a point that teachers with minimal computer backgrounds can place lesson sequences directly on the computer for lesson delivery in the classroom. Several off-the-shelf software packages allow for multimedia integration into a computer-delivered lesson. Text, graphics, photographs, sound, animation, and video can be incorporated into a multimedia lesson that is individually and interactively provided on a computer.

The Potomac Edison Company, in partnership with schools in Virginia, West Virginia, and Maryland, has developed an authoring system for education. The system, now in its third generation, is a HyperCard-based program for Macintosh computers. It was designed so that educators could rapidly learn and utilize the applications on the computer. The authoring system development software (development refers to teachers developing instructional sequences for student use) uses the MacRecorder for sound, Photoshop for graphics and color photographs, and Macromedia Director for animation. Video and related compression technology is placed into the system by using the system extension QuickTime, an Apple Computer product. With QuickTime, videotape can be converted to a digital compressed format and saved on a disk. Premiere editing software is used to edit video and sound sequences. The HyperCard-based authoring system combines all of the mentioned off-the-shelf programs into one interactive, instructional sequence.

Sound, color, picture, and video sequences take up an enormous amount of disk space. The best cost-benefit arrangement for utilization of such storage-intense applications is to provide a network server and a high-speed network system. This can be accomplished by using a large storage file server such as the one our partner, the Potomac Edison Company, has provided: a Digicard server with a 1.2-gigabyte hard drive. By using a high-capacity file server, student computers can be cheaper machines. The only additional requirement is a high-speed network system to rapidly transfer files from the server to student computers. This can be accomplished by using an ethernet network system and coaxial cable.

For this project, the Potomac Edison Company has provided an authoring system, file server, development computer, and some related software to Rappahannock Elementary School. Two fourth grade teachers, as well as four other teachers, have already been trained by Potomac Edison personnel in utilization of the authoring system. Since the elementary school's installed base, file server, and training all relate to Macintosh computers, and since Macintosh has the only off-the-shelf system-supported format for digitized video, the natural alternative for student use is the Apple Macintosh LC III computer with four megabytes memory, an eighty-megabyte hard drive, and an ethernet network–ready configuration.

Quality improvement theory indicates that in any given process variance will occur. The process of instructional delivery can have significant variance from one child to the next. For example, children can have different prerequisite backgrounds; they have different learning styles and different abilities. However, even more mundane variance can occur: the student can be absent from instruction or mentally inattentive at the time of instruction. When considering fourth grade instruction, variance exists from one teacher's instruction to another's, and from one teacher's instruction during one period to that of the same teacher during a different period.

Rappahannock County Elementary School, along with the rest of the school system, has been in partnership with the Xerox Corporation. The Xerox Corporation has helped move the school and system toward the concept of Total Quality Management and continuous improvement. The Xerox training focuses on three areas. The first area is composed of developing a teamwork environment, team communications, and productivity. Problem solving is the second area. A problem-solving model is presented to show how to reduce and remove special-cause variation from a process. By removing special-cause variation, a process will move toward stability. Quality improvement is the third process that is taught. Quality improvement moves a stable process toward identified customer requirements. The quality improvement process has been applied to education for the development of an instructional sequence.

The Quality Improvement Process for Instructional Process is composed of nine steps. The steps are more easily understood when applied to a specific unit of study. For example, in a fourth grade mathematics class, currency is studied. An activity could be designed on the computer to teach a student (in the role of waiter or waitress) how to add up a customer's menu choices and prepare a bill that clearly and correctly reflects the amount owed. In this case the nine steps would be interpreted as follows:

Step 1: Identify Instructional Output—"What's to be done?"

The output in this lesson could be, "Bill preparation learned."

Step 2: *Identify Customers of Instructional Output—"For whom is it to be done?"*

The primary customers would be the students receiving the instruction. The secondary customers could be the future employers of these students or the schools of higher education receiving these students.

Step 3: *Identify Customer Requirements for Instruction—"What does the customer want, need, expect?"*

The primary requirement: accurate information for adding the amount of the menu selections and preparing the bill; the opportunity to apply those instructions and produce a quality product (accurate bill); any specific training she or he might need to follow the instructions (i.e., how to add currency).

Step 4: *Translate Customer Requirements into Specifications—"What precise characteristics will the output have?"*

This would include the specific concepts to be taught, i.e., steps to be followed in adding currency; practice problems to be solved; steps to be followed in preparing the bill; how to present the information; how to build self-correction opportunities into the lesson, etc.

Step 5: *Identify Steps in the Work Process—"How will the work be accomplished? (Who, in what order, with what resources?)"*

For example, step 1 could be: The project staff will design the mathematics unit on currency. Step 2 could be: The staff will place the written plan on the computer. Detailed steps would follow in order.

Step 6: *Select Measure for Critical Process Step—"How will errors be prevented? How will we know if requirements will be met?"*

- Determine at what points accuracy can be checked.

- Determine where errors may occur in the instructional process.

Step 7: *Determine Process Capability to Meet Requirements—"Does the work process actually produce a product/service that meets customer requirements?"*

- Have teachers run through the completed computerized sequence.

- Have selected students run through the completed computerized sequence. Determine if the process is capable of meeting requirements. Were the teachers and students in the process capability study able to follow the directions and do the correct computation? Did they receive the help they needed when they hit a snag? Were they able to produce an accurate product (customer bill)? Was the instructor able to determine which students needed additional assistance with the concepts?

- If the process is determined to be incapable of meeting requirements, problem solving is initiated to find out what is wrong and how to correct it.

- If the process is determined capable of meeting requirements, the instructional process will be used with all appropriate students.

Step 8: *Evaluate Results—"Is the process still working? Any change needed? Any new problems? Customers satisfied?"*

The instructor will determine if the students are finding the instructions accurate and easily understood. Are they able to work through the process and come up with a quality product (customer bill)? Do they feel that their needs have been met by the program, or have they needed a significant amount of additional instruction? Have they had fun working on the program or have they found it a drudge? If there is a problem, problem solving is initiated to correct it.

Step 9: *Recycle—"Could we do even better? Could other outputs be included? Could it be used for additional customers (students)? Are there better ways to measure student success?"*

For the first time, classroom teachers have the ability to document an instructional process and minimize variation by computerized delivery. And, for the first time, teachers can cooperatively apply quality improvement to an instructional delivery process to improve student achievement. A multimedia authoring system allows educators to place nearly all instruction on a computer for individualized and interactive applications. Lectures, examples, illustrations, reteaching techniques, practice, resource material, and research can all be provided on the computer in an interactive mode. This process guarantees that every fourth grade student receives the same instruction with much less variance. The computer can interweave text, digitized sound (voice, music, etc.), graphics, pictures, animation, and video to create an instruction process.

Since the computerized instructional process is interactive, the student must be mentally attending in order to proceed. If a student is absent, the same computerized instruction presented to the class awaits his return. The entire instructional process will be the same, regardless of teacher or period. However, while it is a singular process, it will be individually applied. Students can proceed at their own rate, branching off for reinforcement or review and alternating teaching and reteaching as individual needs dictate.

This concept provides for a completely documented instructional process that is constant for instructional delivery. A documented stable process is one that can be applied to quality process improvement. In an environment of a stable instructional process, it will be possible to achieve educational quality control. That is, all students will be predictably successful based on customer-driven specifications. Student success will vary only within a predetermined acceptable range attributed to natural variance within the learner and the system.

Furnishings in a computer-centered classroom will require development. Currently computers are used in lab facilities. Thought should be given to "form following function," with student furnishings being designed around a computerized medium of instruction.

The Next Century School desk looks different from today's school desks. Today's desks are used for writing and for holding student books, classroom materials, or related classroom projects. This project stresses the vision of the next-century computerization in instruction. Just as the form of student desks followed their function in this century, so will form follow function in the next century.

Student desks hold a computer and are designed so that the keyboard and mouse are in a functional location and yet retractable when not in use. The computer is concealed and protected from tampering, yet well ventilated for proper operation. Desks have access to electrical power and network wiring. Electrical and network wires are concealed. The desks are designed so that they are not limited to computerization use only, since paper-and-pencil exercises will still exist in the classroom at certain times. One possible design is presented in figure 6.

This project has every indication of success since Rappahannock County Elementary School has al-

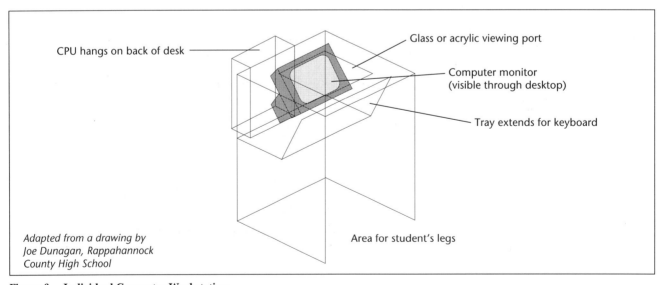

CPU hangs on back of desk

Glass or acrylic viewing port

Computer monitor
(visible through desktop)

Tray extends for keyboard

Adapted from a drawing by
Joe Dunagan, Rappahannock
County High School

Area for student's legs

Figure 6   Individual Computer Workstation

ready experienced some success by using computerized mathematics instruction on the sixth grade level. For years prior to the 1988–89 school year, Rappahannock County Elementary School provided a traditional mathematics program for sixth grade students. The nationally normed percentile scores, as determined by the mathematics section of the Science Research Associates (SRA) test, for eight years prior to 1989 are shown below.

1976	43	1985	55
1977	46	1986	61
1978	41	1987	63
1984	49	1988	54

During the 1988–89 school year, the elementary school changed sixth grade instruction from a traditional process to a computerized process. Nearly all mathematics instruction was provided on the computer from 1988–89 to the present. The scores for the years of computerization of sixth grade math made a significant increase as follows: 1989—72; 1990—72; and 1991—68. Using a control chart to plot the results (see fig. 7), it indicates that the system was within the upper and lower control limits until the process was changed. In effect, the results of computerization have placed the improved student achievement outside of the limits of expectation for the traditional system. One caveat is needed. It is understood that in order to produce an XR control chart, a minimum of twenty initial data points should be used. Only eight data points were available, since only eight prior years had been tested at the sixth grade level.

THE BIRTH OF INSTRUCTIONAL QUALITY CONTROL

Educators have traditionally considered instruction as being an unpredictable process. Teachers

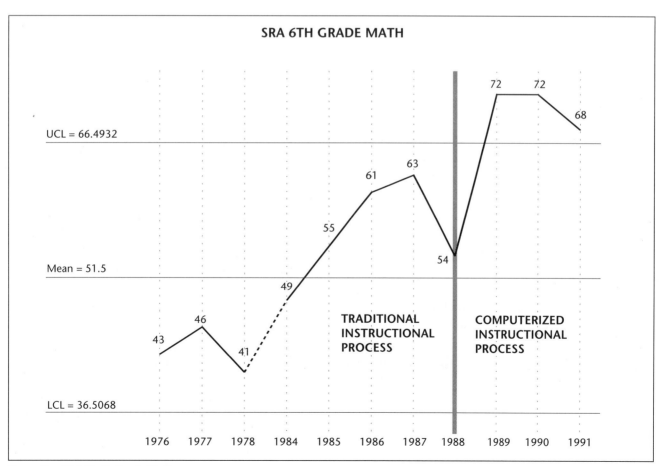

Figure 7   SRA Sixth Grade Math

have provided some sort of instruction, and students either learned it or they did not. Perhaps remedial or reteaching strategies were then applied, but whether learning took place or not was largely unpredictable. Individual teachers may eventually acquire insight into what could be a successful lesson, but this is only after years of experience, and there is still no way to communicate or measure the insight. Statistical measures of education are mainly descriptive or inferential and not predictive. Educational statistics describe what a data set looks like or how the results of a small group of data relate to a larger unmeasured data set. Educational statistics are not predictive. Statistical measures do not accompany an instructional process that will give the educator insight as to how successful the instruction process will be at fostering student learning. Schools accept new instructional programs without any knowledge of predictability of success with their students.

Statistical quality control strives to be predictive. Analytical procedures such as control charts help people understand the boundaries of variation in a process (Shewhart 1939). Every system produces variation. Some variation is inherent in the system, or sources of variation come from outside influences on the system. Once the types of variations and the boundaries of variation are understood, improvement can be focused on changing or limiting variation by changing the process. An example of how statistical quality control works is easily understood in an industrial context. In order for a machine to produce manufactured parts that are consistently defect free, two things must happen: First, the machine must be designed so that it's aim is to produce defect-free parts. In other words, product quality must be designed into the machine. Second, once the machine is in operation, data must be collected and statistical analyses such as control charts must be used to determine the parameters of variation in the parts the machine produces. The process of using the machine and the machine itself are then adjusted until the parameters of variation of the parts produced are within the desired limits specified by the customer. At this point the process and the machine are predictable and can produce defect-free parts.

Educators certainly do not like to consider students as defects, but we certainly have students who do not learn and become defectors or dropouts. Statistical quality control in instruction is first designing a process that will generate the desired learning results, that is, designing instruction aimed toward the desired learning outcome. Next, use the instructional process to determine the parameters of variation. Then, improve the instructional process by removing as much undesirable variation as is specified by the customer.

The notion of statistical quality control is valid in the industrial age of mass production. It was not part of the preindustrial age of local craftsmen. Industrial mass production and quality control have produced more products at a cheaper price and of higher quality than could be provided through local craftsmen. Today, education is in the age of local craftsmen or teachers. Computerization will provide the platform for mass instruction where statistical quality control can be applied. The promise of statistical quality control in instruction is the same as in other sectors. For instruction it means more learning at a cheaper price with less failure.

Educators will find this concept undesirable. Local industrial craftsmen didn't like the concept of industrial mass production either. In addition, educators will say that people do not behave like machines and they are not always predictable. While people are not always predictable, generally they behave as though they are. If people were not at least partially predictable, commonly used statistical sampling techniques would be useless. The following is offered as an example of human learning that is predictable. Two years ago norm-referenced standardized test scores were requested from the Virginia Department of Education for every school system in Virginia for grades four, eight, and eleven. The data for each system and grade level was then placed into a control chart. Generally, the scores for each grade level in each system were stable and future results could be predicted between parameters unique to the grade level and system.

Aside from the point of predictability, this experience goes a long way toward understanding the futility of annually trying to explain why standardized test scores are either up or down. Generally, the change in test scores for most school systems was a result of variation within a stable system. Every system has variation, and within a stable system it is neither good nor bad. It is just variation. Stated in the vernacular, "variation happens." Yet each year educators feel good or bad based on variation from within the system. Educators must first understand variation and then through the use of computerization move to control learning variation by improving the instructional process. By focusing teachers on strategies for improvement of instruction instead of on repetitive instructional delivery, the quality improvement process in the RJR-Nabisco school provides a means of substantial systemic change.

REFERENCES

Chappell, R. 1993. Impact of the implementation of quality on the Rappahannock County Schools. Dissertation prospectus, Blacksburg, Virginia.

————. 1995. Increase in public school market share linked to quality principles. *Critical linkages II newsletter.* Chestnut Hill, Mass.: Center for Essential Linkages and Learning.

Deming, W. 1986. *Out of the crisis.* Cambridge, Mass.: M.I.T.

Hailey, W., J. Horine, and L. Rubach. 1993. Transforming schools. *Quality Progress,* October, 23.

Rappahannock County Public Schools. 1991. School board policy manual. Sperryville, Va.

Rappahannock County Public Schools. 1991. Parent survey. Sperryville, Va.

Shewhart, W. 1939. *Statistical method from the viewpoint of quality control.* Washington: The Graduate School, The Department of Agriculture.

U.S. Department of Commerce. 1992. *Malcolm Baldrige: 1992 award criteria.* Milwaukee: American Society of Quality Control.

Xerox Corp. 1990. *Commitment to quality: Virginia Public Schools in partnership with the Xerox Corporation.* Stamford, Conn.: Xerox Corp.

RIDING THE ROLLER COASTER OF EDUCATIONAL CHANGE
Evaluation and the Learning Organization

—

Hallie Preskill

Four months into the implementation of one school's efforts to transform education, the four lead teachers offered the following metaphor:

> We're like the Super Orient Express train traveling at five hundred miles per hour. As we go along, the environment changes . . . the climate changes too. . . . Some people get left off (we're moving so quickly). Some of the people who manage to stay on are held on by outreached hands and ropes that are thrown out to them. We've had a couple of people fall off. We haven't thrown anyone off yet. When people enter the train, they expect to see a dining car. Either they adapt to what we are or they go to the back and jump off. We're constantly redecorating the train. If the train stopped, it would fall apart, we need to keep it moving, keep the energy. If we did stop, we'd end up looking like everything else.

This chapter is a story of how one school attempted to implement systemic change within a large city district environment, and how, had it exemplified a learning organization, it might have been able to deal more effectively with the many challenges it faced. The context for the story is the formative evaluation conducted for this school over a three-year period. In this chapter I suggest that school change efforts need a learning organization model to follow for implementation. I also suggest that evaluation should be developmental in nature, so that it provides the necessary information for making programmatic improvements.

PLANNING THE SCHOOL OF THE FUTURE

The Marston School (a pseudonym), located in a large, midwestern inner city, opened in September 1989 with 162 students in grades four through six. By its third year it had grown to nearly 300 students by adding grades seven and eight. The concept of the school emerged from a belief that each student can learn and must be better prepared for the twenty-first century. The three goals outlined in the school's early development were: (1) students would choose and attain achievement levels commensurate with their unique abilities and needs as specified in their personal growth plans; (2) staff would receive intensive and ongoing training in the use of current, highly effective teaching/learning practices; and (3) state-of-the-art technology would be made available for both instructional and managerial purposes.

The Marston School case is unusual because it is not an attempt to change or restructure an existing school. Rather, it is an experiment in transforming education. It started from scratch, bringing together teachers with varied educational and teaching backgrounds who had never worked together. Master's level university interns with little or no training in education or teaching experience were brought together with 162 students in a renovated space within another school (it has since moved into a downtown building that was purchased and renovated specifically for Marston). The school has tried to redefine teacher, student, parent, and community roles in addition to the way curriculum is designed and delivered. It received national attention in May 1991, when President Bush and Secretary of Education Lamar Alexander toured the school and spoke to over 1,000 Marston School and community members, and President Bush signed the *America 2000* education bill. In addition, several journal and magazine articles have been written applauding Marston's efforts to reform education.

As a third-party evaluator, I began with the school's initial design. Funded for the first two years by a local foundation and by the district for the third year, the evaluation's major focus was formative. The negotiated purpose of the evaluation was to document the school's implementation and to provide feedback to assist in its development. I viewed this task as "the careful and systematic monitoring of appropriate components, processes, and interactions of program implementation, so that the innovation, program effectiveness, and future reform efforts can be improved" (Clark 1988, 21). The philosophy and approach guiding this evaluation reflected the current literature on educational reform, which stresses the need to understand educational change as a process and not as an event (Fullan 1991). It also stresses that the perceived failures of past educational innovations and reforms have failed not because of their intent or philosophy, but because of a failure in the implementation process (Cuban 1990).

The evaluation's design included the collection of quantitative data in the form of (1) closed-item responses on student and parent surveys, and (2) students' standardized test scores for each of the three years. Qualitative data resulted from interviews with teachers, parents, and students throughout the three years, plus open-ended data from the parent and student surveys. In addition, I spent over four hundred hours on site observing teachers, students, and parents; took over four hundred photographs; and collected numerous internal and external documents.

Throughout the evaluation, I was presented with numerous challenges and opportunities. At times, I questioned the value of my role and wondered if it made any discernable difference. Yet there were times when I truly believed that my evaluation work was contributing to the school's development. Throughout this up-and-down experience, two questions continually emerged that I have grappled with in hopes of gaining a better understanding of how evaluation findings can be more useful for program staff making bold attempts to change traditional ways of educating students:

1. What effect does the degree to which a school is a "learning organization" have on that school's use of formative evaluation information?

2. What is the role of formative evaluation in systemic change efforts? Are there other role options?

Before I begin to address the above questions, I believe it is necessary to provide the reader with a glimpse of what it has been like for the teachers at Marston to construct their approach to education.

LIVING THROUGH EDUCATIONAL REFORM

The school is led by four teachers—one lead teacher and three associate teachers—who have specially negotiated twelve-month union contracts and are paid $55,000–$60,000 a year. At the end of the third year of the evaluation, there were twelve generalist teachers with nine-month contracts, five paraprofessionals, and several consultants who had individual contracts with the school. The school has engaged over forty other adults who have provided students with small group or individualized instruction and other support services.

The curriculum at Marston is developed from information gathered from students and parents, which is documented in the students' personal growth plans (PGP). From the students' PGPs, teachers brainstorm topics. Individual teachers are responsible for developing course objectives and content and for communicating this information to parents and students prior to the time of course registration for each term. For most teachers this has meant teaching new courses every ten weeks and having approximately four days to plan new courses between each term. It has been a goal of the school to utilize the downtown area and to provide students with internships and mentorships within the community.

Throughout the school's three years, the teachers have used numerous metaphors to describe their experiences in implementing educational reform. Many of these metaphors reflect the lack of time and the uncertainty of their "journey" through the change process. The metaphors used in the first two years focused on four themes: the fast pace of the implementation effort, the uncertainty and ambiguity of their mission, the perseverance and courage needed to implement reform, and the vulnerability of teachers engaged in major reform efforts (Preskill 1991). Interestingly, other educational researchers have also found teachers using the metaphor of journey in their studies of educational reform, especially in a program's early stages (e.g., Fullan 1993; Stacey 1992; Wincek 1995).

The teachers have had to move quickly in establishing the school's structures, processes, and policies, not to mention negotiating their own roles and responsibilities, since none of this had been planned prior to the first week of school. In describing the *fast pace* of their task, they used numerous transportation metaphors (speeding train, stationary bicycle, whitewater raft, kayak, broken bus). These metaphors imply the need for energy and stamina to successfully accomplish the goals of systemic change.

Many of the staff spoke about Marston as a journey or new adventure without a map. They reflected

that while the journey was exciting, it was also imbued with great *uncertainty* and *ambiguity*. These descriptions emphasized the importance of establishing a clear vision for the staff and the need to continually share it with others in the school community.

In spite of the challenges and stresses in starting a new school, the teaching and paraprofessional staff exhibited great *perseverance* and *courage*. They likened the experience to building a house with the people already in it, giving birth, or tracking through mud.

The fourth category of metaphors were associated with how *vulnerable* these teachers have felt. With the national attention they have received, teachers said it was like being in a goldfish bowl. Instead of being allowed to make mistakes and try new approaches and materials, they often felt that they were being held up as a model school. Yet in their own reality, they were merely a research and development site.

As with any school that brings in people who do not know one another, time was needed to establish a healthy working climate. The school intended the four lead teachers to work as a team to set the direction for the other staff members. For three years, however, the lead staff painfully sought to define their roles and responsibilities and to learn how to work together, while trying to deal with the interpersonal communication issues between and among the staff and parent community. Though some of the staff wanted the adult climate to be more social and friendly, several of the lead staff publicly stated that they were not interested in building friendships with the staff; their job was solely to teach and lead.

THE LEARNING ORGANIZATION

As I watched Marston grow and change, I wanted to understand how the formative evaluation information was being used and if there was any relationship to Marston's use of it and the degree to which it exemplified a learning organization. For the last twenty years, organizational theorists have been writing about organizational learning and change. Marsick and Watkins (1992a) write that organizational learning is the ongoing and informal acquisition, both on and off the job, of individual, team, and organizational skills, knowledge and abilities. It includes a mindset that views experience as potential learning; a value that encourages individual and team learning and involvement; an attitude that encourages the routine reexamination of individual, team, and organizational assumptions, values, methods, and policies. (p. 11)

Dixon (1992) believes it is important to look at organizational learning as a process instead of an outcome because it focuses on the system rather than the individual. Argyris and Schon (1978) suggest the following for organizational learning to occur:

Learning agents' discoveries, inventions, and evaluations must be embedded in organizational memory. They must be embedded in the individual images and shared maps of organizational theory-in-use from which individual members will subsequently act. If this encoding does not occur, individuals will have learned but the organization will not have done so. (p. 19)

Marsick (1987) discusses a similar concept but calls it action learning. She describes this as "a cyclical process by which a group of people jointly identify a problem, experiment with a solution, monitor the results, reflect critically on the process, and use the resultant information to reframe the problem and try out a new solution" (p. 20). A sign of a learning organization is the continual measure of its success and its members accountability for its progress. Wick and Leon (1993) also suggest that a "learning organization is hungry for knowledge," and that this knowledge must be communicated quickly to members with honesty and openness (p. 130).

It is important to note that while the above definitions focus on the organization, and groups or teams of people, these authors point out that individual learning is a prerequisite to organizational learning, and only after individuals critically reflect on their own experiences can organizational learning occur.

There are several models in the literature of how organizations learn (see Dixon 1992 for an excellent review of literature on organizational learn-

ing), and while they may indeed lend important insights into understanding organizational learning, educational reform, and formative evaluation, I have chosen the work of Argyris and Schon (1978) in which to ground my thoughts for this chapter. Following are three ways they believe organizations learn.

The first is described as *single-loop learning:* "Organizational learning occurs when individuals, acting from their images and maps, detect a match or mismatch of outcome to expectation which confirms or disconfirms organizational theory-in-use" (p. 19). When errors are detected, individuals attempt to correct these errors through an inquiry process. To correct the errors, they must invent new strategies based on new assumptions and then evaluate those strategies.

When people within organizations keep information to themselves, have little trust in others, are afraid to make issues or problems public, try to communicate issues but feel they are not listened to, or do not wish to solve problems collaboratively, they may learn, but they are unable to act as agents of *organizational* learning. Single-loop learning appears to be sufficient in organizations that operate within a constant framework of norms for performance. They are interested in "how best to keep organizational performance within the range specified by existing norms" (p. 21), not in systemic change.

Double-loop learning, on the other hand, involves inquiry that resolves conflicting requirements. The results of the inquiry are used to restructure organizational norms, strategies, and assumptions. An important feature that differentiates double-loop learning from single-loop learning is confrontation of conflicts. In organizations with double-loop learning, individuals come together to confront and resolve conflicts. "In this sense, the organization is a medium for translating incompatible requirements into interpersonal and intergroup conflict" (p. 23). Members of the organization are able to come to some sort of agreement, or at least an understanding of conflicting philosophies and/or practices. When this is accomplished, members of the organization can move on and adapt to the new images and maps of the organization.

The third type of organizational learning described by Argyris and Schon is *deutero-learning*. This type of learning requires organization members to use previous contexts. They reflect on and inquire into previous episodes of organizational learning, or failure to learn. They discover what they did that facilitated or inhibited learning, invent new strategies for learning, produce the strategies, and evaluate and generalize the results of the strategies. The results become encoded in individual images and maps and are reflected in organizational learning practice. This type of learning is often linked to double-loop learning because the conversations about previous learning take place in the context of collaborative inquiry.

In summary, single-loop learning is focused on effectiveness. Individuals may learn but the organization doesn't, and established norms of performance exist. Double-loop learning focuses on joint inquiry into resolving conflicting norms of performance and making new norms more effectively realized. And, finally, deutero-learning adds to the process critical reflection and dialogue that produces new insights for future action. It would seem, therefore, that for schools and programs undergoing significant change, double-loop and, if possible, deutero-learning would be the preferred model for becoming a learning organization.

FORMATIVE EVALUATION AT MARSTON

I entered into Marston's evaluation believing that the information I collected would be of use to the school community in its decision-making processes as it grew and developed. I knew that the district and staff saw my role as the documenter of the school's implementation. As I got to know the staff and school organization better, particularly after the first year, I found myself becoming the "confidant" or the "much-needed outlet" for several of the generalist and paraprofessional staff. I would often walk into the school and have a staff member ask if we could talk. We would find the closest unused room and the person would tell me his or her concerns, with little more prompting than "How's it going?" The individuals would typically end the conversation by saying it was good to talk to some-

one and they appreciated my role in documenting the school's evolution so others could see what it had been like. I don't believe they expected me to share this information with the lead staff; rather, I believe they saw me as someone with whom they could share their concerns and who could help them reflect on their daily challenges.

My early negotiations with the school centered on gaining the staff's acceptance of the data-collection efforts, which included making random observations, conducting formal and informal interviews with students, attending staff and parent meetings, and taking photographs. While I offered to provide feedback as requested during the evaluation, I did not negotiate an ongoing mechanism for disseminating the evaluation findings. On and off during the first year and a half, the lead staff and I met to discuss various issues; yet, due to the staff's lack of time and the increasing interpersonal conflicts among the four lead teachers, I did not pursue additional feedback sessions. In the third year, little feedback was provided. Since the evaluation wasn't authorized and funded until March, data wasn't being collected until between April and June, which left me virtually no time or opportunity to analyze, interpret, and share information before the school year finished.

The results of each year's formative evaluation were presented in a final report that focused on the extent to which each of the school's goals were being achieved, what was working particularly well, what obstacles they were encountering, and what they still needed to work on. The final drafts of the reports were reviewed by the lead and generalist teaching staff and parent members of the school council. Their suggested additions and changes were used to clarify issues or to correct inaccurate information. Though I would have been pleased to do so, I was never asked to discuss and verbally present to the staff or school council the implications of the findings (though I did make presentations to a subcommitee of the school board each year). In part, this may have been because I was unable to provide the staff with a draft of the final report until August of each year.

By the second year, however, I became frustrated by the evaluation's seeming inability to positively affect the school. I was sitting on so much data—information from all perspectives that seemed to be sealed within individuals or small groups of people. My role seemed to be that of an archivist and information broker for the district and outside educational community (the evaluation reports were made public and were being requested by and sent to various educators throughout the country). I felt increasingly ineffective in my ability to do what I had hoped—to provide ongoing information to the teachers and staff about how things were going and to help them implement their mission more effectively.

MARSTON AS A LEARNING ORGANIZATION

Reflecting on Marston's history, its evolution, and my understanding of organizational change and learning, I now believe that some of my frustration with formative evaluation and the use of its results may be related to Marston's being an example of single-loop learning. While members within the school were continually learning what worked for them individually, the school as a whole was unable to develop an ongoing inquiry process that allowed the staff to reflect collaboratively on issues and problems. As a result, individuals learned to cope and adapt to situations as best they could, but their learning and action had little positive impact on the organization as a whole. Marston ended up developing a "self-reinforcing cycle in which conditions for error in organizational theory of action provoke individual members to behaviors which reinforce those conditions" (Argyris and Schon 1978, 46). That is, the same organizational issues (errors) continued to be areas of great concern and clouded the real successes the school was experiencing. There may be examples that prove the exception to this, but when it comes to the major issues the school faced throughout its first three years, it clearly exhibited more of the conditions of single-loop learning than double-loop learning. To explain this further, I will describe two issues that continually presented challenges to the school: the staff's roles and responsibilities, and student discipline.

As described earlier, the lead staff came to the school without much, if any, training in leadership. They had varied educational backgrounds and were struggling to define who they were within this change effort. From the beginning, they found they had the following: (1) conflicting values; (2) unclear notions of how they wanted to develop the school's structures, processes, and policies; (3) communication problems with one another and other staff; and (4) a dislike for conflict and personal confrontation (although they did communicate their grievances via e-mail). Adding new teachers each year and a new half-time principal the third year further contributed to the leadership and management struggle. When the four lead teachers came together, they talked a lot about working as a team to make decisions on the school's development and implementation. Yet they never publicly defined what they meant by "collaboration" or "team." As Fullan (1993) points out, "Collaboration is one of the most misunderstood concepts in the change business" (p. 82). Adding to this confusion was the fact that the lead teachers also never talked about what it means to *lead* versus *manage* a school. As much of the literature on leadership argues, the competencies and dispositions of these two activities are quite different. The lack of agreed-upon definitions to these critical processes eventually led to a Balkanization of the teaching and paraprofessional staff. Pockets of dissatisfaction began to grow as various staff found themselves excluded from the "team" and expecting certain leadership functions from the lead staff, who felt it was not their job. Fullan (1993) suggests that Balkanization occurs when "strong loyalties form within a group with a resultant indifference or even hostility to other groups" (p. 83). The resultant behaviors of several staff, most notably the lead staff, were a complex system of defensive routines that further stymied the development of the school as a learning organization.

Student discipline was also a serious recurring issue over the three-year period. There were competing philosophies among the lead, generalist, and paraprofessional staff concerning the management of inappropriate student behavior. For three years the school (teachers and parent council) worked on developing a discipline policy that could be agreed to by all staff. (The policy was eventually written, but generally not implemented.) In spite of the teachers' desire to create a safe and respectful environment for the students, they did not share the same goals for achieving this mission. Schein (1992) suggests that "to achieve consensus on goals, the group needs a common language and shared assumptions about the basic logical operations by which one moves from something abstract or general as a sense of mission to the concrete goals . . . " (p. 56). Because of the staff's inability to communicate effectively with each other, their desire to avoid conflict, and their lack of collaborative discussion on core assumptions and values regarding adolescent behavior and discipline, little progress was made on this issue during the three years.

Had Marston been an example of a double-loop learning organization, it would have been able to collaboratively work on developing a shared understanding of these issues by listening to its staff's concerns in an attempt to find real solutions or compromises that could be accepted by all organization members. They would have seen conflict as inevitable and would have engaged in a process of sharing competing philosophies and practices.

Marston was also prevented from being a deutero-learning organization because its lead staff, in particular, rarely drew on lessons shared in the literature on educational reform and middle school curriculum or from other teachers involved in systemic change. Had they reflected on their practice in light of others' experiences, they would have been more proactive in developing solutions to recurring issues. Furthermore, their lack of developing an inquiry process prevented them from having conversations that could critically reflect on the group's experiences and recent learnings. While these two issues consumed many pages in the formative evaluation year-end reports, it appears that little of the information was used to enact positive change.

I have often wondered what else I could have done. Having some familiarity with the role of organization development consultant (one who "seeks to help an organization define and clarify its own issues, values, problems, and resources" [Hanson and Lubin 1989, 21]), I wonder if attempts at systemic change should have an organization development consultant working with the formative evaluator to assume the role of "change agent" (the facilitator of the change process). One situation in particular led me to this point in my thinking. Midway through the first year, several interpersonal issues arose among the staff. I believed I had a good understanding of the issues and wanted to help in whatever way possible. I had a feeling I would be asked to facilitate a discussion that would attempt to deal with the conflicts that had arisen. Even with my twelve years of evaluation experience, I began to wonder what formative evaluation was all about—was facilitating this meeting the right thing to do? I didn't have to think about it very long. One night shortly thereafter, I received a call from one of the lead teachers, who, after discussing whether it would be advisable for me to assume this facilitator role, decided that if I chose to lead this meeting, I would likely "co-opt" myself and lose the credibility I had established as the "neutral" evaluator of the the school's implementation. This teacher felt that the latter role was far more important than the potential outcome of the meeting. After I hung up the telephone, I felt a slight sense of relief that I would not have to try to "fix" the problem myself; I could remain the observer and documenter as initially negotiated. Shortly after this phone conversation, an organization development consultant was hired to interview all the staff and facilitate a discussion regarding issues of concern. Without going into much detail here, suffice it to say that the outcome of this experience was less than satisfactory. The consultant, while having some information from the staff, had little, if any, knowledge about educational change. The consultant was unaware of the deeper currents of dissatisfaction and was not wholly trusted by the staff.

In the second year, another organization development consultant was brought in by the lead teacher and the teachers' union. The hostility that greeted this person was overwhelming. While he visited the school several times and asked my opinion about several people or situations, he only conducted one or two interventions with the entire staff. Most of the meetings he eventually had were with the four lead teachers. Again, there was a feeling of mistrust by many of the staff, and, while he may have helped the lead staff grapple with several leadership issues, thereby helping them gain individual learning, his involvement led to very little organizational learning.

These experiences prompted me to wonder who could help the school staff and parents make sense of the evaluation findings and facilitate their use? I became convinced that there was a need for someone with in-depth organizational knowledge to help the staff translate formative evaluation findings into action and change.

THE ROLE OF EVALUATION IN THE LEARNING ORGANIZATION

It has become increasingly clear that evaluation has an important role to play in supporting learning organizations. Stephen Kemmis (1986) has written:

> A major task for programme evaluation is to harness this self-critical conversation; to collect the perspectives and judgments of those associated with a programme, to reclaim meanings and concerns from the flux of programme experience, and to make this store of understandings available to participants and other audiences. (p. 129)

Kemmis goes on to say that the organization must be willing to engage in critical debate independent from the evaluation. Sirotnik (1987), on the other hand, suggests that evaluation can be the conduit for developing critical knowledge. He describes the process of critique as

> consciousness raising and enlightenment gained through reflection on, and critique of, existing knowledge through the dialectical process . . . it poses both the current and historical context for issues and problems, it suggests the data to inform the process, and it demands explicit consideration of the often hidden values and human interests guiding educational practices. By definition, the *evaluation is the production of critical knowledge through the process of critical inquiry.* (p. 51)

The task for evaluators then becomes

> an educative one, informing and developing the understandings of those associated with the programme. It may report frequently rather than just towards the end of the evaluation, so that the perspectives of participants and audiences can be engaged more or less continually rather than in a single confrontation of perspectives. The recurring "reports" of the evaluator can be regarded as a conversation which develops the points of those it engages. (Kemmis 1986, 130)

This type of role clearly diverges from the more traditional view of the evaluator as the neutral, value-free, objective observer. Instead, it helps organization members become accountable for solving its problems, which is critical for organizational learning. If one believes, then, that an evaluator should assume this different role, it is important to question how well suited formative evaluation is for the task. I believe that formative evaluation does have an important role to play in educational reform. It can document the evolution of a program or school, it can provide important information to program funders and external constituencies, and it can provide feedback to the program's staff at certain intervals in the program's life. Yet it has significant limitations with regard to the learning organization. As Fullan (1993) reaffirms, the reason we need learning organizations is related to the discovery that change in complex systems is nonlinear and full of surprises. Formative evaluation that results in interim or year-end reports, therefore, can rarely meet the frequent information needs and collaborative inquiry process required of the learning organization.

I believe this is particularly true in schools that are developing new and innovative programs that require significant changes in organization members' behaviors and beliefs. While the traditional definition of formative evaluation explicitly states that formative evaluation occurs *during* the program for the purpose of improvement (Scriven 1991), it makes no mention of the role of the evaluator in helping staff understand the findings and implementing the changes indicated by the evaluation's results.

There is another type of evaluator role, however, that I believe should be considered in developing and implementing systemic change. It supports Kemmis's (1986) and Argyris and Schon's (1978) ideas. Michael Q. Patton (in Stockdill et al. 1992) has described this as "developmental evaluation." He suggests that "when a program is exploratory and developmental . . . the evaluation should be exploratory and developmental" (p. 26). An evaluator in this role would become part of the program's developmental process in establishing its goals and strategies for implementation. The evaluator would facilitate the evaluation through a collaborative inquiry process where the program staff and other stakeholders become accountable for "their own goals, claims, criteria, and methods" (p. 27) and data are collected and communicated on a regular basis to build "norms of collegiality and experimentation" (Little 1982). Building on Argyris and Schon's (1978) ideas of using a consultant to facilitate the learning organization's inquiry processes, an evaluator assuming this role would help organization members map out their different and conflicting views. This might involve constructing case histories of the organization in terms of both its successes and failures and then discussing these in light of future action. It would be important for the facilitator/evaluator to bring organization members together to interpret these case histories and the meanings associated with them. Glickman, Hayes, and Hensley (1992) further suggest that

> facilitators can help group members examine their own motives and assumptions relative to any proposed change and to bring new insights to their decisions through exposure to the latest research, relevant journal articles, case studies, visits to other schools, and consultation with recognized experts in areas of interest. (p. 24)

If this developmental evaluation approach had been used at Marston, it would have meant that in the area of student discipline, the entire staff would have come together to lay open their philosophies and assumptions of managing student behavior and appropriate consequences given these philosophies. Teachers and support staff could have developed case studies of situations with individual students where they might have been uncertain of how to act, or of situations where the current policy ran contrary to their values and beliefs. Had these conversations taken place, there might have been far less ambiguity and misperception of what Marston's approach was for managing inappropriate student behavior. More trust and support might have been developed instead of feelings of inadequacy and hostility. In facilitating this process, the evaluator would have engaged organization members in double-loop learning by "reducing the conditions for error which prevented shared perceptions of inconsistency and incongruity in organizational theory of action" (Argyris and Schon 1978, 39).

In terms of applying developmental evaluation to the issue of staff's roles and responsibilities, the evaluator might have begun facilitating discussions early in the first year about individuals' definitions of leadership and management and how they might inform their practice. Early in the first year, the lead staff had been offered leadership training, but chose not to participate. The developmental evaluator could have more easily probed for the staff's underlying reasons and thus have brought about a more productive end. By bringing out organization members' understandings, assumptions, and expectations, they could have developed a context in which to interpret their beliefs and practices within the context of the school's evolution. They would also have been able to develop a strategy for dealing with the conflicts that inevitably arise in new organizational structures. By not engaging in this process, the school's leadership became fragmented, resulting in each staff member's defining his or her role in isolation to the rest of the organization's members. The result was that the staff worked in a context of instrumental action unrelated to personal understanding or organizational learning, which led to greater misinterpretations and misunderstandings (Marsick and Watkins 1992b).

What Marston lacked was what Argyris and Schon (1978) call an "organizational dialectic," which occurs when

> organizational situations give rise to organizational inquiry—to problem setting and problem solving—which, in turn, create new

organizational situations within which new inconsistencies and incongruities in organizational theory of action come into play. These are characteristically manifested in organizational conflict. The organization's way of responding to that conflict yields still further transformations of the organizational situation. (p. 42)

This notion of dialectic also assumes that the organization is always changing and is never static, which is particularly relevant for organizations undergoing systemic change.

DEVELOPMENTAL EVALUATION AND EDUCATIONAL CHANGE

I have now come to believe that for an evaluation of a systemic change effort to be of most use and benefit to program participants and staff, a developmental evaluation approach should be attempted. The educational reform literature is replete with articles emphasizing the time it takes to enact educational change and the need to encourage teachers and administrators to engage in critical reflection and conversation. Heckman and Peterman (1992) have suggested that for educational change to happen, schools need to "create a setting for innovation." Organization members need to question the assumptions of new practices, assess the conditions that lead to innovation, and engage in dialogue that helps individuals gain new insights into current and future practice. As Fullan (1993) said, "Only by tracking problems can we understand what has to be done next in order to get what we want" (p. 26).

Developmental evaluation is ideal for schools that wish to develop processes promoting organizational learning. Evaluation information collected during the program's implementation (by both the evaluator and program staff) can be used by the developmental evaluator in facilitating organization members' discussions of issues through a dialectic process where members of the program staff

> have real opportunities to enter into the discussion; challenge constructively what others have to say and the basis on which they say it; say how they feel and what their own

beliefs, values, interests are, and so forth; and participate equally in controlling the discourse. (Sirotnik 1987, 58)

Evaluation reporting then is no longer an interim or year-end type of endeavor. In Marston's case, while the reports were to be formative in nature (useful for making incremental changes to the program), they were perceived by external audiences as summative reports. As a result, readers of the reports often came to premature conclusions about many of the school's initiatives.

Without a facilitator and an established mechanism for doing this, however, teachers and others involved in systemic change efforts will be hard pressed to find the time necessary to carry out these processes on their own. We have learned from the Marston experience that time is a critical factor for success. If organization members do not establish collaborative critical inquiry and effective problem-solving processes early on, the school is at the mercy of making the same mistakes over and over again, and of creating individual, not organizational, learning. Furthermore, when problems and issues are not publicly addressed and resolved, individuals' dissatisfaction may go underground, leading people to become passive-aggressive in their behavior and prompting increased interpersonal conflicts. When this occurs, the organizational culture is negatively affected, which in turn makes critical conversation even more difficult.

SUMMARY AND RECOMMENDATIONS

The time has come for schools engaging in reform to become more deliberate in their approaches to evaluating their development and implementation progress. If we are truly serious about transforming education through systemic change, then we must find ways to support teachers, parents, students, district staff, and the community in their struggles to bring about this change. The educational research literature has confirmed over and over again that significant educational change takes at least five to ten years. By applying more traditional forms of evaluation to school change efforts, we endanger their survival by providing too much information to external audiences and not enough to internal program staff. What I hope to have made clear in this chapter is that by helping schools become learning organizations and by using a more facilitated approach to evaluation, the results of any inquiry process will be useful information that can be immediately applied within the context of the evolving change effort.

Yet, as is true of school change, nothing is quite as simple as it sounds. In spite of what I see as strengths of the developmental evaluation approach, there remain several issues that should be addressed by program staff and evaluators who wish to implement this approach to evaluating systemic change. The role outlined in this chapter suggests that evaluators, in addition to their methodological and evaluation design and analysis skills, must be competent in facilitating group and conflict management processes. Negotiating the developmental approach with program staff might also prove to be a challenge if the staff believes they will not have, or do not wish to make, the time to engage in the collaborative critical inquiry processes, or if they are concerned they may feel vulnerable as a result of the process. Prior evaluation negotia-

tions should clearly delineate the requirements of participation in the evaluation so that organization members' roles in the inquiry process are clear. Should a formative evaluation also be requested as a means of documenting the program's implementation, resources must be allocated to cover both development and formation (if not also summative). This will have to be addressed by those contracting for, and with, the program evaluation staff. As with other forms of evaluation, issues related to confidentiality and to prior expectations and experiences with evaluation should be discussed.

In conclusion, the fundamental value of developmental evaluation is teachers' becoming real change agents; that is, they become self-conscious about the nature of change and the change process, rather than the "victims of change" (Fullan 1993, ix). As Fullan reminds us, "The factor that distinguishes those that move ahead is whether they *learn* from their experiences. To be able to do this depends very much on the learning orientations and capacities of the organization's members" (p. 103). Somehow, this approach seems to make the most sense given the roller coaster experience of many systemic change efforts.

REFERENCES

Argyris, C. 1993. *Knowledge for action.* San Francisco: Jossey-Bass.

Argyris, C., and D. A. Schon. 1978. *Organizational learning: A theory of action perspective.* Reading, Mass.: Addison-Wesley.

Clark, T. A. 1988. Documentation as evaluation: Capturing context, process, obstacles, and success. *Evaluation Practice* 9 (1): 21–31.

Cuban, L. 1990. A fundamental puzzle of school reform. In *Schools as collaborative cultures: Creating the future now,* edited by A. Lieberman. New York: The Falmer Press.

Dixon, N. 1992. Organizational learning: A review of the literature with implications for HRD professionals. *Human Resource Development Quarterly* 3 (1): 29–49.

Fullan, M. 1993. *Change forces.* London: The Falmer Press.

Fullan, M., and S. Stiegelbauer. 1991. *The new meaning of educational change.* New York: Teachers College Press.

Glickman, C. D., R. Hayes, and F. Hensley. 1992. Site-based facilitation of empowered schools: Complexities and issues for staff developers. *Journal of Staff Development* 13 (2): 22–26.

Hanson, P. G., and B. Lubin. 1989. Answers to questions frequently asked about organization development. In *The Emerging Practice of Organization Development*, edited by W. Sikes, A. Drexler, and J. Gant. San Diego, Calif.: University Associates.

Heckman, P., and F. Peterman. 1992. Inventing context, inventing practice: Altering patterns for success. Paper presented at the annual conference of the American Educational Research Association in San Francisco.

Kemmis, S. 1986. Seven principles for programme evaluation in curriculum development and innovation. In *New Directions in Educational Evaluation*, edited E. R. House. London: The Falmer Press.

Little, J. W. 1982. Norms of collegiality and experimentation: Workplace conditions of school success. *American Educational Research Journal* 19 (3): 325–40.

Marsick, V. J. 1987. New paradigms for learning in the workplace. In *Learning in the workplace*, edited by V. J. Marsick. New York: Croom Helm.

Marsick, V. J., and K. E. Watkins. 1992a. Continuous learning in the workplace. *Adult Learning* 3 (4): 9–12.

———. 1992b. Towards a theory of informal and incidental learning in organizations. *International Journal of Lifelong Education* 11:287–300.

Preskill, H. 1991. Metaphors of educational reform implementation. Paper presented at the annual conference of the American Evaluation Association in Chicago.

Schein, E. H. 1992. *Organizational culture and leadership*. 2d ed. San Francisco: Jossey-Bass.

Scriven, M. 1991. *Evaluation thesaurus*. 4th ed. Newbury Park, Calif.: Sage.

Sirotnik, K. A. 1987. Evaluation in the ecology of schooling: The process of school renewal. In *The ecology of school renewal*, edited by J. I. Goodlad. Eighty-Sixth Yearbook of the National Society for the Study of Education, Part 1. Chicago: University of Chicago Press.

Stacey, R. 1992. *Managing the unknown*. San Francisco: Jossey-Bass.

Stockdill, S. H., R. M. Duhon-Sells, R. A. Olson, and M. Q. Patton. 1992. Voices in the design and evaluation of a multicultural education program: A developmental approach. *New Directions for Program Evaluation* 53:17–33.

Wick, C. W., And L. S. Leon. 1993. *The learning edge*. New York: McGraw-Hill.

Wineck, J. 1995. *Negotiating the maze of school reform*. New York: Teachers College Press.

WHERE SYSTEMIC CHANGE IN EDUCATION BEGINS
Leadership Systems Management

—

Carol Gabor and Greg Meunier

Spruce Hill is a comprehensive high school situated in an older suburb of a large midwestern city. The school is thirty years old and serves 1,800 students in grades nine through twelve. The community is predominantly middle class with increasing ethnic diversity. Spruce Hill offers traditional courses in mathematics, science, English, social and behavioral sciences, and the arts. In addition, there is a dwindling core of vocational education courses. In the past year Spruce Hill lost its International Baccalaureate Program to another high school in the district. Each year about 65 percent of the graduating class go on to some form of postsecondary education. Statewide, statistics show that 25 percent of those who enroll in four-year degree programs actually receive degrees.

Last year Spruce Hill's district floated a bond referendum for capital improvements. With their part of the money Spruce Hill hoped to replace old carpeting, build a student commons, and significantly upgrade the science and computer labs. The referendum was rejected by the community. Some months later the district announced a budget shortfall of $1.3 million. As a result, Spruce Hill expects to reduce staff and curtail extracurricular activities. Further, this will increase class size and reduce the number of elective offerings.

The district superintendent has stated publicly on many occasions that the district vision is to develop a "world class" student body. This will happen, she believes, when learning is personalized, active, experiential, and relevant to real life. She is especially concerned with the large number of students in the community who comprise the "forgotten half"—those who are not best served by an academic, college preparation-focused education. For this reason she has said that the district will effect a results-oriented, outcomes-based educational transformation within the next five years. Spruce Hill has several outcomes-based committees working to revise its curriculum and learning processes. This latest budget crisis is jeopardizing aggressive movement on the superintendent's goals. She hopes to encourage faculty and administration throughout the district to make efficiencies in creative ways, and has thrown her support behind site-based management. It is her belief that grass-roots empowerment is the only way to help the district rise above its financial difficulties.

The principal of Spruce Hill wholeheartedly endorses the district vision and agrees with the superintendent about the need for school-level empowerment. Several things have convinced him that major change is due at Spruce Hill. Over the years there has been a slight, but steady, increase in the drop-out rate. Class size has grown. Many students seem to wander through the school's curriculum with no direction or focus. Most say they intend to go on to college after graduation, but few have clear career objectives.

Planning is underway to offer a Technology Preparation (Tech Prep) option at Spruce Hill. The principal views this as one positive way to meet the needs of his "general track" students. Through a combination of the Tech Prep initiative and the conversion to outcomes-based education, he intends to restructure a school that offers fragmented curriculum that is tied to separate disciplines and departments and is served up to students in single course offerings. The principal knows that such major restructurings cannot occur without substantial support from faculty and staff. He hopes to gain that support by giving them a larger stake in school administration. To that end he has established a site-based management team representing faculty from each department, maintenance and support staff, and parents. He has asked the team to develop a site-based management plan for the school.

The principal is finding it more and more difficult to generate faculty enthusiasm for these new projects. He tends to ascribe this to the inherent conservatism of teachers. The worsening financial climate has also made people wary of the future. Some have been very vocal about their anxiety, and the principal feels that morale is being eroded. He finds it impossible to rally everyone around the successful implementation of even one project, and hopes that site-based management will change all this.

Community involvement in the school varies and is unpredictable. At times, it seems to the principal that he sees parents only when they have a complaint or when their child is disciplined. The decision to move the International Baccalaureate Program caused an uproar among parents of high-potential students. These same parents are rallying against the cause of outcomes-based education because they see it as undermining enrichment opportunities for their children. Parents of the rest of the student body usually come to the school only for concerts and sporting events.

As part of the Tech Prep initiative the principal intends to offer youth apprenticeship opportunities for some students. He realizes that this will require strong links with the business community. At the moment those links are largely nonexistent, except for a few sponsored scholarships and some donated equipment. Both he and members of his faculty have on numerous occasions met with individual business leaders to discuss partnership possibilities. In his mind, none of these meetings has yielded anything more than a vague philosophical exchange about the problems of the educational system.

For their part, faculty and staff say that the increasing financial uncertainty at Spruce Hill is frustrating because they have no sense of what the future will bring. Many suspect that the administration has plans and agendas in place that will affect them, but they are unwilling to disclose those plans. In staff meetings, issues around poor communications come up over and over again. Faculty also feel that the demands on them are continually increasing while the support they get is not keeping pace. They say that they are working harder than they ever have before with fewer and fewer tangible results.

Spruce Hill is organized into departments aligned to separate disciplines. Faculty identify strongly with their individual departments, and their primary allegiance is to their own discipline. Most consider the classroom as their real workplace, as opposed to the school or the school district. They tend to filter all policies and decisions through the lens of "How will this affect me in my classroom?" On a daily basis they worry about classroom discipline and the transmission of subject matter. The increasing amount of diversity within their classes, both in terms of ability and cultural background, is beginning to overwhelm them. Yet they feel enormous pressure to move students through to graduation.

Students are not able to articulate very clearly their expectations of the school. Most will say they appreciate interesting teachers who can maintain order in the classroom. They are vocal about what they do not like, but their complaints center mainly around individual policy decisions and individual teacher actions. Some students, usually with the help of their parents, have developed very definite career goals and strategies for achieving those goals. These students claim that Spruce Hill provides ample opportunities for success. On the other hand, there are large numbers of students who do not know how to plan for their future or what will be demanded of them beyond high school.

Parents, for the most part, do not understand how Spruce Hill operates or why things happen the way they do. Those parents who had been active volunteers when their children were in elementary school, claim that the high school is a very distant place and that connecting to it is difficult. They do not know how to influence direction or policy except through the electoral process or through the force of their complaints. Those parents who neither want to run for the school board, nor have specific complaints, accept on faith the belief that the school knows what is best and has the interests of their child at heart.

The business community is frustrated. Business leaders cite the many times they have met with education officials to state their needs. They claimed to have argued over and over again that high school graduates are poorly prepared for the workplace and for further education. They cannot read. They cannot compute. They cannot solve problems; and they do not communicate very well. The business community does not see anyone actively engaged in solving these problems, and they feel that educators are not listening to them.

Everyone—the district superintendent, the principal of Spruce Hill, faculty, students, parents, and the business community—agrees that change is needed. What they cannot agree on is how this change will come about, what needs to happen first, or where the most strategic improvement opportunities lie. No one is claiming that Spruce Hill is a bad school. In fact, as high schools go, they find

much to be proud of in Spruce Hill. What people do share is a feeling of disappointment that results from a sense of missed opportunity. This feeling is summed up in a general conviction that the school could be so much more than it is at present.

SYSTEMIC IMPROVEMENT IN EDUCATION

Many systems exist side by side in a school and work together to form the unique culture of that school. Curriculum and instruction systems, counseling and student support systems, evaluation and assessment systems, and administrative systems are some common examples. Each of these systems is made up of people and work processes that interrelate to mold the experience that the student, staff person, parent, or administrator will have when coming in contact with the school. The principal of Spruce Hill senses, probably accurately, that the experience of the middle band of students in his school is not as rewarding as it could be. The complaints and the lackluster results indicate that these students are not being well served. He does not know where the specific problems lie or what the root causes might be. Nonetheless, he hopes that by instituting Tech Prep and outcomes-based educational initiatives he can change key systems and improve the educational experience for students.

Educators are beginning to realize that major improvement seldom results from fixing isolated problems. Things—people and processes—are interconnected. Actions taken in one area can have unforeseen consequences somewhere else. Lasting, fundamental change involves whole systems. Thus the notion of "systemic change" is gaining currency in educational circles. The principal is attracted to the promise of these new initiatives precisely because they do not appear to be a "quick fix." They offer a large-scale approach to large-scale problems. He hopes that in adopting them, he will promote lasting systemwide improvement.

At Spruce Hill new activities are being added on top of existing activities. In his support of these new initiatives, the principal is unknowingly applying solutions before clearly understanding how his own systems function and what the problems really are. In effect, he is increasing the amount of variation in systems that are already highly variable. This is what the teachers see when they complain of too many new programs. It is not that they are resistant to change; they are only resisting what seems to them to be the too-often-repeated experience of moving in one direction one week and an opposite direction the next. This is probably why staff continually complain that they are working harder than ever before and seeing fewer and fewer positive results. They fail to understand that as they are forced to deal with increasing amounts of variation, in course offerings, in instructional approaches, and in students, their capacity to serve individual needs is systematically being eroded.

Students see a number of new courses being introduced, but they do not know how to choose. From the counselors and from other students they know which courses have math components and which courses require essay writing. They know that in some courses students take exams, in others they do portfolios or projects. They know that some courses offer opportunities to work outside of the school. And they know which courses have heavy homework and which ones do not. But, because they do not know why certain courses are offered, and how these courses relate to other course offerings, they end up making decisions for the wrong reasons. In effect, their choice has not been increased, it has been paralyzed, because they do not have enough of the right kind of information.

Variability and variation is *not* the same as variety and the ability to meet individual needs. Offering multiple options to students is only effective as a way of meeting individual needs when what is offered fits into, and is supported by, all of the other systems and processes in the school. The language of systematic process management, on which all planned, as opposed to fortuitous, change must be based, tells us that improvement comes when the variation in processes and process outcomes is understood and controlled. Once we have observed our processes long enough to know how they currently work and what it is they regularly and predictably produce, then we are in a position to discover which outcome variations can be attributed to special causes and which are the result of

common causes. Special causes of outcome variation are those that are extrinsic and accidental to the system. Poor learner outcomes resulting from interaction with a poorly trained or inexperienced teacher is an example of a special cause of variation. Common causes of variation are those which result from the way the system or process is designed. Instructional systems that teach to students who benefit from an abstract, theoretical approach will make little impact on students whose learning styles favor hands-on techniques. This would be a common cause of variation in learner outcomes for classes made up of students with diverse learning styles.

Systemic change is brought about by attacking common causes of variation—those things inherent in the design of the system that make different or improved outcomes impossible. However, common causes can only be identified and dealt with once special causes have been eliminated. Rewriting curricula to address a variety of learning styles would make no appreciable improvement in learner outcomes if teachers were unable to identify learning style differences in students, or if they did not have the time to teach to different students differently. In this case, teacher training and lack of time are special causes of variation that, unless identified and eliminated, would render curriculum revision efforts fruitless. In fact, curriculum revisions made without any understanding of how instruction really works in a particular setting simply adds an extra dimension of special cause variation to systems already plagued with too many inconsistencies.

Educators are attracted to the promise of change held out by such initiatives as Tech Prep, outcomes-based education, and site-based management. They learn how these things were implemented elsewhere and, without knowing how things actually work in their own situation, adopt these methods wholesale. Then the very programs aimed at producing much longed-for systemic change end up as a set of newly introduced, special causes of variation that produce unpredictable results, only some of which may count as an improvement. This is not in any way to disparage the insights that produce new ways of thinking about educational problems and that have resulted in innovative Tech Prep, outcomes-based education, and site-based management approaches. It is only to warn against the temptation to search for recipes or formulas within these approaches. In the end, recipes and formulas are rejected by people and systems ill equipped or too overburdened to accept them. This is happening with Tech Prep, outcomes-based education and site-based management at Spruce Hill. They can only flourish on ground that has been carefully prepared to accept them. That ground has not yet been cultivated.

No one at Spruce Hill knows anything, other than on an intuitive level, about how the processes and systems with which students have daily contact actually work. Although opinions and anecdotes abound, no one can answer any of the following questions definitively:

- How do our students experience instruction?

- What kind of variation do they see from class to class, day to day, year to year?

- Which of our processes are contributing most to student learning at Spruce Hill?

- How do they operate?

- Who is involved in operating them?

- How do the people and processes relate to each other?

- What are the bottlenecks and disconnects?

- How will making changes in one area affect other areas?

To answer these questions, it is necessary to see both the forest and the trees. Information must be gathered. Processes must be documented and outcomes measured. All this requires discipline—a discipline that will end up involving everyone in the school.

In most schools there are hundreds of processes in place, each one having some individual or group responsible for it. Spruce Hill is no exception, and it is becoming clearer every day that it is not possible to give everything the time and attention it deserves. People's energies must be directed and focused. The discipline that continuous im-

provement imposes cannot be exercised unilaterally in every process; some things are more important than others. But how will staff know what is important to measure and improve? An organizational vision and a set of clear values help employees to understand what has priority. It is the responsibility of school leaders to see that focus and direction is provided. They do this by helping the school surface its vision and articulate its values.

A shared vision can help a school create a new future. A vision is a desirable state for the school—one that paints a picture different from the way things are now. A vision is concrete. People will know when they are there. A vision is reachable, but it is a stretch. A compelling vision will spur action and drive everyone's job. But everyone must understand the vision in the same way. A clearly articulated, well-defined vision helps everyone to learn what is important, where the school is going, and what needs to be changed. It provides focus and direction. It is an emotional "hook" that gives people the will to change and makes any improvement efforts meaningful because it provides a framework for identifying the important things that need to be improved.

It is clear that the superintendent and the principal both have some kind of vision for the district in general and Spruce Hill School in particular. What is not clear is how well these leaders have connected each other and the rest of the employees to their personal visions. The superintendent speaks of creating a world-class student body. Spruce Hill's principal says he agrees with this aim. In addition, he has committed the school to three major educational initiatives. The unspoken assumption is that by participating in any or each of these initiatives world-class status will be achieved. However, as it stands at the moment, there are as many different interpretations of "world-class student body" as there are administrators, faculty, staff, students, and community members to interpret the phrase.

Organizational values are as important as vision in providing focus and direction. Values address the way everyone will work together to attain the vision. The superintendent has listed a set of values that the principal says he endorses. These values describe the way learning is to be achieved. Learning must be "personalized," "active," "experiential," and "relevant to real life." In fact, staff working in the school will say that learning is centered on control and discipline, textbook based, abstract, and measured by grades. The values that are really at work in a school are brought to life in the everyday operation of its systems, not by proclamations by leadership.

At Spruce Hill the systems which support learning do not support the values the superintendent is promoting. Something about either the values or the systems has to change. These changes must be consciously made and everyone must take part in the discussion. Together, vision and values provide a clear framework within which the work of individuals has meaning. They lay out the domain of appropriate activity. When employees share common vision and values, they know how their work fits into the school's larger purpose; they know what is important and what is not important; and they know how the work is expected to be done.

In summary, broad, systemic change demands two things: an understanding of how the existing systems in the organization currently work, and a framework of meaning within which priorities are established. In other words, systemic change happens when continuous process improvement is guided by shared vision and values. Without a clearly articulated, compelling, and shared vision of the desired future state, it will be impossible for those who must make the change occur to know where the most strategic improvement opportunities lie and what will count as an improvement. On the other hand, without an honest, fact-based assessment of the capacity of existing systems, it will be impossible to distinguish between a realizable vision and an impossible dream.

A NEW ROLE FOR LEADERS

Framing the vision and understanding the discipline required for accurate self-assessment requires a unified response by the organization. It cannot be delegated to task teams or subcommittees. A general conversation, bringing in everyone who will ultimately be involved in making change

happen, must be opened. This does not mean that the school is a democracy or that all decisions are driven to consensus or brought to a vote. Nor does it mean that empowerment is something that leaders dole out to employees like scoops of ice cream. What it does mean is that an organizational dialogue in which there is a free exchange of knowledge and learning must occur so that everyone can contribute to the growth and development of the school. When vision retreats to the classroom and teachers work in isolation, the school stagnates.

Spruce Hill is not a united organization, nor is it unusual in this. Most schools are not cohesive organizations. They are simply administrative umbrellas, concerned primarily with payroll processing, contract negotiation, purchasing, and facilities management. As a living organism, and as a system, an organization is more than the sum of its parts. It has a life force that must be nurtured and sustained. When the life force of an organization is neglected, the possibility of self-determination evaporates. Things just happen. This is the state in which the majority of educational organizations find themselves today. Things just happen to them. Lacking an organizational consciousness, and with leaders who, for a multitude of reasons, are isolated and disconnected, they are becoming victims of forces beyond their control.

Schools must be managed as organizational systems. This means everyone's efforts must be connected, focused, and mutually supportive. These kinds of connections can only be made by a leadership team that understands organizational development to be a primary leadership function. Leaders play a critical role in uniting the school. They provide a framework within which everyone's work becomes meaningful. They also make possible the kind of continuous improvement that releases creativity. Leaders have work to do that is different in kind from the work of other individuals in the school. They are responsible for developing their school as an organization. Their role is not to be the expert technician. That role is already filled by the faculty and staff. When employee's efforts are focused they have more than enough expertise and energy to carry out the mission and achieve the vision of the school. It is the responsibility of leadership to understand how the organization is working and use that knowledge to bring everyone together. They do this by managing their own leadership systems.

Just as there are organizational systems through which faculty and staff carry out the work of the school (e.g., curriculum and instruction systems, counseling and student support systems, administrative systems, and evaluation and assessment systems), there are leadership systems through which leaders do their leadership work. They are leadership information systems, organizational focusing systems, communication and influence systems, and evaluation systems. Leadership systems exist in every school by virtue of the fact that it is an organization. Unless these systems are managed on a daily basis, effective leadership is impossible. Some very successful leaders manage their leadership systems instinctively. However, conscious management of leadership systems will allow leaders to improve their own leadership, predict how the organization will react to their decisions, and, in the end, build a school whose success is independent of any one leader's personality.

Leaders must understand how the school is working in order to plan for the future. The leadership information system is the system through which leaders receive information about their markets and their customers, about the environment within which they operate, about employees, about organizational performance and capacity, and about their own leadership effectiveness. While leaders have access to important information about the "big picture," other, equally valuable information is in the hands of employees who work in processes and interact daily with students and the public. However, only some of what employees know is necessary for leaders to know. They should not be concerned with using information for micromanagement. They need predictive information—information about key trends—for this is what enables them to set direction, assess the systemwide implications of individual process improvements, and manage the other leadership systems.

The articulation and surfacing of vision and values, as well as the identification of primary customers, occurs within the organizational focusing system. Within this system, leaders work with employees to compile customer profiles, set direction for the organization, and build a framework of values that will determine how the work will get done. Breakthrough goals and priority activities are selected, and essential processes for improvement are identified. When the vision and values are clear, and all employees understand them in the same way, the reasons for selecting certain processes to improve rather than others also becomes clear. An effective organizational focusing system permits the connection between vision and values and continuous process improvement to be made.

Through the communication and influence system leaders initiate an ongoing organizational dialogue that both empowers employees and enables leaders to set direction. The point of establishing an organizational dialogue is not to appease people or to make them feel included but to put to use important information that could significantly impact the future of the school. This information resides with faculty and staff and is dispersed throughout the organization. An effective communication and influence system provides a mechanism through which organizational knowledge can be consolidated and learning enhanced. Everyone knows and understands the priorities and is able to use his or her particular expertise and information to influence decisions before they are made. Mutual expectations are communicated. All employees understand and connect to the vision and can focus their continuous improvement efforts on important work.

The evaluation system allows leaders to assess progress on several levels. This system helps them determine the contribution of individual process improvements to the expansion of organizational capacity. It helps them to evaluate the school's progress toward attainment of the vision. It helps them to examine the way organizational values are being actualized through the work. Finally, it helps leaders evaluate their own leadership effectiveness by giving them answers to such questions as these:

- Are we doing the right things?
- Do people understand?
- Is the school focused?

- Do people have the information they need to do their jobs?

- How well are we managing our leadership systems?

The leadership systems at Spruce Hill have been neglected for some time, and the school's inability to attack problems in a disciplined, single-minded manner is the evidence of this. Unfortunately, the superintendent, the principal, and the site-based management team, who together seem to bear the responsibility for leadership, are unaware of the existence of these systems and of the need to manage them. One result of this is that they lack any useful information about how the school works, what employees think and feel, how students and stakeholders perceive them, what the customers and stakeholders need, and how the school is performing. What leaders receive in the way of information is largely anecdotal. They are therefore forced to rely on gut-level feelings rather than on facts when making decisions. More specifically, the superintendent, the principal, and the site-based management team only have a vague understanding of the people they serve. Except for financial figures, they do not know what counts as a performance measure and have no idea what would tell them that the school as a whole is improving.

The principal of Spruce Hill has, on more than one occasion, voiced a difficulty with pulling faculty, staff, and the community together around any of his favorite programs. The site-based management team, as he sees it, has been given every opportunity to effect fundamental change. However, they seem to spend most of their time discussing school issues without ever resolving anything or producing a plan of action. What the principal sees as empowerment, faculty and staff see as lack of leadership. The role of the site-based management team at Spruce Hill has never been made clear. Faculty at large are confused about its leadership responsibilities. Members of the team are similarly confused. They wonder what it is they are supposed to be doing.

The principal has suggested many new programs and initiatives. Some people see these suggestions as a way of controlling and manipulating the team. They are reluctant to support any of his ideas. Others have been inspired by the possibilities inherent in one or the other of the principal's projects and have gone off and made some beginnings. The result is that a number of disparate activities are occurring throughout the school. Each is vying with the others for time, attention, priority, and resources. Multiple programs, processes, and initiatives send people running in opposite directions. However, a school that cannot martial *all* of its resources on behalf of a compelling shared vision cannot hope to improve. Faculty and staff at Spruce Hill are disconnected. Their work is unfocused and has little meaning beyond individual classrooms. As a result, customers—students, parents, the community—experience extreme variation in service provision.

So much is happening at Spruce Hill that the leadership cannot possibly communicate on all fronts. The principal says he needs to share information better. He has toyed with the idea of a newsletter, but no one has the time to staff it. In the meantime, faculty and staff say that they are not being communicated with. However, these feelings stem more from the fact that they are not able to influence decisions before they are made than from the fact that they are not receiving enough information. Memos are almost epidemic at Spruce Hill. But with the institution of each new project and initiative, plans are made, decisions are formulated, and employees are left to implement ideas within systems that are largely out of control. Secrets and rumors abound, and people begin to feel as if "management by innuendo" is the new style. In the site-based management team, members are afraid to express their true feelings and ideas. They just nod in silent agreement to plans that are clearly flawed.

While there is no outward dissent, the leadership at Spruce Hill is isolated. They have not stopped to learn what is happening in the school. They sometimes ask themselves, "Why is this like this?," but the only answer they will accept is that certain people are just not doing their jobs. Then they fall back on the notion that their hands are tied by teacher contracts and seniority rules. In the end, they feel hopeless and helpless.

In order to be effective, leaders must open the organization and themselves up to a high degree of self-awareness. They have a responsibility to evaluate the way in which the systems and processes (as opposed to the people) work, and their own efforts at developing the school as an organization. Because this means asking and answering some tough questions, the evaluation system is frequently the most underdeveloped of the leadership systems in a school.

Just as in Spruce Hill, these leadership systems exist in every organization. Every school has processes, formal and informal, through which leaders receive information, determine important work, communicate to employees, and assess their own effectiveness. Oftentimes, these systems are ignored, with the result that only some employees know what the priorities are and only some of the organizational knowledge is tapped. Leaders are isolated. They hear only selected voices.

The leadership systems are interconnected and mutually reinforcing and must be managed with this in mind. This means that the "results" of well-managed leadership systems are not as important as the integrity of the processes that underlie them. Having a vision is not as important to the organization as visioning. Setting up formal communication channels is not as important as communicating. Having an information system is not as important as the free flow of information. Finally, conducting peer and subordinate reviews is not as important to the organization as is the openness and humility that invites leadership self-examination.

When we speak of the necessity to manage leadership systems we are speaking about the process of leadership. When management processes are consciously enhanced and improved, the results—an effectively led school—will take care of themselves. When leaders are focused on discovering how informing, visioning, communicating, and evaluating happens in the school and on improving those processes, they are managing their leadership systems. The work of leaders is to focus, connect, and learn from the organization, its systems, and its people. It is for this, not for troubleshooting or for

being the chief technician, that leaders get paid. It involves exposure and a certain vulnerability that can be frightening at first. But over time it gives way to an assurance that everyone in the school is moving together along the same path. Leadership systems management driven by educational leaders who live the core values moves the organization toward attainment of its vision and, ultimately, toward systemic change and improvement.

The careful management and improvement of leadership systems is the glue that holds the organization together as an organization and connects leaders with those who do the work. When attention is not paid to leadership systems, leaders and leadership activities are effectively disconnected from the organization. The information leaders get about employees and process capacity is unreliable. Therefore, any vision created is created with no real understanding of what can possibly be achieved or of whether the organization as a whole stands behind it. Leaders learn selectively, listen selectively, and set up unrealistic visions based on poor information. From their point of view, faculty and staff see leaders who act primarily on behalf of self rather than on behalf of the school. The vision is a vision for the leadership team only. Continuous improvement furthers an agenda known to leaders, but not to faculty and staff. At best, these employees "go along to get along." At worst, they ignore what leaders have to say.

Spruce Hill is a typical school with typical problems. The ability to produce systemic change and to make real improvement lies well within its grasp. They have no need to look outside for new answers. If they concentrate on learning how things are working and on making disciplined improvements in priority areas, they will take the first steps toward systemic change. Spruce Hill will then put itself in a position to benefit from the promise contained in exciting new initiatives such as Tech Prep, outcomes-based education, and site-based management. But first it must understand and optimize what is already important in the school. The will to do this will be created by leaders whose job is to develop the school as a single organization.

REFERENCES

Block, P. 1991. *The empowered manager: Positive political skills at work.* New York: Jossey-Bass.

———. 1993. *Stewardship.* San Francisco: Better Koehler.

Covey, S. 1989. *The 7 habits of highly effective people.* New York: Simon and Schuster.

Deming, W. E. 1982. *Out of the crisis.* Cambridge, Mass.: MIT Press.

Senge, P. M. 1990. *The fifth discipline.* New York: Doubleday.

Walton, M. 1986. *The Deming management method.* New York: Putnam Publishing Group.

SOUTH DAKOTA'S PROCESS OF SYSTEMIC CHANGE
A National Science Foundation Statewide Systemic Initiative

—

David Anderson, Robert Caldwell, Molly Linstrom, David Makings, and Katherine Pedersen

Change has been the byword of American education almost since its beginning. When the American colonists first constructed one-room schools, they saw them as a necessary social element that would provide the country's new citizens with the skills and knowledge they would need to survive in the New World. This is still true more than two hundred years later. Citizens continue to look at public education as a critical component in developing the skills and knowledge needed to excel in a global economy. Policy makers and researchers are now focusing on "systemic change" as the conceptual basis for the most current policies and approaches to educational development.

South Dakota is currently involved in systemic change through two programs: the state's Modernization Project and its Statewide Systemic Initiative (SSI), supported by the National Science Foundation. This chapter will focus on the SSI program. In order to understand the vision of South Dakota's SSI program, it would be helpful to provide some information about the context of that initiative effort and about South Dakota itself.

South Dakota grew into statehood in 1889 due to the influx of goldminers and homesteaders. Today, it has a population of slightly more than 700,000 (51 percent female). There are approximately 60,000 Native Americans residing on nine reservations in areas remote from even small population centers. Almost 28 percent of South Dakota's total population is concentrated in three cities: Sioux Falls (105,000), Rapid City (54,000), and Aberdeen (25,000). The state covers a geographical area of more than 75,952 square miles, is traversed by the Missouri River, and is governed by two time zones.

This chapter seeks to define the context in which many of the educational changes are being carried out, to discuss some of the national initiatives that have been a response to the educational change movement, and to detail how South Dakota has initiated its systemic change efforts.

INFLUENCES ON SYSTEMIC CHANGE IN SOUTH DAKOTA

The motivation for the current South Dakota educational change efforts is the result of various influences at both the national and state level.

National Influences

While there has been a regular wave of reform movements within the educational community in the United States, the release in 1983 of *A Nation At*

Risk, a report by the National Committee on Excellence in Education, prompted a broader, nationwide concern for a "rising tide of mediocrity" in America. As a result, the country launched a decade of school reform. This period of change has led to the realization that change must be systemic in nature. In other words, successful change efforts require the entire system to change, not simply discrete components of the system.

Around 1985, professional educators became more aware that how mathematics is taught is just as important as what is taught. Two important documents helped focus a new vision for school mathematics: *Everybody Counts: A Report to the Nation on the Future of Mathematics Education* by the National Research Council (1989), and *Curriculum and Evaluation Standards for School Mathematics* by the National Council of Teachers of Mathematics (1989). Similarly, in the area of science, two documents helped shape a comparable vision for science education: *Project 2061: Science for All Americans* by the American Association for the Advancement of Science (1989), and *Getting Started in Science: A Blueprint for Elementary School Science Education* by the National Center for Improving Science Education (1989).

As a result of these and other reports, the professional education community has been galvanized into action and many systemic change issues have been initiated. These initiatives have touched almost every aspect of schooling, including curriculum, teaching methods, teacher preparation, school leadership, and financing. Many of these national initiative-inspired reforms are only now reaching their apex and are bringing about sweeping systemic changes on a national and statewide basis.

State Influences

While most state education initiatives have been based largely on marked declines in overall achievement, particularly in mathematics and science, South Dakota youth have held their own. From 1980 to 1990, students in South Dakota have done remarkably well, maintaining an average score of 551 on the math section of the Scholastic Aptitude Test, which in 1980 was 105 points above the national

average. By 1991, the national average had narrowed the gap to 77 points, but even at their lowest average in 1989, South Dakota students remained a comfortable 67 points above the national average.

The same can be said for scores on the Stanford Achievement Test. In 1991, South Dakota students scored consistently in the 60th percentile in math and science achievement. In addition, nearly half of all high school students in South Dakota enroll in four-year colleges or some other form of postsecondary schooling. South Dakota ranks fifth in the United States for the fewest number of high-school dropouts. Most states would envy this type of performance from their young learners. Why, then, is South Dakota so focused on a systemic initiative to improve the teaching of mathematics and science? The answer to this question falls into three broad categories: (1) the needs of Native American students; (2) economic issues; and (3) the need to develop critical thinking skills in all students.

The Needs of South Dakota Native American Students

While traditional measures of achievement indicate that most South Dakota students are well above national averages, this is not the case for all South Dakotans. The following is a sample of the degree to which the state's Native Americans lack adequate academic preparation in math and science:

- The performance of many children living on reservations ranks in the lowest 4 percentile on the Stanford Achievement Test.

- Administrators report that teachers still have lower expectations of Native American and minority children than other students, particularly in math and science.

- Native American learners do not have substantive contact with role models in science and engineering.

- Only 2 percent of Native Americans who graduate from high school will have sufficient preparation in math and science to meet college entrance requirements.

- Few Native Americans enter postsecondary mathematics, science, or technology programs.

- Dropout rates for Native Americans are 50–70 percent in many areas of the state and are at least three times higher than other minorities.

Clearly, these are important problems that must be addressed in any educational change initiative.

Economic Issues

The age of technology offers expanded economic development opportunities for many parts of the United States, particularly for rural areas that have not been participating fully in economic activities because of their remoteness. In South Dakota, a well-skilled labor force has proved that, through technology, rural areas can prosper. Workplace demands and the increasing complexity of society have forced an emphasis on cooperative learning, teamwork, and communication skills.

Overall, limited career opportunities are not restricted to the state's Native American population. Even though many South Dakotans between the ages of 18–24 are well prepared for careers that take advantage of their mathematics and science preparation, few opportunities currently exist in South Dakota to find jobs in a highly technological or scientific field. As a result, some of South Dakota's best talent leaves the state to seek employment elsewhere.

Thus, there are serious problems in South Dakota that remain unaddressed. Specifically, South Dakota has the following: (1) inadequate technological infrastructure and resources; (2) the fewest scientists and engineers of the fifty states; (3) the lowest federal research and development spending in the nation; and (4) an unacceptably low level of economic diversity.

For these reasons, one of the principal goals of the systemic change movement in South Dakota is to help the state's transition from a predominantly rural economy and job base to a more diversified and highly technological environment that can absorb the talented graduates of its schools. To do this, South Dakota must have among its goals a concerted effort to attract diverse industry and to encourage the development of small entrepreneurial companies that are founded and run by graduates of South Dakota universities and colleges.

The Need to Develop Critical Thinking Skills in All Students

Finally, even though traditional measures of achievement indicate that most South Dakota students are well above national averages, these measures do not address the degree to which students have developed critical thinking skills (called for in national reform documents). South Dakota educators, in particular, have recognized that the current school system does not effectively or consistently develop critical thinking skills in students. As a result, the educational community has produced several state documents to respond to the national initiatives and focus on the needs of South Dakota's students. These documents include the *South Dakota Science Framework Draft* (SD NSF SSI 1991) and the *South Dakota Mathematics and Science Benchmarks* (SD NSF SSI 1992).

SYSTEMIC CHANGE IN SOUTH DAKOTA

In order to respond to the South Dakota needs outlined in the previous section, South Dakota initiated a series of activities to change the teaching of mathematics and science. Following are those activities:

- In 1990, South Dakota's governor and legislature developed several education-related initiatives, including the National Science Foundation (NSF) Grant, the Office of Child Care Services, the Governor's Youth At Risk Trust Fund, the Modernization K–12 Education Program, and additional state funding for adult literacy.

- In 1990, the governor and the legislature approved the concept of the Rural Development Telecommunications (RDT) Network, a fiber-optic system linking all school, university, and state buildings via two-way interactive video-audio communications. The existence of the RDT Network served to minimize the obstacles to collaboration that might have been expected in South Dakota because of its vast geographical area. Thus, it was possible to think of statewide initiatives that could be locally originated but at the same time directed toward a common goal.

- The High Plains Center was established at the South Dakota School of Mines and Technology in Rapid City with the purpose of enhancing the competitiveness of South Dakota industries by keeping them linked to cutting-edge technology and information.

- The South Dakota Futures Fund was established in 1987 to directly nurture and finance the implementation of technology-based research concepts and business ventures that are coordinated at the university level. This multimillion dollar fund has served as a catalyst in fostering needed academic actions and business partnerships.

As a result of these activities, in 1991 South Dakota was awarded a five-year, $7.5-million competitive grant from the National Science Foundation to address systemic change. As one of the initial ten states to receive funding, the South Dakota National Science Foundation Statewide Systemic Initiative (NSF-SSI) became a major statewide effort to encourage improvements in science, mathematics, engineering, and technology education through comprehensive reforms in the educational systems of the state—kindergarten through university.

The vision and direction of South Dakota's original NSF-SSI came about through the statewide collaborative efforts of more than one hundred parents, teachers, legislators, administrators, business leaders, university faculty and administrators, Board of Regents, and Department of Education and Cultural Affairs members. Maintenance of collaborative relationships has become the cornerstone of the state's systemic efforts.

The vision and goals of the South Dakota NSF-SSI program have been largely framed by the docu-

ments described in the previous section, including the *Curriculum and Evaluation Standards for School Mathematics* (NCTM 1989), *Project 2061: Science for All Americans* (AAAS 1989), *Educating Americans for the 21st Century* (NSB 1983), the *South Dakota Science Framework Draft* (SD NSF SSI 1991), and the *South Dakota Mathematics and Science Benchmarks* (SD NSF SSI 1992). In general, these documents call for better communication skills and problem-solving skills within both mathematics and science using technology.

Specifically, based on these documents, the original goals for systemic change in the NSF-SSI initiative for the teaching of mathematics, science, and technology include:

1. integration of mathematics and science;

2. integration of mathematics and science with written and oral communication skills, arts education, social studies education, and Native American culture;

3. teaching of mathematics and science—kindergarten through university—in a hands-on, inquiry-based, cooperative learning environment;

4. effective and appropriate use of technology teaching;

5. addressing the mathematical and scientific needs of the underserved;

6. implementation of student assessment strategies that include performance-based assessment, authentic tasks, and alternative assessments such as portfolios and journals.

These goals, in turn, are being reinforced by the various components of the NSF-SSI program.

Program Components of the SSI Initiative

Through a cooperative agreement negotiated with the National Science Foundation in 1991, the original goals of South Dakota were distilled into specific expectations. These target areas, interpreted within the state's NSF-SSI vision, are currently the following:

1. A competitive grants program

2. Curricular change models

3. Postsecondary partnerships

4. Computer networking and telecommunications

5. Alternative assessment strategies

6. Public relations

First, the *competitive grants program* is viewed as a multiyear process and program of the SSI. Through an annual application process, school districts are encouraged to develop their own interpretive model for classroom and systemwide change in the teaching of mathematics and science. Proposals that are funded are obligated to implement their efforts through a collaborative partnership consisting of K–12 and postsecondary community members. Through the enactment of a competitive grants program, local educational leadership has been recognized and financially rewarded. The competitive nature of the grant program prompts a "cutting-edge" quality of proposals.

Second, through competitive funding, *curricular change models* have been developed in which locally initiated projects are based on the strengths and collaborative plans of the local community, school, and postsecondary institutions. It is through the implementation of various curricular change models that the state hopes to develop integrated mathematics and science curriculum frameworks that present authentic application of concepts that have been "field tested" and allow consistent implementation at the local level.

Both the *competitive grants program* and *curricular change models* reinforce and illustrate the broad scope of the NSF-SSI goals for mathematics and science education. For example, in the Lake Central School District (Madison, S. Dak., pop. 6,257), student journals, surveys, reports, and portfolios are being utilized using mathematics concepts and scientific results from experiments. In White River (pop. 595), the predominately Native American student body is integrating technology into all curricular areas, as well as making a concerted effort to educate parents and community members about

the relevance of mathematics, science, and technology in daily living.

Third, a number of *postsecondary partnerships* have been developed through various funded grant sites as well as the establishment of the Higher Education Council, a committee that is responsible for the collective view of *all* postsecondary institutions in South Dakota. Postsecondary institutions play an important role in local curricular models by facilitating teacher training, resource and materials evaluation, technical assistance, and local program assessment. These partnerships foster local leadership and nurture the K–16 hands-on, inquiry-based cooperative learning that is an important goal of the NSF-SSI.

In addition, through postsecondary partnerships, educational stakeholders can be drawn to the table to examine the methods, contents, and practices in higher education and to evaluate how these elements address the continuing needs of schools and communities.

Fourth, in a large, sparsely populated state like South Dakota, communication between all the stakeholders in systemic change is critical but difficult. Clearly, communication is an important part of systemic change and all the stakeholders in a change process need to have an avenue to contribute to the reform process. This is necessary for their commitment and contribution to the change process. In order to facilitate this type of communication in South Dakota, *a computer bulletin board system and a telecommunications network* with two-way interactive audio and video are being extensively used. These network systems have served to increase effective communication throughout the state.

Fifth, a driving force behind the NSF-SSI program is a belief that *all* students from across the state deserve an education that will enable them to communicate and fully participate in a society full of technological, mathematical, and scientific advances. In order to participate in this changing and technologically advanced society, students must develop critical thinking skills. Even though these skills may be emphasized in the curriculum and instruction, they are not usually the focus of assessment. In this case, because of the importance of assessment as a focus for curriculum, any curricular change efforts will be limited. Unfortunately, traditional approaches to assessment do not measure the necessary skills, attitudes, and knowledge. Thus, the South Dakota NSF-SSI project is emphasizing the development and implementation of appropriate *alternative forms of assessment,* such as performance assessment, portfolio assessment, and other authentic assessment strategies. These forms of assessment allow teachers to evaluate the critical thinking skills of individual students based on their own learning styles. The South Dakota NSF-SSI believes that by providing teachers with a more formal way to do the types of assessment they do every day, teachers will have their teaching and assessment strategies to support each other, and teachers and students will receive valuable information on the effectiveness of their teaching and learning activities.

Sixth, developing a comfortable vocabulary and working knowledge that can lead to a widespread public acceptance of the state's program goals has been a challenge. *Public relations* efforts have had to be initiated at the state level with examples that can be translated into meaningful local dialogue. The umbrella of public relations includes community relations, constituency building, governmental affairs, "recruitment" of new participants, and accountability. It is essential that both the process and the purpose of the NSF-SSI program components, emerging classroom models, and curriculum development be communicated in a manner that encourages realistic adaptation and implementation at the local level.

Accomplishments

As a result of the work in these various components, the NSF-SSI program can already point to some concrete accomplishments.

South Dakota Mathematics/Science Benchmarks

Because of its involvement with the integration of mathematics and science programs, the NSF-SSI program was asked by the state's Department of Education and Cultural Affairs to work collaboratively with teachers to develop a working document of the South Dakota mathematics and science benchmark.

Unlike other states that have developed scholastic benchmarks from a top-down perspective, South Dakota's initial efforts relied on the experience, judgment, and insight of sixty-five teachers from across the state. Benchmark development team members identified a collective vision of what the performance in mathematics and science could be in South Dakota.

The development of state-level benchmarks for both mathematics and science, as well as *integrated* math/science benchmarks, is an important accomplishment. These benchmarks provide an important framework for the vision and goals that drive the change process. Success depends on a clearly articulated vision so that appropriate activities and evaluation strategies can be implemented. South Dakota's benchmarks also maintain a focus on what students are learning—not just what teachers are teaching.

Changing Assessment Methods

In order to address the need for alternative forms of assessment, the South Dakota National Science Foundation Statewide Systemic Initiative, in conjunction with the Psychological Corporation, implemented a performance-based assessment system in twenty-five school districts (as well as a group of nonpublic schools) during the fall of 1992. Approximately eleven thousand students were assessed.

The implementation of performance assessment at a variety of demonstration sites is perhaps the most visible success of the initiative to this point, not only as an evaluation tool, but also as a tool for change. In other words, the performance assessment not only provided appropriate information for the state's overall program evaluation, but it also provided a clear example to teachers and students of South Dakota's vision for systemic change.

In fact, this performance assessment is an excellent example of an activity that supports many of the overall goals of the program:

1. Participants (in this case, local school districts) have been provided with a vehicle that

allows them to document their strengths in a positive manner. For example, performance assessment models good instruction and good assessment and offers an example of how instruction and evaluation methods can integrate and shape curriculum.

2. Both personal and professional development has been facilitated. Through various training workshops and seminars, teachers have assumed responsibility for conducting local workshops.

3. A broad spectrum of players have been involved in the systemic change efforts of the state. Not only were all the players recognized, but the playing field was level.

4. Activities that present an opportunity for growth at the local and individual level have been implemented.

5. The value (and prestige) of all activities has been identified. Many of the state's NSF-SSI activities are identified as critical elements to the state's overall thrust for educational change as evident in legislative funding, governor initiatives, and cabinet-level support.

Computer Networking and Telecommunications

The use of computer networking and telecommunications is another accomplishment that emphasized the importance of technology in education. With the implementation of a computer network for all teachers across South Dakota, each funded grant site must develop and share their development and evaluation plans with other schools over the network in order to qualify for continued funding. This has encouraged participants to use the networking capabilities and has provided a structure wherein they can appreciate its potential.

In addition, South Dakota has begun to take advantage of the RDT Network, which links most of the postsecondary institutions in the state. This has become a valuable forum for communication and sharing. Currently, the NSF-SSI sponsors a weekly two-hour session on the RDT Network to hold meetings, present information, and provide a

forum for different sites to showcase their activities. Through the use of both forms of technology, South Dakota educators, students, and community members are able to experience firsthand the effective and appropriate use of technology.

Infrastructure

One of the most important goals of the South Dakota NSF-SSI is that local initiatives must be built on solid models of change, demonstrate the broadest involvement of key players, and make the maximum use of state and local resources. These local initiatives will only thrive within environments that encourage risk taking and provide continual support for reform initiatives. Such environments depend upon an appropriate *infrastructure*. The NSF-SSI program is developing an infrastructure in the state around three main components:

1. administrative support at all levels;

2. sufficient working capital to implement plans; and

3. appropriate leadership to translate a vision of change into models of capacity building.

First, *administrative support* has been an essential ingredient at all levels. Active partners in the state's systemic change initiatives have included the South Dakota Board of Regents and their affiliated universities; the Department of Education and Cultural Affairs and their associated programs, such as Vo-Tech and Tech Prep; the Governor's Office; independent, privately run colleges; a national-level advisory board composed of representatives from the National Science Foundation and the Educational Development Center (EDC); and statewide, professional organizations that are educational and business orientated.

Support that is evident at the local level includes school superintendents, principals, governing boards, parent organizations, teachers (some of which are collectively organized), students, community members, and service organizations.

In addition, the state's NSF-SSI office has also developed a number of *working* committees that support and codevelop many of the materials and products needed by the initiative. These committees include the South Dakota NSF-SSI Board of Directors, Higher Education Council, Benchmark Development Committee, and Systemic Change Leadership Committee.

Second, South Dakota is fortunate to have a *capital base* from which to finance many of its educational reforms. Included in this base are legislative appropriations for the Modernization Program (a companion and parallel program to the SSI), Bush Foundation Grants, Eisenhower Grants, and project-specific funding from McREL.

Third, *educational leadership* is being fostered in South Dakota through such activities as the initial "Thinking Beyond Tomorrow" conference held in 1992. At this conference, South Dakota's educational community focused its attention on change in the teaching of mathematics, science, and engineering—kindergarten through university. Recently, the SSI office cosponsored and developed the first annual Conference on the Teaching of Undergraduate Mathematics and Science, which was held to provide a forum for postsecondary educators to gain exposure to national ideas and trends and to discuss the impact and opportunities of educational reform in South Dakota.

Other Accomplishments

Other accomplishments that have been generated by the state's NSF-SSI efforts include the following: a series of workshops on the appropriate use of calculators in the classroom (South Dakota began using calculators for statewide assessment in the spring of 1993), a series of one-page promotional "briefs" that highlight the specific initiatives of each curricular change and staff development site, the establishment of a supportive and knowledgeable Board of Directors, and the development of a broad-based professional team of NSF-SSI staff members.

Overall, these accomplishments represent specific achievements that resulted from a clear understanding of the needs of South Dakota and a clearly defined vision of systemic change.

Barriers

By its nature, change frequently brings with it elements that can threaten even the most noble intentions. The acceptance of change as an agent of daily living, in a broad context, needs the recognition that change can occur as a result of a personal need or as a result of more complex organization needs.

Barriers that impede the implementation of systemic change in South Dakota can be divided into two principal categories: performance obstacles and organizational obstacles.

Performance obstacles are barriers that directly block and hamper the performance of a teacher, student, or governing body in the implementation of systemwide change. They include: (1) absence of appropriate models of change; (2) lack of support by colleagues or administration; (3) lack of time or money for the preparation of a changed environment; (4) lack of vision for the desired direction of change; (5) the belief that change is not necessary or beneficial; (6) insufficient knowledge of how to bring about change; and (7) the expectation that the effects of change will be evident immediately.

Organizational obstacles are barriers to the development of collaborative relationships with existing organizations. They include the following: (1) "turf" protection, usually motivated by a fear that change will cause an organization to become obsolete; (2) conflicting priorities among organizations for change; and (3) organizational accountability, which often takes the form of a system of rules and regulations supported by substantial "paperwork." Even though these systems were designed for accountability, they usually serve to preserve the status quo. The rules and regulations can address such activities as length of class, qualifications of teachers, and the collaborative structure of school. Unfortunately, organizational accountability can result in an inability to react to an existing need.

Because of these barriers to reform, implementing systemic change can be a slow, painful, and, at times, frustrating process. Often, drastic changes in existing political structures and agencies are necessary before even "simple" changes in the schools can be attempted. This difficulty in changing established procedures (overcoming organizational and performance barriers) is an excellent example of organization "inertia." Organizational inertia can be metaphorically summarized by a simple physical principle: an object at rest tends to stay at rest.

However, once reforms are in place, this inertia can work to support change (an object in motion tends to stay in motion). Thus, in spite of the frustrations, there have also been some very encouraging aspects of the NSF-SSI activities. In addition to the accomplishments listed in the previous section, the NSF-SSI office continues to initiate new activities that promise to support the continued inertia of change.

REFLECTIONS

This section will provide a summary of some of the new and continued activities that represent the NSF-SSI attempts to overcome the previously identified barriers as well as to establish the basis for a useful legacy that the NSF-SSI program hopes to provide in South Dakota.

One current project, "Algebra with Applications," represents an attempt to provide appropriate curricular materials that integrate mathematics and science using hands-on applications. The high points of this effort are the teachers who have put in time and effort (and taken risks) to make changes as well as the students who have been fortunate enough to be involved. "Algebra with Applications" represents a valuable link with business. The tremendous effort involved in getting the project up and going has demonstrated the commitment of all the participants.

The NSF-SSI has also succeeded, in some small ways, in bringing about change in areas other than the K–16 educational institutions. Specifically, the NSF-SSI office has provided an important example of teamwork and collaboration. Furthermore, it has demonstrated how a collaborative unit can reach its objectives with the educational system, which is usually perceived as linear and "top down" in nature.

The NSF-SSI will continue to support most of the activities that have already been established:

> In each year of operation in South Dakota, SSI is prepared to fund additional curricular change and staff development proposals and planning grants. Each proposal represents the strengths of the school, community, and postsecondary institution and the local com-

mitment to implement a process that supports the vision of the SSI.

> All funded project sites will continue to participate in performance-based assessment in both science and mathematics at grades 3, 5, 7, 9, and 12—approximately 23,000 students in 1993.

> The South Dakota Mathematics and Science Benchmarks and the South Dakota Mathematics and Science Curriculum Frameworks will be developed, or completed, by 50–60 South Dakota teachers.

What is expected in three more years? The NSF-SSI hopes to leave a lasting legacy of its reform efforts, which will continue to draw together the components of the state's stakeholders. It is important to realize, however, that the nature of these "legacies" may change as the needs and constraints within South Dakota evolve. Currently, there are six principal legacies envisioned by the NSF-SSI project:

1. The NSF-SSI will have facilitated the implementation of integrated mathematics and science classes in the K–16 education system. This will include a variety of demonstration sites where students are experiencing mathematics and science consistent with the state's systemic initiative vision. For example, high schools will have set up two- and even three-hour blocks of time in which students work in collaborative teams, sharing information and expertise on problems or situations that require them to use mathematics, science, technology, and communications skills.

Example: A group of students are working on a project entitled "Greenhouse Gases and Global Warming." The South Dakota students are doing some actual, accurate data collection on methane production at a local feedlot. This information is shared, via modem, with students in Los Angeles and several other sites. The students do not necessarily "finish" the experiment and write a conclusion. Instead, they continue, in an ongoing process, to gather and share information, develop hypotheses, debate the relative impact of beef cattle feedlot operations on global warming, and even discuss the economic and social impacts of possible steps to reduce global warming.

2. A sufficient infrastructure will have been generated to support continued reform throughout the state. This infrastructure will include a group of teacher-leaders who can continue the leadership of the NSF-SSI. This infrastructure will also require all the stakeholders of education to be committed to systemic change. In particular, the public must be convinced of the necessity to provide the tremendous resources (including both money and time) to move forward and continue with these types of educational activities.

3. The NSF-SSI project will have implemented a computer information network and telecommunications system that will be used and supported by the education community. However, giving a school a computer and a modem will be of no value unless the school can use it and supports its use. Thus, this effort must provide not only the necessary equipment, but also the commitment and skills to effectively use the equipment. Ultimately, every classroom will have one computer for every four or five students (these computers will be desktops as well as laptops and even palmtops).

4. In order to realize the vision of systemic change, business and industry must also change. Students of the very near future will be leaving school (temporarily, for all people *must* be lifelong learners) with cooperative teamwork skills and the ability to think and communicate. However, this type of person may not fit well into many of the jobs of tomorrow, or even of today. Although the concept of restructuring the workplace is a common theme, the bottom line is that most jobs (especially in a rural state like South Dakota) are in small businesses with very tradi-

tional organizational approaches. These traditional organizational approaches must evolve parallel with the reform in education. Thus, the changes in both education and industry must complement and support each other for successful systemic change.

5. Alternative approaches to assessment and certification will be part of the educational establishment. In particular, South Dakota will have performance assessment as one element on its state report card.

6. Finally, teacher preparation programs will be reformed. In particular, technology will impact the delivery of specific mathematics and science courses—at both the K–12 and postsecondary levels. Thus, South Dakota will have teachers who are comfortable with change and with professional leadership.

CONCLUSION

It may be fitting to bring this chapter to a close by reconsidering the "why" of systemic change. Right now, there is a unique confluence of forces for systemic change, including social, political, and educational forces. This confluence of forces is occurring because of a perceived need for educational reform, which has led to a vision of systemic change supported by diverse stakeholders in education: funding agencies, academic institutions, governmental groups, and the public. Empowered by this vision, these stakeholders have provided money, expertise, and a commitment to change.

Although it is true that time makes everything obsolete, it is crucial to continually question whether the current educational system is meeting the needs of students and the public as a whole, both within South Dakota and across the country. As a nation, we must take full advantage of this opportunity to realize the vision of systemic change by connecting and productively harnessing these convergent forces for change.

REFERENCES

American Association for the Advancement of Science. 1989. *Project 2061: Science for all Americans.* Washington, D.C.: American Association for the Advancement of Science.

Chief of the Bureau of Statistics, Treasury Department. 1992. *Statistical abstract of the United States.* Washington, D.C.: Government Printing Office.

Governor's Office of Economic Development. 1991. *South Dakota manufacturers and processors directory, 1991–1992.* Pierre, S. Dak.: Governor's Office of Economic Development.

National Center for Improving Science Education. 1989. *Getting started in science: A blueprint for elementary school science education.* Washington, D.C.: National Center for Improving Science Education.

National Commission on Excellence in Education. 1983. A *nation at risk: The imperative for educational reform.* Washington, D.C.: U.S. Department of Education.

National Council of Teachers of Mathematics. 1989. *Curriculum and evaluation standards for school mathematics.* Reston, Va.: National Council of Teachers of Mathematics.

National Research Council. 1989. *Everybody counts: A report to the nation on the future of mathematics education.* Washington, D.C.: National Academy Press.

South Dakota Board of Regents and Department of Education and Cultural Affairs. 1990. *South Dakota statewide systemic initiative.* Pierre, S. Dak.: South Dakota Board of Regents.

South Dakota Division of Elementary and Secondary Education. 1993. *South Dakota Educational statistical digest, 1992–93.* Pierre, S. Dak.: South Dakota Division of Elementary and Secondary Education.

South Dakota National Science Foundation Statewide Systemic Initiative and Department of Education and Cultural Affairs. 1991. *South Dakota science framework draft.* Pierre, S. Dak.: South Dakota National Science Foundation Systemic Initiative.

———. 1992. *Request for proposals.* Pierre, S. Dak.: South Dakota National Science Foundation Systemic Initiative.

———. 1992. *South Dakota mathematics and science benchmarks.* Pierre, S. Dak.: South Dakota National Science Foundation Systemic Initiative.

———. 1992. *South Dakota science and mathematics teachers' network: User manual.* Pierre, S. Dak.: South Dakota National Science Foundation Systemic Initiative.

AUTHORS

David Anderson received his Ed.D. from the University of Michigan. He is currently an assistant professor of education at Salisbury State University in Salisbury, Maryland. Formerly, David worked at the South Dakota National Science Foundation Statewide Systemic Initiative as the associate director for assessment. He has also worked as an executive associate for assessment and research at the National Board for Professional Teaching Standards. David specializes in the areas of assessment, educational technology, foundations of education, science education, and school finance.

Bela H. Banathy is president of International Systems Institute and professor emeritus of systems science at the Saybrook Graduate School. Both his research and development work and his teaching have focused on the application of systems and design theories in systems of learning and human development. He is a research fellow at the European Institute of Evolutionary Studies. Banathy is also on the International Editorial Advisory Boards of *Systems Practice* and *World Futures* and is honorary editor of *Systems Research*.

Robert O. Brinkerhoff is a professor of education at Western Michigan University, where he coordinates graduate programs in human resources development. An internationally recognized expert in training effectiveness and evaluation, Robert has provided consultation in training effectiveness and project management to dozens of major companies and organizations in the United States and around the world. He is author of nine books on evaluation and training, including his most recent work, *The Learning Alliance: Systems Thinking in Human Resources Development*.

Michael L. Burger has been a high school science teacher, a principal, and a professor in both undergraduate and graduate teacher education programs. As director of the Learning Technology Center at Texas A&M University from 1984 to 1991, he directed a research project that utilized information technologies as productivity tools for educational practitioners. The university commercialized the technology developed in the center, and in 1991 he left public education to continue to lead the research and development efforts. Michael holds a master's degree in education administration and a doctorate degree in administration, curriculum, and instruction from the University of Nebraska-Lincoln.

Robert Caldwell began his career in education as a classroom teacher in Pittsburgh, Pennsylvania. Soon after acquiring his Ph.D., he joined the Division of Educational Studies faculty at Southern Methodist University in Dallas, Texas. Robert specialized in teaching cognitive psychology, instructional systems design, learning theory, and the application of computer technology to learning. Robert was also a senior research associate with the National Science Foundation Statewide Systemic Initiative, where he worked to help establish educational reforms in the teaching of mathematics and science in twenty-six states and Puerto Rico.

Alison A. Carr is an assistant professor in the Instructional Systems Program at Pennsylvania State University. She has published and presented on topics ranging from school restructuring and systemic design to electronic performance support systems and hypermedia applications. Her current interests focus on research in areas of parental influence on public schools. Alison is currently working closely with Dr. Kyle Peck on the establishment of an educational systems change program at Pennsylvania State University.

Edward W. Chance is a professor of educational administration at the University of Nevada-Las Vegas. He was previously at the University of Oklahoma. His research interests include leadership development, collaborative vision building, and rural education. He has received several national awards for his work with technology and rural schools. Edward serves as a consultant to numerous school districts in the areas of school improvement, vision, and team building. He is the author of *Visionary Leadership in Schools* and editor of *Creating the Quality School.*

Robert Chappell is superintendent and quality trainer for the Essex County Public Schools, Tappahannock, Virginia. He completed doctoral studies at Virginia Polytechnical and State University on the effects of the implementation of Total Quality Management on the Rappahannock

County, Virginia, Public Schools. While serving as assistant superintendent of the Rappahannock schools, Chappell was certified by the Xerox Corporation to provide new employee quality training. Robert is the author of an article published in *Quality Progress,* "Will TQM Survive in Public Education without Co-Production?"

Patricia Cloud Duttweiler is assistant director of the National Dropout Prevention Center at Clemson University. She spent eight years with the Southwest Educational Development Laboratory (SEDL) in Austin, Texas, where she conducted research on barriers to organizational change, developed the Learning Climate Inventory, and coordinated "partner" teams that developed a process for implementing systemic change and promoted restructuring efforts in each of the five states in the Southwestern region.

David M. Fetterman is professor and director of research at the California Institute of Integral Studies and director of the MA Policy Analysis program at Stanford University. David works in the fields of educational evaluation, ethnography, and policy analysis and focuses on programs for dropouts and on gifted and talented education. He is the author of *Empowerment Evaluation: Knowledge and Tools for Self-Assessment and Accountability; Speaking the Language of Power: Communication, Collaboration, and Advocacy; Ethnography: Step by Step;* and *Qualitative Approaches to Evaluation in Education.*

Carol Gabor is director of the Minnesota Quality Award, a Baldrige-based state-level award that recognizes exemplary practices in customer satisfaction and operational management. The Minnesota Quality Award is the state's highest honor for businesses and schools. Carol is widely published and frequently gives presentations on quality-related matters to businesses, professional groups, and conferences around the nation. She is also a senior evaluator for the education pilot of the 1995 Malcolm Baldrige National Quality Award.

David Gangel has served as superintendent of the Rappahannock County Public Schools since 1987. A pioneer in Total Quality Management in education for the past five years, he has written articles and spoken at national conferences on the this topic. David is also a member and officer of the American Society for Quality Control, Education Division.

Joe B. Hansen is executive director of the Division of Data and Technology Systems for the Colorado Springs Public Schools, where he oversees the functions of management information systems, planning, evaluation, research, and assessment. Joe has twenty-seven years' experience in edu-

cational research, evaluation, and assessment. He has more than fifty major conference presentations and publications, many of which take a systems perspective on educational problems and issues.

Patrick M. Jenlink consults with school districts in the area of educational systems design, systemic change, and leadership development. Formerly, he was an assistant professor in the Department of Educational Leadership at Western Michigan University, where he taught courses in organizational leadership in a graduate-intensive program. His expertise includes leadership theory, personnel administration, human resource management, and school finance. Dr. Jenlink currently serves on the board of directors for the International Systems Institute, an organization dedicated to systems design and its use in improving educational systems.

D. Thomas King is director of technology and employee training for the St. Paul Public Schools. His educational career spans thirty-three years and includes service as a secondary mathematics teacher, department chair, curriculum associate, and coach and several administrative positions. He holds a Ph.D. in curriculum from the University of Wisconsin-Madison and serves as an adjunct professor in the graduate education department at the University of St. Thomas. Thomas is the founder of the nationally recognized Saturn School of Tomorrow and continues to speak and write on the topic of technology and school reform.

Molly Linstrom is media relations and program development coordinator for the South Dakota NSF-SSI. Her chief responsibility is to communicate and relate SSI program elements that illustrate the vision and objectives of the South Dakota program. Molly initiates, develops, and implements marketing programs, business/community partnerships, and legislative activities on behalf of the SSI. She has won national and state press association awards for writing and advertising.

David Makings is a consultant for Star Schools and Telecommunications at the Idaho Schools sites and provides support to all K–12 districts and the Department of Education in the area of internet and general telecommunications. Formerly, David worked with the South Dakota NSF-SSI as a research associate and project site coordinator. Coordination included mentoring and providing support to classroom teachers and administration and monitoring of the overall project.

Greg Meunier is director of customer satisfaction and organization effectiveness for AmeriData, Inc., a leading nationwide provider of value-added personal computer products. Prior to assuming his role at AmeriData, Greg was a classroom teacher, held senior executive positions with the Minnnesota Technical College System, and was a principal consultant and assistant vice president with First Bank System. In 1995, he was awarded Master Examiner status with the Minnesota Quality Award. He is a member of the Minnesota Council for Quality Administrative Board.

Laurie Miller Nelson is an associate instructor and a Ph.D. student in the Instructional Systems Technology Department at Indiana University. Her interests in systemic educational change include creation of professional development materials for facilitators and design teams, refinement of a systemic change process model, promotion of a systemic change process model, and promotion of systemic educational change at local, state, and national levels.

Katherine Pedersen was awarded the Illinois Council of Teachers of Mathematics Max Beberman Award for outstanding research and service to mathematics education and received the Southern Illinois University Alumni Great Teacher Award. Katherine has published and presented extensively in mathematics and in other areas such as equity, teaching strategies, and technology support for the teaching of mathematics.

Hallie Preskill is an associate professor of education in the University of New Mexico's graduate program in Training and Learning Technologies and teaches courses in program evaluation and instructional systems design. Her consulting and research interests include program evaluation theory and methods, organizational learning and culture, and the transfer of learning. She has recently coauthored a book on communicating and reporting evaluation findings (to be published by Sage Publications in 1996).

Charles M. Reigeluth has been a professor in the Instructional Systems Technology Department at Indiana University since 1988 and is currently chairman of the department. He taught science at the secondary level for three years and spent ten years on the faculty of the Instructional Design program at Syracuse University, ending as chair of the program. He has also served as an educational restructuring consultant for state and local education agencies and as an educational technology consultant for corporate, health, public, and higher education institutions.

Rosalie T. Torres consults nationally with educational and business and industry organizations. Rosalie has written numerous papers and articles on evaluation and is currently coauthoring a book on communicating and reporting evaluation findings. She has worked as an internal evaluator for the Dallas Independent School District, the Chicago Public Schools, and Colorado Springs School District Eleven. Currently, she teaches evaluation and research methodology courses at the University of Colorado.

Ray Williams is a principal partner of Ray Williams and Associates, Educational and Management Consultants. He has been a secondary school teacher and principal, a university professor, and superintendent of schools for Chilliwack School District, British Columbia. Ray currently serves as a consultant to school systems, postsecondary institutions, and private sector organizations in the areas of strategic planning, organizational and systemic change, staff development, quality systems, and personnel practices. He is the author of *The Leadership Edge: Strategies for School Reform* and *The Quest for Quality Schools: Total Quality Management in Education.*

INDEX

—

NOTES

NOTES

NOTES

NOTES

Learn from Our Books *and* from Our Authors!

Bring Our Author/Trainers to Your District

At IRI/Skylight, we have assembled a unique team of outstanding author/trainers with international reputations for quality work. Each has designed high-impact programs that translate powerful new research into successful learning strategies for every student. We design each program to fit your school's or district's special needs.

Training Programs

Gain practical techniques and strategies for implementing the latest findings from educational research. IRI/Skylight is recognized around the world for its commitment to translating cognitive and cooperative learning research into high-quality resource materials and effective classroom practices. In each program IRI/Skylight designs, participants learn by doing the thinking and cooperating they will be asking their students to do. With IRI/Skylight's specially prepared materials, participants learn how to teach their students to learn for a lifetime.

Networks for Systemic Change

Through partnerships with Phi Delta Kappa and others, IRI offers two Networks for site-based systemic change: *The Network of Mindful Schools* and *The Multiple Intelligences School Network.* The Networks are designed to promote systemic school change as practical and possible when starting with a renewed vision that centers on *what* and *how* each student learns. To help accomplish this goal, Network consultants work with member schools to develop an annual tactical plan and implement the plan at the classroom level.

Training of Trainers

The Training of Trainers programs train your best teachers, those who provide the highest quality instruction, to coach other teachers. This not only increases the number of teachers you can afford to train in each program, but also increases the amount of coaching and follow-up that each teacher can receive from a resident expert. Our Training of Trainers programs will help you make a systemic improvement in your staff development program.

To receive a free copy of the IRI/Skylight catalog, find out more about the Networks for Systemic Change, or receive more information about trainings offered through IRI/Skylight, contact

IRI/Skylight Training and Publishing, Inc.
200 E. Wood St., Suite 274, Palatine, IL 60067
800-348-4474
FAX 708-991-6420

There are
one-story intellects,
two-story intellects, and three-story
intellects with skylights. All fact collectors, who
have no aim beyond their facts, are one-story men. Two-story men
compare, reason, generalize, using the labors of the fact collectors as
well as their own. Three-story men idealize, imagine,
predict—their best illumination comes from
above, through the skylight.
—Oliver Wendell
Holmes

SkyLight

TRAINING AND PUBLISHING, INC.